THE
SAILBOAT OWNER'S
EQUIPMENT CATALOGUE

THE
SAILBOAT OWNER'S
EQUIPMENT CATALOGUE

St. Martin's Press
New York

Book Cover and Design by David M. Nehila

Library of Congress Cataloging in Publication Data

Stevenson, Edward P.
      The sailboat owner's equipment catalogue.

      1. Boats and boating—Equipment and
supplies—Catalogs.   2. Sailboats—Catalogs.
I. Title.
VM351.S697   623.8′223′0288   81-21469
ISBN 0-312-69673-6   AACR2
ISBN 0-312-69674-4 (pbk.)

First Edition
10   9   8   7   6   5   4   3   2   1

CONTENTS

1

AMENITIES

Airguide Instrument Company
2210 Wabansia Avenue
Chicago, Illinois 60647

CLOCKS AND WEATHER INSTRUMENTS

HYGROMETERS/ THERMOMETERS

No. 121-B (Ship's Wheel)
No. 122-B (Traditional)
Thermometers show from 20° to 120°F.; −5° to 49° C. Relative humidity is shown as a percent.

BAROMETERS

No. 215-B (Ship's Wheel)
No. 216-B (Traditional)
Compensated for temperature variation. Large white dial with easy-to-read graphics is calibrated in inches of mercury, millibars (mb) and kilo Pascals (k/Pa).

CLOCKS

No. 1215-B (Ship's Wheel)
No. 1216-B (Traditional)
Large white dial is scaled to 2400 hours. Super accurate quartz movement with sweep second hand runs 9–12 months on a single C-cell (not included). Back removes for easy access to battery

and for mounting to bulkhead if desired.

No. 1298 Ship's Wheel Clock and No. 298 Ship's Barometer
Hand-rubbed wood finish is complemented by golden bezel and silvery spun finished dial. Clock uses quartz movement with an AA battery (not included). The wood spokes are highlighted by brass accents. Cases are 7″ round with an overall diameter of 11 7/10″.

No. 1244 Ship's Quartz Clock and No. 244 Ship's Barometer
Rugged molded cases crafted to duplicate the exact appearance of solid brass. These models have the look, luster, and rich beauty of real brass.

Clock runs 9–12 months on a single C-cell battery (not included). Twist-off back plate with curved back. Matching barometer has open face to show temperature compensated movement and brass set hand. Scaled in inches of mercury, millibars, and kilo Pascals.

Each case is 5⅛″ diameter, 3″ deep. Boxed.

Aqua-Temp Corporation
421 North Line Street
Lansdale, Pennsylvania 19446

LO-BOY AIR CONDITIONERS

Lo-Boy units are ideal for installations where space, especially height, is at a premium. It accomplishes this by utilizing a remote water pump that can be mounted in the engine compartment or bilge.

Units are available in a choice of 9,000, 12,000 and 16,000 BTU versions. Each also features standard reverse cycle heating and comes in either free standing or recessed versions. Free standing models include a teak cabinet. Recessed models are somewhat smaller. Each weighs approximately 100 lbs.

Adding to the versatility of these air conditioners is a selection of left, right and top discharge locations. On recessed models, air can be ducted to other parts of the cabin. They operate on conventional 115 volt power.

The LB-Series usually can be self-installed in a few hours. A comprehensive installation and service manual is provided with each unit. The remote water pump is a positive displacement type that does not have to be situated below the waterline.

All units include Aqua-Temp's one year warranty against manufacturing defects. Standard features include a high volume, yet quiet, squirrel cage blower; salt water resistant cupronickle condenser; long life hermetically sealed compressor; full charge of Freon-22 refrigerant; permanent washable air filter; overload protection; thermostatic control and variable speed fan for quiet night time operation.

Beckson Marine, Inc.
P.O. Box 3336
Bridgeport, Connecticut 06605

RAIN SHIELD/ VENTILATOR

This is a simple and permanent solution to the problem of obtaining cross ventilation without rain water entering a boat through open ports. Designed to fit Beckson ports, this new patent pending Internal Rain Shield/Ventilator is easy to install, contains its own non-corrosive fine mesh screen and does not interfere with visibility or protrude outside the port frame. The louvered shield lets the rain drop harmlessly into the water or onto the deck. It works regardless of the intensity of the rain. The port can be closed during severe conditions or cold weather without removing the Rain Shield.

The Shield is made of rugged, scratch resistant marine plastic. The screen is non-corrosive and will not rust or stain. The unit is resistant to salt water, ultra-violet light and ozone, and is available in four models. Those designed to fit Beckson's 3" x 10", 5" x 12" and 4" x 14" opening ports have one clear louvered shield. Units designed for Beckson's large 7" x 14" opening port have two shields.

W. H. Denouden (USA), Inc.
P.O. Box 8712
Baltimore, Maryland 21240

VETUS KBL SHIP'S WHEEL

Made of walnut. With wooden hoop. Provided with a brass hub and a stainless steel cap.
KBL 47—outside diam. 47 cm (18½")
KBL 57—outside diam. 57 cm (22½")

Docker Marine
350 Gate 5 Road
Sausalito, California 94965

FULL-FEND FENDERS & BUMPERS

The fender utilizes its entire length for full fending. No metal parts to mar or scratch. Molded of the finest grade marine vinyl. Can be secured with dual line ties.

The 18 modules may be placed as often as necessary along the dock to give you the best possible protection with a soft cushion of air. Finest quality vinyl with recessed nail holes for extra protection.

VINYL COWL VENTILATORS

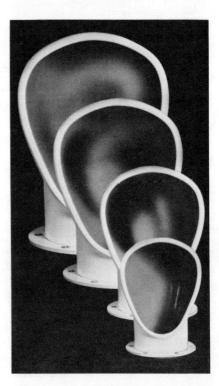

Docker Marine Ventilator Systems are molded of especially formulated new vinyl—unaffected by salt air and abrasion, they require minimum maintenance. Color is an integral part of the molded vinyl which has an ultraviolet stabilizer added to inhibit sun damage.

GO Industries

629 Terminal Way
Costa Mesa, California 92627

WINDOWS AND PORTS

The development of fiberglass boats has freed the yachtsman of much of the care and maintenance previously required for his yacht. Improvements of windows and ports has not kept pace, however, with the rapid advancement in the fabrication of fiberglass yachts. GO Industries was specifically organized by yachtsmen to fulfill this need for improved windows and ports.

The answer to this need was found in the use of a high impact weather resistant vinyl plastic. The use of this plastic has further reduced the care and maintenance required on boats so equipped. No more care is required of GO Industries window frames than is normally used in washing, waxing and polishing the rest of the boat.

Window frames may be fabricated to most size and shape configurations. The window pane material is Lucite A/R (abrasion resistant)—a coated material which is stronger than glass and can resist most chemicals.

Sets of replacement windows can be ordered and may be installed by the owner with a minimum of effort, since the mounting holes are pre-drilled and fasteners are furnished.

Because marine windows must withstand the force of breaking waves in storms, GO Industries designed a test to determine what force a GO window would stand before failing, and how the failure would occur. A large force on the window was required for the test, and this was obtained by applying air pressure to a mounted window.

The window chosen for the test was an irregular shaped one, approximately 14⅝" by 41⅝", giving an opening area of 609 square inches. The pane was 3/16" Lucite A/R. The window was mounted in the box opening with silicone sealant.

One inch of mercury (Hg) vacuum is equal to .491 pounds per square inch air pressure on the top of the window. The area (609 square inches) times the pressure (.491 pounds per square inch) equals the force 299 pounds on the window for each inch of Hg vacuum.

As the vacuum increased, the pane curved down. When the vacuum reached 5" the pane had pulled down over 2" in the center. At a vacuum of 7" Hg, the window had bowed down about 2¾" in the center. At a vacuum of 7½" Hg, the window failed.

The failure occurred at 2,250 lbs. which is more than one ton, and according to information gleaned from Scripps Institute of Oceanography, the force applied to a window in a complete knockdown by a large wave should be approximately 1 lb. per square inch. Since the failure of this window occurred at 2,250 lbs. which is 3.69 lbs. per square inch, it appears fairly safe to state that the window will withstand the force of a complete knockdown or of a boat being hit with a rogue wave.

High Seas, Inc.
4861 24th Avenue
Port Huron, Michigan 48060

DRINK SWINGER

The solution to a classic problem. Spilled drinks are eliminated with the Drink Swinger attached securely to your lifelines. This convenience accessory is of *all-stainless*, polished construction and is available in two sizes: one for regular sized bottles and glasses and a jumbo version designed especially for styrofoam coolers. They come in packages of two and styrofoam coolers are included with the larger version.

ITT Jabsco
1485 Dale Way
Costa Mesa, California 92626

BOAT FENDERS

PAR Pneumatic Boat Fenders are now protected with Bio-Shield, which resists mold, mildew, bacteria and aquatic plant growth. The Bio-Shield additive is safe, having been approved for use in infant's plastic pants.

Available in square and ribbed round designs, the fenders are constructed of smooth, one-piece white vinyl and won't mar or scuff the hull's finish. The vinyl construction has uniform wall thickness and can be inflated to desired pressure to meet individual needs.

The PAR boat fenders give full length working surface from end to end. The center passage design eliminates lost working area used by tying ears and grommets. The larger surface area absorbs and cushions heavy shock loads.

PAR fenders are lightweight, buoyant and tough, and are easy to hang vertically or horizontally. The round ribbed fenders are available in sizes of 6 x 15 in. (152 x 381 mm), 8 x 20 in. (203 x 508 mm), and 10 x 26 in. (254 x 660 mm). The square fenders are available in 6 x 6 x 26 in. (152 x 152 x 660 mm), 8 x 8 x 28 in. (203 x 203 x 711 mm), and 10 x 10 x 30 in. (254 x 254 x 762 mm).

Kenyon
P.O. Box 308
Guilford, Connecticut 06347

ALCOHOL STOVES

Keny One-Burner Non-Pressurized Alcohol Stove—Model 110
"Keny" is a small, single burner non-pressurized alcohol stove. Requires no preheating of burners. Simply open the bottom control and snuffer valve, and light. Holds a maximum of 8 ounces of alcohol. Stove body is aluminum with thermoset plastic finish, available in numerous colors.

Two-Burner Alcohol Stove—Model 126
This model is the smallest of the Kenyon Homestrand pressurized tank alcohol stoves. The tank is brass with integral pump and pressure relief fill cap. Brass burners have adjustable air/fuel ratio. The stove frame is clear anodized aluminum. The "basket" grate is stainless steel and will accept pans up to 8½ inches.

Two-Burner Alcohol Stove—Model 205
The tank and burner assembly of this model are like Model 126 but the tank has a slightly larger capac-

ity. Pans up to 10-inch size will fit within the guard rails. The stove frame is drawn aluminum for strength and easy cleaning, and is anodized against corrosion. Alcohol burners are the standard Kenyon Homestrand design, incorporating the nozzle cleaning mechanism. One-piece aluminum drip tray catches spillage and slides out for easy cleaning. Tabs are provided for fastening the stove to a counter top.

Two-Burner Alcohol Stove with Lid—Model 206
The integral tank, which is pressurized using the built-in pump, holds about a quart of ethyl alcohol. The pan and lid are stainless steel. Tank and burners are brass and are of proven design. The Model 206T has a walnut and birch serving tray lid.

faces. The deep design keeps the wind from blowing food off the plate, or the plate across the boat.
And with the sailor in mind, another unique feature is the patented design permitting the Captain's Table to be mounted on any

winch.* It then becomes a stable and secure auxiliary tray, allowing even the single-handed helmsman to enjoy a beverage or snack.

*Which uses universal winch handles.

Nautical Engineering
Division R&D Enterprises
P.O. Box 5252
Worthville, Michigan 48167

THE ARRANGER

Uses:
Use two about 12″ apart for coiling line in figure eights. Hang wet, heavy clothing and foul weather gear on them. Great for organizing lines and equipment in the lazarette. Perfect for holding oars.

THE CAPTAIN'S TABLE

Made of sturdy injection-molded plastic, the Captain's Table accommodates a dinner for one or snacks and beverages for four. A can or cup fits neatly inside each leg, while a ring of non-skid rubber (just like boat dishes) on the bottom prevents sliding on sloped sur-

North American Nautical Industries, Inc.
10801 Endeavour Way
Largo, Florida 33543

BIMINI TOPS

Specifications

FRAMES
1″ O.D. Stainless Steel Tubing, .065″ wall thickness, Mirror Finish.

FITTINGS
Type 316 Stainless Steel.

FABRIC
Genuine Weblon®. Waterproof, Sun Resistant. Fire Retardant. Has Underwriters' Laboratories Approval and California State Fire Marshall Approval. Dimensionally

Stable. Offers excellent rot and age resistance and can be stored wet or dry without deterioration.

WEBBING
1″ Nylon. 1,500 lbs. breaking strength.

THREAD
Bonded Polyester Dacron.

Pastime Products, Inc.
1035 South 11th Street
Philadelphia, Pennsylvania 19147

RAINSCOOP

A simple and efficient way to replenish fresh water. In a moderate rainfall, the Rainscoop will collect

Shipmate Stove Division
Richmond Ring Company
Souderton, Pennsylvania 18964

CABIN HEATERS

**206CH CABIN HEATER
BULKHEAD MOUNTED**

more than a gallon of water every two minutes.

The Rainscoop requires no installation. It is quick and easy to tie beneath a boom, pulpit, rails or lifelines. By connecting a hose to the built-in drain plug, fresh rainwater is funneled directly into your water holding tanks or jerry jugs. Made of durable, non-toxic coated nylon, the Rainscoop measures six feet long and has a maximum depth of 22 inches. It can be detached and folded for quick and easy compact storage.

SUPER STIX

Here's a boat hook that converts quickly to a mop or brush handle and is now available as a complete marine kit with mop head, deck brush, adaptor and boat hook end. There are two sizes: an expanding model (4–8 feet) and a fixed-length five foot pole. Both high tensile anodized aluminum poles are offered in complete marine kits or separately with free screw-head adaptor included so you can use your own mop or deck brush.

WINDSCOOP

The Windscoop ventilating sail puts an end to hot stuffy cabins and sleepless nights. It is aerodynamically designed to force the slightest breeze down into your cabin to keep you cool and comfortable.

The versatile Windscoop can be hung from halyard, boom or roller furling sheet. Fits any hatch or companionway up to 4 feet wide. Nothing to install. Since it has no tie-downs, once you put it up, it will follow a variable wind. Works with most screens. Complete with nylon storage bag.

This compact SHIPMATE cabin heater is made of heavy gauge stainless steel with polished brass trim for long rust resistant service. The mounting plate is fully insulated to protect the bulkhead. The heavy fire door can be safely closed or opened for a cheery open fire. When the door is closed, the double wall construction allows circulation of warm air.

A fire of pea size coal will last overnight when banked in the large 8" wide by 4½" deep by 5½" high heavy cast iron firebox. The stainless steel ash pit drawer can be removed for easy cleaning. The SHIPMATE cabin heater will burn charcoal, coal, or wood. It weighs 52 pounds.

**701CH
SHIPMATE CABIN HEATER
KEROSENE**

The SHIPMATE bulkhead mounted kerosene cabin heater will keep your cabin dry and cosy during early spring and late fall cruising.

This compact cabin heater is made of stainless steel for rust resistance. It is only 7½" wide, 8½" deep and 15" tall. It weighs 18 pounds. The double wall construction promotes warm air circulation throughout the cabin. It has the famous Primus self-cleaning silent pressure kerosene burner which delivers 10,000 BTU per hour.

The two quart brass pressure tank is complete with brass hand pump and pressure gauge. It is mounted in an insulated compartment in the heater eliminating the necessity of installing a separate tank and tubing. The cabin heater will operate for 9 hours on one filling.

A fully insulated mounting plate is provided to protect the bulkhead woodwork. A stainless steel safety vent pipe is supplied. Both the stainless steel through deck fitting and stainless steel vent cap are also provided with each heater.

STOVES

**Two Burner
With Oven
2782**

The SHIPMATE stainless steel kerosene stoves with ovens are designed for the long distance cruising yachtsman. They appreciate the worldwide availability of inexpensive kerosene with its high BTU content. Both the two burner with oven and three burner with oven stoves have the famous Optimus silent kerosene burners. These burners are operated under low pressure and have the clean burning wick lighting tubes. The special SHIPMATE tubing system assures trouble free service.

Both the SHIPMATE models 2782 and 2783 have adjustable stainless steel pot holders. These pot holders can be locked in any postion on the rail to accommodate different size pots and pans.

The SHIPMATE kerosene stoves are designed exclusively for marine use. One of these compact stoves will fit the most limited galley but still inspire the cook. The clean functional design of the quality handcrafted SHIPMATE stove will be a compliment to your galley and a convenience to the cook.

**Three Burner
With Oven
2783**

The SHIPMATE stainless steel kerosene stoves are made from heavy gauge rust resistant stainless steel. The back, bottom and inside parts are stainless steel as well as the top, front and sides. All the tubing and fittings in both

these stoves are also rust resistant for long service in the corrosive atmosphere of ocean cruising. Both stoves have sturdy stainless steel sea rails which incorporate the mounting gimbals. The high gimbal pivot point provides stability and superior gimbaling action in the roughest weather. When not in use, the gimbals can be locked to prevent all motion of the stove.

The oven compartment of both the SHIPMATE models 2782 and 2783 is fully insulated. The stoves have a large easily read thermometer mounted on the oven door to indicate the interior oven temperature. Both models have a spacious oven which is 17" wide by 13½" by 8" high. This oven will please the most ambitious cook.

Cast-Iron Ranges

Shipmate cast iron ranges for coal or wood are available in eight sizes ranging from 21 to 42 inches wide. Most of the sizes are available equipped with an oil burner. Bulletin available.

Gas Ranges

Shipmate bottled gas ranges are made of stainless steel and aluminum. There are two, three or four burner hot plates. They also are available with two, three, four or six surface burners with an oven above or below the surface burners. The oven and broiler can be in the same compartment or in separate ones. Bulletin available.

Alcohol or Kerosene Stove

These Shipmate alcohol or kerosene stoves are made of stainless steel and aluminum. They are available with two or three burners and have a brass pressure tank. They can be equipped with gimbals. Bulletin available.

Enameled Ranges

Shipmate enameled ranges are coppertone or white. They are made for alcohol, bottled gas or kerosene. They can be free standing, gimbaled or built into your galley. Bulletin available.

Fireplace

The Shipmate Open Fireplace will keep the cabin cozy on chilly spring and fall days. It can burn coal, wood, briquets or coke. It is black enamel with polished brass trim. Bulletin available.

Skippy

The Shipmate Skippy is an efficient small size cabin heater. It can burn coal, wood or briquets. It also can be equipped with a natural draft oil burner. Bulletin available.

Soderberg
Manufacturing
Company
20821 Currier Road
P.O. Box 506
Walnut, California 91789

RAIL CADDY

An adjustable bracket and clip assembly that can be used for a variety of applications. It securely holds your coffee mug, beer can, drinking glass, beverage or wine bottle, thermos, etc. It can be hung on your rail or stanchion, or permanently mounted to your bulkhead, kitchen counter, or dashboard. (Hook can be removed.) The clip location and length are fully adjustable to accommodate a variety of objects, from light fixtures, fire extinguishers, to your favorite beverage cans.

VDO-ARGO Instruments, Inc.

980 Brooke Road
Winchester, Virginia 22601

CABIN CLOCK

Features:

Polished brass case

Diameter of 7 3/32″ (180 mm)—
Radio Operator's Clock

Diameter of 5 1/16″ (129 mm)—
Cabin Clock

Electronic quartz mechanism,
battery-operated, with quartz
oscillator frequency of 4.194 304
MHz

One-step-per-second central
second hand

Circuit design: integrated C-MOS
technology

Operational voltage range: 1.2 V
to 1.7 V

Operational temperature range:
+14° F to + 140° F (−10° C to
+60° C)

Current consumptions at nominal
voltage of 1.5 V: 270 uA

Battery type: 1 dry cell 1.5 V
(1EC R 14 DIN 40 865)

Average life of battery: 1 year

Mounting position: optional

Permissible vibrational load: 0
dB, at 20 to 1000 Hz

Permissible shock load: max. 100 g,
triangle impulse, duration 3 ms

Accuracy: 1 sec/24 hrs. at 23° C
± 3° C, 3 secs./24 hrs. at + 14°
F to + 140° F (−10° C to 60° C)

Accuracy of the alarm: ± 3
minutes

Duration of ringing tone: approx.
30 minutes.

Alarm Features:

Nominal voltage: 1.5 V DC

Current consumption: 1.5 mA

Operational voltage range: 1.1 V
to 1.65 V

Sound level within 20 cm:
approx. 70 dB.

RADIO OPERATORS CLOCK

This battery-operated clock offers
the same accuracy and resistance
to temperature and shock as the
cabin clock. Alarm feature. Alternating red and blue sectors on face
mark periods of radio silence for
emergency signals, meeting the requirements of International Marine Communication. A single
1.5v battery (included) powers the
chronometer for a full session. 6″
(152.40 mm) diameter x 3¾″
(95.25 mm) deep. Shatterproof
glass face.

BAROMETER

Housed in a 5 1/16″ (129 mm) case
of polished brass, the barometer's
clear, highly readable dial in international styling gives weather
trends at a glance. Atmospheric
pressure is indicated in both milli-
bar and millimeter of mercury.

2

ELECTRICAL SYSTEMS

Free Energy Systems, Inc.
Holmes Industrial Park
Pine and Prince Streets
Holmes, Pennsylvania 19043

129 SL SOLAR BATTERY CHARGER

Specifications:

18 Volts o/o 600 m/a, 10 Watts

Dimensions:
8″ x 30″ x 1/2″

The Free Energy 129SL is the standard photovoltac marine battery charger in the industry exclusively designed for the recreational field.

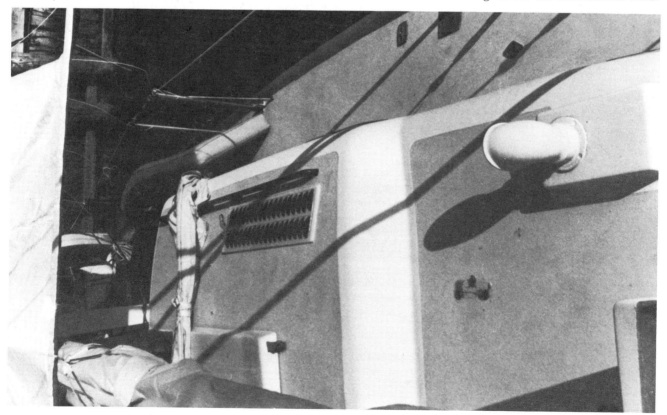

This unit incorporates 36 1/2–3″ high quality silicon solar cells. The cells are imbedded in a surgical grade silicon rubber and covered with shatterproof plexiglas for strength, impact and corrosion resistance. The covering is a non-reflective, non-skid surface. The edges are completely leveled for safety. The unit will conform to the curve of the deck of most marine vessels. Once the panel is mounted, it can be walked on without harm.

Model 129SQ

Specifications:

18 Volt o/o, 600 m/a, 10 Watts

Dimensions:

15¼″ x 15¼″ x ½″

This panel is preferred where hatch mounting is desirable or necessary.

Raritan Engineering Company
1025 North High Street
Millville, New Jersey 08332

CONVERTERS AND POWER ACCESSORIES

CROWN CONVERTER

Fully automatic solid state marine converters supply onboard DC power from dockside AC power line. Charges up to three separate banks of batteries automatically charging only those batteries that are below full charge. Includes an isolation transformer to help prevent electrolysis. Circuitry is included in each converter to allow engines to be run safely at dockside with the converter turned on. DC output automatically shuts down when engines are running to protect engine alternators. 50/60 cycles, 115V. (50/60 cycles, 230V available by special order.)

Model	Rated	DC Volts	Size-Inches (L x D x H)	Weight
R2012-3	20 Amps	12	13 1/2x7 1/4x8 1/4	33
R2024-3	20 Amps	24	17 1/2x8x10	56
R2032-3	20 Amps	32	17 1/2x8x10	57
R3012-3	30 Amps	12	13 1/2x8 1/4x9	39
R3024-3	30 Amps	24	17 1/2x8x10	61
R3032-3	30 Amps	32	17 1/2x8x10	69
R4012-3	40 Amps	12	17 1/2x8x10	54
R4024-3	40 Amps	24	17 1/2x8x10	69
R4032-3	40 Amps	32	17 1/2x8x10	69
R6012-3	60 Amps	12	17 1/2x8x10	62

CONVERTER REMOTE CONTROL

Provides remote control station for Raritan Crown Converter. Use with either shore line or onboard generator. Indicator lights show current flow, charging.

Model RMC

POWER LINE FILTER

Filters DC power supply noise from ship-to-shore radio. Easily installed by any competent electrician or electronic service technician.

Model PLF

SONIC POLARITY INDICATOR

Prevents electrolysis damage and dangerous shock hazards by warning of reversed polarity in shore line hookup. Alarm stops when connection is properly made. Hermetically sealed. Easily installed. Thousands in use.

PUSHBUTTON SWITCH

Single pole pushbutton switch for through-panel mounting. Fits in panels to 3/4″ thick. When used on heavy amp draw, such as Crown Head, use a Continuous Duty Solenoid.

Model RM726

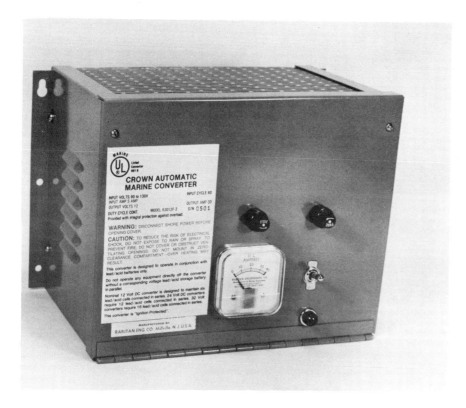

CROWN II CONVERTER

The "Crown" Converter line can operate under short circuit conditions without blowing fuses or tripping breakers. They will compensate for input voltages, of anywhere between 90 and 130 volts AC with the finishing voltage remaining constant.

In addition, the new Crown Converters have several safety features. Units are designed so that batteries cannot be overcharged should a part fail within the converter. A varistor protects the internal circuitry from lightning surges and spikes in line voltage. Units have no fans, switches, or

relays to wear out or malfunction. An isolation transformer eliminates a possible source of electrolysis. Output voltage is built into the transformer at the factory.

These converters can maintain up to three banks of batteries. They are designed to maintain batteries at 2.2 volts per cell. Ignition protected, they can be mounted above or below deck. UL listed.

The ferroresonant transformer is constructed of high quality "silicon steel laminations" and high quality insulation. Efficient heat sinks are used throughout.

Models are available with 12, 24, or 32 volt and 20, 30, or 40 ampere outputs; 12 volt available in 60 ampere output.

SUNWATER, Inc.
P.O. Box 732
Northridge, California 91328

WINDERATOR— MODEL 101

Features:

Generates power anytime there is a breeze. Eliminates trickle charger and extension cords for dock power connection.

3

HARDWARE

Cruising Design, Inc.
65 Rear Walnut Street
Peabody, Massachusetts 01960

THE REEFER

Designed to reef and furl almost any headsail, the reefer allows even lightly crewed or single-handed boats to achieve maximum sail area in variable wind conditions. The reefer performs so well because it's a grooved aluminum extrusion that fits right over the existing headstay. This ensures minimal sag in the sail's luff. The reefer's high torsional strength means negligible twist as the sail is reefed. No twist and little sag mean an even rolling of the sail for optimal reefed shape. So sailors can adjust the size of their sails to match the wind condition without leaving the cockpit.

The design of the reefer makes it the safest and most reliable furling system available. It has a self-contained halyard, led internally down the grooved headstay to the furling drum. By eliminating the connection between halyard and mast, the chief cause of failure in other systems is avoided. Loads on the bearings are also greatly reduced, eliminating the need for rust-prone steel bearings. The reefer is constructed of totally non-cor-

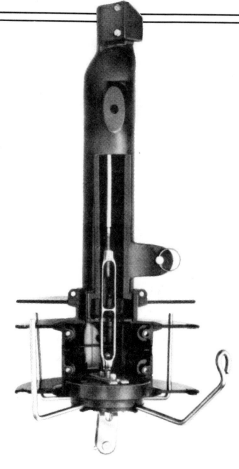

rosive materials (tough GE Lexan), and fits over almost any headstay and turnbuckle.

MODELS FOR YACHTS 18–55 FT.

Models R4/R6

Available for boats 18–27 feet

Fits headstay diameters 1/8 and 5/32 (#4), 3/16, and 7/32″ (#6)

Complete with halyard and all parts necessary for installation.

Tensioning unit is an optional accessory

Models R8/R9/R12

Available for boats 26–55 feet

Fits headstay diameters, 7/32, 1/4 (#8), 9/32 (#9), 5/16, and 3/8″ (#12)

Complete with halyard and tensioning system

Standard equipment on many high-quality yachts

THE TAILER

For a fraction of the cost of buying a new self-tailing winch, the tailer™ will convert an old winch into a state-of-the-art self-tailer . . . in just a few minutes, using only simple hand tools. It is designed to perform every function of a self-tailing winch and works on any size winch—one, two and three speeds—and any size line.

The tailer™ is constructed of durable engineering plastics and anodized aluminum, to provide years of carefree use. The unit consists of a ribbed flange which secures easily to the winch without structurally affecting it, and a stripper arm, which mounts on the surface next to the winch.

Sizing:

Size 1
Fits wenches with drum diameters of 2 1/2" to 3 7/16"
Lewmar 6-24
Barient 10-24
Barlow 16-24
Size 2
Fits winches with drum diameters

of 3 1/2" to 4"
Lewmar 43-44
Barient 26-28
Barlow 26
This list shows only some of the more popular model winches. The tailer™ fits and works well with almost any winch. It is only necessary to know the drum diameter to select the correct size.

W. H. Denouden (USA), Inc.
P. O. Box 8712
Baltimore, Maryland 21240

BOW-ROLLERS

Two models of stainless steel bow-rollers that make weighing the anchor an easy task. They also enable the anchor to be held in position on the Nylon rollers, instead of lying around on deck.

Specifications:

Type Asterix
Length: 328 mm (13")
Width: 106 mm (4")
Suitable for rope and chain up to 8 mm (5/16")
Type Obelix
Length: 445 mm (17 1/2")
Width: 150 mm (6")
Mx. chain size: 12 mm (1/2")

Falcon Safety Products, Inc.
1065 Bristol Road
Mountainside, New Jersey 07092

HALYARD HUSH-UPS

Halyard Hush-Ups provide a simple, effective way to restrain halyards and silence slapping noise. A few turns of Hush-Ups around shrouds and halyards will encircle both. Enclosed lines cannot bang or slap . . . results: Quiet! Rugged, weatherproof and economical, Hush-Ups never ride up, and refuse to get lost since they store conveniently on turnbuckles when not in use.

MOOR-SECURER

The Moor-Securer doubles the strength of the mooring system for boats moored at permanent anchor—cuts chafe by half while making mooring with two lines easy and tanglefree. The Moor-Securer consists of three rugged PVC links, ingeniously designed, to be set at intervals along parallel mooring lines, and all strongly secured with stainless steel hardware.

MOORING CINCH

This Mooring Cinch is an easy on/easy off secure way of preventing mooring pendants from lifting off their cleats. No need to lash lines; no need to strain, even in the heaviest weather. For double security, the Falcon® Mooring Cinch can be used even when pendant is double-looped over cleat. Made of sturdy PVC, the Mooring Cinch is available in two sizes to accommodate lines from 3/8" to 1".

SHOCK CORDS

These marine shock cords are covered in durable, bright blue nylon and feature non-rust, non-staining clamps, all inset to prevent snags. Non-marring, solid nylon hooks are guaranteed against cracking or peeling.

The Stretch Tie™ is a 3/16″ pre-assembled tie-down featuring open nylon hooks at each end. The hooks can be locked together instantly to form custom lengths for unlimited uses. Ideal for lashing down any kind of gear, Stretch-Tie is available in 12″, 18″ and 24″ lengths.

Super Stretch Tie™, the hefty 5/16″ version, is pre-assembled with large nylon hooks at either end, featuring the super-secure SnapLock. Two or more cords can be snapped together to form any desired length and, for even greater versatility, it is available in both 24″ and 36″ sizes. Any kind of heavy equipment—on board or on shore—can be quickly and easily secured with it.

The Lock Tie is a handy 1/4″ cord featuring a versatile wooden ball knot that completely eliminates knot tying. The ball knot secures any loop supertight, yet releases it instantly. This cord can be used to tie up or lash down just about anything from an anchor to a duffle because it's completely adjustable.

Tiller Tie™ is a simple-to-use shock cord system that keeps the tiller securely in place to prevent damage while the boat is docked. Recommended for boats 25′ and over, the fully adjustable system is quickly and easily installed.

The Sail Tie™ is a tie-down for the mainsail. Made of sturdy 3/16″ cord, Sail Tie comes completely assembled with fully adjustable fittings. It can be instantly attached and stays conveniently flush under the boom while the boat is under way.

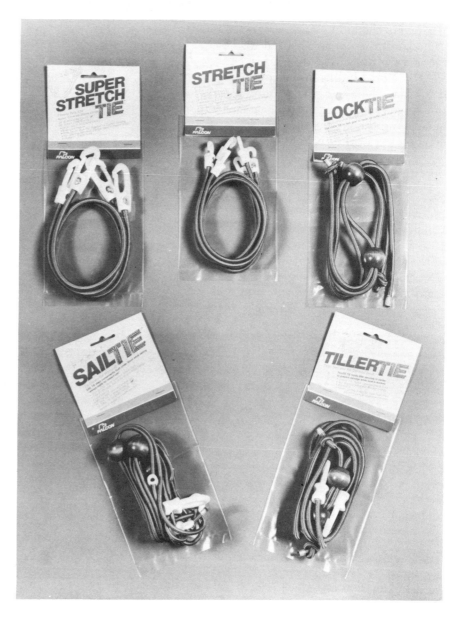

Hyde Products, Inc.
810 Sharon Drive
Cleveland, Ohio 44145

STREAM-STAY ROLLER REEFING/ FURLING SYSTEMS

The Hyde Stream-Stay® double groove headsail system makes your boat a versatile cruiser or racer. Stream-Stay requires no extra rig-ging—you have a dependable reef-ing/furling system and a double groove rod headstay for flat-out racing.

The double groove rod headstay allows you to sail downward with two headsails. This arrangement provides tremendous drive without the risk or inconvenience of setting a spinnaker. If sailing single handed is your style, the Hyde Stream-Stay system makes it easy and safe. Just pull on the sheet to set your sails. To reduce sail, simply haul in the furling line and reef as much of the sail as you need to meet varying wind conditions. When wind conditions become dangerous, there's no need for anyone to go forward because you can quickly furl the sail from the safety and comfort of the cockpit.

Specifications:

Stream-Stay is a single or double-groove, extruded aluminum rod which replaces the conventional wire forestay. It is sized according to the strength of the existing stay. Vertical reefing/furling systems for mainsail applications normally use size #9 or #10. Stream-Stay may also be adapted for staysails and other special sails.

Standard end terminals swivel on radial roller thrust bearings, 3 per terminal in sizes 8, 12 and 16; 2 per terminal in sizes 9 and 10.

Halyard swivels are fitted with two deep groove ball bearings, one each at the top and bottom to eliminate the possibility of cocking.

Materials:

Rod—Aluminum type 6061—T6
Terminals—Stainless steel
Type 316
Furling Drum and Halyard Swivel—Aluminum castings AL, MAG 35

Imtra
151 Mystic Avenue
Medford, Massachusetts 02155

V1000 and V3000 VERTICAL POWER WINDLASS

Nilsson's vertical design allows these high-capacity units to be thru-deck mounted, saving deck

space, reducing height and resulting in a striking appearance. Yet each is intended for the heaviest duty, constructed of bronze with stainless steel shafts and chrome-plated finish to exposed surfaces.

A single, folding lever operates both clutch and brake, eliminating separate clutch lever or mallet. A non-reversing mechanism in the gearbox prevents a backrunning when the motor is stopped under load. A heavy ratchet and pawl secure the chain when the warping drum is in use.

The rugged chain stripper and thru-deck chain pipe are included as standard, along with waterproof foot deckswitch, precision-generated oil-bathed reduction gears, bronze main-shaft bearings, sealed deck bearings and gearbox (to en-

sure waterproofness), drain provision, and heavy-duty isolated earth motor.

Features:

12v, 24v or hydraulic drive. Vertical space saving design. Foldaway clutch handles given snag-free operation. Clean cut functional and attractive appearance. All above-deck parts stainless steel or bronze. Sealed, self-locking gearbox and isolated earth motor fitted under deck, positions optional. Independent drive chainwheel with cone clutch/brake. Permanent drive warping capstan. Emergency hand wind.

ACCESSORIES

Sealed footswitch (electric models). Chain pipe and stripper.

Hand wind lever. Chain run indicator. Overload protection. Roving hand control. Fiberglass deck cover. Teak deck mounting pad.

OPTIONAL BUILDS

Extra length deck clearance. Dual direction on V1000 only. Reversed rotation with chainpipe opposite side. Low profile—(less capstan) chainwheel only model.

FINISH

Above deck, natural bronze or chrome. Underdeck, primed and enamelled.

CHAINWHEEL RANGE

V1000, all sizes up to ⅜″ (10mm)
V3000, all sizes up to ½″ (12mm)

SIZE

V1000 up to about 40 ft (12m)
V3000 up to about 65ft (20m)

ITT Jabsco

1485 Dale Way
Costa Mesa, California 92626

BALL-TYPE SEACOCKS

Jabsco now offers a full line of "ball-type" bronze seacocks. A hard chromed-bronze ball is seated in Teflon to provide low operating torque and eliminate the periodic lubrication needed with other types of seacocks. The surrounding body and handle are constructed from bronze and stainless steel to withstand harsh marine environments.

The handles of the seacocks are vinyl-coated and rotate ¼ turn to positive on and off stops. A predrilled triangular base supports the seacock and allows for ease of installation. Drain plugs are included for winterization.

RATING

V1000 12v: 1000 lbs at 12 rmp, 24v at 24 rpm
V3000 12v: 3000 lbs at 15 rpm, 24v at 20 rpm
No load amps 50 approx. No load speed approx. 70 rpm
V3000 Hyd: 3000 lbs at 35 rpm given 2000 psi at 6 gpm

Standard Equipment:

Chrome 12v, Chain Pipe, Foot Switch, Emerg. Crank Handle. Stock Nos. V1000C, V3000C.

Options:

Chain Meter, Stock No. V9010C, Fiberglass Cover, Stock No. V9005C, ¾″
Teak Spacer, Stock No. V9025C and 24v specify

Each valve is tested to 400 psi (2700 kPa) and 29 in. (1.0 kg/sq cm) of mercury vacuum. The valves are U.L. listed.

Six models are available in the Model 45560 Series of seacocks, ranging in size from ¾ in. (19.1 mm) to 2½ in. (63.5 mm).

Mr. Z's Products

22322 Basset Avenue
Canoga Park, California 91303

RIGGING VICE

Features:

Available in aluminum or bronze models
Size, 5½″ x 6″, for easy storing
Aluminum model weighs under 3 lbs.; bronze, 8 lbs
Vice capable of forming up to ½ inch cable around thimbles
Can be used to keep cable in place for Nicro press clips
Easy to use aboard ship or in workshop
Can be clamped vertically or horizontally.

Nashmarine

32906 Avenida Descamso
San Juan Capistrano, California

TRIGGER CLEAT

Trigger Cleat™ releases line when you pull down on tail. Allows you to ease sheets, vang, traveler, foreguy, etc. without removing line from cams. When tail is tensioned down on trigger, "geared" cams open and free line for easing through cam gap. When tail is raised, stainless steel cams regrip line. Line always stays between cams even when operated from up to 6 feet away. Allows you to trim from off axis and from high side of boat, keeping boat in balance. For lines to ½″. Weight 5½ oz. Bolt spacing 2.0″.

R & D Enterprises

Nautical Engineering Division
P.O. Box 5252
Northville, Michigan 48167

ANCHOR-LOK

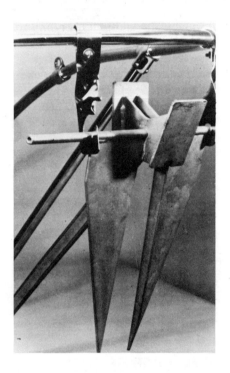

Each Anchor-Lok set consists of two (2) marine-grade stainless brackets, friction straps (to hold brackets in their adjusted position), and stainless steel attaching hardware. The set will accommodate fluke-type anchors with stock diameters up to and including ¾″ (i.e., 22S Danforth).

The brackets are easily installed on any 1″ or ⅞″ rail (bow or stern). By pivoting the brackets fore or aft, they adjust to fit many combinations of rail height and anchor size. This adjustability allows you to position your anchor so that the shank can be secured to a third point, i.e., tied to the base of the forestay, a pad eye, stemplate, or any similar hardware.

The third point attachment provides an added margin of safety in heavy weather. To keep the anchor from moving side to side, secure the brackets within approximately ½″ of each fluke.

MIDSHIP CLEAT I AND II

A moveable cleat available in 2 models. The first has a cleat of cast aluminum with an improved corrosion-resistant epoxy coating. The newest is made of injection-molded plastic. All other components on both models are marine-grade stainless steel.

Designed to fit a 1″ or 1¼″ T-Track, it can be moved to any position along the track in seconds, then secured in place by a standard thumb screw mechanism. No extra hardware is needed for installation or use.

When rafting off (port or starboard) run the cleat forward and tie up securely. When docking, use them for tying spring lines. Tie off fenders with no lifeline foul-ups.

REEF HOOKS

These handy hooks, because they are designed with a twist in two planes, are well-suited for such uses as:
Main or headsail tack points (use singly or back-to-back to make headsail changes smooth and easy)
Downhaul (or Cunningham hook)
Outhaul hook
Reef Hooks come in two sizes: *Large* for boats 25′ and over and *Small* for boats 24′ and under.

REEF-LOK

Uniquely designed to simplify main and headsail reefing when used at the tack. The need for standard reefing gear is eliminated along with the usual confusion of lines.

Simple to use, just bolt the Reef-Lok to your gooseneck or boom and lower sail to reef cringle. No more looking for pre-marked positions or making halyard adjustments after setting the main. Shaking out the reef is simpler and faster, too.

The Reef-Lok is available in two sizes: *Large* for boats 25' and over and *Small* for boats 24' and under.

TACK HOOK

Designed for speed and efficiency, the Tack Hook allows greater sail control for the racing sailor. The unique construction of marine-grade stainless steel enables 2 hooks to be bolted back-to-back so twin headsails can be hoisted.

One end of the Tack Hook is flat and pre-drilled for attachment to the gooseneck and/or stemplate. The opposite end is rounded to prevent damage, tears, and chafing.

The Tack Hook also eliminates the danger of flying shackles.

Pastime Products, Inc.
1035 South 11th Street
Philadelphia, Pennsylvania 19147

THE GRABBER

The slim, non-bulky Grabber adjusts quickly and securely to any length over its heavy duty elastic cord. Use the Grabber to furl a sail, hold gear or a drink on deck, keep a tarp in place or any of scores of uses around your boat.

PB Nautical Innovations, Inc.
262 Cardinal Leger
Pincourt, Quebec
J7V 347, Canada

MAST WALKERS

Features:

Specifically designed for sailing masts.

Comfortable and easy to use without assistance. Perfect for the singlehander.

Permanently fastened to masts with flat, oval, or round external surfaces.

Can be mounted on masts made of wood, aluminum alloy, carbon fiber, or glass fiber, etc.

Designed and fabricated to a 5:1 safety margin, i.e., a safe working load of over 1,000 lbs (454 kg). Documented stress tolerance test data available on request.

Die-cast of non-corroding aluminum for maintenance-free service. They cause no electrolysis.

Open and close without hinges. There is only one moving part which never wears out.

Present a very low profile against the mast when retracted to achieve minimum windage.

Contoured and smooth to reduce the risk of lines fouling and chafing.

Rungs cannot fall out of their support brackets regardless of how much the mast is heeled.

Installed on the mast with only four fasteners. Holes and fasteners cannot be seen when the rungs (steps) are in the folded position (closed).

Tamper and child proof. A security feature on the first few Mast Walkers prevents unauthorized climbing of the mast. One small screw does the job.

Have long (6 ¼ in.), and wide 1⅜ in.) rungs.

Bracket dimensions are: length 4⅝ in., width 2¾ in., thickness (depth) 1 in.

Weigh 12 oz. (330 g) per set (one rung and bracket, contour A).

Guaranteed for the life of your boat.

Ronstan Marine, Inc.
P.O. Box 3449
Clearwater, Florida 33515

DOUBLE AND SINGLE ROPE JAMMERS

Ronstan rope jammers are designed for use with halyards and reefing lines on large trailable yachts and keel boats to 33 feet in length. They allow multiple utilization of a minimum number of winches.

Suitable for ropes from six mm to twelve mm in diameter, they have serrated jaws on both the cam and the base for exceptional holding power, and they are easily operated under even extreme loads. Shown are models RF1394 (top) and RF1390 (bottom).

HALYARD TURNING BOXES

Ronstan's halyard turning boxes are designed for re-directing halyards aft from the mast-step area to the winches on the cabin top. They are available in two sizes, both in double and triple models. Each model features black stainless-steel cheeks flared to minimize rope chafe, as well as strategically placed freshwater wash holes. Both sizes have ¼-inch diameter fastening holes strong enough to handle the heaviest conditions. And for those who prefer rope-to-wire splices, the boxes also come with alloy sheaves grooved for wire.

SEALOC TURNBUCKLES

Ronstan's "Sealoc" turnbuckles feature improvements in tension capacity, ease of adjustment, weight, wind resistance, and metal fatigue. The toggle end of each turnbuckle is attached directly to a small stainless-steel barrel, and the threaded end is connected to the barrel with a hexagon coupling nut. The coupling is free to swivel on the barrel, and turning the coupling nut adjusts tension on the stay. Patents are pending on this design.

STAINLESS STEEL BLOCKS

These four blocks feature an innovative, electro-statically applied black nylon coating. Clockwise, from top, center, are the triple ratchet block (RF1494M), three-sheave fiddle block with snapshackle and becket (RF1172), single-ball-bearing block with universal head (RF1458), and the ratchet block with double roller block (RF1484M). This new coating method diminishes corrosion problems and provides higher tensile strength, longer life and superior impact resistance.

VERTICAL "I" TRACK

The vertical design of the Ronstan "I" track provides greater strength designs by transmitting loads in straight shear force to traveller wheels. Angular track/wheel designs tend to wedge the traveller open due to the 45-degree ramp effect, making them weaker and less dependable.

Available in four sizes with a complete selection of cars, blocks, camcleats and stops for boats up to seventy feet in length, the Ronstan "I" tracks are electrostatically coated with black nylon to improve corrosion resistance and longevity.

Shown on the RF830 large "I" track are (left to right) the Ronstan RF832 spring stop, RF874 stand-up block on slide, RF827 ball-bearing traveller car, RF853M double traveller control block with metal cam-cleat, and another RF832 spring stop.

SNAPSHACKLES

These snapshackles are designed with the pivot position at the side of the shackle for quick opening and high strength. Cast from certified 17-4PH stainless steel and heat treated to an ultimate tensile strength of 180,000 lb. P.S.I., they combine light weight, great strength and high corrosion resistance. They're easy to operate with wide opening arms and feature a guard around the plunger head along with a heavy-duty spring to prevent accidental flogging undone in bad conditions.

VANG KITS

Ronstan Marine offers vang kits suitable for a variety of purposes on boats up to forty-five feet in length. Ideal in applications such as a spare mainsheet system, backstay adjustment, trapeze height adjustment, centerboard or keel uphaul, hoisting a dinghy or lifting and moving other heavy equipment, the kits feature Ronstan stainless-steel blocks with electro-

statically applied black nylon coatings.

Pictured are the RK12-330 kit with 3:1 purchase and 30' x ⅜" line for yachts to thirty feet (top) and the RK12-440 kit with 4:1 purchase and 40' x 7/16" line for yachts to 45 feet (bottom).

Sea Spike Anchors, Inc.
994 Fulton Street
Farmingdale, New York 11735

THE SEA PLOW ANCHOR

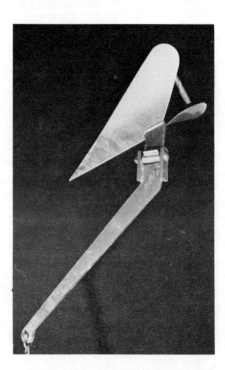

This compact anchor is contoured and balanced for quick setting and worry-free holding. If the boat is swung by wind or tide, the Sea Plow burrows in deeper. It can hold up to 300 times its weight. When the shank is pulled directly upward, it breaks out easily and clean. The Sea Plow is of all-welded steel construction and hot dipped galvanized to protect it against corrosion.

SEA SPIKE AND SEA SPIKE SLIDING RING ANCHOR

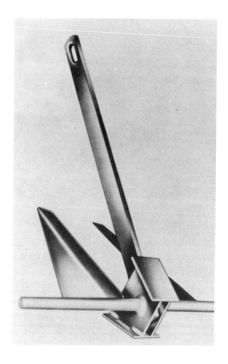

Features of both anchors:

Because the widely spaced flukes are not easily bridged, very little is brought up from the bottom. The anchors can't clog or jam with mud, shells or small stones.

The small flukes, made possible by the extra drag of the center section, requires far less effort to break out than does the ordinary anchor.

It digs in faster and holds better . . . line pull on shank causes center section to act in a tripping fashion thereby forcing flukes down.

There is more holding power made possible by the extra drag of the center section.

YACHTSMAN'S ANCHOR

Size: 7 lb. 15 lb. 25 lb.
35 lb. 50 lb. 75 lb.

Spartan Marine Products, Inc.

160 Middleboro Avenue
East Taunton, Massachusetts
02718

CLEATS

BRONZE CLEATS

Spartan Marine bronze cleats are tumble finished smooth and inspected individually. Available in burnished, polished bronze or bright chrome on bronze.

DESK CLEATS

Cast bronze. Traditional styling in two-hole and four-hole configurations.

HERRESHOFF CLEATS

Cast bronze. Each cleat has four-hole mounting requiring FHMS.

JAM CLEATS

3" Jam Cleat adequately handles up to ¼" line. Two-hole mounting for #8 FH fastener. 6" Jam Cleat adequately handles up to ⅜" line. Four-hole mounting ¼" fasteners.

COAMING CLEATS

These coaming cleats make mounting sheet cleats on wood coamings simple and effective. Each cleat houses mounting holes threaded for ¼-20 MS.

LOCKING CHOCK

These chocks are designed to quickly accept an anchor or mooring line and lock it in place. Each chock is solid manganese bronze for a tough cast construction. A strong ⁵/₁₆" stainless steel bolt easily slides to form a large 1½" opening between the chock jaws and slides shut securing and locking the line in place. The wide 1 ⅝" locking chock base has three mount holes for ¼" FHMS. This chock can also be considered for the stern where rising and falling tides can easily cause a dock line to escape a straight open chock.

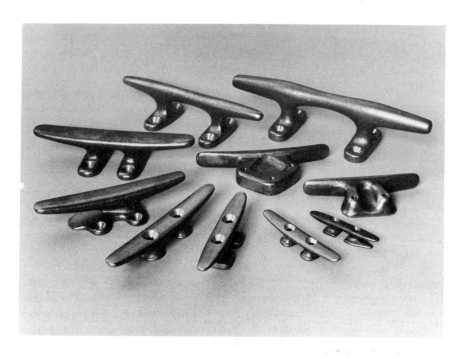

SEACOCKS

Solid brass construction. Each valve base is designed with a caulking groove to improve watertightness about the base. The mounting holes are enclosed slots to fully support a washer and the head of the mounting fasteners. A turning key has a cast bronze handle attached to it with a stainless steel fastener. Our shut-off stop detail ensures the user that the Spartan valve is in the closed position when required.

The hose adapter is grooved for positive hose clamping. The base has a female thread which is a straight pipe thread so a thur-hull can be properly installed in the seacock. Two drain fasteners are located to either side of the seacock housing and can be used to drain the valve during its lay-up period. The full-opening plug type seacock is easily dismantled for annual maintenance.

Specifications:

Maximum Working Load—
600 lbs.

Stall Rating—1,000 lbs.
Motor—1.3 HP
Voltage—12 Volt DC
Gear Ratio—123:1

Superwinch

Connecticut Route 52, Exit 95
Putnam, Connecticut 06260

WINDLASS

Features:

Weatherproof deck-mounted foot switch.
Permanent magnet 12-volt motor.
Permanently lubricated and sealed gearbox.
Finish is Imron* polyurethane over epoxy primer.
Tenzalloy aluminum gypsy with clear anodized finish.
For sailboats 20-40 feet.
Note: Wildcats are not intended for all chain anchor rode, only for leader chain.

*Dupont registered trademark.

Declercq Marine Systems, Inc.

Winch Tailer Division
7144 South Shore Drive, South
St. Petersburg, Florida 33707

WINCH TAILER

In the demanding sport of offshore yacht racing, winning can usually be attributed directly to crew and equipment efficiency. The sophisticated technology influencing modern yacht and sail design has produced a dramatic increase in sheet and halyard loads. Ultimately, all this loading ends up at one point, a line which the crew has to move in or out to control sail trim. The speed and efficiency of both crew and equipment is critical at this point.

Competition spawns innovation and Winch Tailer was originally developed to meet the needs of competition. The cruising community was also quick to realize the advantages of our system.

Winch Tailer is a new accessory which expands the performance of any winch by providing both self-tailing and instant cleating capabilities. Four years of intense research and product evaluation has produced the only system which keeps the line, winch and tailer perfectly prepared to perform all winch functions in any sequence. And these functions are performed instantly from any distance.

Easing out your line is simply accomplished with an upward flip on the line. This action releases your line from the roller's grip while a downward snap relocks it. The line can be released, eased and relocked from any distance away, in the time it takes to snap the line twice.

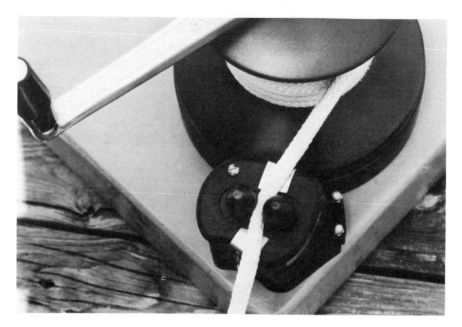

tailing winches. Also, cranking a winch fitted with a Winch Tailer requires half the effort compared to self-tailing winches. And Winch Tailer's rollers do not chew up your line by dragging it through an obstacle course.

An added feature of Winch Tailer is its ability to automatically grip any size line. No adjustments are required. Once your line is removed from the rollers, Winch Tailer retracts from contact and your winch becomes free spinning.

Winch Tailer will add versatility and greater efficiency to your existing winches with demonstrated advantages over new self-tailing winches. Winch Tailers are available in five models which adapt to any size winch. A complete mounting kit which includes do-it-yourself instructions, spacers and fasteners to simplify the installation, is furnished with each Winch Tailer.

The winch handle can remain in the winch during the complete procedure without interference.

The ability to ease-out or cast off instantly without prior preparation is important to the safety of both your crew and your yacht. Winch Tailer is doubly safe in this respect because your line is less likely to accidentally unlock than on self-

4

NAVIGATION AIDS

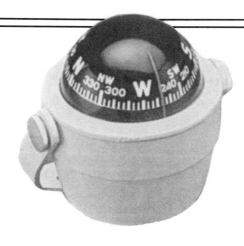

Airguide Instrument Company
2210 Wabansia Avenue
Chicago, Illinois 60647

COMPASSES

NOS. 57-B, 57-W
NOS. 57-BI, 57-WI
With illumination.
Direct reading dome type card for excellent visibility. Can be quickly removed from bracket for safekeeping. Built-in compensators. Case and mounting bracket finished in either black or white. 3 ⅜″ (86 mm) high, 3 ¼″ (83 mm) wide.

NO. 61 FOR SMALL BOATS HAS QUICK RELEASE FEATURE
A quick twist and you can remove this compass from its base plate for safekeeping. Clear white graduations read to 5° on black compass card. Bright red 45° lubber lines aid in observing wind shifts. Card pivots freely to accommodate heeling up to 35°. Designed for small fiberglass or wood craft, it has no compensating mechanism. 4″ (102

mm) across base, 3″ (76 mm) high. Not illuminated. Removable plugs open holes in case to allow Cunningham to pass through when necessary. Non-corrosive black Cycolac® case.

NOS. 62-B, 62-W
NOS. 62-BI, 62-WI
With illumination.
An extremely visible and dependable small boat compass. Easily removed for safe storage. Built-in compensator system. Metal case and mounting bracket finished in black or white. 3 ⅜″ (86 mm) high, 3 ¼″ (83 mm) wide.

NO. 64 HAND BEARING COMPASS
Accurate, lightweight and illuminated. A useful accessory for any

craft. Plot your position on the water by sights or bearings on distant landmarks. Or relocate the spot where the big ones are biting.

Big 3″ (76 mm) diameter compass turns on a jeweled bearing and is damped in oil for precise and steady readings. Clear sight vanes superimpose bright yellow sight lines over the white-on-black card. The rugged Cycolac® handle is formed to fit the hand and a wrist lanyard gives added security. On-off switch controls the self-contained battery powered night light (battery included). A Dacron® tote bag protects the instrument when not in use. Overall height is 5 ½″ (140 mm) and the spread of the sight vanes is 4 ½″ (115).

No. 70 BULKHEAD MOUNT COMPASS
A large surface mount bulkhead compass. Requires no large holes to mount. Merely fasten to vertical or inclined surface with 4 screws. Movement is jeweled and internally gimbaled. Built-in compensators. Additional 45° lubber lines aid in navigation and sailing. Inclinometer shows angle of heel. Rhe-

ostat controlled night light is built-in. Rugged black phenolic binnacle and sunshade. 7″ (180 mm) high, 6″ (153 mm) wide, 4 ½″ (115 mm) deep.

No. 78-C FOR ONE DESIGN AND SMALL CRUISING CLASS RACING
Rugged black Cycolac® case. Centerline gimbal allows compass to level when heeling. Compass snaps from anodized aluminum U-bracket for safe stowage.

Red 45° lubber lines indicate the amount of "lift" or "header" the boat is receiving from a shifting wind. The helmsman can then pick his way through shifting winds to reach the windward mark in the shortest time possible.

Jeweled movement. AG-1000 alloy pivot and powerful Alnico V card magnets. Adjustable compensators in base. Case is 3 ⅜″ (85 mm) diameter, 4 ⅝″ (125 mm) high. Illuminated.

NOS. 87-B, 87-W
Ideal for small sail and power boats, and useful as a repeater or standby on larger craft. Popular direct reading card. Built-in compensating system. Jeweled movement. Easily removed from U-bracket for safe storage. Black or white molded case, black anodized gimbal ring and bracket. 3 ⅜″ (86 mm) high, 3 ½″ (90 mm) across bracket.

NO. 97-A LOW PROFILE LARGE DIAMETER COMPASS
Five lubber lines allow the sailor to remain on course while on the raft or in a trapeze. Internal gimbals keep the compass card and lubber lines level at almost any angle. Inclinometer shows angle of heel. Has no internal compensating system, as most racing and day sailing boats have little ferrous metal or electronic gear to deflect the compass. Low set for non-line fouling.

Easy to mount. Stands only 3 ⅝″ (92 mm) high, yet is a big 6″ (153 mm) across its flange.

No. 919 WINDIAL WIND SPEED INDICATOR AND COMPASS
WinDial hand anemometer shows wind direction and speed, quickly and accurately. Just point WinDial into the breeze and read the big 3 ½″ white-on-black dial. Lightweight and self-contained, there are no batteries, electrical circuits or recalibration necessary. Scaled 5–70 MPG. Black Cycolac® case is 7 ½″ high. Boxed.

Alden Electronic and Impulse Recording Equipment Company, Inc.
Alden Research Center
Westborough, Massachusetts
01581

WEATHER CHART RECORDER

The Alden Marinefax IV is the most compact fully integrated weather chart recorder available with a built-in radio. Its rugged shock mounted construction features solid state circuitry and simple electro-mechanical design to insure long trouble free operation in the marine environment. The printing process is quiet and free from fumes, smoke or odors. No venting is required. Its small size and light weight allow the Marinefax IV to be installed in any convenient location on the bridge, in the navigator's area, radio room or even in the Captain's quarters. The system can be mounted on a table-top or vertically on a bulkhead.

The Alden Marinefax IV provides Captains of pleasure craft and commercial vessels with radiofacsimile weather charts and oceanographic charts 11 inches wide by any length on a worldwide basis. Weather charts provide information on existing and forecast wind intensity and direction, as well as wave heights. Surface maps indicate the actual and predicted location of major storms and fronts. Ice information is broadcast where pertinent. Satellite cloud pictures are available in many areas.

The built-in radio is designed specifically for the reception of radiofacsimile weather charts. It features solid state, phase locked, digital synthesized tuning combined with "winking" lights to permit easy tuning of all frequencies worldwide from 100 kHz to 29.999 MHz. Coverage is continuous with no gaps. You no longer need to buy and store expensive crystals. All the frequencies you'll ever need are available at your fingertips.

The radio may also be used to copy long wave weather transmissions, marine coast station voice weather broadcasts as well as WWV time ticks. Broadcasts from ships at sea and from worldwide amateur radio operators may also be monitored.

The Marinefax IV is very simple to install. Since the radio and recorder are fully integrated in one package, installation consists of locating the system in the desired position and plugging it into the available power source. Connecting the Marinefax IV to a suitable whip or long wire antenna completes the job. Alden also offers a compact 4 ft. 8 in. (1.4 m) all wave antenna as an option.

All operating controls are located on a central control panel. To operate the Marinefax, simply turn the system on, select the operating speed desired and dial-in the desired frequency utilizing the digital thumbwheel switches. The rest is automatic. The system starts, prints and stops upon command from the transmit site. When transmitting or radio propagation conditions are less than optimal, the fine tuning control feature brings in a clear, sharp chart.

The Alden Marinefax IV uses Alfax electrosensitive paper packaged in handy disposable cassettes. To reload paper, simply drop in a replacement cassette. No threading of paper is necessary.

Specifications:
RECORDER
Recording Rates:
60, 90, 120 SPM.

Index of Cooperation:
Automatic with manual override switch. IOC 576 CCIR, 169 lines per inch. IOC 288 CCIR, 84 lines per inch.

Control Signals:
Automatic and manual start, phase and stop.

Start:
Signal shifting between 1500 Hz and 2300 Hz at a 300 Hz or 675 Hz (for 288 IOC) rate for 5 seconds.

Phase:
A 1500 Hz signal interrupted by a short burst of 2300 Hz each scan line. Duration: 20–30 seconds immediately following start signal.

Stop:
Signal shifting between 1500 Hz and 2300 Hz at a 450 Hz rate for 5 seconds.

Circuitry:
Solid state.

Input Impedance:
600 ohms balanced.

Input Level:
−25 dBm to +10 dBm.

Scanning Electrode:
Stylus belt.

Recording Paper:
Alfax electrosensitive paper in throw-away cassettes with built-in printing electrode. Each cassette contains 35 ft. (10.7 m) of 11 in. (27.9 cm) wide paper.

Size:
4¼ in. (10.7 cm) H x 16 in. (40.6 cm) W x 9¾ in. (24.7 cm) D.

SYSTEM CHARACTERISTICS
Input Power:
115 VAC ±10% 50/60 Hz.
220 VAC ±10% Hz.
12 VDC ±2 Volts

Maximum Power Standby Mode:
25 Watts.

Maximum Power Operating Mode:
47 Watts.

Net Weight:
17.8 lbs. (7.9 kg).

Dimensions:
4¼ in. (10.7 cm) H x 16 in. (40.6 cm) W x 9¾ in. (24.7 cm) D.

OPTIONAL ANTENNA
Frequency Coverage:
50 kHz to 30 MHz continuous.

Antenna Height:
4 ft. 8 in. (1.42 m).

Output Impedance:
Switch selectable. 50, 100, 500 ohms.

Power Required:
115 or 220 VAC ±10% switch selectable, 50/60 Hz, 4 Watts.

Control Module Dimensions:
6.5 in. (16.5 cm) W x 3 in. (7.5 cm)

Dimensions:
H x 7.5 in. (19.0 cm) D.

Shipping Weight:
9 lbs. (4.1 kg).

RADIO RECEIVER
Frequency Coverage:
100 kHz to 29.999 MHz continuous.

Reception Modes:
Upper sideband, lower sideband, FSK, CW.

Frequency Readout:
Digital thumbwheel switches to 1 kHz resolution.

Frequency Selection:
10, 1, .1, .01, .001 MHz steps—±1 kHz fine tune.

Frequency Stability:
±50 Hz. At constant ambient of 25°C in any 8 hour period after ½ hour warm up.

Image Rejection:
80 dB.

RF Blocking:
120 dB to 1 uV. Desired signal 60 dB above 1 uV with blocking signal removed 20 kHz and its amplitude adjusted to reduce desired signal by 3 dB.

AGC Range:
Audio output is flat within 5 dB, with an RF input level from 3 uV to 1V.

Intercept Point:
The level of an input signal required to drive the RF stages of the receiver nonlinear: 20 dBm.

RF Bandwidth:
2.4 kHz at 6 dB.
4.8 kHz at 60 dB.

Audio Active Filter:
An audio active filter insures that noise component from the mixer outside of the normal audio bandwidth is attenuated.

Audio Output:
a) Fax Recorder Drive: 0 dBm from 600 ohm source.
b) Monitor Audio: 2 Watts RMS into internal 4 ohm speaker.

Power Source:
Derived from recorder. 13.8 VDC ± 10% at .4 amp.

Sensitivity 10 dB (S + N)/N:

RF Bandwidth:	100 kHz	200 kHz
4 kHz SSB-CW:	10 uV	5.0 uV
Nominal:	5 uV	1.5 uV

400 kHz–20 MHz	20 MHz–29.999 MHz
1.0 uV	1.0 uV
.5 uV	.6 uV

Brookes and Gatehouse, Inc.

154 East Boston Post Road
Mamaroneck, New York 10543

HALCYON ELECTRONIC COMPASS

The Halcyon repeating compass is an electronic compass system that uses a flux gate sensing unit rather than a conventional compass card. Once installed, the sealed sensing unit need never be touched, and can be mounted anywhere in the boat reasonably free of magnetic influence. Up to three 4″ diameter compass indicator dials can be located at the helm, a second station and in the navigator's area. A bold pointer gives boat's heading, and the indicator is fitted with an adjustable course grid to make steering a course easier. It is illuminated for nighttime use.

Since the sensing unit detects the earth's magnetic field directly, it is not affected by vibration, pitch or roll which cause conventional compass cards to wander and spin. Recovery in a turn is instantaneous. A patented suspension system eliminates errors due to heel. Halcyon is suitable for any hull material, including steel.

Accuracy is ± 2°. The sensing unit contains internal compensators for deviation correction. Voltage is 12 to 24 VDC, less than two watts nominal power draw. Both sensor and indicator are sealed, waterproof units and carry a three year warranty.

HERCULES NAVIGATIONAL COMPUTER

Features:

Data Available:
Boat Speed, Stored Log, Reset Log, Battery Voltage, Apparent Wind Speed and Direction, True Wind Speed and Direction, V.M.G. Reaching and Tacking Performance, Stopwatch, Timer
With the addition of the Brookes and Gatehouse Halcyon 2 Compass: Ship's Heading, Dead Reckoning, Magnetic Heading of the Wind

Analog Readout available as optional extra, and Hercules will interface with the Trimble Loran, to allow Loran data to be displayed anywhere on board.

World-wide Three Year Warranty, parts and labor.
Operating Range:
Humidity 0–100%, Temperature −10°C to 80°C (Internal)

HOMER 5 MARINE RADIO RECEIVER

Homer 5 is a single band marine radio receiver with the remarkable frequency range of 50 kilohertz to 25 megahertz continuous. Yet this sophisticated all-frequency receiver is only 9″ wide, 5″ high and 4 ¾″ deep. It is double-sealed for completely weatherproof operation. It can be tuned digitally from the sealed keypad or manually with the variable rate tuning knob, which can cover the entire range in just a few seconds, yet at slow speed offers the fine tuning necessary for SSB reception.

Sophisticated microprocessor-based circuitry allows for the elimination of complicated controls. All receiver functions except frequency and volume are automatic. Tuning frequency is digitally synthesized, with an accuracy of better than ten parts per million. A built-

in quartz clock gives an accuracy of ± seconds per week. Separate modes are provided for optimum reception of all principal marine transmissions: AM, FM, upper and lower Single Sideband, CW and DF.

The microprocessor memory function stores up to 24 radio frequencies and modes for instant push button tuning, including 6 radio-beacon frequencies in an automatic 6-minute radio-beacon tuning program, as well as nine alarm times per 24-hour period to automatically turn on the radio on a predetermined radio watch schedule. Provision is made for outputs to headphones, external speaker, recorder and weatherfax equipment, with automatic start-stop signals to the recorder or facsimile machine.

The Homer 5 radio can also be used with G & G's hand held Heron RDF. Heron covers the entire 190 to 415 kHz radio-beacon band and features an extremely sharp null, indicated as a digital bar chart on the LCD display.

HORIZON SATELLITE NAVIGATOR

Features:

Simple operation.
Compact display unit with pressure tested, waterproof case.
Low power "stand-by" mode.
Non-volatile data memory with continuous running clock.
Interfaces directly to B & G instruments for automatic dead reckoning between fixes.
Long aerial lead available—up to 150 feet standard.
Three year, world-wide guarantee.

CURRENT NAVIGATIONAL DATA

Present latitude and longitude, also last position fix.

GMT or local time plus date.
Manual entry of tide direction and speed; the unit will calculate tide after two fixes.
Course (true or magnetic); speed made good and time from fix before last.
Present speed and heading entered manually or automatically from, for example, the Hercules system 190.

WAYPOINTS (1–9)
Waypoint number, course to steer to waypoint (allowing for tide; time to waypoint at present speed). Rhumb line bearing and distance to waypoint.

Latitude and longitude of waypoint.
Speed made good in direction of waypoint on present heading.
Speed made good on a new heading (e.g. on the other tack).
Great circle bearing and distance to waypoint.

SATELLITE STATUS
Past: Latitude; longitude; quality and time of last 3 good fixes
Present: Greenwich mean time or local time also status and number of satellite including rise and set time of present or next satellite.
Future: Catalog of satellite numbers, rise times, elevations and quadrants of next 100 Satellites.

Cybernet International, Inc.
7 Powder Horn Drive
Warren, New Jersey 07060

CTX-1000 MARINE HAILER/INTERCOM

Simple push button operation allows the operator to choose and se-

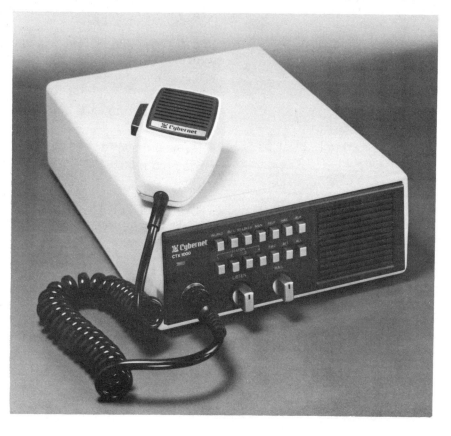

lect a function with ease. Its compact size allows it to be placed almost anywhere onboard the boat. The CTX-1000 was designed with the most advanced marine electronic circuitry available today. A full 25 watts of hailing power allows the CTX-1000 to be clearly heard at great distances. A full intercom system is also incorporated in this hailer-system.

Specifications:

Input voltage: 12 VDC (13.8 VDC nominal)

Polarity: Negative ground

Input power:
Listen (zero signal): 1.0A
Listen (2 watt output): 1.2A
Intercom: 1.2A
Loud Hall (25W output): 6.0A
Foghorn (25W output): 6.0A

Output impedance: 8 ohms

Microphone (Dynamic): 600 to 2000 ohm w/PTT switch

Foghorn frequency: 400 Hz ± 100 HZ

Amplifier characteristics:
Hail sensitivity (1 kHz): 6 mV for 25W output
Hail distortion (1 kHz): 10% at 25W output
Listen sensitivity (1 kHz): 1 mV for 2W output
Listen distortion (1 kHz): 5% at 2W output

Dimensions: 7½"W x 3"H x 9¹³/₁₆"D (190 x 76 x 250 mm)

Weight: Approx. 7.7 lbs. (3.5 kg)

CTX40 + 4 RADIO TELEPHONE

The CTX-40+4 Citizen Band Radio was designed with the mariner in mind. It is equipped with all 40 channels plus 4 VHF marine band weather channels for continuous monitoring of weather information. Compact and rugged, it is ideally suited for recreational and commercial vessels requiring a heavy duty CB.

Specifications:
GENERAL
Number of channels:
CB: 40
Weather: 4

Systems:
CB: PLL digital synthesizer
Weather: Crystal controlled

Supply Voltage: 13.8 volts DC negative ground

Microphone: Dynamic with PTT SW

Operating temperature:
CB: −30°C—+50°C
Weather: −20°C—+50°C

Built in speaker: 8 ohms

Controls: Volume w/on off, squelch, channel selector, mode SW, weather SW

Connectors: Ext. SP jack 3.5 mm
Hailer SP jack 3.5 mm
Antenna receptacle for PL-259
DC power connector

Circuit protection: Prevents transistor burn out when transmitting w/o antenna (5 minute limit)
2 amp. fuse in DC power cord

ANL: Built in automatic noise limiter

Dimensions: 6¼"W x 2⁹/₁₆"H x 7¾"D (160 x 66 x 198 mm)

Weight: Approx. 3.3 lb. (1.5 kg)

TRANSMITTER
FCC-DOC approved
Frequency range: 26.965–27.405 mHz

Frequency response: 400–2.5 kHz

Transmit power output: 4 watts FCC max.

Modulation capability: Up to 100%

Frequency tolerance: ± 0.003%

Spurious emission: −60 dB

SENSITIVITY
0.7 uV at 10 dB S+N/N
Frequency range: 26.965–27.405 mHz

Adjacent channel selectivity: −50 dB

Audio output @ 10% THD: 3.5W (8 ohms at ext. spkr. jack)

Spurious rejection: −50 dB

Image rejection: −50 dB

Squelch range: 0.5–2000 uV

IF frequency:
1st: 10.695 mHz
2nd: 455 kHz

WEATHER RECEIVER:
Sensitivity 20 dB NQ: 1.2 uV (measurable at antenna terminal)

Frequency range: 161.650–162.55 mHz

Spurious rejection: −40 dB

Image rejection: −30 dB

IF frequency:
1st: 10.695 mHz
2nd: 455 kHz

CTX-1200 VHF/FM RADIOTELEPHONE

The CTX-1200 is a low-cost VHF/FM radiotelephone for coastal cruising, with 12 channels to meet the most popular communication's needs and 25 watts of power. Ruggedly constructed, the CTX-1200 has been engineered and manufactured to perform in the harshest marine environment. It's the ideal radiotelephone for all types and sizes of boats.

Specifications:

GENERAL
Frequency range:
Transmitter: 156.00–157.50 mHz
Receiver: 156.00–163.00 mHz

Number of channels:
Transmitter: 12 (10 supplied)
Receiver: 12

Supply voltage: 13.6 volts DC negative ground

Antenna impedance: 50 ohms

Modulation: 16F3

Microphone impedance: 600–2000 ohms

Current drain:
Transmitter H/L: 5.0A/2.0A
Receiver stby/rated: 0.4A/1.0A

Temperature range: −20°C to +50°C

FCC: Part 83 & 15

DOC: RSS 182 V

Dimensions: $6^7/_{15}$"W x 2½"H x $9^5/_{16}$"D (164 x 63 x 237 mm)

Weight: Approx. 4.8 lbs. (2.2 kg)

TRANSMITTER
Output power: 25 W/1 W

Deviation: ±5 kHz max. @ 1 kHz

Spurious & harmonics: −65 dB

Audio frequency response: +1, −3 dB, 300–3000 Hz

Distortion: 5%

RECEIVER
Sensitivity:
−12 dB sinad: 0.3 uV
20 dB quieting: 0.35 uV

Squelch sensitivity:
Threshold: 10 dB noise quieting
Tight: 2 uV

Modulation acceptance bandwidth: ±7 kHz

Spurious & image rejection: −65 dB

Intermodulation rejection: −60 dB

Selectivity: −70 dB

Hum & noise: −50 dB

Audio frequency response: +1, −8 dB, 300–3000 Hz

Audio output 10% THD 4 ohms: 5 watts

CTX-2400 VHF/FM RADIOTELEPHONE

The CTX-2400 incorporates all the features needed for the captain requiring dependable communications and the flexibility of channels, but who doesn't want the expense of synthesized radios. The CTX-2400 comes equipped with 24 channels that may be changed at any time, if desired, whether it be U.S. or International. A full 25 watts of transmit power is ready for distance communication, especially when safety is critical. Ideally suited for both commercial and recreational use.

Specifications:
GENERAL
Frequency range:
Transmitter: 156.00–157.50 mHz
Receiver: 156.00–163.00 mHz

Number of channels:
Transmitter: 20
Receiver: 24

Supply voltage: 13.6 volts DC negative ground

Antenna impedance: 50 ohms

Modulation: 16F3

Microphone impedance: 600–2000 ohms

Current drain:
Transmitter H/L 5.0A/2.0A
Receiver stby/rated: 0.4A/1.0A

Temperature range: −20°C to +50°C

FCC: Part 83 & 15

DOC: RSS 182 V.L.C.

Dimensions: 7½"W x 3"H x $9^{13}/_{16}$D (190 x 76 x 250 mm)

Weight: Approx. 7.7 lbs. (3.5 kg)

TRANSMITTER
Output power: 25 W/1 W

Deviation: ±5 kHz max. @ 1 kHz

Spurious & harmonics: −70 dB

Audio frequency response: +1, −3 dB, 300–3000 Hz

Distortion: 5%

RECEIVER
Sensitivity:
−12 dB sinad: 0.3 uV
20 dB quieting: 0.35 uV

Squelch sensitivity:
    Threshold: 10 dB noise quieting
    Tight: 2 uV

Modulation acceptance bandwidth: ±7 kHz

Spurious & image rejection: −70 dB

Intermodulation rejection: −70 dB

Selectivity: −70 dB

Hum & noise: −50 dB

Audio frequency response: +, −8 dB, 300–3000 Hz

Audio output 10% THD 4 ohms: 5 watts

CTX-5000 VHF/FM RADIOTELEPHONE

Fully synthesized for all U.S. marine channels with the turn of a dial. The large LED channel readout has been designed for maximum visibility in all light conditions. The CTX-5000 also incorporates the dual watch feature of monitoring channel 16 distress and any desired channel selected.

Specifications:

GENERAL
Frequency range:
    Transmitter: 156.00–157.50 mHz
    Receiver: 156–163.00 mHz
Number of channels:
    Transmitter: 45
    Receiver: 50
Supply voltage: 13.8 volts DC negative ground

Antenna Impedance: 50 ohms

Modulation: 16F3

Microphone impedance: 600–2000 ohms

Current drain:
    Transmitter H/L: 5.5A/2.2A
    Receiver stby/rated: 0.5A/1.5A

Temperature range: −20°C to +50°C

FCC: Part 83 & 15

DOC: RSS 182 V.L.C.

Dimensions: 8½"W x 3¹/₁₆"H x 10⅞"D (216 x 78 x 277 mm)

Weight: Approx. 7.7 lb. (3.5 kg)

TRANSMITTER
Output power: 25 W/1 W

Deviation: ± kHz max. @ 1 kHz

Spurious & harmonics: −70 dB

Audio frequency response: +1, −3 dB, 300–3000 Hz

Distortion: 5%

RECEIVER
Sensitivity:
    −12 dB sinad: 0.3 uV
    20 dB quieting: 0.35 uV

Squelch sensitivity:
    Threshold: 10 dB noise quieting
    Tight: 2 uV

Modulation acceptance bandwidth: ±7 kHz

Spurious & image rejection: −70 dB

Intermodulation rejection: −70 dB

Selectivity: −70 dB

Hum & noise: −50 dB

Audio frequency response: +1, −8 dB, 300—3000 Hz

Audio output 10% THD 4 ohms: 5 watts

CTX-5500 VHF/FM RADIOTELEPHONE

Fully synthesized, the CTX-5500 is designed to meet the requirements for simple operation, yet incorporates all the capabilities of a full function keyboard VHF/FM radiotelephone. The micro-processed synthesizer has been engineered to make available all U.S. and Canadian channels. Ideally suited for the application where flexibility in channels is mandatory.

Specifications:

Model number CTX-5500

GENERAL
Frequency range:
    Transmitter: 156.00–157.50 mHz
    Receiver: 156.00–163.00 mHz

Number of channels:
    Transmitter: 55
    Receiver: 59

Supply voltage: 13.6 volts DC negative ground

Antenna impedance: 50 ohms

Modulation: 16F3

Microphone impedance: 600–2000 ohms

Current drain:
    Transmitter H/L: 6.0A/2.5A
    Receiver stby/rated: 0.6A/1.5A

Temperature range: −20°C to +50°C

FCC: Part 81 & 15, 83

DOC: RSS 182 V.L.C.

Dimensions: 9¹³/₁₅"W x 3⅜"H x 12⅞"D (250 x 84 x 327 mm)

Weight: Approx. 8.6 lbs. (3.9 kg)

TRANSMITTER
Output power: 25 W/1 W

Deviation: ±5 kHz max. @ 1 kHz

Spurious & harmonics: −70 dB

Audio frequency response: +1, −3 dB, 300–3000 Hz

Distortion: 5%

RECEIVER
Sensitivity:
    −12 dB sinad: 0.3 uV
    20 dB quieting: 0.35 uV

Squelch sensitivity:
    Threshold: 10 dB noise quieting
    Tight: 2 uV

Modulation acceptance bandwidth: ±7 kHz

Spurious & image rejection: −70 dB

Intermodulation rejection: −70 dB

Selectivity: −70 dB

Hum & noise: −50 dB

Audio frequency response: +1, −8 dB, 300–3000 Hz

Audio output 10% THD 4 ohms: 5 watts

CTX-7800 VHF/FM RADIOTELEPHONE

Incorporating the latest designs in micro-processing technology, the CTX-7800 provides continuous performance and reliability with minimal current consumption. Because of its corrosion resistant construction, the CTX-7800 is well suited to the harshest marine environment. An optional full function remote is available where an additional station may be required.

Specifications:
GENERAL
Frequency range:
  Transmitter: 156.00–157.50 mHz
  Receiver: 156.00–163.00 mHz

Number of channels:
  Transmitter: 55
  Receiver: 78

Supply voltage: 13.6 volts DC negative ground

Antenna impedance: 50 ohms

Modulation: 16F3

Microphone impedance: 600–2000 ohms

Current drain:
  Transmitter H/L: 6.0A/2.5A
  Receiver stby/rated: 0.6A/1.5A

Temperature range: −20°C to +50°C

FCC: Part 81 & 15, 83

DOC: RSS 182 V.L.C.

Dimensions: 9¹³/₁₅″W x 3⅜″H x 12⅞″D (250 x 84 x 327 mm)

Weight: Approx. 8.6 lbs. (3.9 kg)

TRANSMITTER
Output power: 25 W/1 W

Deviation: ±5 kHz max. @ 1 kHz

Spurious & harmonics: −70 dB

Audio frequency response: +1, −3 dB, 300–3000 Hz

Distortion: 5%

RECEIVER
Sensitivity:
  −12 dB sinad: 0.3 uV
  20 dB quieting: 0.35 uV

Squelch sensitivity:
  Threshold: 10 dB noise quieting
  Tight: 2 uV

Modulation acceptance bandwidth: ±7 kHz

Spurious & image rejection: −70 dB

Intermodulation rejection: −70 dB

Selectivity: −70 dB

Hum & noise: −50 dB

Audio frequency response: +1, −8 dB, 300–3000 Hz

Audio output 10% THD 4 ohms: 5 watts

Falcon Safety Products, Inc.
1065 Bristol Road
Mountainside, New Jersey 07092

FALCON PILOT

Mounted anywhere on bridge or cockpit with powerful, non-marring suction cups, the Pilot becomes the on-deck navigation log. An easily erasable #2 pencil is all that's required for logging and charting. Handsome, weatherproof, white polystyrene, the Pilot features a handy time/speed/distance calculator. Conveniently compact at only 7 ½″ x 9″, the Pilot is ideal for pre-race/pre-cruise planning.

FALCON SELF-STEERER

So lightweight and compact, it can be carried in a jacket pocket, the Falcon Self-Steerer easily mounts on the tiller or can be quickly and easily adapted to the wheel. It will steer a 15′–50′ boat on any angle to the wind for hours or days at a time. The Steerer simply links to the traveller to convert the full power of the mainsail to steer the boat on a beat, a reach or a run. On boats not equipped with a traveller, the Falcon Self-Steerer links to the mainsheet for close haul sailing, and with the jibsheet on off-wind courses.

WIND INDICATORS
CHALLENGER PLUS
For sailboats with masts under 30′. Features exclusive Fin Turbulator design for added stability. Non-corrosive one-piece molded construction, with highly visible reflective reference tabs. Adjustable balance. Includes Falcon Adjustable Tacking Arms with reflective tabs as standard equipment.

CHALLENGER-2 PLUS
For sailboats with masts of 30′ and over. Exclusive Fin Turbulator design for added stability. Non-corrosive one-piece construction, with highly visible reflective reference tabs. Adjustable balance. Includes Falcon Adjustable Tacking Arms with reflective reference tabs as standard equipment.

CHALLENGER
Same as Challenger Plus, for sailboats with masts under 30′. Fin Turbulator design, noncorrosive one-piece construction. Reflective reference tabs, adjustable balance. Does NOT accept Falcon Tacking Arms.

CHALLENGER-2
Same as Challenger-2 Plus, for

sailboats with masts over 30'. Fin Turbulator design, non-corrosive one-piece construction. Reflective reference tabs, adjustable balance. Does NOT accept Falcon Tacking Arms.

PRO-12
For sailboats with masts under 30'. Exclusive GyraMount maintains vertical position of indicator at all times. Eliminates heel lift. Unique Fin Turbulator design for unmatched accuracy and stability. Adjustable tacking arms with reflective reference tabs. Adjustable balance. Ideal for racing boats.

PRO-15
For sailboats with masts 30' and over. Features exclusive GyraMount which maintains vertical position of indicator at all times. Eliminates heel lift. Unique Fin Turbulator design provides unmatched accuracy and stability. Adjustable tacking arms with reflective reference tabs. Adjustable balance. Ideal for competition.

ARROW
Unique aerodynamic design and feather-weight construction for excellent sensitivity. Factory balance. The perfect choice for centerboard sailboats.

QUICK-RELEASE SIDE MOUNT
Mounts to mast to allow quick, easy attachment or removal of Falcon Wind Indicators (Models Arrow and Challenger series.) Especially useful when mast is lowered to trailer sailboat. Stainless steel construction.

Furuno U.S.A., Inc.
P.O. Box 2343
271 Harbor Way South
San Francisco, California 94080

LORAN LC-70
Furuno's new computerized Loran system, the LC-70, puts an unri-

valled position fixing capability at a navigator's fingertips. The compact, easy-to-use unit features a touchpad control (an electronic "beep" confirms each entry) and the exceptionally large LCD presentation is clearly visible day or night.

Scaled down in size to fit comfortably on the smaller pleasure boat, the LC-70 sacrifices none of the navigational features of larger units. It gives a readout of the ship's position in latitude and longitude, the range and bearing from the ship's position to any waypoint, or between any two selected waypoints, ground speed and course made good, as well as cross track error and time-to-go between any waypoints.

The LC-70's memory can handle up to 32 waypoint entries in latitude/longitude, and a buzzer sounds when a waypoint is approached. Cross track error facilitates the swift return of the vessel to its intended track. The rechargeable battery ensures that stored coordinates are preserved for more than 30 days in the unit's memory, in the event that the main power supply is cut off. Stored coordinates are also instantly available for subsequent voyages. Operating on 10-42 VDC, the LC-70 draws a frugal 35W.

ULTRA COMPACT RADOME RADAR
Furuno has introduced the Model 1600 radar with a weatherproof, wind resistant radome antenna. Designed primarily for small coastal vessels and pleasure crafts, the 1600 provides performance unmatched in this type radar. A totally new microwave 1C circuit in the transceiver doubles receiver sensitivity, thereby equalling the performance of much larger radars. The very bright 7" CRT (12" equivalent with integral magnifi-

er), full 3kW output power, 6 range scales to 16 n. mi. and dual pulse lengths produce a truly superb picture. Consisting of just two units, interconnected by a single flexible cable, the Model 1600 is simple to install and the compact display is easily unplugged for safe storage. This radar contains a universal 11-40 VDC power supply and draws an extremely low 50 W., making it feasible for some sailing vessels.

Specifications:
ANTENNA RADIATOR

Type: 80cm center-fed slotted waveguide array, enclosed in radome.

Revolution: 24 rpm

Wind Load: Relative Wind 100 knots

Beam Width: 2.7° (HOR), 25° (VERT)

Sidelobe Attenuation: 21 dB within ±20° of main beam, 26 dB outside ±20° of main beam

Polarization: Horizontal

RF TRANSCEIVER (Contained in the Radome)

Transmitter Tube: E3513,M599F or 9M302/E3513

Frequency: 9410 ± 30 MHz (X-band)

Peak Output Power: 3 kw

Pulse Length and Repetition Rate: 0.08 μs with 3300 Hz P.R.R. (1/2, 1 and 2 n.m. ranges), 0.5μs with

800 Hz P.R.R. (4, 8 and 16 n.m. ranges)

Intermediate Frequency: 40 MHz, Bandwidth 7MHz (0.08μs), 3 MHz (0.5μs)

Mixer and Local Oscillator: Microwave Integrated Circuit

Duplexer: Circulator with limiter diode

Modulator: Solid state

Tuning: Manual

DISPLAY UNIT

Picture Tube: 7" PPI Scope (12" presentation with magnifying lens)

Range Scales: Range: 1/2, 1, 2, 4, 8, 16 n.m.
Ring: 1/8, 1/4, 1/2, 1, 2, 4 n.m.

Range Discrimination: Better than 25m

Range Accuracy: 1.5% or 70 meters, whichever is the greater

Minimum Range: 25m

Ambient Temperature: −15° to 55°C

POWER SUPPLY
11-40VDC universal, 50W
110/220 VAC, 70VA (with extra rectifier)

Ray Jefferson
Main and Cotton Streets
Philadelphia, Pennsylvania 19127

DEPTH COMPUTER

This compact unit includes a sensitive 2 foot to 300 foot capability with a keel offset, depth alarm and anchor watch as standard features. As a depth computer, the Model 240 takes advantage of computer type circuitry for precise pinpoint readings on a bold Liquid Crystal Display panel. A switchable night light makes the panel easy to read after dark. The unit also has an automatic gain control that compensates for changes in water depth and a blanking circuit that turns off the display should it be unable to obtain an accurate depth reading. This eliminates potentially confusing random digits from being displayed. A noise reject circuit does away with engine shallow water, the Model 240 can be set to read in .1 foot increments. The unit also has internally sealed toggle switches for maximum moisture protection and long life.

The keel offset feature is ideal for sailboats and large power vessels. This automatically deducts the depth of the keel from the depth of the water assuring you of a true reading for your particular vessel, regardless of where the transducer is located. This control can be adjusted up to 9 feet.

The depth alarm on the Ray Jeff Model 240 is adjustable down to 99 feet and provides the captain with a loud warning when the boat

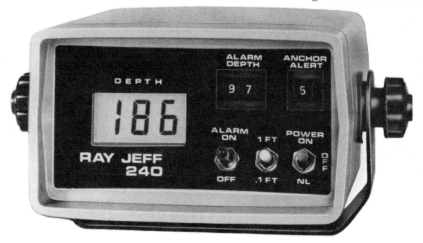

nears shallow water or potentially hazardous objects drift beneath the boat.

The anchor watch can be your boat's insurance against disaster, especially if you like anchoring overnight, near channels or close to shallow areas. This adjustable feature also sounds a loud alarm when the boat has drifted from its anchored position within a ± 9 foot differential, allowing valuable time to save the craft from possibly going aground or drifting into a shipping channel.

The Model 240's compact size makes it easy to mount, even in a small electronics box. It measures 4½" wide x 2½" high x 5" deep and weighs less than 1 pound. The case and front panel are made of high impact plastic. It is supplied with a gimbal mounting bracket, sensitive transducer and all necessary power and transducer cables.

LCK-99 KNOTMETER

The Model LCK-99 utilizes a Liquid Crystal Ciode display to present boat speed in bold reflective and back lighted digits that are easy to read, even in direct sunlight or in darkness. It is completely solid state for unmatched accuracy, and power consumption is an exceptionally low 12 mA with the night light off and just 60 mA with the light on.

The Model LCK-99 comes complete with non-fouling paddle-wheel transducer that can be removed for easy cleaning, heavy duty bronze thru-hull fitting, screw-in cap for use when the transducer is removed and 20 feet of power and connecting cable.

KL-12 AND KL-24 KNOTMETERS/ LOGMETERS

Both units provide the helmsman with a highly accurate reading of

his boat's speed as well as a resettable log that precisely measures the distance travelled up to 9999.9 nautical miles.

The Model KL-12 reads speeds to 12 knots and is designed especially for sailboats. The Model KL-24 is engineered for high performance sailboats and powerboats and records speeds to 24 knots. They feature an extra large dial with white numerals on a high contrast black background for easy reading, even at high speeds. There is a low drain red light for night time use.

Both the KL-12 and KL-24 have a resettable log that reads to 1/10th mile increments. The KL-12 is calibrated in ½ knot increments, while the KL-24 is calibrated in one knot increments.

The 4½" brushed aluminum bezel is weather resistant and the dial glass is shatterproof. Each comes equipped with a non-fouling paddlewheel transducer that may be removed for cleaning after installation by use of the screw-in seal cap. The Units also feature heavy duty bronze thru-hull fitting and 20 feet of power connecting cable.

L-99 LOGMETER

The Model L-99 Logmeter provides the boater with an accurate

record of distance travelled, up to 9999.9 nautical miles. It features a

resettable log and the mileage is indicated in white numerals on a black dial. A low current red light provides for easy night viewing.

The Model is easy to install and its 4" brushed aluminum bezel is weather resistant. The unit operates off the boat's 12V DC electrical system, drawing just 30 mA with the light off and 100 mA with the light on. It comes complete with non-fouling paddle-wheel transducer that may be removed for easy cleaning, heavy duty bronze thru-hull fitting, screw-in seal cap for use when the transducer is removed, 20 feet of connecting cable and red night light.

WS-60 WIND SPEED METER

The Model WS-60 is a precision instrument providing accurate readings from 0 to 60 knots. It is designed for bulkhead mounting and the brushed bezel and case are corrosion resistant aluminum. The unit has a bezel diameter of 4¼". The case measures just 2⅛" deep.

The meter comes with a masthead unit with anemometer cups and 60 feet of connecting cable. It operates from any 12V DC source, drawing just 100mA with the night light off and 170mA with the light on. The unit is easy to read with large white numerals on a black dial face, and it is calibrated in 2½ knot increments.

The WS-60 also is available as a Wind Speed/Wind Direction package with the companion Model WD-30 Wind Direction Meter. The WD-30 is not available as a separate unit.

Metz Communication Corporation
Corner Route 11 and 11C
Laconia, New Hampshire 03246

VHF MARINE AND MASTHEAD ANTENNAS

VHF MARINE ANTENNA

The Manta 2 by Metz offers mariners an alternative to the large white fiberglass antennas for VHF/FM marine radio. Manta 2 is a slim stainless steel 26″ whip mounted to a silver plated post into a 1½″ stainless steel coil. Fed with common top quality RG-8X coaxial cable, Manta 2 will transmit and receive further than a 6db gain 9 foot fiberglass antenna.

VHF MASTHEAD ANTENNA

Manta 6 is a slim stainless steel 34″ whip mounted to a gold plated post into a 1½″ diameter stainless steel coil.

Features:

No ground plane radials needed. Precut whip tunes entire 216-220 MHz marine band. Outperforms 54″ fiberglass "3db gain" masthead antennas. Low angle of radiation beams signals *over* horizon. Stainless steel construction of whip, coil, and hardware. Lightning protection aloft second antenna function. Ideal for racing-required emergency antenna. Less wind load aloft than fiberglass antennas. Epoxy sealed coil assembly. Silver plated whip lock. Antenna stores easily. ½ wavelength, shunt fed. SWR less than 1.3 to 1 over 216-220 MHz marine band. Radiation/reception gain compares to "6db" gain antenna. Radiation angle ideal to minimize rolling effects. Stainless steel cover over coil eliminates SWR on steel masts. #16 wire used in windings rated at 500 watts output. 17-7ph whip seldom takes a set when bent 360 degrees. 8 oz. aloft total weight for racing enthusiasts. SO-239 at base for mating to PL-259. Silver used for "skin effect". Whip and mounts easily detach.
Manta 6: Same features as Manta 2, except: Precut whip tunes entire VHF/FM marine band. Gold plated whip lock. SWR less than 1.3 to 1 over 156/162 MHz marine band. Gain compares to "6db" antenna. Stainless steel cover over coil eliminates SWR on steel masts. Gold used for "skin effect."

Micrologic
20801 Dearborn Street
Chatsworth, California 91311

ML 2000 LORAN-C

The ML-2000 Loran-C is available in three versions, to satisfy almost every type of user requirement. The economical ML-2000R provides the basic receiver outputs of time differences, which can be used for high-precision position fixing with Loran C charts. This enables the user to chart his course manually.

In addition to incorporating all of the ML-2000R features, the ML-2000S provides a steering display, distance to go in Micro-seconds, and time-to-go. Ten waypoints, specified as time differences, can be entered into memory and will be retained even when power is switched off.

For the serious navigator, the ML-2000N supplies complete navigational information. Instantly, you can obtain time differences, latitude/longitude, range and bearing to your destination, cross-track error, ground speed, true course and velocity made good. The liquid crystal display on the ML-2000N also acts as a graphic steering display. Ten waypoints, entered as TD's or LL, are retained with power off.

The ML-2000N solves a variety of navigational problems—whether or not Loran signals are being received. You can convert Lat/Lon to TD's, TD's to Lat/Lon, or TD's from one chain to another. The ML-2000N will also compute great-circle range and bearing between any two points on earth!

The Micrologic engineers designed each of the three versions so that the ML-2000R receiver and the ML-2000S receiver versions can be upgraded with an internal circuit board change. Each of the three versions has the same external appearance. If you're learning about Loran C navigation, you can begin with the ML-2000R receiver version. As your skills and knowledge develop, a circuit board exchange quickly converts your ML-2000R receiver into an ML-2000S receiver, with the advantages of 10

Current	Backlighting Intensity
0.65 amps	Very dim
1.05 amps	Full brightness

ANTENNA COUPLER UNIT
Mounts with standard 1″–14 hardware. Waterproof. Sealed in epoxy.

Dimensions
12.8 x 1.6 inches (Height, diameter)
32.5 x 4.1 cm.

Weight
1.6 lbs.
0.7 kg.

Operating temperature
−40° to +158°F
−40° to + 70°C

R & D Enterprises
Nautical Engineering Division
P.O. Box 5252
Northville, Michigan 48167

SIGNAL-MATE EMERGENCY REPLACEMENT ANTENNA

waypoint memory storage and auto-steering. As your navigating skill develops, your ML-2000S receiver can be converted into the full-function ML-2000N Navigator to give you complete navigational information.

Sailboats cannot generally sail directly toward a destination, but instead must take a series of tacks. The ML-2000 provides a direct readout of the groundspeed component toward the destination. This is referred to as Velocity Made Good or VMG. By adjusting the tack to maximize VMG, sailboats can substantially improve their performance.

Specifications:

PERFORMANCE
Meets or exceeds all Type I receiver requirements of the RTCM-70 specification. (Report of special committee No. 70, Minimum Performance Standards Marine Loran C Receiving Equipment, July 19, 1979, Radio Technical Commission for Marine Services, Washington, D. C. 20554).

Sensitivity: 1 microvolt
Dynamic Range: 110 dB
Four internal notch filters
No error due to velocity

PHYSICAL
Welded-aluminum and stainless steel construction, with mylar and polycarbonate front panel.

DIMENSIONS
10.7 x 2.9 x 12.2 inches (WHD)
27.1 x 7.4 x 31.0 cm.

WEIGHT
6.8 lbs., 3.1 kg.

OPERATING TEMPERATURE
−5° to +55°C
+23° to +131°F

POWER SUPPLY
Input Power:
10–18 VDC continuous (negative ground)
Receiver will track down to 8 Vdc with degraded signal-to-noise ratio. Short surges to 35 Vdc will be tolerated.

Signal-Mate is a coil-stored VHF emergency replacement antenna with automatic uncoiling action. Ready for emergency use in just seconds. No extra hardware is required. It can normally broadcast and receive signals up to 15 miles. The concave spring steel construction terminates in a connector which is mechanically compatible with the antenna input and/or output of any VHF-FM radiotelephone. The protective coating guards the antenna against corrosive elements. Its design accommodates a center frequency of 156.8 MHz (Marine Emergency Channel).

To store, simply roll the antenna toward the connector and fasten. Signal-Mate requires less storage space than a pack of cigarettes. The weather-resistant, reusable package insures safe storage.

Navidyne Corporation
11824 Fishing Point Drive
Newport News, Virginia 23606

ESZ-7000 LORAN-C

The ESZ-7000 uses a CRT (cathode ray tube) screen to display all navigation and routing information at the same time. The operator does not need to memorize any call-up codes or constantly refer to an operator's manual to obtain essential information from the computer.

The CRT provides a constantly updated readout of all pertinent information, including latitude and longitude, date and time, course and speed made good, course-to-steer and distance to any of 25 preselected waypoints (great circle and rhumb line), distance run, estimated time to destination, the number of Loran-C LOPS in use, and a confidence index based on signal strength and network geometry.

All information on the screen is updated automatically as the ship moves through the water. The CRT even provides left-right steering instructions to maintain desired course.

An alternate display, available at the touch of a button, shows all Loran-C time difference readings, with signal-to-noise ratios and secondary phase factor corrections for each.

The ESZ-7000 is the only Loran-C navigator that uses *all* available Loran-C lines of position to compute latitude and longitude, thus providing improved accuracy, especially in the vicinity of base line extensions. Accuracy can be further enhanced through the use of secondary phase factor corrections. With the ESZ-7000, these corrections can be computed automatically or entered manually.

Initialization of the ESZ-7000 is automatically prompted on the CRT screen. It is only necessary to turn the set on and enter the appropriate GRI and a rough position estimate. The receiver immediately begins to acquire and track the master and all available secondary stations.

The ESZ-7000 contains only five plug-in circuit boards. Field repairs can be made quickly and easily by replacing circuit boards. A complete inventory of spares is maintained by Navidyne agents at strategic locations throughout the world. The ESZ-7000 carries a three-year warranty.

Specifications:

RECEIVER CHARACTERISTICS
Sensitivity: <1 microvolt

Dynamic Range: >110db

Differential Signal: >70db for <0.1 microsecond phase error

Self-Test: Automatic, computer-controlled diagnostics

Notch Filters: 2 internal, 2 external

Antenna Coupler: Active circuit (50 ohm output)

Search Mode: Fully automatic

Display Resolution: 0.01 minute (latitude/longitude)
0.1 microsecond (time-difference)

Signal Outputs: 75 ohm composite video for remote CRT display(s)
RS-232 I/O for printer or integrated navigation computer

PHYSICAL/ ENVIRONMENTAL DATA

	Main Unit (including trunnion mount)	Antenna Pre-Amp*	Power Supply (AC operation only)
Size	11.9H x 16.9W x 16.3D (inches)	3.5D x 9.0H (inches)	5.4H x 7.6W x 10.4D (inches)
	302H x 429W x 414D (mm)	89D x 229H (mm)	137H x 193W x 264D (mm)
Weight	32 lbs. (14.5 kg)	2.5 lbs. (1.1 kg)	16 lbs. (7.3 kg)
Temperature	0° to +55°C	−50° to +70°C	0° to +55°C
Humidity	95%	100%	95%

*For use with a 108-inch fiberglass whip antenna (3/8 inch-24 mounting stud).

X-Y plotter output
Speed/heading outputs suitable for
Satnav dead reckoning
- speed: 200 pulses/nautical mile
- heading (course made good): stepper

Input Power (DC): 10–40 volts, 65 watts

Input Power (AC): 100–240 volts (selectable), 47–400 Hz
Single phase, 100 watts
Optional full-battery backup

ESZ-3900 SATELLITE NAVIGATOR

The Transit Satellite system is internationally recognized as the standard in precision navigation.

The system is comprised of a constellation of satellites orbiting some 700 miles above the earth with their nearly circular paths intersecting at both poles. A shipboard satellite navigator receives signals from these satellites to provide worldwide position fixing with an accuracy of about 0.25 miles.

It is the only dependable, all-weather navigational system with worldwide coverage. And its record of uninterrupted service means safe and reliable navigation to the world's largest ships.

Now, with Navidyne's ESZ-3900, this unmatched system can mean the same to your yacht.

Navidyne's ESZ-3900 draws heavily on the proven technology of the ESZ-4000, our satellite navigator designed for commercial ships. The ESZ-4000, chosen for fleetwide installation by many major shipping companies, is now the world's best-selling satellite navigator.

There's a good reason why. No other satellite navigator can provide more information in such an easy-to-use format. And that's the very same advantage you'll find with the ESZ-3900.

One look at the screen will tell you why the ESZ-3900 is the most advanced satellite navigator you can buy for your yacht. It is the only one that gives you all navigational information on a cathode ray tube (CRT) display.

Just one glance will tell you where you are, where you've been and where you're going. And because all the information appears simultaneously and continuously on the screen, no call-up codes are ever required. Even manual inputs for geoidal height have been eliminated.

Concise Information, Continually Displayed

It takes less than a minute to set-up the ESZ-3900. A visual prompting sequence leads you step-by-step through data entry:
Date
Greenwich Mean Time
Approximate Latitude
Approximate Longitude
Speed and Heading

Once set-up is complete, a high speed microcomputer takes over, constantly updating the information on the screen. You'll see all the facts, all at once, in three easy-to-read groups (see center photograph). The top group lists date and precise GMT, your present latitude and longitude, dead reckoning time, and course and speed (manually updated).

The middle group contains waypoint information, plus automatically computed set and drift, and gives you course-to-steer and distance to any waypoint or between any pair of waypoints, both great circle and rhumb line.

The bottom group shows the magnitude and angle of the last lead reckoning correction as well as all pertinent information concerning the last satellite fix and the next satellite pass.

Navidyne's CRT screen also fea-

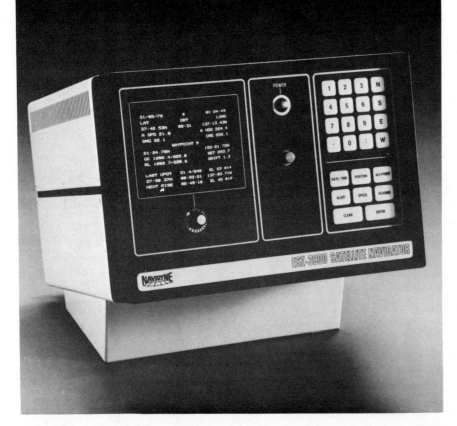

tures a unique two-page format. At the press of the ALERT switch, a comprehensive display of satellite data will appear. At the top of the screen is a list of the next ten available satellites. At the bottom is a list showing the last six accepted fixes.

The ESZ-3900 fits beautifully and effectively into the yachting environment. The crisp design features sealed membrane switches for improved dependability.

Inside the ESZ-3900, the beauty is in the simplicity. Like the ESZ-4000, it contains fewer internal parts, just five plug-in boards and three functional modules. And to make certain these parts meet Navidyne's reliability standards, each set is subjected to at least 240 hours of factory burn-in.

The compact antenna/preamp for the ESZ-3900 is extremely lightweight and fully sealed for protection. The unit mounts easily in any clear, above-deck location.

Should you ever need service or assistance, you'll get prompt response from Navidyne in virtually any major port. Navidyne also maintains a total inventory of spare parts in strategic locations around the world. That means no undue wait for parts shipment. And no need to send the ESZ-3900 back to the factory for service.

In addition, the ESZ-3900 is backed by a six-month field service warranty, and all parts are guaranteed for a full year.

Safety and reliability are more than important to the crew of an ocean-going yacht. They are absolutely crucial. Navidyne's unmatched technology already means safe and reliable navigation to the crews of some of the world's largest ships. And now, with the ESZ-3900, your crew can navigate with the same confidence.

The ESZ-3900 combines the best of Navidyne's innovative design and worldwide service network to make it the first truly professional satellite navigator for yachts.

No other satellite navigator can offer you more for your money. Because no other company has had more seaworthy success in satellite navigation than Navidyne.

Performance Specification:

Satellite Fix Accuracy: 0.05 NM plus 0.2 NM per knot of speed error (RMS)

Receiver Frequency: 400 mHz

Sensitivity: 152 dbm (measured in 40 Hz noise bandwidth)

Self Test: Automatic; computer controlled diagnostics

Input Power:* 10–40 VDC: 75 watts maximum

Receiver Tuning: Fully automatic; computer controlled

Nelco Nautical Electronics Company, Inc.

7095 Milford Industrial Road
Baltimore, Maryland 21208

AUTOFIX 900 LORAN C RECEIVER

The Autofix 900 loran, a dual display computer-controlled loran, is ideal for the basic user or the advanced navigator. It automatically tracks up to 5 slaves with fast accurate cycle identification and provides the navigator with the most desired computer NAV features, including a versatile steering mode and complete waypoint navigation ability. The battery powered memory holds the last used slaves, GRI, as well as 30 waypoints and 8 waypoint programs for 5-10 years. An easy-to-understand keyboard provides all the input necessary to store, recall, manipulate or steer to any waypoint or series of waypoints and the steer mode provides a left-right indicator with a distance off-course readout as well as time and distance to destination.

The Autofix 900 has a universal DC power supply (10–50 volts) and uses only 8 watts of power. Its 4″ x 8″ x 9½″ rugged metal case weighs only 6½ lbs.

Physical/Environment Data:

	Receiver/Display (including mounting yoke)	Antenna/Preamp
Size	13.6(h) x 13.4(w) x 17.8(d) inches 345(h) x 340(w) x 452(d) mm	Diameter 3.5 inches (89 mm) Height 28.9 inches (734 mm)
Weight	27 lbs (12.2 kg)	5.1 lbs (2.3 kg)
Temperature	0° to +55°C	−30° to +70°C
Humidity	0 to 95%	0 to 100%

*External power supply for AC operation, with optional battery backup, is also available.

RECEIVER

Frequency: 100 KHz

Sensitivity
   Tracking: 1 UV/M
   Acquisition: 10 UV/M

Resolution of time difference: 0.1 microsecond

Interference elimination: 4 Notch filters (2 pre-set, 2 front panel adjustable)

Signal lock time
   Turn on to tracking in less than 1.5 minutes with S/N better than +10 db
   Turn on to tracking in less than 5 minutes with longest GRI rate and S/N of −10 db

ELECTRICAL

Voltage: 11 to 50 volts DC

Power consumption: 8.0 watts

DISPLAY

Numeric: Vacuum fluorescent

Interference meter: L. E. D.

TEMPERATURE

Receiver: 0°F (−18°C) to 130°F (+59°C)

Antenna coupler: −4°F (−20°C) to 149°F (+65°C)

MECHANICAL

LORAN RECEIVER

Height: 4.2″ (.107 m) less mounting bracket

Width: 8.2″ (.203m)

Depth: 9.5″ (.241m)

Weight: 6.5 lb. (2.95 kg)

Construction: Aluminum

Control panel: Lexan laminated face; aluminum subpanel

ANTENNA COUPLER

Length: 3.3″ (.084m)

Diameter: 2.0″ (.050m)

Weight: .5 lb (.227 kg.)

Construction: PVC plastic Hermetically sealed

Terminations: Antenna input waterproof connector

Antenna cable: Supplied as standard 25′ (7.62m)

Trunnion addition: 1.4″ (036m)

Okeamos, Inc.
8361 Vickers Street, Suite 301
San Diego, California 92111

SHIPMATE SATELLITE NAVIGATOR

Shipmate includes interface for automatic speed and heading input as standard hardware. It is the only low-cost system able, without modification, to accept input from all modern speedlogs and speedometers. For heading input, the distributor who imports this system from Denmark has developed a special very low cost compass. This is the Model OK15C Course-Minder™, a highly reliable and accurate fluxgate device.

   The value of full automation is easy to calculate. With it, users can obtain the 0.05 nautical mile

Meets US Coast Guard MPS TYPE 3 CLASS B

One-year limited factory warranty—parts and labor

accuracy claimed by SatNav manufacturers. Without automatic speed and heading input, errors are likely to be two-tenths of a mile or more.

COURSEMINDER

Developed specifically for use with the new Danish import Model RS5000 Shipmate Satellite Navigator, CourseMinder™ is a highly accurate and reliable fluxgate device. CourseMinder™ is housed in heavy duty gold-anodized aluminum and is easily installed without technical assistance. Location may be virtually anywhere in the vessel. Since all satellite navigation systems must ded* reckon between satellite passes, automatic input of heading information means very much improved position accuracy as well as easier operation. For

those with the Shipmate Model RS5000 Satellite Navigator, CourseMinder™ is an excellent alternative to earlier electronic compass systems costing three times the price, or more.

*According to Nathaniel Bowditch, "American Practical Navigation" when allowance is made for current and wind, this is a deduced position. Therefore, commonly-used "dead" reckoning should instead be "ded".

Ranging, Inc.
Measuring Systems
90 Lincoln Road North
East Rochester, New York 14445

RANGING 1000 DISTANCE FINDER

The Ranging 1000 lets user navigate unfamiliar waters, obtain fast accurate range fixes, determine speed and distance off-shore. Works at night, too. Also computes a fix from a single known object using distance, speed and course.

To use, sight on target (no need to know target height), turn dial until target is sharply defined, read dial for distance in yards. 10½" x 1½" x 1¼". 22 ounces. 6 x 18 power removable scope. Two-year warranty.

Raritan Engineering Company, Inc.
1025 North High Street
Millville, New Jersey 08332

RUDDER ANGLE INDICATORS

Meter indicates rudder angle at all times. Aids in setting up for sharply changing winds and tide conditions. Compact and easy to read. Easy to install. For all voltages 6 to 32V DC.

Comes with complete meter, calibration box, sealed sending unit, and connecting wire.

Interchangeable repeater units available consisting of a complete meter with 15' of connecting wire.

Flush mount edgewise meter
3 3/4" x 2" x 2 3/4" deep   Model MK4
Repeater unit using MK4 meter
Model MK4R
Console mounted edgewise meter
4 1/4" x 2 5/8" x 3" deep   Model MK4C
Repeater Unit using MK4R meter
Model MK4CR
Flush mount 4 1/2" two color panoramic
meter 4 3/4" x 3 5/8" x 1 5/8" deep
Model MK5
Repeater unit using MK5 meter
Model MK5R
Flush mount 3 1/2" two color panoramic
meter 3 3/8" x 2 5/8" x 1 5/8" deep
Model MK6
Repeater unit using MK6 meter
Model MK6R

Regency Electronics, Inc.
7707 Records Street
Indianapolis, Indiana 46226

NC 6000 VHF DIRECTION FINDER

FEATURES

- Turns your VHF transceiver into a VHF direction finder for navigating to other ships and coastal VHF stations.
- Shows relative bearing of signals received on your VHF transceiver in normal, priority or scan modes.
- Permits normal operation of transceiver even when NC 6000 is in use.
- Hold features displays direction after received signal has stopped.
- Supplied with DF array antenna, 30 ft. of connecting cable plus 8 ft. mast with mounting hardware.

- One year limited warranty.
- Made in U.S.A.

SPECIFICATIONS

Frequency Range: 155-163 MHz

DF Antenna: 4 element dipole array

Antenna Switching: Electronic scanning, phase detection

Display System: 36 LED's indicate relative bearing

Display Speed: one second (typical)

DF Sensitivity: 1 μV (with .3 μV @ 20db sinad transceiver)

Accuracy: ±5° @ 5μV/m input
Audio: 5W @ 10% into 3.2 Ω
Power: 13.8VDC, 1A max.

Ricker Instrument Company

P.O. Box 52
Clifton Heights, Pennsylvania
19018

CLINOMETERS

These instruments aid Loading (both Fuel and Cargo), Sailing and Cruising. In Sailing, they enable the Skipper to maintain proper Heel angle at all times. In Cruising, mounted on the Beam axis they will assist turning and fuel tank selection. Mounted on the Keel axis, the instrument will save fuel by maintaining proper Trim angle.

MODEL No. 2055   6″ x 2½″

ONE SCALE, ONE RANGE
55° x 0° 55°
Raised Markings at 5° intervals,
    ¼ of an inch apart.
Readable to 2°, at a distance of 12
feet.

MODEL NO. 2056   6″ x 3¾″

TWO SCALES, TWO RANGES
1–6° x 0° x 6°
Raised Markings at 1° intervals,
    ⁷/₃₂ of an inch apart.
Readable to ½°, at a distance of 12
feet.
2–55° x 0° x 55°
Raised Markings at 5° intervals,
    ¼ of an inch apart.
Readable to 2°, at a distance of 12
feet.

TRIM-HEEL-LIST INDICATOR

Models Nos. 2060-P and 2060-S
6″ x 1¼″
By using two Clinometers, (Port and Starboard), with reversed markings, the Skipper has a useful range of 40° with readability and accuracy doubled. Parallax errors are minimized. Parallax errors occur when readings are taken from a position which is not perpendicular to the instrument. With these two, one Clinometer is always dead ahead.

Features:

Large, easy to read dial with markings at 2° intervals
Clear markings a full ¼″ apart
Readability to 1° at a distance of 12 feet
All models are complete with protective covers

Ritchie Navigation Instruments

Pembroke, Massachusetts 02359

COMPASSES

EXPLORER

Designed with the small boat owner in mind. Highly visible dials. 5° increment markings. Large numer-als. Sapphire jewel bearings. Stainless steel, molded plastic, and traditional brass.

The S-15, with conventional open face dial.

The S-15-A, with direct reading dial allowing increased viewing angle.

Cast bronze mounting bracket external gimballed, and a brass spring plate for easy removal. Ideal for day sailors.

GLOBE MASTER

Spherical shaped bowls with special light weight aluminum gimbal system. Non-coloring damping fluid for maximum card stability. Phosphor bronze bellows-type expansion chamber prevents bubbles and bowl pressure caused by temperature fluctuation, aiding performance and long life. Red filtered night lighting. Special optical design eliminates eyestrain caused by glare and reflection. Special mounts on models C-453 and C-463 cushion compass unit from shocks and vibrations, giving longer life to pivot and jewel and less card oscillation from engine, weather, and rigging vibrations. Several lamp voltages and two card styles available.

NAVIGATOR

The Navigator compass with its large 4″ dial is a dependable, accurate instrument designed for offshore piloting. Materials used in construction are traditionally seaworthy, like cast bronze brackets and bezels, brass spherical bowls, phospher bronze expansion cham-

bers, and built-in Navy type night lighting and compensators. The

Navigator series offers a full range of mounting options for both sail and power, and is one of the more popular compasses among knowledgeable mariners around the world.

SR-1—RACING COMPASS

Here is an excellent compass for small racing sailboats. Large, easy to read 3½″ blue dial with extra large markings allows good visibility from many angles. Internal gimbals provide excellent performance at extreme angles of heel and special alloy pivot and jewel bearing dial assure accurate trouble-free performance.

Night lighting and built-in compensators are not available.

Scammar Marine Products
298 Harbor Drive
Sausalito, California 94965

MONITOR WINDVANE

Many different ways have been tried to get a sailboat to steer itself. The Monitor self-steering is a so-called servo-pendulum vane gear, a system that has increasingly emerged as the most powerful and reliable self-steering method in the past ten to fifteen years.

Imagine yourself holding an oar with its blade in the water on a boat that travels forward. You will do fine as long as the edge of the blade is aligned with the direction of the boat. If you twist the oar, even a fraction, the water will hit the flat surface of the blade and you will be unable to keep the oar in the water. A tremendous leverage is created from the blade, through the shaft to the end of the oar where you are holding on. A

servo-pendulum gear uses this great leverage to keep the yacht on course. An oar is suspended like a pendulum from the stern of the boat. As long as the yacht is on course, the oar blade trails on the centerline, its edges aligned in the direction of travel. The windvane sensor controls the servo-pendulum oar and rotates it when the boat wanders off course. The flow of water hitting the blade broadface causes the pendulum oar to swing to the side with great force. The pendulum is connected through lines to the wheel or tiller and the resulting movement of the yacht's rudder brings the boat back on course.

Practically the entire Monitor is made of heliarc welded and electropolished stainless steel. The advantages are obvious. Corrosion is avoided. The material combines great strength with comparatively light weight. Everything is easy to take apart and, in the unlikely event of damage, repairs are usually possible even at sea or in remote places.

On most yachts the Monitor attaches to the hull with four separate support tubes and universal hull brackets, which easily conform even to complex compound curves. This four point attachment is extremely strong and rigid. At the same time the installation is very easy to perform and can generally be handled in a short time. The vane gear can be removed very simply by unbolting four bolts, leaving only the small universal brackets on the hull.

Canoe sterns are no problem. Even outboard rudders and boomkins can be handled in a fairly easy fashion by bending the attachment tubes or welding additional tangs or attachment plates to the Monitor frame. With the necessary measurements or drawings at hand, the appropriate tubes, welds and bends can be prefabricated at the factory.

The vane of the Monitor is operated remotely from any chosen spot on the yacht. Remote control is often necessary, such as in boomkin installations, and it should definitely be possible to make small adjustments to any degree desired. The vane control provides such infinite adjustment capability through a stainless chain and sprocket drive. This feature is especially valuable when going to weather. A small change in the vane setting may then lead to a proportionately much larger change in course, as the apparent wind stays nearly the same over a wide range of headings on a boat. By allowing exact vane adjustment, the boat can always be kept on the desired heading.

To protect the pendulum, it has been hinged in its middle, to allow it to be moved out of the water when not in use. A latch mechanism locks or unlocks the hinge. This latch has been designed from experience with similar airplane fittings. A simple push with a boathook releases the pendulum. Under way, the latch is self-energizing, locking harder as the pressure on the pendulum increases.

The servo blade is the muscle of the servo-pendulum vane gear. In the Monitor the stainless pendulum has been given a NACA high lift profile and the blade has been semi-balanced to allow the windvane to turn a larger surface in lighter airs. The result is greater power and sensitivity. A side bonus is that the pendulum can be fixed in the center position and used for emergency steering.

Although the signals from the vane-sensor are very light they are sufficiently strong to rotate the servo-pendulum, unless friction interferes in the linkages between vane and pendulum. Friction will affect the performance of a vane gear in a very negative manner, particularly in light airs. Maintenance free delrin roller bearings and ball bearings are used in all critical places. The result is a completely smooth connection between the vane and the pendulum.

Any control system needs a feedback mechanism to prevent it from overreacting. The Monitor provides feedback through the bronze master gearset, which gradually neutralizes the rotation of the pendulum blade during the swing of the pendulum, preventing over-steering and "fishtailing."

The tiller and wheel attachments are engineered like the rest of the windvane; in stainless steel, both provide split second disengagement of the self-steering gear through a quick release clutch pin. The small wheel adaptor is designed for mounting on the inside of the steering wheel, where it is out of the way and hardly noticeable.

Features:

Pivoting on inclined horizontal axis for maximum sensitivity and stabilization. Fabricated on ¼″ marine plywood, sealed and finish coated. Spare vane included. Semi-balanced NACA high lift profile. Stainless shaft and skin with polyurethane foam core.

TIG-welded and electropolished AISI 303 and 304 stainless steel. Delrin and teflon bearings and bushings. Bronze master gearset. Total mounted weight 50–52 pounds depending on installation requirements. Break tube mounted between pendulum latch and pendulum blade. Spare tube included. No greasing or oiling. Hose down with fresh water after long use. Check pendulum sheet lines and blocks and sheaves occasionally.

SAILOMAT

Sailomat was designed to meet the challenge of real self steering in all weather conditions on sailboats under 60 feet l.o.a. It will maintain the yacht on a desired heading relative to the wind and with the auxiliary rudder design, it will do so independently of the yacht's ordinary rudder. Course corrections are performed with unequalled accuracy, often better than a helmsman himself.

Features:

Servo pendulum-oar driving an auxiliary rudder. Totally independent of yacht's ordinary rudder.
Powered by wind and water forces alone. All mechanical design (patented). No gears.
Exceptionally high steering power and rapid response. Sets new standards in high sensitivity.
High directional stability. High yaw damping.
Accurate course holding, even in weak winds.
Easy to set. Instant return to manual steering. Safe. Can be used as backup emergency steering.

High quality materials. Corrosion resistant.
Easy installation to any transom. Detachable rudder, oar and vane. Strong. Overload safety system, preventing damage to either yacht

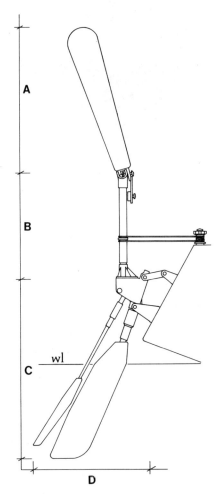

or major Sailomat components. Compact. Lightweight.
Dual-axis wind-vane actuating oar. Variable vane-to-oar angular ratio. Low water drag. Efficient high-lift profiles.

Stephens Engineering Associates, Inc.

7030 220th Southwest
Mountlake Terrace, Washington
98043

AUTOMATIC ANTENNA COUPLERS

The first is the SEA 1603, which will handle up to 150 Watts PEP and tune over the range of 1.6-25 MHz. The 1603 requires only 50 ohm input, 12 VDC and any an- tenna length from 23 to 75 feet. It can be used therefore, with any transceiver without special modifi- cation. It is believed that with this universal adaptability the 1603 will be in substantial demand for new installations as well as in-service updates. The 1603 tunes on voice so that both operation and installa- tion are extremely simple. The product measures 12″ wide, 14″ long, 5″ high, weighs only 10 lbs. There are also two models designed for the international market. The models 1601 and 1602 handle a bandwidth of 1.6-25.0 MHz. The 1601 operates on VDC, and the 1602 on 12 VDC; all other specifi- cations are the same as the 1603.

The second automatic coupler is the SEA 2100 designed for use as an external automatic coupler with the new SEA-209 transceiver. The 2100 will automatically tune any- where in the 2–9 MHz range with an antenna of 28–35 feet in length and handle up to 150 Watts PEP.

As with the 1600 series of coup- lers the 2100 requires only 50 ohm input and 12 VDC and will operate with any transceiver covering 2-9MHz. It measures 9″ wide, 11″ long, 4″ high, weighs 7 lbs.

Specifications:

		SEA 1603	SEA 2100
FREQ. RANGE		1.6–25 MHz.	2-9MHz.
RF POWER HANDLING CAPABILITY		150W PEP. Maximum.	150W PEP. Maximum.
TUNING TIME		1–3 seconds, nominal.	1–3 seconds, nominal.
INTERNAL MATCHING NETWORKS (Micro-computer controlled)		"pi" or "L".	"pi" or "L"
INPUT IMPEDANCE		50 ohms.	50 ohms.
USABLE ANTENNA LENGTHS		23 to 75 feet. (7 to 23 meters).	28 to 35 feet. (8.5 to 10.6 meters)
POWER REQUIREMENTS		13.8VDC @ 0.3A (typ.) 13.8VDC @ 0.6A (max).	13.8VDC @ 0.3A (typ.) 13.8VDC @ 0.6A (max).
INTERCONNECTIONS		RF: RG/8U coax. Power, 2 cond. #18 shielded.	RF: RG/8U coax. Power, 2 cond. #18 shielded.
GROUND LEAD		2″ copper strap not over 3 ft. (1 meter).	2″ copper strap not over 3 ft. (1 meter).
LEAD-IN LENGTH		Total length of ant. and lead-in should not exceed 75 ft. (23M)	Total length of ant. and lead-in should not exceed 35 ft. (10.7M)
DIMENSIONS	Inches MM	11.5 W, 14.0L, 5.5D. 292W, 356L, 140D.	9.5W, 13.5L, 4.5D. 241W, 343L, 114D.
WEIGHT:	Pounds KG	9.2 pounds. 4.2 kilograms.	5.5 pounds. 2.5 kilograms.

SEA 209 SYNTHESIZER TRANSCEIVER

The Sea 209, a 2–9 MHz marine transceiver, holds 1024 channels, either simplex or semi-duplex, in memory in 32 groups of 32 channels each. The groups are field programmable so that as long as the user only needs frequencies up to 9 MHz, he can operate virtually anywhere in the world with the channels in memory when the radio is delivered. The Sea 209 has a built in antenna coupler which comes in two versions, pre-set or automatic. The automatic coupler, which tunes on voice, represents a significant step forward in reducing the installation complexity of single sideband equipment. A complexity which, to date, has materially reduced the broader use of SSB especially for non-commercial applications.

Other features of the Sea 209 include 150 Watts PEP, voice activated squelch, LED frequency readout, A3A/A3J, clarifier and a specially designed new chassis designed to provide exceptional

strength and rigidity. The SEA 209 measures 14″ wide, 4.5″ high, 13″ deep and weighs 18 lbs. (8.1 Kgs.).

Specifications:

GENERAL

FREQUENCY RANGE: 2 to 9MHz.

CIRCUITRY: Single conversion (10.7008 MHz).
Dual loop synthesizer with PROM memory.

CHANNEL CAPACITY: 32 simplex or semi-duplex frequencies per memory page. 16 pages programmed in each radio.

CHANNELS IN MEMORY: 1024, maximum.

FRONT PANEL CONTROLS: Volume ON/OFF, Squelch ON/OFF, Channel selector, Band selector, A3A/A3J, LED readout, Clarity.

OPERATING TEMP. RANGE: −30° to +60°C.

FREQUENCY STABILITY: 20 Hz.

OPERATING MODES: A3A (SSB, −16db carrier). A3J (SSB, −40db carrier).

PRIMARY VOLTAGE: 13.6VDC ±15%. Neg. gnd.

CURRENT DRAIN: Receive:
Standby: 2.0A
Full audio: 2.5A
Transmit:
Average voice: 11A.
Two-tone: 19A

SIZE: Inches: 14.0W, 4.5H, 13.OD.
MM: 356W, 114H, 330D.

WEIGHT: Pounds: 18.0
KG: 8.2

TRANSMITTER

POWER OUTPUT: (Into 50 ohms).
150W PEP, A3A or A3J.

INTERMODULATION: −32 db below PEP.

SPURIOUS EMISSIONS: −64 db below PEP.

CARRIER SUPPRESSION: −46db below PEP.

UNDESIRED SIDEBAND SUPPRESSION: −60 db below PEP.

AUDIO RESPONSE: 300 Hz to 2400 Hz, ±3 db.

RECEIVER

SENSITIVITY (SSB): 1μV for 12db SINAD.

SELECTIVITY (SSB): −6db, 300 to 2400 Hz. 60 db at 4kHz.

AGC: Audio output varies less than 10db for signals between 10μV and 100 MV. Fast attack, slow release.

INTERMODULATION: At least −80 db.

SPURIOUS RESPONSES (Including image): At least −60 db.

NOISE LIMITER: Diode limiter.

AUDIO OUTPUT: 4W @ less than 10% distortion.

ANTENNA COUPLERS/ SYSTEMS

ANTENNA COUPLER #1.

TYPE: Built-in, pre-set.

ANTENNA LENGTHS: 23 to 75 feet. (7 to 23 meters).

VSWR CIRCUIT: Built-in for easy tuning.

OPTIONAL ANTENNA COUPLER #2.

TYPE: Built-in, fully automatic:

ANTENNA LENGTHS: 28 to 35 feet. (8.5 to 10.6 meters).

TUNING TIME (Typical): 1 to 3 seconds

OPTIONAL ANTENNA COUPLER (SEA 2100).

TYPE: External, fully automatic.

ANTENNA LENGTHS: 28 to 35 feet. (8.5 to 10. 6 meters).

TUNING TIME (Typical): 1 to 3 seconds

TRANSCEIVER 50 OHM OUTPUT: 50 ohm output provided on rear chassis for resonant antennas or for external antenna coupler.

HF/SSB TRANSCEIVERS

Stephens Engineering Associates now has the only complete line of synthesized HF/SSB transceivers covering each of the frequency range models generally called for by sailors. The six model line includes three 2-23 MHz units, Sea 106, Sea 106-1, Sea 106-2, one 2-16 MHz model, Sea 116, one 2-12 MHz model, Sea 112 as well as the 2-9 MHz transceiver, the Sea 209.

SEA 112

2 to 13 MHz 150 Watt PEP synthesized SSB radiotelephone. Channel capacity—640 channels. Supplied in pre-programmed memory 80 channel sets for eight regions. Standard are voice-activated squelch, pin diode receiver protection, trunnion mounting bracket, operation and maintenance manual. For operation on 13.6 VDC negative ground. Canadian D.O.C. approved.

SEA 112/w FD OPTION

As above with liquid crystal frequency display.

SEA 116

2 to 17 MHz 125 Watt PEP synthesized SSB radiotelephone. Channel capacity—192 simplex or 96 duplex. Supplied with pre-programmed frequency memory for standard marine channels, voice activated squelch, pin diode receiver protection, trunnion mounting bracket, operation and maintenance manual. For operation on 13.6 VDC negative ground.

SEA 106

2 to 23 MHz 125 Watt PEP synthesized SSB radiotelephone. Channel capacity—384 simplex or 192 duplex. Supplied with preprogrammed frequency memory for standard marine channels, 6 digit LED frequency readout, voice activated squelch, pin diode receiver protection, trunnion mounting bracket, operation and maintenance manual. For operation on 13.6 VDC negative ground.

SEA 106-1

Sea 106 as above with thumbwheel frequency selectors added to provide continuous frequency coverage in 100 Hz steps and preprogrammed frequency memory.

Sea 106-1
Option 2

Sea 106 with thumbwheel frequency selectors providing 100 Hz frequency increments in lieu of preprogrammed frequency memory and LED display.

Tiller Master
P.O. Box 1901
Newport Beach, California 92663

TILLER MASTER AUTOPILOT

Tiller Master was developed over a 20-year period and tested extensively by an experienced sailing enthusiast with an electronics background. Built with materials of the highest quality, Tiller Master is made to stand up under exposure and to use little enough current to be practical on sailing boats with limited battery capacity. Tested thoroughly before shipment, it can steer in a variety of conditions and temperatures under both sail and power.

The components of Tiller Master are corrosion resistant and have low current drain. The case is #5052 aluminum, irridited and painted. The fittings are of stainless steel and passivated. The compass is oil-damped with a Ritchie magnet and jewel, with optical sensing. The electrical circuit board is all solid state on a fiberglass printed board. The contracts of the board are gold-plated. It is plugged into an amphenol plug which also has gold-plated con-

tacts, and the board is easily removed for service. The mechanical feedback system is calibrated for the characteristics of the boat to be steered and can be recalibrated easily for another boat. The motor is a high efficiency aircraft servo motor with a 25:1 reduction gear. It is protected from moisture by a custom-made vinyl cover. The jack screw is made of stainless steel especially selected for its non-magnetic qualities. This is not a threaded rod bought by the yard, but a precision-ground revised standard stub-acme thread, working on a bronze nut brazed in a stainless tube. Thus it is long-wearing and powerful.

igator. Advanced technology features include instant lat/lon read out; dual programmable displays; course, speed and distance information; waypoint programming/sequencing and built-in steering indicator. Exclusive with the TI 9900 is the position resolution alarm (PRA) which warns of nearness to the baseline extension so that alternate TD's may be selected. The Constant Memory™ feature stores system operating data even when the unit is turned off. The entire package is about the size of a major city telephone book.

TI 2100 VHF MARINE RADIO TELEPHONE

The fully synthesized TI 2100 is a microcomputer controlled VHF (156-164 MHz) marine radiotelephone with 55 transmit and 76 receive frequencies, including 4 weather and all US and international channels. The Programmable Scan allows the user to monitor channel 16 and any other selected

Texas Instruments Inc., Marine Division

P.O. Box 226080
Dallas, Texas 75266

TI 9900 LORAN C NAVIGATOR

The TI 9900 is a fully automatic computer controlled Loran C Nav-

channel. Other features include maximum legal output power channel memory, easily-read, gas discharge display and superior receiver sensitivity to improve weak signal reception. The lightweight, weatherproof design has a reversible front panel to allow mounting in any position and a special anti-theft tray, yet weighs only 9 pounds.

TI 3000 RADIO TELEPHONE

The TI 3000 fully synthesized HF SSB radiotelephone covers 234,951 frequencies, from 1.605 to 25.1 MHz. The two-part design features a combined amplifier/antenna coupler unit which makes its

125 Watt PEP out perform even higher powered units by delivering full power right to the antenna. The receiver/exciter/control unit can be installed as simply as a VHF radio.

Other features include a fully automatic antenna coupler; reversible front panel, Constant Memory feature which stores channel frequencies and mode assignments, antenna coupler settings, and last channel used. You can store data for up to 48 simplex channels, 24 duplex channels, or any combination in between. Simple pushbutton tuning permits installation as short as one hour. Only low-cost RG 58 cable need be used between the receiver/exciter unit and the power amplifier/antenna coupler unit.

Trimble Navigation
1077 Independence Avenue
Mountain View, California 94043

TRIMBLE LORAN MODEL 100A

Turn the Trimble on, push the LAT and LON buttons, and you have your position. It does not require TD selection or filter tuning as do so many other "fully automatic" Lorans. The Trimble's fully automatic operation increases your margin of safety because anyone on board can use it, without training and without an instrument manual. Your latitude and longitude are displayed to a resolution of 0.01 minute (60 feet).

Enter the LAT/LON of your destination and the Trimble will calculate the great circle route (shortest distance) to your destination, and display course and distance from your present position.

The Trimble doesn't ask you to select the best TDs—it does it for

you. All Loran stations in a given chain are acquired; the two best TDs are automatically selected on the basis of the best crossing angles and the highest signal-to-noise ratio (SNR) for most accurate position. Fully automatic operation eliminates operator error.

Before every LAT/LON reading, four notch filters are automatically and electronically tuned to eliminate all local interference. Neither operator nor dealer will ever need to calibrate notch filters when moving into a new area. Fully automatic filter adjustment eliminates operator adjustment, one of the most common causes of poor Loran performance.

Although many manufacturers claim "fully automatic" operation for their Loran-C units, only the Trimble receiver and one other high quality unit are truly automatic. "True automatic operation" means that the Loran system selects the best TDs, tunes its filters and presents positions with abso-

lutely no operator decisions required. Operator mistakes are eliminated. The Trimble units work anywhere in the Loran-C coverage area without ever needing any dealer or operator adjustments.

The receiver's unique design provides extended range because it is able to work with low SNRs. The Trimble has provided good groundwave fixes in Bermuda, Jamaica, all the way between California and Hawaii, to Cedros Island, halfway down the Baja coast, and halfway to the Azores from the Atlantic Coast at 32° N, 50°W. All of these locations are beyond normal groundwave reception area as designated by the U.S. Coast Guard. Skywave fixes with sextant accuracy potential extend the range.

Only 15 watts, 1.2 amps, at 12 VDC, are required. The Trimbles do not need to be on continuously in order to track and to obtain their best accuracy. They save power because they can be used intermittently for the few minutes that are required to obtain position.

The Trimble also warns when a skywave is detected, when a marginal signal is being used, or when the Coast Guard "blink" conditions is notifying users that transmitted data may be inaccurate.

The large liquid crystal display (LCD) allows selection and holding of a reading or gives two readings alternately every four seconds. The LCD is clearly visible in bright sunlight and is dimly backlit for easy night reading. This specially designed military grade display has never had a field failure.

Specifications:

PHYSICAL CHARACTERISTICS:

SIZE
5"H x 10⅝"W x 12⅛"D (excluding

mounting brackets and connectors)

WEIGHT
12 pounds

POWER
11-30 VDC at 20W

DISPLAY
7-digit liquid crystal with soft yellow backlight

OPERATING TEMPERATURE
0–50°C
Antenna: 1″ x 14 threaded coupler accepting standard 8-foot fiberglass whip; 40′ coax-supplied; longer cable available on special order. Rigid coupler/antenna 48″ long is recommended for mizzen mast mounts and bridge mounts on power boats.

ELECTRICAL CHARACTERISTICS
Notch Filters: Four, automatically tuned
Acquisition Time: Three minutes or less for a readout of LAT/LON
Update Rate: Less than 10 seconds
LAT/LON Accuracy: Typically well under 0. 15 nautical mile
Repeatability: Approaches the limits of display resolution—50 to 100 feet under ideal conditions but varies with location, SNRs, crossing angles, etc.

TIME DIFFERENCE
0.01 microsecond (10 feet)

RESOLUTION
LAT/LON Resolution: 0.01 minute (60 feet)
Secondaries Tracked: All available
Loran Chain Selection: Local chain can be preset; all others from front panel entry
LAT/LON Coverage Area: All existing chains; Pacific, Atlantic, Great Lakes, Mediterranean, Gulf of Mexico, Norwegian Sea

VDO-ARGO
Instruments, Inc.
980 Brooke Road
Winchester, Virginia 22601

ELECTRONIC SUMLOG

The Electronic Sumlog offers the advantage of eliminating the speedometer cable with its attendant drag and maintenance requirements. Compared to the Mechanical Sumlog, it can be located farther from the sending unit without measurable error. An additional feature of the Electronic Sumlog is a calibrating screw which permits compensating for minor inaccuracies caused by hull turbulence. Gauge Diam.: 4″ - 100 mm.

Dual station installation is possible by simply wiring an additional instrument head to the existing sending unit.

ELECTRONIC SUMLOG II

Installation diameter 4″ (100 mm). Installation depth 4″ (100 mm). Dial diameter 4″ (100 mm). Customer's design option 4 15/16″ x 4 15/16″ (125 x 125 mm) bezel module or 4 23/32″ (120 mm) diameter bezel ring. (Both are included with instrument.)

Available in various dial ranges. The Sumlog II head incorporates 2 distance counters to record:
a. total distance travelled;
b. individual journeys (resettable).

Adjustments to compensate for turbulent flow of water may be made by means of the adjustment screws located at the back of the instrument.

The transducer is contained in a through-hull skin fitting, which is to be sited where the tiny vanes at the tip of the low-drag transducer will get full flow of water at all times. To mount the unit, an opening 1 17/32″ (39 mm) in diameter is required.

The water passing under the hull drives the exposed vanes in proportion to the speed of the boat. The paddlewheel's revolutions are converted into corresponding electrical signals. Receiving these signals via the connecting cable, the instrument head translates them into readings of speed and distance.

MECHANICAL SUMLOG

Utilizing the log principle handed down through centuries of seafaring, this accurate instrument indicates not only speed, but total distance and trip (or racing leg) mileage as well, combining in a single unit all the non-directional navigational information needed for safe, on course cruising or competitive racing.

Completely independent of outside power sources, the Mechanical Sumlog operates regardless of external conditions. Equipped with an adjustable reference pointer which serves as a further guide to boat trim, it can be used in the following ways: (1) Set pointer on a given speed to indicate instantly whether boat speed is increasing or decreasing with changes in sail settings, trim tabs, jets, stern drive, or load distribution. (2) Indicates top speed corresponding to the rated maximum engine RPM. (3) Hold speedometer needle to reference pointer to maintain steady speed. (4) Mark posted speed limits. Gauge Diameter: 3⅜″ (85 mm).

TRIM INDICATOR

Installation diameter 3 21/64" (85 mm). Installation depth 3½" (89 mm). Dial diameter 4" (100 mm). Customer's design option, 4 15/16" x 4 15/16" (125 mm x 125 mm) bezel module or 4 23/32" (120 mm) diameter bezel ring. (Both are supplied with instrument.) Current consumption approximately 65mA.

The Sumlog indicates the speed of the boat. However, any slight change in the setting of the sails can affect the speed. These very slight changes are extremely hard to discern on the speedometer, and this is where the greatly enlarged scale of the trimming unit comes in.

The unit is push-button operated (push-button is separately fitted, for instance, in the instrument panel). The pointer goes initially to the "0" position and it then indicates variations in the current speed of the boat within a range of ± 1 knot. The trimming unit may be fitted as a supplement to previously installed electronic Sumlog sets.

Version for use with the Electric Sumlog:

The trimming unit is adjustable for measuring ranges of 10 and 15 knots and is to be connected in parallel via the transducer input terminal of the electronic Sumlog head.

Version for use with Electronic Sumlog II:

The Sumlog-II Trim Indicator permits universal application for measuring ranges of 8, 12, or 18 knots, and connects to the Sumlog II head.

VDO WIND INDICATOR SYSTEM

All components are protected from spray and are salt water resistant.

The face diameters are 4"—100 mm, install. diameter 3⅜" (85 mm). The complete system consists of:

WIND SPEED INDICATOR

Indication of wind velocity is relative to the speed of the boat and to the direction of the wind. Dual scale readings: Inner—Beaufort notation; Outer—in knots.

WIND DIRECTION INDICATOR

On a scale divided into two 180° segments, the pointer deflection corresponds to the side of the boat from which the apparent wind is blowing.

CLOSE HAULED AND RUNNING INDICATOR

This instrument shows the precise angle of the wind for port and starboard, both upwind and downwind.

COMBINED MASTHEAD UNIT FOR WINDSPEED AND DIRECTION

The upper portion of the masthead sending unit houses a transducer for wind direction. Adjusting to the apparent wind direction, its sensitive vane controls the reading of the Wind Direction Indicator and Close Hauled and Running Indicator. The lower part of the unit accommodates a transducer for wind speed indication. Ideally, the masthead sending unit should be located on the top surface of the masthead toward the bow coinciding with the fore and aft line.

ELECTRICAL CONNECTING CABLE

75 ft. special connecting cable. Do not use other type; inaccuracy will occur.

Vexilar, Inc.
P.O. Box 2208
Hollywood, Florida 33022

VECTA RADIO DIRECTION FINDER

The Vecta system by Vexilar is a portable, self-contained, hand-held radio direction finder that makes navigation by radio bearings simple and foolproof.

It will receive and read out a compass bearing toward any AM radio transmission from 190 to 1600 kHz, whether a marine radiobeacon, aerobeacon, or AM broadcast station with absolutely no chance of a mistake in station identification.

Key to that claim, and to Vecta's accuracy and popularity, is Vecta's pretuned, single-frequency, plug-in receiving modules. Each module will receive *only* the signal for which it is built.

Taking a radio bearing with the Vecta is just as easy as taking a visual bearing on a landmark. And it can perform the same anywhere in the world that a radiobeacon is transmitting and you have the module to receive it—the Atlantic and Pacific coasts, the Gulf coast, the Great Lakes, Europe, the Mediterranean, and many other waters around the world.

The Vecta unit is completely self-contained in its shock-resistant and weatherproof Lexan case. It contains a sensitive AM radio receiver with a sensitive internal ferrite bar antenna for maximum accuracy and sharpness of null, a sensitive null meter as well as a speaker for both audible and visual null readings, and a small but accurate magnetic compass from which you can take a positive bearing on the signal at the moment of null.

The case also contains a battery pack for six AA pencells, usually enough for a full season's use, and on-off-gain control, and an internal light for the compass and null meter for use at night or in poor visibility.

Make Vecta navigation even easier with Vecta charts. These are special adaptations of National Ocean Survey Charts, modified to simplify RDF navigation. All marine and aero radiobeacons and major broadcast stations are precisely located, and a large compass rose is centered on each, with its name, broadcast frequency, dot-dash identification code, "on" time, and effective range in miles. Pick out the correct module, find the null, read the compass, and the rose helps plot the exact bearing on your chart. The 13 by 21-inch charts are laminated in durable, waterproof plastic and printed on both sides. Position plots and other marks wipe off easily after use.

Armchair Sailor Bookstore
Lee's Wharf
Newport, Rhode Island

ZEISS FREIBERGER SEXTANT

Ideally suited to yachts due to its low power telescope and compact size. The index arm is behind the frame for better protection, instrument errors are listed on the certificate for every 10° of arc, both mirrors are fully silvered and are the same size. All 3 mirror adjusting screws have lock nuts. The optional light can be attached at any time in less than a minute.

Specifications:

Frame: special aluminum alloy, anodized and painted. Arc: divided from −3° to 123°. Black degree marks on aluminum. Radius: 5.6″. Micrometer drum: attached firmly to shaft with spanner nut and locking screw. Single index mark. Mirrors: 57 mm x 29 mm. Shades: 3 index, 2 horizon, neutral tint. Telescope: 2.4 x 25 with screw focusing and rubber eye cup. Weight: 1.9 lbs. Case: plywood finished, dovetailed joints, lock.

5

SAFETY

ACR Electronics, Inc.
3901 N. 29th Ave.
Hollywood, Florida 33020

ACR/ACL-4 ANTI-COLLISION LIGHT

All ACR/strobe lights have been designed and engineered to meet the severe environmental requirements set forth by various government and civilian agencies.

Pulsating, high intensity flashes are visible for several miles. The brilliant light is directed through a specially designed fresnel lens 360°. During inclement weather, the xenon flash penetrates rain, fog, or haze like no conventional light can. This powerful light can signal a warning or significantly enhance visual sighting and recovery.

A compact, non-corrosive and shock resistant case may be secured in a base or side mounting position. Its appearance is smooth to touch, easy to clean, and resistant to stain. Color is international orange.

Specifications:

Model No. ACR/ACL-4

SIZE
2.13" (5.4 cm) wide x 6.25" (15.9 cm) high x 1.5" (3.8 cm)

BASE
4 mounting holes—.201" (.5 cm) diameter for upright or side mounting

WEIGHT
8 oz. (227 gms.)

LIGHT INTENSITY
750,000 peak lumens per flash

FLASH RATE
60 flashes per minute @ 10

VISIBILITY
360°; up to 8 miles on a clear night

WEATHER-AND-WATERPROOF
Impervious to humidity and moisture

DURABILITY
Completely encapsulated electronics. High impact plastic case.

TEMPERATURE RANGE
−40°F to 140°F (−40°C to +60°C)

LENS
Clear, durable plastic

POWER SOURCE
External

OPERATING VOLTAGE
12 VDC ± 2 VDC

CURRENT DRAIN
Nominal .15A at 12 VDC

ACTIVATION
External switch (not supplied)

CASE COLOR
International orange

CREW LIGHT

Description:

The ACR/Crew Light is powered by two standard AA Alkaline Batteries which are easily replaceable. A lanyard fastened to a Velcro backed stainless steel pocket clip on the back of the flashlight allows convenient methods of portability for the user. Lamp extraction/insertion tool is provided at the top of the unit. A positive action lever switch is located at the top of the unit for easy one hand operation. The bottom cover of the FA-11 Crewlight is designed to serve as a spanner wrench for the removal of the lens. Two small teeth on either end mate with indentations in the lens. All ports and openings are sealed with "O" rings for a watertight enclosure. For other than occasional replacement of the bulb or battery, there is little which is required in maintaining the flashlight. Should the lamp burn out, replace with G.E. type 243 or equivalent. Under cockpit situations it may be desirable to use the red filter over the flashlight lens to avoid excessive brightness when the eyes are accustomed to subdued lighting. The red filter may be slipped over the lens by pushing upward on the filter button with the thumb.

Specifications:

NOMENCLATURE CREW LIGHT
Model No. ACR/FA-11

SIZE
3 5/8" x 1 5/8" x 1 5/16" (9.21 cm x 4.12 cm x 3.33 cm)

WEIGHT
4.6 oz. (130 gms) including batteries

BATTERY
Two, Size "AA", 1.5V/Cell. Recommended: Alkaline, Mallory MN1500 or equivalent

LAMP
GE Type 243 or equivalent (Min. Screw)

INTENSITY
25 Foot Candles at 1 ft. minimum

BEAM
Oval Shape, 10" x 5¼" at 3-ft. nominal

CASE
Durable plastic, International Orange

ATTACHMENTS
Pocket clip, lanyard, Velcro

ACCESSORIES
Lamp Extraction/Insertion tool, spanner wrench for lens removal

DISTRESS MARKER LIGHT

The ACR Distress Marker Light is a lightweight, compact, battery operated man overboard light. When dropped overboard, it automatically rights itself and begins flashing. The light is used to mark a position in the water. This type of light is standard equipment in ocean races; a life saver for any boater.

Electronic strobe module produces a high intensity, with a 360° flashing light visible for several miles. The brilliant flash has the same color temperature as the sun. Its intensity provides greater penetration power in rain, fog, or haze like no conventional light can.

The Distress Marker Light essentially consists of a case, internal ballast and flotation, electronic strobe module with integral end cap, and stainless steel hanging clip.

The case made of a touch corrosion resistant plastic will withstand a 150 foot air drop. Watertight in-

tegrity is assured by an "O" ring seal between surfaces. A standard 6 volt lantern type battery may be replaced without the need for tools. Three stainless locking swivals provide easy access to the battery compartment.

Specifications:

MODEL
ACR/566

SIZE
15.75" (40.0 cm) length; 4.0" (10.16 cm) diameter

WEIGHT
2.0 Lbs. (.91 Kgs); 3.38 Lbs. (1.53 Kgs) with battery

LIGHT OUTPUT
250,000 peak lumens per flash

FLASH RATE
55 ± 10 per minute

VISIBILITY
Horizon to Horizon

OPERATIONAL LIFE
50 Hours

ACTIVATION
Automatic gravity switch

BATTERY
6 volts DC Lantern type with screw terminals. Recommended: NEDA #925 or 915.

MATERIALS
Lexan lens, stainless steel hanging clip, stainless steel locking swivals, poly vinyl chloride case.

OPTIONAL ACCESSORY
The ACR Waterproof Whistle only measures 2″ x ¼″ x ⅞″. Non-corrosive, retainer ring. Model ACR/WW-2.

SM-2 ILLUMINATION MARKER

The ACR-SM2 Illumination Marker is a durable, bright orange emergency flasher designed for a variety of safety and rescue uses at sea. It is precisely constructed and balanced to float upright even in rough seas. Upon deployment, it immediately begins flashing an easy-to-see, powerful strobe light through a 360° Lexan lens for total directional coverage.

Unit is mounted on a quick access bracket for immediate availability in any emergency. A stainless steel cable-ring on the bottom of the case permits rope or lanyard attachment.

The ACR SM-2 meets U.S. Coast Guard 161.010 requirements and provides 50 hours of repeated flashes with a 6 volt battery. A high voltage discharge principle

generates an exceptional penetrating brilliance in a xenon gas tube.

Specifications:

SIZE
12″ (30.5 CM) length; 3.5″ (8.9 CM) diameter

WEIGHT
3¼ lbs. including battery; 1¾ lbs. excluding battery

OUTER CONSTRUCTION
PVC Casing and Lexan Lens

BATTERY
Standard 6 Volt Lantern

OPERATION LIFE
Up to 50 hours

LIGHT INTENSITY
250,000 peak lumens

RANGE
Up to 15 miles

LENS
360° visibility

ACTIVATION
Automatic gravity switch

BRACKET
Plastic non-magnetic and non-corrosive mounting bracket

OPTIONAL ACCESSORIES
USCG Approved E.P.I.R.B., 161/.011 9/0 Class A, Automatic Float-off/Activation, includes Mounting Bracket

SPECIFICATIONS SUBJECT TO CHANGE.

ACR-RLB 12 EPIRB

Battery operated and self-buoyant, the beacon transmitter is an item of survival equipment and is designed to be carried aboard vessels at sea and in port so as to be readily available in any emergency. It is intended to be installed in its bracket so that it will automatically float off and actuate in the event of a sinking craft. It may also

be manually extracted and attached to personnel, or survival craft, with provided lanyard.

When turned "On" by removal from the bracket and inverted, it transmits sweeping tone distress signals (VHF/UHF) to civil and military aircraft. Rescue craft can "home" to the transmitting unit.

Construction is of materials designed and tested to withstand climate and weather. It is corrosion and mildew resistant and built for a long life top side. The beacon case with its external antenna is water-proof.

Operating readiness of the beacon can be tested intermittently or on a periodic schedule by using the built in Press to Test switch and indicator light (LED). Access to the longer life, magnesium battery is also made simple for periodic replacement.

Specifications:

TYPE ACCEPTED
FCC Part 83, Class "B"

SIZE
16″ x 3.5″ (40.7 cm x 8.9 cm)

WEIGHT
4.75 pounds (2.16 Kgm)

OPERATING FREQUENCIES
121.5 and 243.0 MHz, simultaneously

DISTINCTIVE TONE
Variable audio sweep from 1300 to 300 Hz in accordance with RTCA Regulations.

INITIATION
Toggle type (3 Position) switch. Test-Off-On. Push to test.

OUTPUT POWER TOTAL
200 Milliwatts

OPERATING LIFE (Minimum)
48 hours at −20°C

BATTERY
Magnesium, nominal 6 V. Shelf life 6 years, replacement interval 3 years.

ANTENNA
18″ (45.5 cm) flexible, ¼ wavelength each channel. Folds against case when not in use.

ATTACHMENT
20 foot lanyard

COLOR
International orange body with bright yellow ends

ACR/RLB-14 EPIRB

RLB-14 meets U.S. Coast Guard/FCC requirements. Approved "Class A" EPIRB. Maximum realiability; foolproof operation. If vessel sinks, EPIRB floats free from bracket; automatically activates. Manual operation; remove from non-metallic, non-corrosive bracket; invert. May be attached to personnel of survival craft with provided lanyard. Permanently deployed flexible whip antenna design. Power output 200 mW/channel P.E.R.P. Test circuit with indicator light (LED) assures operating readiness. Magnesium battery system has 6-year storage life. Dependable EPIRB provides fully automatic operation, durability, and freedom from service.

Specifications:
CERTIFICATION
U.S.C.G. 161.111/9/0 Class "A" FCC Part 83 for Marine use

SIZE
16″ x 3.5″ (40.7 cm x 8.9 cm)

WEIGHT
5.75 pounds (2.61 kg) installed; 5.0 pounds (2.27 kg) less bracket

OPERATING FREQUENCIES
121.5 and 243.0 MHz, simultaneously

MODULATION
Type A9

DISTINCTIVE TONE
Variable audio sweep from 1300 to 300 Hz in accordance with RTCA regulations

FREQUENCY STABILITY
005T crystal controlled

ACTIVATION
Automatic on deployment or when manually inverted (antenna "up")

BRACKET
Automatic float off

TEST CIRCUIT
Push to TEST switch, Internal dummy load, indicator light (LED)

POWER OUTPUT
200 MW/Channel PERP

OPERATING LIFE
48 hrs minimum at −4°F (−20°C) much longer at higher temperatures

OPERATING TEMPERATURE
−4°F to +130°F (120°C to +58°C)

BATTERY
Magnesium battery, nominal 6V. Shelf life 6 years, replacement interval 3 years.

OPERATION RETENTION
Lanyard for securing to person or survival craft

COLOR
International orange body

ACCESSORIES
ACR/SM-2 Automatic man overboard light. U.S.C.G. approved 161.010/610. Flashes a 360° high intensity xenon strobe light up to 50 hours. Includes non-metallic mounting bracket.

ACR/RLB-15 RESCUE LOCATOR BEACON

A new dependable emergency transmitter that attaches to survival craft for semi-permanent installation. Compact, lightweight. Features automatic activation, magnesium battery pack with proven six year storage capacity and test circuit with indicator light. U.S.C.G. approved as equivalent Class "A" EPIRB. (161.011/10/0).

ACR/4F FIREFLY RESCUE LITE

Description:

The ACR/4F Firefly introduces advanced dimensions in visual recovery. Brilliant, white, strobe light flashes pulsate 50 times a minute.

Night visibility extends to 700 square miles, if viewed from altitudes of 2500 feet or more. 250,000 peak lumens of light cut through fog and rain better than conventional lights.

Powerful mercury battery drives the Firefly continuously for nine hours. Encapsulated battery allows quick and easy battery change.

Made of tough butyrate plastic, the Firefly is totally waterproof. Resists stains and all environmental corrosive agents.

Optional equipment such as a day-glow orange carrying pouch, styrofoam float, flash guard, and color treated, snap-on lenses make

our xenon strobe light suitable for a variety of uses.

No larger than a pack of cigarettes, the Firefly goes with you anywhere. Utilized by military and civilian pilots in downed-airman recovery, firefighters in inner-structure utility work, motorists to signal emergencies, and mariners for emergency anti-collision and man-overboard situations.

The Firefly meets the requirements of FAA TSO-C85. Thousands of strobe light users have found that the ACR/4F Firefly Rescue Light meets the most rigorous demands of visual rescue and distress requirements.

Specifications:

SIZE
4½" x 2" x 1" (11.4 cm x 5.1 cm x 2.5 cm)

WEIGHT
6.6 oz. (187 gm) including battery

LIGHT OUTPUT
250,000 peak lumens per flash

FLASH RATE
50 flashes per minute (nominal)

OPERATING LIFE
9 hours continuous

VISIBILITY
5 miles (8 Km) line of sight on a clear night.

WATERPROOF
Impervious to humidity and liquid submersion.

TEMPERATURE RANGE
+32° to 140°F (0°C to +60°C)

POWER UNIT
4RM1B mercury battery (encapsulated, with integral metal end cap). Also fits Model SDU-5/E

SHOCKPROOF
Unit is completely encapsulated in shock and vibration resistant plastic.

CASE COLOR
International orange

LENS
Durable butyrate plastic

ACTIVATION
Bonneted push-push switch

OPTIONAL EQUIPMENT
Carrying pouch (Orange Day Glow w/Lanyard), colored snap-on lenses (red, amber, blue, green), styrofoam float, flash guard, extra duty battery (216 MG)

ACR/4G FIREFLY RESCUE LITE

Description:

The ACR/4G Firefly is the only personal rescue strobelight designed exclusively for underwater applications.

Accepted and used by the Navy UDT and SEAL teams and commercial salvage divers, the Firefly meets the most stringent demands.

A totally sparkproof sliding magnetic switch allows the Firefly to be used around highly combustible liquids and gases. Slides back and forth with enough resistance for easy on-off manipulation, yet will not turn off or on inadvertently.

A xenon gas-filled tube flashes 250,000 peak lumens with each pulse. Can be seen horizontally up to 50 feet in clear water. Cuts through murky waters better than conventional lights.

Made of tough, durable butyrate plastic, the ACR/4G Firefly takes all the knocks and abuse active divers can dish out. It's impervious to stains and corrosive agents that may originate from weather conditions and from most man-made chemicals. Completely water-tight with encapsulated semiconductor circuitry, the Firefly is operational down to 200 feet.

Flashes continuously for nine hours on one powerful mercury

battery, yet the unit is smaller than a pack of cigarettes. Batteries are replaceable and easy to change, even underwater.

Specifications:

SIZE
4½″ x 2″ x 1″ (11.4 cm x 5.1 cm x 2.5 cm)

WEIGHT
7 oz. (199 gm) including battery

LIGHT OUTPUT
250,000 peak lumens per flash

FLASH RATE
50 flashes per minute (nominal)

OPERATIONAL LIFE
9 hours continuous

VISIBILITY
Up to 50 feet (15 m) underwater; up to 5 miles (8 km) line of sight on a clear night.

WATERPROOF
Impervious to humidity and liquid submersion. Operational at depths down to 200 feet (61 m).

TEMPERATURE RANGE
+32° to 140°F (0°C to +60°C)

POWER UNIT
4RM1B Mercury battery (encapsulated, with integral metal end cap)

SHOCKPROOF
Completely encapsulated in shock and vibration resistant plastic

CASE COLOR
International orange

LENS
Durable butyrate plastic

ACTIVATION
Magnetic slide switch

OPTIONAL EQUIPMENT
Carrying pouch (Orange Day Glow w/Lanyard), colored snap-on lenses (red, amber, blue, green), flash guard, styrofoam float

ACRO/L-10A S.O.S. LIGHT

Fully certified by the U.S. Coast Guard as a Nighttime Distress Signal, the ACR L-10A Automated S.O.S. Light represents the finest safety instrument of its kind.

It is 5 times brighter than

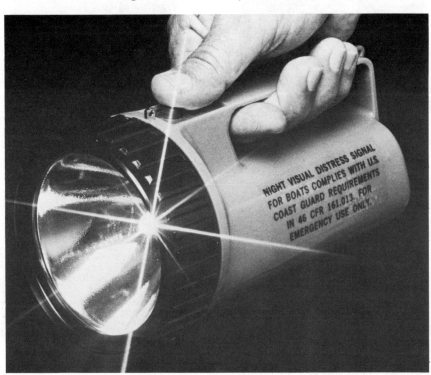

USCG specifications require and is designed to last 2 times longer.

Powered by six standard "D" cell batteries, it is designed to function as a fully automated S.O.S. flasher. It is completely waterproof and will float beam-up if dropped overboard.

Includes snap-on red filter and adjustable carrying strap.

Atlantis Weathergear, Inc.
Bay Street at the Waterfront
Sag Harbor, New York 11963

PERSONAL RESCUE PACK AND FLOTATION DEVICES

The Atlantis Personal Rescue Pack fits on your belt or inside your jacket pockets to maximize your chance of rescue from boat, aircraft or shore. Meeting USCG Carriage requirements (through 1982), it contains 3 self-launching red aerial flares (no gun needed), signal mirror, dye marker and whistle with lanyard, packed with emergency instructions in a vinyl pouch.

UL-listed USCG-approved Type III Personal Flotation Devices (PFD's) are available in two styles utilizing continuously nylon fabric shells and closed-cell foam for light weight, comfort, and longevity. The unique ColorSafe® coding system shows at a glance your correct size—a safety extra in any emergency. And both styles have pockets for belongings or the Personal Rescue Pack.

The Signal Classic is waist-length with vertical channels of super-soft PVC foam in front, polyethylene closed-cell foam in back. The SuperSport Vest is longer and uses narrow channels of ultra-light weight polyethylene; in addition, SOLAS-grade reflective tape across the shoulders increases nighttime visibility.

Imtra Corporation
151 Mystic Avenue
Medford, Massachusetts 02155

AVON LIFERAFTS

Avon has taken note of the findings of an extensive liferaft test program carried out in the rugged waters off Iceland and has modified its ballast/sea anchor system, but without affecting seaworthiness. Liferaft ballast pockets have been increased in number, depth and capacity and have been weighted down so as to fill rapidly within 60 seconds of launching. The ballast pockets are in separate sections to allow if necessary (should the bottom buoyancy tube lift clear of the water) a wind passage between the pockets and prevent a build-up of wind pressure against the pockets themselves. The effect of the increased capacity of the pockets and their slight re-positioning outwards on the bottom of the liferaft is to increase the actual weight of water in the pockets and the anti-capsizing forces by 300 to 400%.

Emergency Pack YM(E):

1 Knife—to cut painter.
1 First Aid Pack. Drinking water—1 pint per person (½ litre). 2 Plastic Lids—for re-sealing water cans. 2 Safety

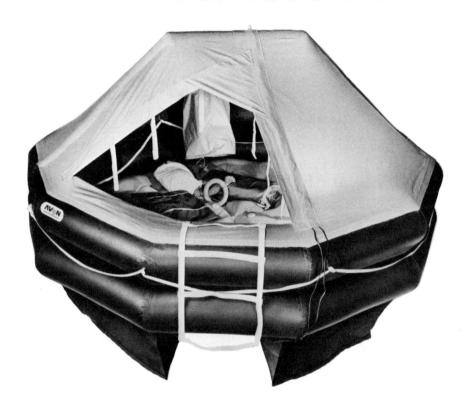

Can Openers. 1 Graduated Drinking Cup. 6 Plastic Storage Bags. 1 Signalling Torch (flashlight). 2 spare batteries and bulb. 2 Paddles. 2 Parachute Flares. 3 Hand Flares. 1 Sun Signalling Mirror. Distress Signal Table.

1 Bailer. 2 Sponges. 1 Sea Anchor. 1 Rescue Quoit on 100′ (30m) line. 1 Bellows. 1 Repair Kit incl. leak stoppers for rapid repairs. 6 Anti-sea Sickness Pills per person. 1 Fishing Kit. Instructions on how to survive.

Specifications:

		4 Persons		6 Persons		8 Persons		10 Persons	
Weight	Valise	66 lbs	30 kg	86 lbs	39 kg	104 lbs	47 lbs	115 lbs	52 kg
	Canister	79 lbs	36 kg	101 kg	46 kg	121 lbs	55 kg	135 lbs	61 kg
Length	Valise	24″	61 cm	28″	71 cm	30″	76 cm	33″	84 cm
	Canister	31″	79 cm	32″	81 cm	32″	81 cm	32″	81 cm
Diameter	Valise	16″	40.5 cm	16½″	42 cm	17½″	44.5 cm	18½″	47 cm
Width	Canister	17″	43 cm	23″	58.5 cm	23″	58.5	23″	58.5 cm
Height	Canister	11″	28 cm	11″	28 cm	13″	33 cm	14¼″	37.5 cm

Falcon Safety Products, Inc.
1065 Bristol Road
Mountainside, New Jersey 07092

SENTRY BOAT BURGLAR ALARM

Keep your boat "armed" whenever it's unmanned or anchored. Falcon Sentry is the ideal way to protect yourself, your boat, and your valuables against unwanted intrusions and thefts. Sentry, when activated, lets out a piercing blast, audible up to one mile away, that will frighten away the most brazen intruder. This unique protection device is dependable, effective, and inexpensive.

SOUND OFF! BOAT HORN

Up to 300 sonic blasts can be heard from Sound Off!'s replaceable 3 oz. canister. Its sturdy, high-impact plastic trumpet is guaranteed unbreakable, and like all Falcon portable boat horns, meets U.S. Coast Guard requirements for Classes I, II and III. Sound Off! is small enough for carry-along convenience, yet delivers its emergency signal up to a mile away.

Givens Associates
3198 Main Road
Tiverton, Rhode Island 02878

GIVENS BUOY LIFE RAFT

With its patented dual-stabilizer, the Givens Buoy Raft has saved hundreds of lives. Its increased stability and lowered center of gravity

make it the only raft suitable for the mariner to carry in all weather conditions. Standard Features:

1. The patented GIVENS/NASA buoy water ballast stabilization system
   a. 1st and 2nd stage ballast chambers
   b. 297 gallon capacity buoy ballast system for 1-6 man; 375 gallon-capacity for 1-8 man
   c. 3/16″ stainless steel cable sewn in spiral configuration to form and facilitate deployment of buoy chamber.
2. One way flapper valve (valve on bottom of buoy chamber—controls water intake)
3. Because of this specially designed buoy ballast system the raft will stay in the proximity of the disaster—will favor current and not varying winds (gives you a better chance of being found by search and rescue teams after given mayday and Loran readings)
4. Deballasting line (will facilitate easier towing and padding if needed)
5. U.S.C.G. spec. 16-AA material used on all rafts (under Federal spec. 160.051)
6. The full "A" deluxe survival package (except where noted)
7. Automatic CO2-nitrogen inflation system (for inflation in cold and warm weather)
8. Cam operated firing inflation system
9. Inside/outside water activated dome lights (SB model, outside only)
10. Canopy mounted rain catch (for drinking water, except SB model)
11. Inner/outer nylon web boarding ladder
12. Hand life ring with 100 ft. of heaving line

13. Interior/exterior life lines

14. Canopy mounted line cutting knife

15. Patented quick opening velcro door entrance (closed during inflation to prevent swamping of occupant area prior to entry)

16. International orange canopy

17. Sea anchor (automatically deployed upon inflation of raft)

18. Stainless steel pressure relief valves for each inflation chamber

19. Hand pump for topping off raft when needed

20. View port hole (also for ventilation)

21. 60 ft. braided nylon painter line (allows you to clear vessel in case of fire)

22. 500 lb.—breaking strength weak-link (on all deck mounted cannister packs)

23. Stainless steel cable attached to weak-link and shackle mounted to deck. Gasket and cable prevent water from entering life raft through nylon painter (firing) line

24. Dodecagon shape (12 sided) lessens resistance of raft in rough and breaking seas. Model A and USCG (only) Double floor and canopy, once floor is manually inflated, it will act as insulation, as will the double canopy to prevent hypothermia; the lowering of body core temperature due to exposure, eventually resulting in death. Three separate inflation chambers (the upper tube and arches, bottom tube and inflatable floor)

The Guest Corporation
17 Culbro Drive
West Hartford, Connecticut
06110

NAVIGATION LIGHTS

Guest Marinaspec navigation lanterns feature high intensity quartz halogen bulbs that provide 25 percent more lumens per watt. Other lanterns feature conventional tungsten filament bulbs. This bulb will operate on 20 percent less current than other navigation lanterns with the same rating.

Mounting:

The twist-off base allows for easy mounting and alignment, as well as simple removal for storage or bulb replacement.

Unique Optical Features:

Guest Marinaspec lanterns are designed with grazing incidence optics to ensure the maximum utilization of light generated by the quartz halogen bulb. This feature allows a high degree of visibility maintained even at a 30 degree angle of heel.

SEA BEAM II SPOTLIGHT

The new Sea Beam II is waterproof, lightweight and floats. It features a high impact yellow case and a brilliant 12,000 candlepower

beam. A handy light for emergencies. Uses 6 volt spring terminal lantern battery (Eveready #509, Ray-O-Vac #941, not included). 8½″ long.

High Seas, Inc.
4861 24th Avenue
Port Huron, Michigan 48060

SEA STEP

Features all-stainless welded construction, buffed to a high polish. Mounting flanges are drilled for ¼″ machine screws and the pins are easily removed. Two adjustable support arms hold the ladder off the transom when in the lowered position.

While designed primarily as a convenience, the Sea Step fulfills a valid safety function by providing rigid, fast access to and from the water in emergency situations.

ITT Jabsco
1485 Dale Way
Costa Mesa, California 92626

MARINE AIR HORN KIT

The Model 46070-0000 marine air horn kit contains a 25 inch solid brass, triple chrome-plated horn; a 12 Vdc compressor in the 80 to 100 psi range; an air storage tank; an electric air valve with button; 30 feet of 5/16 inch tubing; 4 feet of ¼ inch hose, and all necessary fittings. It meets U.S. Coast Guard Navigational Rules CG-169 as they apply to "sound signal intensity and range audibility" for vessels under 246 ft. (75 m). The horn's sound level at 1 meter is 130 dB.

Audibility range is one nautical mile.

MARINE SEARCHLIGHTS

These cabin-controlled 7 inch (178 mm) and 8 inch (203 mm) sealed beam searchlights feature a quick-action control lever for 380° horizontal sweep and 70° vertical sweep, with horizontal and vertical locking devices. Light housing, base, control rods and escutcheon plate are all of high quality brass, with a heavy nickel-chrome plated finish or tough epoxy-type paint finish.

Light movement is friction-dampened for ease of operation. The entire unit is weather proofed. Designed for cabin roof mount, these searchlights feature standard base and control rods for up to 5 inch roof thickness. Height above the surface for the 7 inch model, number 43630, is 15-3/8 inch (391 mm), and 15-3/16 inch (386 mm) for the 8 inch model, number 43640.

Monarch Moor Whips
P.O. Box 6
Normandy Beach, New Jersey 08739

MOORING LINE MATES

A quick, easy and sure way for mooring lines. As a boat owner, you've experienced the hassle of docking (or trying to dock) during strong winds with the boat rocking and you can't reach or even find those mooring lines. Mooring Line Mates solve that problem and guarantee that your lines will always be right where you need them . . . when that split second timing while docking means everything. Easy to reach, they swing to and away from you. Adjustable stop with friction clutch. Fiberglass rods, stainless steel hooks and tenzaloy mounts. All hardware is stainless steel.

Sea-Fire Extinguishing Marine Products
Division of Metalcraft, Inc.
718 Debelius Avenue
Baltimore, Maryland 21205

HALON 1301 FIRE EXTINGUISHER

Stop fire where it starts with a new SEA-FIRE system in your boat engine compartment; complete automatic operation, with self-contained heat sensor and protective guard, puts out fires in seconds whether your boat is in or out of the water. Using Du Pont Halon 1301 which chemically blocks the process of combustion, this agent is recognized as the most effective against Class B flammable liquids and Class C electrical fires. Three times as effective as CO_2. Leaves no messy residue for costly cleanup and will not damage internal engine parts. Easy to install by boater. Can lower insurance premiums. Compact, lightweight design allows for *vertical* or *horizontal* installation in most engine compartments. No piping or electrical connections needed. Installation hardware with heavy duty aluminum and stainless steel mounting bracket included. Five convenient models.

Construction:

Noncorrosive baked enamel aluminum DOT approved cylinder. Other components of rust free bronze and anodized aluminum. Passed 240 hours salt spray test. From the leading manufacturer of Halon 1301 portable extinguishers.

MODEL E-75
75 cubic feet (2.1 cubic meters) capacity, contains 1.5 pounds (.68 kg) Halon 1301. Actuation temperature 212°F (100°C). Dimensions: 3-inch diameter by 12 inches high. Weight less bracket: 3 pounds (1.4 kg).

MODEL E-250
250 cubic feet (7 cubic meters) capacity, contains 5 pounds (2.3 kg) Halon 1301. Actuation temperature 165°F (74°C). Dimensions: 4-inch diameter by 15.62 inches high. Weight less bracket: 7.75 pounds (3.5 kg).

MODEL E-350
350 cubic feet (9.9 cubic meters) capacity, contains 7 pounds (3.2 kg) Halon 1301. Actuation temperature 160°F (74°C). Dimensions: 5-inch diameter by 16.5 inches high. Weight less bracket: 11 pounds (4.9 kg).

MODEL E-500
500 cubic feet (14 cubic meters)

capacity, contains 10 pounds (4.6 kg) Halon 1301. Actuation temperature 165°F (74°C). Dimensions: 5-inch diameter by 19.62 inches high. Weight less bracket: 14.5 pounds (6.6 kg).

Construction:

Heavy-duty, DOT approved, steel cylinder and mounting bracket finished with electrostatic applied baked enamel. Other components of rust free bronze and anodized aluminum. Passed 240 hours salt spray test.

MODEL E-150A

150 cubic feet (4.2 cubic meters) capacity, contains 3.0 pounds (1.4 kg) Halon 1301. Actuation temperature 212°F (100°C). Dimensions: 3½-inch diameter by 13½-inches high. Weight less bracket: 6.75 pounds (3.1 kg).

Shewmon, Inc.
P.O. Box 755
Dunedin, Florida 33528

SEA ANCHOR

Shewmon sea anchors are designed, tested, and made for all types of vessels, both private and commercial, from liferafts to ships. Self-opening, these sea anchors produce maximum pull at minimum speeds, and are used for emergencies, drift fishing, and sea layovers. They are shipped in their own tote bags, and require little storage space.

Sea anchors made by Shewmon, Inc., are available in diameters of from 2 to 25 feet. Others can be made on request. Since a sea anchor is a survival tool, its size should be chosen conservatively. Larger sea anchors will permit less drift and will wear better than smaller ones.

Generally, a 2-foot sea anchor is appropriate for liferafts; the 3 and 4-footers for small boats; the 5 and 6-footers for large boats. The 10-foot sea anchor will perform well for very large boats, and even for small ships that point towards the wind while drifting.

DROGUES

Shewmon self-opening drogues are designed to be deployed from the sterns of sailboats maintaining course in strong following winds. Their purpose is to greatly reduce the chances of broaching or pitchpoling.

At drifting speeds, the pull of drogues is minimal. For this reason, they should not be used as sea anchors except in emergencies.

Shewmon drogues are either 2 feet in diameter for medium sized boats, or 3 feet for large boats.

Their canopies are extremely rugged, weighted to reduce rotation, and can be tripped while under full load.

Tripping can be accomplished by pulling an extension of the 5/16th-inch trip line. Drogues under load require tripping forces of many hundreds of pounds, necessitating the use of a winch. Tripping may also be accomplished by cleating the trip line and slacking off on the main drogue rope.

Soderberg Manufacturing Company

20821 Currier Road, P.O. Box 506
Walnut, California 91789

MINIBUOY S1223 FLOATING INCANDESCENT LIGHT

Features:

Lights automatically in upright position or when thrown into the water. Operates up to 50 hours on 2 "D" cell flash light batteries. Visible for several miles.

Corrosion resistant bracket made of polished stainless steel and black enameled aluminum conveniently holds the Minibuoy inverted until needed, or in operating (upright) position. Bracket can be permanently affixed to bulkhead or securely hung on any rail.

The high impact rugged housing is molded of "international orange" butyrate. Color will never fade.

A clear acrylic lens produces a brilliant light pattern. Lens will not yellow.

"O" Ring seal assures total water tightness.

Can be used as a man overboard light, slip, dock, buoy, net, or channel marker—or as an onboard emergency light.

Specifications:

DIMENSIONS
3.5" Dia x 12 " long

WEIGHT
(less 2 "D" cells) 1.5 lb.

SEAFLARE 5 1707B MASTHEAD AND ANCHOR STROBE LIGHT

22 Million Peak Candle Power. (10 Joules)

This all solid state xenon strobe light is combined with an incandescent anchor light and each can be operated independently.

Rugged corrosion resistant construction—aluminum alloy housing finished with durable epoxy paint. All stainless steel hardware. Unit is designed to withstand high vibration and shock environment.

High impact high temperature glass lens.

Low power requirements—draws less than 1 amp.

Convenient mounting provision—mounts to ½ inch pipe thread or to ¾ inch tube. (special mounting bracket available)

Incandescent lamp and Xenon flash tube easily replaceable.

Reverse polarity protected.

Specifications:

DIMENSION
3″ Dia x 6″ long

WEIGHT
1.5 lb.

FLASH RATE
30 (±10) flashes per minute

POWER
Model S1707B/12 12-14 VDC
Model S1707B/32 32 VDC

SEAFLARE II S1890 MASTHEAD STROBE LIGHT

Features:

Trim, light weight, all solid state xenon strobe light especially suited for sailboats and racing applications. Weighs only 10 oz.

Flash rate can be changed with the flip of a switch (not included).

Rugged, corrosion resistant construction—aluminum alloy housing finished with durable epoxy paint. All stainless steel hardware. Unit is designed to withstand high vibration and shock environment.

High impact, high temperature glass lens.

Low power requirements—draws less than 1 amp.

Convenient mounting provision: mounts to ½″ pipe thread or to ¾″ tube. (special mounting bracket available).

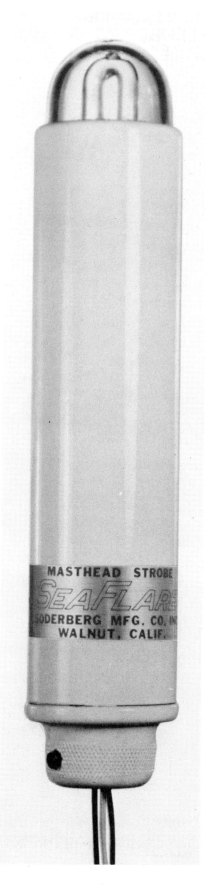

MASTHEAD STROBE
SeaFlare
SODERBERG MFG. CO. INC.
WALNUT, CALIF.

Xenon flash tube easily replaceable.

Reverse polarity protected.

Specifications:

DIMENSIONS
1⅝″ Dia x 8″ long

WEIGHT
10 oz.

FLASH RATE
Recognition 20 (±10) flashes per minute
Emergency 60 (±10) flashes per minute

POWER
12-14 VDC

UNIVERSAL MOUNTING BRACKET

This versatile bracket was designed for the models S1707, and S1890, "Seaflare" Masthead strobes, for mast-top, bulkhead, or deck mounting. It can be installed with mounting tab upward or downward—or on a horizontal surface. It is also ideal for antennas, wind indicators and instrumentation, horns, flags, flood lights, etc.

Features:

Constructed from superior corrosion resistant marine grade stainless steel and polished to a high gloss finish.

½—28 threaded nipple and two nuts provide versatility and numerous mounting configurations. The nipple can be plugged with a ½inch pipe-cap or attached to standard conduit for a water tight installation.

MINISTAR S1694 FLOATING STROBE LIGHT

Features:

The all solid state electronic strobe flashes automatically in upright position or when thrown into the water.

Operates up to 50 hours on 2 "D" cell flash light batteries.

Visible for several miles.

Corrosion resistant bracket made of polished stainless steel and black enameled aluminum, conveniently holds the Ministar inverted until needed, or in operating (upright) position. Bracket can be permanently affixed to bulkhead or securely hung on any rail.

The high impact rugged housing is molded of "international orange" butyrate. The color will never fade.

A clear acrylic lens produces a brilliant light pattern. Lens will not yellow.

"O" Ring seal assures total water tightness.

The electronic module is replaceable and serviceable.

Can be used as a man-overboard light, slip, dock, buoy, net or channel marker, or as an onboard emergency beacon.

Specifications:

DIMENSIONS
3.5" Dia x 12" long

WEIGHT
(less 2 "D" Cells) 1.5 lb.

FLASH RATE
60 (±10)flashes per minute.

SEASTAR S1307 STROBE WATER LIGHT

Features:

Coast Guard Approved (No. 161-010/5/2)

The all solid state electronic strobe flashes automatically in upright position or when thrown into the water.

International orange vinyl coated stainless steel mounting bracket holds the Seastar in an inverted position until needed.

The rugged high impact housing is molded of "international orange" polycarbonate. Color will never fade.

An acrylic lens provides a brilliant light pattern. Lens will not yellow.

"O" Ring seal assures total water tightness.

Manufactured under the most stringent aerospace quality control program for the highest reliability.

Each unit is individually pressure checked, triple function tested, and aged for a 16 hour "burn in" period before leaving the factory.

Specifications:

DIMENSIONS
3.5" Dia x 16" long

WEIGHT
(less 6V lantern battery) 3 lb.

FLASH RATE
60 (±10) flashes per minute

Winslow Company
P.O. Box 578
Osprey, Florida 33559

CANOPIED OBLONG LIFE RAFTS

20M—2MAN

Winslow rafts are made of bright yellow rubber coated nylon, visible for miles. Light weight and compact, the 20M is ideal for small air-

craft. The carrying case, as in all Winslow life rafts, includes hand pump along with attached CO_2 cylinders. The case acts as a sea anchor after raft inflation.
Package 8" x 10" x 23"—inflated 3'4" x 7'4"; buoyancy 500 lbs.

40M—4MAN

The 40M has dual inflation cylinders. Four strap handles provide for easy access and floating safety for additional passengers. There are four nickel "D" rings attached to the compact, soft, carrying case providing convenient bulkhead mounting.
Package 7½" x 11" x 25"—inflated 5' x 8'; buoyancy 1,000 lbs.

80M—8MAN

The eight man raft is designed for the cruising yachtsman who wants the ultimate in safety equipment in an emergency. It provides vital protection against immersion in freezing waters or shark infested seas.
Package 8" x 14" x 30"—inflated 5'2" x 12'6"; buoyancy 2,000 lbs.
Package size 7½" x 13" x 29"—inflated 5'4" x 10'8"; buoyancy 1,500 lbs.
All M and MCR Rafts are Double Bulkhead

120M—12MAN

100M and 120M have two separate buoyancy compartments.
Twelve Man Raft—Here is maxi-

mum security for a large crew in emergency.
Package 11" x 30" x 18½"—inflated 512" x 17'; buoyancy 3,000 lbs.

RADAR REFLECTOR LIFE RAFT

Features

1. Radar reflector canopy
2. Double CO_2 inflation cylinders
3. Ventilation part and fresh water catch
4. Self inflation canopy support tube
5. Interior and exterior life lines

Ten Man Raft—similar to 120M but slightly smaller.
Package 8" x 14" x 30"—inflated 512" x 14'6"; buoyancy 2,500 lbs.

New design for all canopied oblong rafts:
In order to facilitate immediate entry in an emergency, we have opened one entire side of the oblong raft. This will have dual zippered closures that can be operated either from inside or outside. In the closed position, the radar reflective canopy offers full weather protection.

6. Stabilizing pockets.
7. Watertight nylon zippered entrance
8. Dual floatation tubes (Not shown but included)
   Boarding ladder
   Canopy entrance ties
   Hand pump valve
   Hand pump
   Rigid instant release canister
   Tie-down and deck hdw.

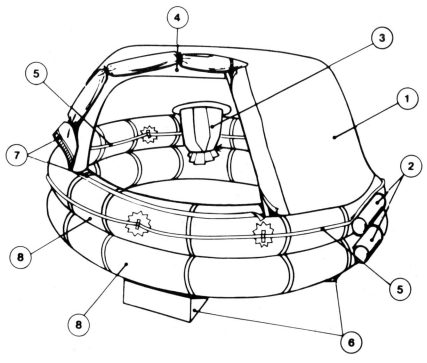

CR-RADAR

The Winslow Radar Reflector Life Raft Model CR-Radar provides the yachtsman with space-age materials developed and tested by NASA under the most rugged weather conditions and proved to provide the best known thermal environment. The self-erecting radar-reflector canopy material, high visibility orange-dyed mylar on rip stop nylon, affords maximum protection against wind, rain and sun, being water proof, rat proof, non-porous and heat reflecting. The canopy will also maintain body warmth in frigid climates. It features underwater stabilizer packets and a fresh water rain catch. Nylon life lines surround the raft and there is a boarding ladder for easy access.

Wolsk Associates, Ltd.
P.O. Box 11741
Lexington, Kentucky 40511

SAFEGUARD SYSTEMS

Safeguard Systems monitors simultaneously the percentage of Halon Extinguishers; provides warning of the build-up of explosive or life threatening vapors; serves as an intruder alarm; warns of bilge flooding and provides back-up to the bilge pump relay and informs the operator of a refrigeration or engine oil pressure failure. All of these functions are performed by a solid-state "brain" housed in a flame retardent ABS case that measures just 8″ wide and 2″ high.

Since the installation of Halon Fire Extinguisher system can reduce the insurance premium on a boat by 10% in many cases, Safeguard Systems quickly pays for itself in lower insurance rates. Many companies offer additional reductions in premiums when the complete Safeguard Systems is employed.

As a battery monitor, Safeguard Systems keeps the operator of the boat informed on the exact percentage of charge on his batteries through a digital display that monitors the battery condition on a regular basis. A separate status button permits the operator to monitor the condition of the batteries at any given instant. As the percentage of charge falls to the point where operation of the boat and its equipment becomes questionable, Safeguard Systems sounds a pulsating alarm alerting the operator to the condition.

As a fire detector, the unit doubles as a monitor of the vessel's Halon fire extinguisher system, warning visually and with a steady audio tone of heat build-up over 135°F or the discharge of the Halon extinguisher through accident or extinguishing failure. With Safeguard

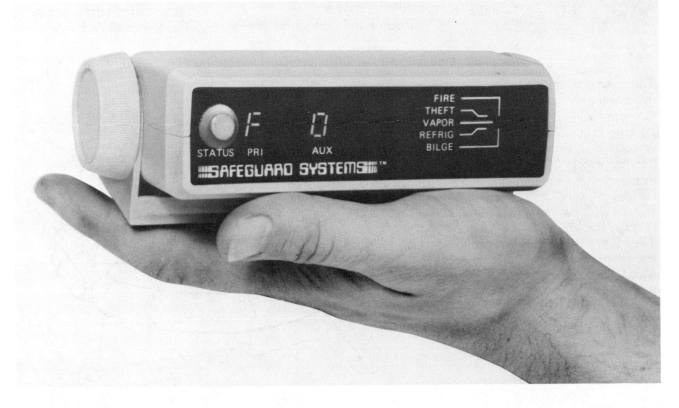

Systems, the operator knows his Halon unit is operational without having to personally inspect the bottle. Safeguard Systems is available with a Halon extinguisher or it may be used with existing bottles.

Safeguard Systems can be used with a variety of switches to warn of intruders. As little as ⅛" of movement in these switches triggers a visual indication and a steady audible alarm in the control head. With the use of an optional hailer relay, the audible alarm is sounded through an external loudspeaker horn. The hailer relay also can be tied to a strobe light system to assist authorities in locating the boat, a sometimes time consuming problem, especially in crowded marinas. The hailer horn and strobe also can be tied into the other Safeguard Systems functions.

Safeguard Systems comes with a sensor for detecting explosive gasoline fumes. The purchaser also may specify sensors for detecting propane fumes or carbon monoxide. Safeguard Systems warns of the fume build-up visually and audibly.

The bilge alarm feature includes a float-type sensor which warns of rising water and also has the capability of providing a back-up to the bilge pump relay in the event that switch is inoperative or fouled with dirt or debris. It can also be wired to cut in a secondary bilge pump by the use of an additional relay (optional).

Finally, Safeguard Systems provides warning of failure of the vessel's refrigeration system, allowing time for the operator to take steps to prevent loss of food or bait. At the owner's option, the refrigeration sensor may be replaced with a sensor to warn of a drop in engine oil pressure in many types of engines.

Safeguard Systems control head comes with a matching universal gimbal mounting bracket that permits the unit to be installed on any flat surface, even overhead. It may also be flush mounted. As protection against accidents or unauthorized disabling of Safeguard Systems, the on/off switch easily can be removed from its position on the rear of the mounting bracket for placement in a remote location.

Sensor hook-up is made easy through a color coded terminal strip. Unused functions can be bypassed. Simple instructions for wiring and by-passing are included. Safeguard Systems can be used with existing compatible sensors, making it unnecessary to dispose of previously purchased devices. Multiple sensors of the same type may be wired in series for extended coverage. The purchaser must specify 12, 24, or 32 volt DC operation.

Safeguard Systems comes standard with the control unit; battery both primary and auxiliary; fire detector/Halon monitor; refrigerator sensor; anti-theft sensor and bilge float switch, plus necessary cables, simple to install color coded terminal strip and gimbal mounting bracket.

6

YACHTS

Alajuela Yacht Corporation
5201 Argosy Drive
Huntington Beach, California
92649

PASSPORTE 48

Designed by Raymond H. Richards

General Description:

The design is that of a first quality, high performance sailing yacht of fiberglass construction and suitable for ocean cruising and racing.

The hull is a blend of classically styled topsides with a modern, hydrodynamically efficient underbody. Its raking stem and patrician sheer and proportions are finished with a modified canoe or cruiser stern. Breadth increases above the waterline and the topsides tumblehome amidships. The deck line is reasonably full into the ends and produces a gentle flaring in the bows.

The underbody is relatively shoal and has good deadrise and easy bilges. The keel has an advanced foil which generates the lift (lateral force) necessary to windward performance while minimizing its aggregate residuary and lift related drag. It is short enough to

be efficient and yet long enough for easy dry-docking (the center of gravity of the vessel is about the one-third length of the shoe). These proportions allow the ballast to be placed very low for greatest effectiveness. Total wetted surface, hull, keel, and appendages, is reduced (re frictional resistance) but not minimized to the detriment of behavioral characteristics. The residuary component of the total resistance spectrum of this combined hull and keel form is remarkably low. That coupled with the moderate to light displacement—length relationship ensures excellent speed potential under sail or power.

Three rigs are offered: cutter, ketch and schooner. Rig proportions are tall, efficient and generous in area, taking advantage of the powerful righting moment spectrum the hull will develop. Forestays are fitted to releasing gear to facilitate tacking large lapping sails. The cutter can, of course, be treated as a sloop.

Spaciousness is evident throughout the vessel. This is particularly so where it counts—on deck. The wing decks are broad and protected by deep bulwarks. The cockpit has two levels. The helmsman is placed a head taller than the sheet handlers and even taller when using the saddle seat on the center line. Right aft and with unobstructed access from side to side, he is given the fullest possible frame of reference for handling the vessel. A variety of winches, cleats, handling gear and instrumentation display options are possible on the unusually large coaming flats along the cockpit.

Among the unique features of this design is the "lido" deck. It is bounded by a coaming topped with a fixed rail. While it provides security to and from the companionway and additional working deck space

it is named for its third function, lounging.

Many of the more pleasant aspects of life onboard will revolve around the saloon. It is huge. Paned cabinets, lockers, drawers, book shelves, sideboards, tufted upholstery and a fine brass lamp swinging below the skylight over the table will make this an outstanding saloon. Of more than their obvious aesthetic value in lending the tradition, spaciousness and a feel of a great cabin, the settees and the quarterberths will be fine sea berths. The settees have an effective length of some 16 feet. With two folding or stake-mounted chairs, the table can be set for ten. The table does not go up and down. There is ample berthing without it. Its fixed center portion incorporates flatware and wine drawers and stowage. The drop leaves are segmented to provide various table areas.

Due attention has also been given to navigational needs. A large chart table along with ample provisions for books, instruments and electronic equipment is a part of the saloon area. It is protected from weather coming down the companionway and yet the navigator has but to step around the ladder to gain the deck.

To port, and just as a sea cook would like it, the galley is also by the ladder. A buffet is worked over the sinks to increase counter space and to screen the mess but not the cook from the saloon. Even though a guard rail is provided, there is ample space to work without being in way of the range. A portable rail extending from the sink counter provides security when rolling in a seaway and a place to lean while on a port tack. The galley features numerous drawers, lockers and cupboards, twin sinks that drain on either tack and a refrigerator/freezer, trash compactor and microwave oven. Finally, the galley has its

own skylight (as do the staterooms and the owner's head).

Characteristic of the detail in this design is the grating covered drain pan at the foot of the ladder. There is also a seat topped boot locker and a large hanging space for wet gear. Adjacent to and forward of this area is a large guest head and shower, drawers, lockers, mirror and pull-out towel racks. To port, forward of the galley is the guest stateroom with upper and lower berths. A portion of the upper can be relocated to the lower, forming a double berth.

The owner's stateroom, to starboard, amidships, has a private head. The berth is a full double which can be divided by a portable sea or "bundling" board to provide single sea berths. Connecting the owner's head and the guest's stateroom is a large bulkheaded shower space. It can be fitted with hinged seats and other features as a sauna for two.

The foc's'le has full headroom in way of the hatch. A variety of options are available for fitting it out. The standard is with lockers and bins for ground tackle, bosun's stores and sails. A hinged pipe berth can be added, or it can have one or two fixed berths and other features as a cabin.

Arranged on a priority of physiological and operational function basis, the accommodations are remarkably effective and spacious. Freedom of access is achieved throughout and with virtually no space lost to single purpose passageways.

The machinery arrangement is equally notable. The propulsion engine is located below the cabin sole, in the tuck of the keel, amidships. This placement has three significant advantages. First, is the virtually ideal accessibility to all the normal maintenance and operational features of the engine. Second is the contribution of its mass (weight) to the transverse stability and to the directional and seakeeping behavioral dynamics of the vessel. Finally, the virtually level shaft line and the propeller location ensure optimum propulsive efficiency. Space is provided forward of the engine for a variety of optional, engine-driven accessories.

Other optional equipment, such as generator, heating and air-conditioning sets can be fitted right aft, in the lazaretto. They will not materially reduce the stability or behavioral characteristics of the vessel because of their relatively light weights. There they will have ample maintenance and operational accessibility and the desirable level of noise attenuation can most effectively be achieved. There will be plenty of space left in the lazaretto for other uses.

Features:

HULL, DECK & DECK HARDWARE

Standard Gel-Coat, white with red & blue boot stripe

Hand-laminated hull

Hand-laminated fiberglass deck with ½" marine plywood core

Alajuela hull to deck connection, fiberglassed and bonded to form a single unit

10,600# of all lead ballast, sealed and bonded to hull with fiberglass mat and roving

Unique vented propane locker with two bottles

Self-bailing cockpit, deck drain and scuppers made possible due to alajuela hull to deck connection

High-density foam, steel reinforced rudder attached with custom heavy-duty manganese bronze gudgeon

Two 150-gallon stainless steel water tanks with inspection plates are mounted under the sole

40-gallon holding tank with mascerators for each head

Custom-designed heavy-duty stainless steel stem fitting with bronze bow rollers

Heavy-duty custom stainless steel chainplates and hardware

All opening bronze ports

Custom painted bowsprit with teak walkway (on staysail schooner only)

Wheel steering with brake, engine controls and provision made for autopilot

6" compass mounted on pedestal

Emergency tiller

Heavy-duty aluminum hatches

Translucent companionway hatch with teak seahood

Seven dorade ventilators with chrome cowls

Contrasting molded-in non-skid deck surfaces

Deluxe custom stainless steel bow and stern pulpits

Double-wall stainless steel stanchions through-bolted through gunnel, with double lifelines and port and starboard opening gates

Six custom alajuela bronze hawse pipes

Three large cockpit locker hatches

Deck prisms

Deck washdown

Bronze thru-hulls and seacocks, double clamped with stainless steel clamps

Bottom hand-sanded and prepared for bottom paint

Bottom paint

Teak: Coamings, caprail, eyebrow, handrails, lido deck, cockpit, great aft cabin skylight, dorade boxes, rub-rail, sea hood, planked forward bow hatch

Exterior bright work varnished

ENGINE AND ELECTRICAL
Perkins 4-236M 85 HP diesel

150-gallon diesel capacity (two tanks) with water separater

Deluxe instrument panel

Four heavy duty 12V batteries

Automatic battery charger

Voltmeter for battery banks

Acoustical insulation for machinery space

Engine room blower

110V outlets with circuit breakers

Sea water strainer

Vented engine compartment

110V shore power cord with dockside power

Grounding system on all thru-hulls, seacocks and all factory installed electronics

Alarm system

Engine automatic fire control system

Counterpoise

3-Blade prop

Manual shaft brake

SPARS AND RIGGING
Aluminum through deck mast with extra heavy-duty boom (polyurethane coated)

Coaxial cable

Heavy-duty PVC conduit in mast for all masthead wiring

Internal halyards

Complete set working sails

Mainsail cover

Anchor and bow lights

Spreader lights

International navigation lights

Strobe or tri-color lights

Stainless steel gooseneck fitting

Standing rigging 1 x 19 stainless steel

Running rigging (blocks, track, traveler, halyards)

Running backstays

Stainless steel turnbuckles and toggles

All sail track with cars and stoppers

Storm trisail track

Spinnaker track

Topping lift

Flag halyards

Sheets

Reefing lines

Standard winch package

PLUMBING
Hot and cold pressure water

Bronze underwater thru-hulls and seacocks

Saltwater pump

Freshwater hand pumps in heads and galley

Water purification system

Manual bilge pump

Electric bilge pump

12-gallon, galvanized, insulated water heater

Warm teak interior with milled corner post, searails and trim

Hand-rubbed, varnished interior joinerwork

Two coats of paint inside all lockers and cabinets

Complete set of 6" zippered cushions. Seat cushions will be buttoned and tufted. (Choice from our standard samples)

Formica covered counter tops and bookshelves

Large private master stateroom with vanity, mirror and hanging locker

6'6" headroom throughout the vessel

Large chart table with drawers, shelves, lift-up top and deluxe chart light

Adjustable pompanette chair at navigation station

Leaded, paned glass doors and hanging brass ship's lantern in great aft cabin

Oilskin locker with drain

½" thick teak and holly sole laid over ¾" thick marine plywood, with lift-out hatches for accessibility

Owner's choice of three foc'sle arrangements

Insulated overhead

Insulation applied to all areas of the hull down to the cabin sole in all living spaces

The stove well will be lined with stainless steel on the outboard and bottom surfaces. Stainless steel will be installed under the deck over the stove

Three exhaust fans—one in each head and one in the galley

Refrigerator/freezer, 110V only.

Specifications:

Length Overall, molded hull	48'4"
Lenth Design Waterline	40'6"
Length Between Perpendiculars	39'3"
Breadth Over Rub Rails	13'10"
Breadth at Design Waterline	12'0"
Draft to Design Waterline	6'9"
Displacement at Design Waterline	29,500#
Ballast, lead	10,600#
Displacement-Length Ratio	220
Prismatic Coefficient, fairbody	0.58
Complement berthing	8 persons
Fuel (diesel) capacity	150 gallons
Potable (fresh) water	300 gallons
Sail Area, with 100% of the foretriangle & roach:	
Cutter	1140 sq. ft.
Ketch	1190 sq. ft.
Schooner, with fisherman topsail	1250 sq. ft.

Mechanical system available as an option

Stainless steel three-burner propane stove

Deep double stainless steel galley sinks

Trash compactor

Microwave oven

Stereo system throughout the vessel

Acoustical bulkheads in stateroom and head spaces

Proper interior hand rails

Generous locker and storage areas

Fresh and saltwater foot pumps in galley

Louvers will be installed on all locker doors as necessary for ventilation

NOTE: Custom interior changes are on a material and labor basis only.

AMF Alcort Sailboats
South Leonard Street
Waterbury, Connecticut 06708

PUFFER

Built-in safety features include full foam flotation to keep the boat from sinking if capsized. (If it does capsize, it can be self rescued by one person in seconds.) Puffer also comes fully equipped at a remarkably low price. Mainsail and jib, vang, anodized aluminum mast and boom, oar locks, outboard motor mount are standard. So are the brightly varnished mahogany board and rudder, the stainless steel rigging and the gleaming-smooth fiberglass hull with accent stripe.

Specifications:

LENGTH
12 ft., 6 in.

BEAM
4 ft., 10 in.

SAIL AREA (MAIN)
55 sq. ft.

SAIL AREA (JIB)
35 sq. ft.

HULL WEIGHT
160 lbs.

CREW CAPACITY
450 lbs. (1–3)

FORCE 5

A powerful single-handed racing machine with a cockpit big enough for two. High-styled in hand-laid fiberglass and rich mahogany. The deck and hull feature rigid, yet light-weight hand-crafted fiberglass construction. (Weighs only 145 lbs.) Stores easily in a garage and cartops anywhere. Standard equipment includes North sail, Harken blocks with Harken hex-aratchet, 8 part vang, dual outhaul and cunningham and full-width, mid-cockpit roller bearing traveller.

Specifications:

LENGTH
3 ft., 10½ in.

BEAM
4 ft., 10 in.

SAIL AREA
91 sq. ft.

HULL WEIGHT
145 lbs.

CREW CAPACITY
500 lbs. (1–3)

TRAC 14

Trac 14 is an all-new speedster that delivers all the excitement of a true performance cat in an easy-to-handle fourteen-foot package. Trac 14 packs all the punch of the leading sixteen. It gives you a list of standard extras the others haven't even thought of yet. And none of the hassles that have kept you away from catamarans before. Single-handed, its lightning responses will start the sprayflying. For two, it delivers a double dose of hull-flying sailing fun and excitement. But getting ready to set a record on the water shouldn't take you all day.

With Trac 14 you're fully rigged and ready to get underway in twenty minutes or less. Shrouds attach with trouble-free snaphooks, while an efficient Harken roller furling system on the job takes the tangle out of setting sail.

Trac 14 features a sophisticated sailplan and fully adjustable rig for complete precise control. The main is fully battened with a window. The jib lets you tack easier and faster, and gets the crew into the fun too. The main halyard locks at the top of the mast to guarantee proper shape of the main in any wind.

At the heart of the four-part mainsheet system is the famous Harken hexaratchet with all roller bearing blocks. And "tweaker" lines let you adjust mast rake instantly—even while under way.

There are lots of extra touches to make Trac 14 a pleasure to sail.

Instead of bouncing around on a hard metal crossbeam for instance, you sit comfortably out on the smooth, fiberglass hull. Built-in storage compartments keep refreshments and accessories dry and handy, yet out of the way. Should you go over, righting takes a minimum of time and muscle.

Trac 14 moves through the water with an exhilarating, confident swiftness. Because of the fullness of the flotation, the bows don't have that tendency to submarine. So there's less bucking and pitch poling.

When you're ready to head for home, this cat just curls up on the top of your car. The twin hulls fold under and reduce the width of the boat from just over seven feet to just over six. And the hull and crossbeam weight has been engineered down to a manageable 150 pounds.

Specifications:

LOA
4 ft., 1 in.

BEAM, TOTAL
7 ft., 6 in.

BEAM, CAR TOP
6 ft., 3 in.

MAST HEIGHT
22 ft., 8 in.

SAIL AREA (MAIN)
119 sq. ft.

SAIL AREA (JIB)
29 sq. ft.

WEIGHT, FULLY RIGGED
195 lbs.

WEIGHT, CAR-TOP
150 lbs.

APOLLO

Designed by Bruce Kirby
The Apollo has sails by Hans Fogh, with main and jib windows, cunningham, leech lines and telltales. "Wrap-around" seats for daysailing comfort. Kick up centerboard and rudder for easy beaching. Roller furling job. Harken "Magic Box" for jib tensioning. Internal wire halyards for reduced windage and easy mast stepping. And spars that are color coordinated with the hull and coated to help prevent corrosion. A storage compartment keeps accessories or refreshments handy.

Specifications:

LENGTH
15 ft., 9 in.

BEAM
5 ft., 11 in.

SAIL AREA (MAINSAIL)
90 sq. ft.

SAIL AREA (JIB)
39 sq. ft.

HULL WEIGHT
300 lbs.

CREW CAPACITY
(2–4)

SUNBIRD

The Sunbird features a low profile, fully encased and weighted centerboard, hinged, rudder, outboard motor mount, and a paddle that doubles as the boom crutch for one-person rigging. Forward there's a seven foot long dry cuddy with vinyl hatch. The cockpit is self-bailing—which means it empties itself of any water that gets in even when the boat is standing still. There is also a generous amount of foam block flotation, and the very best in marine hardware. All based on hand laid up fiberglass construction for years of dependability and low maintenance.

Sunbird trailers with no trouble and rigs in minutes. The mainsail and jib are standard equipment.

Specifications:

LENGTH
15 ft., 11 in.

BEAM
5 ft., 9 in.

SAIL AREA (MAINSAIL)
92 sq. ft.

SAIL AREA (JIB)
42 sq. ft.

HULL WEIGHT
575 lbs.

CREW CAPACITY
900 lbs. (1–6)

AMF ALCORT 2100

Designed by Ted Hood
In the design of 2100, the whole sailing experience is taken into account. Take ease of handling, for instance. The ⅞ rig of the 2100 requires less muscle and a smaller inventory of needed sails for cruising and racing. You'll notice an unusually generous amount of usable deck space. The high freeboard makes for dry comfortable sailing even in windy conditions. The cockpit is roomy and comfortable, with seating for six adults and high seat backs for long-range comfort. Other features include a bridge deck to stop water on its way below. A gas tank storage locker that keeps fumes out of the cabin. And split backstay to give the helmsman all the elbow room he needs.

The 2100 is easy to handle and remarkably responsive. All lines needed to control the boat lead back to a console at the companionway where the winches are situated. Jib sheets can be led to either the windward or leeward winch for ease of sail trim. And the other controls—all of them standard—include vang, cunningham and internal halyards. All with stoppers for fast, precise and simple control.

The 2100 sleeps four in surprising comfort and room—a far cry from the usual day sailing accommodations. You'll like the four full-

Specifications:

LOA
219"

LWL
177"

BEAM
8'

DRAFT-UP
17"

DRAFT-DOWN
4'

BALLAST
850 lbs. Lead internal

DISPLACEMENT
2200 lbs.

SAIL AREA
209.25 sq. ft.

Bangor Punta Marine
P.O. Box 991
Fall River, Massachusetts 02722

O'DAY JAVELIN

The Javelin is living proof that "performance" and "family recreation" are qualities that can exist very nicely in the same sailboat. And there's no reason to settle for any less, especially if cost is a significant consideration.

At 14' overall, the Javelin is the smallest daysailer that a whole family can enjoy together in true safety and comfort. The cockpit is over 9' by 5'—huge by any boat's standards—and is high, deep and well protected. The hull is beamy and solidly built.

While the capability of speed is present in every Javelin, newer sailors don't have to be concerned about starting out with too much boat.

Javelin's tall mast can be rigged by one person. Its rig is straightforward and simply trimmed.

size berths, separate head compartments and well-thought-out galley space. Full sitting headroom and ports at eye level provide a feeling of spaciousness and a standard cowl vent keeps things airy and cool.

You'll find a gleaming smooth hull from molds that are hand buffed to assure a flawless finish. Waterline colors are molded in to stay bright.

Barient winches, Harken fittings, Schaefer blocks, Kenyon spars—your 2100 comes equipped with quality hardware that works better and withstands punishment longer. Sails crafted in the one-design loft of Hood Sails of Marblehead, Massachusetts are available. And the bow pulpit, navigational lights, lifelines, and a spring loaded outboard mounting bracket are all standard.

A lockable storage compartment under the deck keeps things safe and dry. An icebox built into the port cockpit seat keeps things cool and wet.

The Javelin is automatically self-bailing. If knocked down, it is also self-rescuing.

Specifications:

OVERALL LENGTH
14'

WATERLINE LENGTH
13'2"

BEAM
5'8"

DRAFT MINIMUM
6"

DRAFT MAXIMUM
3'10"

SAIL AREA
125 sq. ft.

MAX. RECOM. H.P.
8

MAST LENGTH
23'1"

DECK AND EXTERIOR HARDWARE
5" high bulwark w/teak cap and aluminum rubrail

Cast aluminum midship mooring chocks w/cleats for spring lines

4 mooring cleats fore and aft

5 non-corrosive opening ports w/ Lexon glazing and screens

Large fixed ports in galley and navigation area

Custom welded stainless steel bow and stern pulpits w/gates

27" high stainless steel lifelines stanchions w/vinyl coated double lifelines

Stanchion thru-bolted to bulwark for strength and to keep deck clear

Lifeline gates, port and starboard

Custom stainless steel stemhead fitting

Flush anchor and windlass locker w/overboard drain built into foredeck w/RFP lid

Bow skene chocks

Companionway hatch w/inlay and fiberglass cover

Foredeck and amidship hatches of cast aluminum w/transparent Lexon Teak deck handrails

23" wide weather decks

Deck and cabin top reinforced for addition of hardware

Space for 8' dinghy aft of mast

Lazarette stowage locker w/ overboard drain and teak hatch

COCKPIT

350 degree visibility while seated in cockpit

Comfort-designed cockpit seats and coaming

L-shaped cockpit footwell designed for level-footed steering and winching

Extra large self-draining cockpit scuppers

O'DAY 15

The O'Day 15 does two things very well, and simultaneously: 1) handles easily—no urgent surprises for the beginner, and 2) it planes easily—which means it gets up and skims on the water, not through it.

And on the days when the whole family won't be denied, the O'Day 15's huge 10-foot cockpit can accommodate the whole bunch and their lunch (a cooler neatly wedges into the aft cockpit area).

Seats, backrests, and coamings are contoured for comfort. The cockpit is self-bailing when moored. The rudder kicks up on contact and the hull is built to beach without bruises. In the event of a capsize, the 15 is self-rescuing.

Specifications:

OVERALL LENGTH
14'7½"

WATERLINE LENGTH
13'0"

BEAM
5'11"

DRAFT MINIMUM
5"

DRAFT MAXIMUM
3'3"

MAIN SAIL AREA
73.4 sq. ft.

JIB AREA
35'4"

RECOMMENDED MAXIMUM HP
4

MAST LENGTH
21'8"

MAST HEIGHT
22'9"

MAST WEIGHT
23 lbs.

BOOM LENGTH
8'7"

BOOM WEIGHT
10 lbs.

DAGGERBOARD MATERIAL
FG & PVC Foam

DAGGERBOARD WEIGHT (APPROX.)
0: 15 lbs.

RUDDER TYPE
Kickup

RUDDER MATERIAL
Aluminum, FG & PVC Foam

SEATING
4

SAILING DISPLACEMENT
650 lbs.

MINIMUM TRAILERING WEIGHT
380 lbs.

COMPLETE HULL WEIGHT ONLY
295 lbs.

SAFETY FEATURES
SR/SB

O'DAY 19

Designed by John Deknatel
The O'Day 19 combines the economy and ease of operation of a daysailer with spartan but complete accommodations for two.

The O'Day 19 was designed by John Deknatel and his group at C. Raymond Hunt Associates who have very rigid standards about sailing performance. So the 19 is much more than a daysailer with a box over the deck to create an interior. It's a lively centerboard trailerable, specifically conceived for mini-vacationing.

The cockpit is long enough to slouch with legs stretched along the seat. One seat opens to reveal a wet locker. The other opens to accept an outboard motor fuel tank.

The interior is compact, but in fact large enough for two people. A sink, cooler and head can be organized amid ships. The seats continue forward to become quite a comfortable double V-berth.

The O'Day 19 is only 19 feet of maintenance, storage and expense, but miles and years of sailing fun.

Specifications:

OVERALL LENGTH
19'0"

WATERLINE LENGTH
16'8"

BEAM
7'9"

DRAFT MINIMUM
1'0"

DRAFT MAXIMUM
4'4"

SAIL AREA
179 sq. ft.

MAX. RECOM. H.P.
8

MAST LENGTH
26'4"

MAST HEIGHT
29'4"

MAST WEIGHT
45 lbs.

BOOM LENGTH
8'5"

BOOM WEIGHT
10 lbs.

C/B MATERIAL
FG

C/B WEIGHT (APPROX.)
52 lbs.

BALLAST
300 lbs.

RUDDER TYPE
Kickup

RUDDER MATERIAL
FG/AL

SEATING
6

SAILING DISPLACEMENT
2,040 lbs.

DAY SAILER

The Day Sailer is easy to handle—one of those rare boats that does everything well naturally, without the insistence of an expert helmsman. The hull is stable and sure-footed. The helm is responsive and gentle. Its great potential for speed comes from its powerful rig—145 square feet of working sail area.

Under the press of sail on a fair day breeze, the Day Sailer will fly, rooster tails spewing from its rudder. And, yes, this is the same family boat even your kids can handle.

The best safety features of the Day Sailer are its stability, balance and predictability. Permanent foam flotation is built in place, giving the Day Sailer hull positive buoyancy, even if punctured. Should the boat be knocked down, it is self-rescuing by its normal crew, and the cockpit is self-bailing.

There are 89 organized Day Sailer fleets nationwide.

Specifications:

OVERALL LENGTH
16'9"

WATERLINE LENGTH
16'

BEAM
6'3"

DRAFT MINIMUM
7"

DRAFT MAXIMUM
3'9"

SAIL AREA
145 sq. ft.

MAX. RECOM. H.P.
8

MAST LENGTH
24'3"

MAST HEIGHT
24'11"

MAST WEIGHT
27 lbs.

BOOM LENGTH
10'4"

BOOM WEIGHT
10 lbs.

C/B MATERIAL
FG

C/B WEIGHT (APPROX.)
28 lbs.

RUDDER TYPE
Kickup

RUDDER MATERIAL
FG

SEATING
6

SAILING DISPLACEMENT
1.268 lbs.

MINIMUM TRAILERING WEIGHT
628 lbs.

COMPLETE HULL WEIGHT ONLY
575 lbs.

O'DAY 28

Standard Equipment:

HULL AND DECK
Internal lead ballast bonded in place.

Centerboard model: weighted, foam filled fiberglass centerboard; centerboard trunk molded with hull; centerboard hanger system designed so pivot pin does not penetrate hull; centerboard pennant leads to cockpit.

Welded stainless steel stemhead fitting.

4 Fixed ports and 4 opening ports with screens.

2 Barient #18 2-speed chrome genoa winches with cleats.

Mainsheet traveler with mechanical stops.

Laminated wood tiller.

1 Wet storage locker in cockpit.

1 Cockpit seat hatch; lockable.

Stainless steel chainplates.

Genoa sheet turning blocks.

SPARS AND RIGGING
2 Barient #10 halyard winches with cleats.

Mainsail with single reef point.

Working jib.

Split backstay.

V-berth with removable insert, measures 6'3" x 5'3".

4" Fabric covered foam cushions.

Seat backs swing up to increase sleeping space. Each is 6'3" long.

Overhead teak grab rails.

Keel Model—Bulkhead mounted fold-up double leaf table—storage behind table. Centerboard Model—Centerline, floor mounted drop leaf table.

Locker/bureau—converts to convenient chart table with hinged extension.

Curtains on fixed ports.

Headroom—6'.

2 Burner recessed gimballed stove.

Insulated icebox.

Stainless steel sink with manual faucet.

Stainless steel companionway ladder with teak treads; teak companionway grab rails.

OMC Saildrive with 35 amp alternator.

18 gallon aluminum fuel tank with electric fuel gauge.

95 amp/hour battery in plastic box.

Complete electric panel with circuit breakers, battery condition indicator and power-on light.

Battery disconnect/selector switch.

25 gallon deck filled seamless plastic water tank under starboard settee.

International running lights.

Specifications:

LOA
28'3"

LWL
22'11"

BEAM
10'3"

DRAFT
4'6" keel

3'3" c/b (up)
6'10" c/b (down)

DISPLACEMENT
7,300 lbs.

BALLAST
2,350 lbs.—keel
2,725 lbs.—c/b

O'DAY 37

Standard Equipment:

Internal lead ballast bonded into hull cavity. Ballast weight—6000 lbs.

Hull to deck joint is bolted and glassed, then covered with a two-piece gunwale guard.

Welded stainless steel stemhead fitting with integral anchor roller.

Stainless steel double rail bow and stern pulpits, stainless steel stanchions thru-bolted with back-up plates; single lifelines with gate on starboard side.

Genoa sheet turning blocks.

Translucent aluminum framed hatch over main cabin.

Companionway hatch seahood.

Sliding companionway hatch with hinged bifold teak cabin door—removable.

Two #25 chrome Barient genoa winches with cleats.

One chrome Barient #18 mainsheet winch with cleat.

14 Operating ports with screens.

Pedestal wheel steering with 28" stainless steel destroyer wheel, brake and engine controls on pedestal; emergency tiller provided.

Two lockable seta hatches.

#10 Barient main halyard winch with cleat.

#18 Barient genoa halyard winch with cleat.

Foredeck light on mast.

Mainsail with two sets of reef points.

Working jib.

Double V-berth with removable insert; 4" fabric covered foam cushions. Berth is 6'4" long by 6'2" wide at head.

Teak bifold door separates forward cabin from head and main cabin.

Headroom—6'1".

Vanity with stainless steel sink, mirror, pressure hot and cold water, shower with curtain, towel rings, glass holder and toilet tissue holder.

Marine head discharges into 15 gallon seamless holding tank with dock side discharge.

Large hanging locker with teak louvered door.

Headroom—6'1".

Settees with 5" fabric covered cushions. Settees 6'4" long.

Seatbacks, hinged for access to storage behind.

Centerline dropleaf table with two storage bins.

Overhead teak grab rails.

Headroom—6'4".

2-burner countertop gumballed stove.

Dry storage bin.

Double-stainless steel sinks.

Pressure hot and cold water.

Large insulated icebox with sliding tray and hinged cover.

Navigation area.

Large double berth.

Hanging locker with louvered teak door and shelves.

Three drawers.

6' headroom.

Teak companionway grab rails.

Universal 32HP, 4-cylinder fresh water cooled diesel engine; 2:1 reduction gear, 1¼" bronze shaft; 2 blade propeller.

40 gallon aluminum fuel tank.

150 gallons of fresh water in two tanks, with selector valve and self priming pressure pump.

Two 95 amp batteries in plastic battery boxes.

Complete electrical panel with battery switch, branch line.

12 volt system circuit breakers and 110 volt circum. breakers; battery condition indicator; power-on light.

50' power cord for 110V dockside power.

12 interior cabin lights and one engine room light.

International running lights mounted on pulpits.

6 gallon hot water heater operates off 110V system and engine heat exchanger.

Specifications:

LOA
37'0"

LWL
30'4"

BEAM
11'2"

DRAFT
5'0"

DISPLACEMENT
14,000 lbs.

BALLAST
6,000 lbs.

CAL 39

Designed by William Lapworth Bill Lapworth has never designed anything but all-around good boats. The one time he tried his hand at a downwind flyer for the Transpac, it ended up showing an East Coast fleet the way to Bermuda! Even the Cal 40, perhaps the all-time most successful war horse that every took to the seas, was designed with double quarter berths, because that's where the first owner liked to sleep when cruising.

The Cal 39 is expensive, and looks it. It's a powerful sailing platform, and looks every bit that as well. And in a world where money sometimes buys only disappointment, it's both a satisfying dream and sound personal investment.

Aesthetically, the Cal 39 is to early Cals what the White House was to Lincoln's log cabin. The hull lines that define the looks have become crisper, and flow together more evenly. The rake of the bow is more decisive. The coach house is lower, making the boat's attitude more linear and aggressive. In the past few years, Cal's accommodations have taken elaborate leaps in complexity in order to meet the taste of the men who meet in board rooms. But the part of the Cal 39 that's immersed in water has forgotten nothing about how all the Cals that preceded it won races.

Bill Lapworth has spent half a lifetime polishing his design philosophy: give the hull a longish waterline, keep the weight moderate (especially in the ends), plant it in the water with a high-efficiency fin keel, and locate a balanced rudder far aft for decisive control. The boat that results has the volume to accept a well-developed accommodation and the sail carrying power to move the hull through the water in a hurry. On a distance race where crew comfort plays an important part of winning, a Cal 39 can be a formidable weapon.

Even the casual observers will conclude that the builder first created the interior and then considered the cost. While no feature is forced just to say it's there, no feature is left out just to meet a price.

Teak prevails: no other material could impart the same ambience. Good sense prevails as well. The galley permits the cook to work out of range of a rogue pot from the stove. Centerline sinks are convenient for cleanup, and vital in a bailing emergency. A serious nav area befits a yacht designed for serious passage-making.

The family that would own a Cal 39 would both live aboard for extended periods and occasionally entertain as they would in their home. Abundant lockers and drawers store clothes for ship and shore, and the salon welcomes a small crowd without crowding. Sleep—rarely a problem aboard ship—is made a luxury by an array of deep, wide and comfortable single and double berths.

If you were to point a Cal 39 westward and thread it through the world's most fascinating ports, you would, of course, learn a great deal about the boat.

But you'd still be a few man years short of the thinking we've already put into it. In a sense, the 39 summarizes everything Bill Lapworth knows about hulls, decks and rigs, and everything Cal has learned about construction—some 22 years of perceptive application in both instances. A few of the ideas are recent revelations (Lapworth's realization that thinner keels tend to heel a boat less). Many others are ancient history (Cal's conclusion that nothing produces a stronger, lighter hull laminate than resin hand squeezed into cloth, and the excess hand squeezed out).

Specifications:

LOA
39'0"

LWL
32'1"

BEAM
12'0"

DRAFT
6'8" or 5'6"

DISPLACEMENT
17,000 lbs.

BALLAST
7,000 lbs.

STANDARD EQUIPMENT

HULL AND DECK

Internal lead ballast bonded in place.

Flat area on centerline forward for mounting instrument transducers.

Cast aluminum stemhead fitting with double anchor rollers.

Custom extruded anodized aluminum toe rail.

Double lifelines with a boarding gate to starboard. Stern pulpit has integral, fold-down swim ladder.

24" x 24" aluminum framed translucent hatch mounted on foredeck.

20" x 20" aluminum framed translucent hatch mounted over main cabin.

Sea hood for companionway hatch, with integral traveler mount and dorade boxes.

Teak hand rails on cabin top.

Teak eyebrow on cabin house.

2–12' x 1¼" Aluminum sheet tracks mounted inboard on the deck; sheet blocks on each track.

Lockable seat hatch opens to a molded storage bin.

Lazarette hatch aft opens to a molded bin.

Starboard seat hatch.

2 #28 Barient chrome genoa sheet winches with cleats.

Pedestal steering with 32" wheel; pedestal guard, brake and controls mounted on pedestal; emergency tiller provided.

Engine instruments mounted in cockpit include: tachometer, oil pressure, water temperature and amp meter.

Mainsheet traveler mounted on cabin top; controls lead to cockpit.

1 #18 Barient chrome mainsheet winch.

SPARS AND RIGGING

Single spreaders, double lower shrouds, masthead sloop rig.

1 #38 Barient chrome main halyard winch.

1 #22 Barient chrome genoa halyard winch.

2:1 Boom topping lift with adjustment on boom.

4:1 Internal outhaul.

5:1 Mainsheet purchase: 1 #18 Barient chrome mainsheet winch with cleat, mounted on cabin top to port of companionway.

INTERIOR

Removable vinyl headliner in main cabin, galley and aft stateroom.

Varnished teak and holly cabin sole, except in head area.

4" fabric covered foam cushions.

Cedar lined hanging locker with shelf over, and louvered teak door.

6'2" headroom; berth measures 6'6" long and 6'8" wide at head.

Marine head discharges to holding tank with deck discharge.

Vanity with stainless steel sink, pressure hot and cold water, shower, storage under; medicine cabinet/linen locker over; mirrored plexiglass doors.

Teak framed oval mirror on bulkhead.

Teak louvered door.

6'2" Headroom.

Settees with 5" fabric covered foam cushions. Padded seat backs swing up to increase bunk space. Berths measure 6'4" x 3'6".

Alcoves and lockers with louvered doors.

Centerline drop-leaf table finished in teak and white laminate; fiddles on leaves; bin on table top; table hangs on mast and stainless steel clutch post.

Leaded glass liquor locker and bureau forward of starboard settee.

Chart table aft of port settee with hinged top opening to chart storage; shelves for electronics, etc., storage cabinets under; gooseneck navigation lamp with red bulb.

Lights on forward bulkheads, chart table bulkheads and over table.

6'3" Headroom.

Vinyl boot covers mast.

8.0 cubic foot ice box with tray; polyurethane foamed-on insulation.

Double stainless steel sinks with pressure hot and cold water.

3-Burner alcohol stove with oven.

Dorade ventilator over galley.

Teak companionway ladder mounted on removable panel for engine access.

AFT CABIN

Hanging locker with louvered teak door; vanity with sink, pressure hot and cold water, and storage.

Double berth with 5" fabric covered foam mattress. Berth measures 6'5" x 4'2".

Drawer and large storage bins under berth.

Dorade ventilator over forward end of cabin.

6'3" Headroom.

MECHANICAL: ELECTRICAL AND PLUMBING

Pathfinder 40HP 4-cylinder fresh water cooled diesel engine with 1¼" bronze shaft and 2-blade propeller.

45 Gallon aluminum fuel tank.

2-105 amp/hour marine batteries in plastic boxes.

Master electrical control panel. 12 Volt system includes: battery selector/disconnect switch, circuit breakers and battery condition volt meter, 110V system includes: master circuit breaker, branch line circuit breakers and reverse polarity indicator and 50 power cord.

International running lights mounted on pulpits.

Lightning ground.

130 Gallons of fresh water in 2 stainless steel tanks with deck fills; level gauges for each tank.

6 Gallon hot water heater operates off 110V AC system and heat exchanger.

Electric, self-priming water pressure pump, with water tank selector valve.

Gusher 10 manual bilge pump, accessible with all hatches closed.

Electric bilge pump.

Specifications:

LOA
39'0"

LWL
32'1"

BEAM
12'0"

DRAFT
6'8" or 5'6"

DISPLACEMENT
17,000 lbs.

BALLAST
7,000 lbs.

Boston Whaler
1149 Hingham Street
Rockland, Massachusetts 02370

HARPOON 6.2

Designed by C & C Yachts

The Harpoon 6.2 takes full advantage of its 8-foot beam by offering the largest working cockpit in the industry, comfortably seating six adults. With a transom traveler, end boom sheeting and a boom height that gives plenty of head room, the cockpit is a place to relax. Rich mahogany seats and trim further enhance the character of the cockpit. Cockpit storage also includes room for battery, fuel tank and a versatile sole compartment which can hold winch handles, dock lines, cribboards or serve as a cooler.

The hull of the 6.2 Harpoon incorporates the Boston Whaler foam-sandwich construction. Two fiberglass hulls are filled under pressure with a dense, unicellular polyurethane foam that chemically bonds with the inner and outer hulls, which then form a uniquely strong and durable structural unit. The foam also provides an incredible amount of positive buoyancy which easily offsets the 550-lb. keel, resulting in a unique boat— an *unsinkable* fixed-keel boat!

Complementing the Harpoon 6.2 as standard equipment are such quality items as Lewmar winches, Harken blocks, Kenyon spars and Schaefer hardware. Selected options include North sails, roller-reefing, Genoa, life lines and bow pulpit.

In the cabin, two 6'3" berths are standard with insulated storage underneath. Optional overnight amenities include a stove, sink, Porta-Potti, 25-Qt. cooler and a boom tent which increases sleeping accommodations to four adults.

Specifications:

LOA
6.2 m (20')

BEAM
8'

DRAFT
3'6"

LWL
15'10"

BALLAST
550 lbs.

SAIL AREA
210 sq. ft.

Bounty Enterprises, Inc.
15661 Producer Lane/Unit 1
Huntington Beach, California
92649

NORTH ATLANTIC 29

Designed by Angus Primrose and
Col. Blondie Hasler

Three western sailors, Angus Primrose, Col. Blondie Hasler and Jock McLeod have long seen the distinct advantages of the Chinese lug rig as being far superior to the conventional rig for short-handed sailing and cruising. The Jock McLeod version of the Chinese lug rig, combined with the expertise in design of the North Atlantic 29 by Primrose and Hasler offers the best possible hull shape and best possible rig for this purpose.

Designed for the single-handed sailor, it is an ideal cruising rig that can be handled easily by one person without requiring strength or endurance, and without going on deck, so that sailing can be relaxed, safe and enjoyable; single handed or not. It is a rig that is easily reefed, efficient for self-steering and can do anything that modern rigs can do—with much less strain on the crew. Foremost, it is a cruising rig for a seamanlike passage; safe, quick, comfortable, with the easiest ability to handle any emergency likely to be encountered.

At first sight this rig appears to be an archaic and complex lashup of ropes and spars, but in effect it is basically extraordinarily simple, clever and by far the easiest to handle. The lug mainsail has full-length battens which lie across the width of the sail, from luff to leach, and divide the sail into panels.

The top batten is the yard, which is a heavier spar than other battens, as it takes the full weight

of the sail. The bottom batten is the boom, and takes very little loading so it does not have to be much stronger than the other battens. The head of the sail is secured to the yard, and the sail is raised by hauling on the halyard, which includes a purchase system between the yard and masthead. The sail is held to the mast by rope parrels that run loosely around the mast at each batten. The luff of the sail always lies on the same side of the mast and extends forward of the mast, making it a balanced lug sail. On one tack the sail lies against the mast and is held off the mast by the battens. On the other tack, the sail hangs away from the mast and is held by the parrels. A multiple topping lift system (lazy jacks) passes under the boom and lies on both sides of the sail forming a cradle, which holds the sail when it is reefed or furled.

A single sheet system controls the after end of the boom and the five lower battens by a system of spans and blocks. This gives control over the whole leach of the sail, not just the boom, and reduces the twist of the sail. The main part of the sheet system is one long length of line that runs through the blocks and forms a purchase so that the loading on the tail is light. Since the loading is light, smaller size line can be used throughout. The combination of battens, parrels, and topping lifts makes the lug sail the fastest and easiest of all to handle and reef.

To reef the lug sail, the halyard is eased and the sail comes down under its own weight between the lazy jacks, which collect the sail and hold it on top of the boom. The battens prevent the sail from billowing out, and their own weight, plus the sheet span system keeps them down. This makes it unnecessary to tie any reef points or to handle the sailcloth in any

way. As soon as the halyard is eased and the sail starts to lower, the sheets get progressively slacker, automatically, and the sail starts to spill the wind and will eventually weathercock. Unlike other sails, the lug sail will not flog and so will not damage itself. One of the main advantages of the lug rig is the simplicity and speed of reefing. It takes less than a minute to deep reef and it is possible to reef and unreef the sail several times an hour, in variable winds, without feeling overworked. In an emergency, the halyard can be let fly and the whole sail will automatically furl itself in less than ten seconds. And, it will be totally under control with no flogging canvas smothering the deck. With this rig, there is no sail changing to be done. This eliminates the hazardous and exhausting work of changing headsails in bad weather.

The lug rig mast is stepped through the deck to the keel and is designed to stand unsupported. The loadings are taken at the partners where they pass through the deck and at the heel of the mast where they are stepped on the keel. The hull and deck are reinforced in these areas. However, the loadings on the hull are less than those imposed by conventional rigs, with the taut shrouds and high tension in the forestay and backstay, which combine to produce tremendous compression on the mast and stresses on the hull.

The North Atlantic 29 will tack through approximately 90° to windward. A conventional rig will tack through less than this, but the lug rig does not force the boat down to leeward so much. The flat sail, the optimum sheeting angle, which is further outboard than on a conventional rig, develop their maximum drive with less leeward component. This means that the North Atlantic 29 will maintain a

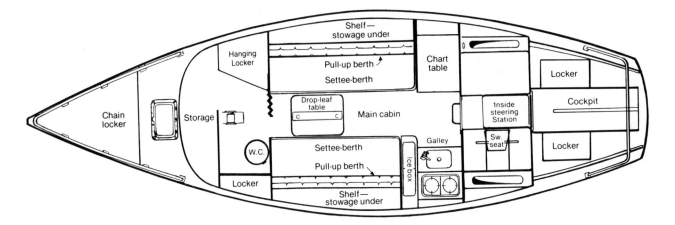

STANDARD INTERIOR LAYOUT FOR THE NORTH ATLANTIC 29

The standard interior layout may be modified to suit your individual needs, as long as the structural bulkheads are not changed. Cost estimates for such changes will be quoted when design is finalized.

windward track with less leeway than a conventional yacht, over the long haul, and will go to windward efficiently.

One of the most unique features is the inside steering station. It removes the helmsman from the elements, hot sun or foul weather. The port or starboard adjustable swing seat enable him to remain level in rough seas, or when the yacht is heeling. These two innovations reduce the "fatigue factor"; long the enemy of ocean sailors. The acrylon pram hoods, that swivel 360°, are directly over the swing seats and afford good visibility and protection. With the aft-led halyard, sheet and reefing downhauls, the yacht can be completely controlled from the inside, or the cockpit. Both the sheet and halyard are led through the deck to the station, and the slack is taken up on aluminum storage reels. In extreme conditions, the prams can be quickly removed and dog-down hurricane hatches secured. There are port and starboard opening ports, teak main hatch lid and cribboards.

Tastefully and completely finished with just the right touch of luxury, the main cabin is wide, deep and roomy. The interior is color-coordinated with painted bulkheads trimmed with varnished mahogany, formica countertops, mildew and water resistant deluxe fabrics and high-grade carpet. A soft vinyl headliner adds insulation. There are ten dog-down opening ports. Designed basically for two, she can sleep four using the swing-up pilot berths. A double-drop leaf dining table with center section serves both port and starboard settees.

The galley is compact and easy to use. There is a two-burner, kerosene, gimballed stove, stainless steel sink, a self-bailing ice box and/or dry storage area, and storage shelves.

The navigator's station has a hinged chart table with instrument storage bin underneath. The table is level and formica-covered for multiple purpose usage. Outboard is a book shelf.

The head is located between the main cabin and forepeak and is closed off from the main cabin with a folding curtain. The marine head has the Microphor sewage treatment system (or equivalent). There is space for an optional stainless steel sink and drop-door cabinet storage, or an optional hanging locker and optional cabin heater.

The forepeak is a huge storage locker and contains the Microphor sewage treatment unit. Forward, the chain locker is partitioned to accept ground tackle.

The North Atlantic 29 is not a production-line yacht. She is built as a semi-custom, one at a time, under the critical eye of Bounty's Bill Noller. The care and precision of her construction reflect her intended purpose. She is hand-laid-up fiberglass using cloth, mat and roving. She is ½″ thick at the keel and tapers up to ⅛″ thick at her topsides. The hull is reinforced with transverse frames on 24″ centers, which are bonded in. The deck is hand-laid-up fiberglass and is reinforced with a ¼″ balsa core sandwich. The boot stripe and non-skid areas are molded in. The 4200 lbs. of lead ballast is internally bonded. The rudder is fiberglass and attached with heavy bronze shoe, gudgeons and pintle. The tiller head is bronze. There are 10 Goiot heavy-duty, tinted, aluminum-framed forward hatch. The cribboards, handrails and retainer rails are solid teak. All thru-hulls are bronze sea cocks. The bow and stern pulpits are stainless steel and thru-bolted to the deck. The bottom is finished with anti-fouling paint. Every component that goes into the North Atlantic 29 is carefully selected to make sure it performs to the builder's specifications, thereby insuring the integrity of the entire yacht.

The yacht is equipped with a 429 sq. ft. lug main and an optional 220 sq. ft. ghoster. In light air (under 10 knots) the optional ghoster provides additional sail power. It has its own wire luff and sheets to port and starboard winches.

The North Atlantic 29 has a hollow spruce mast that is unstayed. There is no need for chain plates, spreders, shroudes, or other failure-prone rigging accessories. It is a cantilevered beam of constant strength tapering from 10½″ at the partners to 4¼″ at the masthead. The mast is stepped through the deck and onto the keel.

Standard Equipment:

Fiberglass hull, hand-laminated w/transverse frames on 24″ centers.

Fiberglass deck reinforced with ¾″ balsa core.

Molded-in gel coat, non skid.

Internally bonded 4200 lbs. lead ballast.

Fiberglass outboard rudder w/ bronze fittings.

Ten Goiot heavy-duty, aluminum opening ports.

Goiot tinted and aluminum-framed forward hatch.

Two cockpit seat lockers w/ latches.

Teak cribboards, handrails and retainer rails.

Two self-bailing cockpit scuppers.

Heavy-duty bronze sea cocks.

Anti-fouling paint.

Rugged, unstayed hollow spruce mast.

Solid spruce boom section.

Fully battened mainsail, 429 sq. ft.

Dacron sheets, halyards and lazy jacks.

Free-standing 220 sq. ft. ghoster.

Sheet and halyard cleats and winches.

Stainless steel bow pulpit.

Oversized stainless steel stern pulpit.

Two aft mooring cleats and chocks.

Two mooring chocks and mooring bit forward.

Rope and chain anchor deck pipe.

Bronze bow roller.

Port and starboard adjustable steering prams w/dog-down hurricane hatches.

Ritchie SFN-44 compass.

13 hp Volvo Penta MD7A diesel engine w/2:1 reduction.

12-volt, 35 amp. alternator.

Sea water strainer.

Stainless steel shaft.

30 gal. aluminum fuel tank.

Morse engine controls.

Engine instrument panel.

12-volt marine battery.

Four-way master safety switch.

US Coast Guard and International approved running lights.

12-volt cabin lights.

30 gal. stainless steel fresh water tank.

Fresh water galley pump.

Water and fuel deck fill plates.

Enameled wood finish w/ varnished mahogany trim.

Soft vinyl headliner.

Inside steering station.

One removable, adjustable, gimballed swing seat.

Two hi-grade vinyl steering station seat cushions.

Two anodized aluminum sheet and halyard storage reels.

Deluxe carpeting throughout.

Four deluxe fabric main cabin sea berths.

Double drop-leaf dining table.

Hinged top-loading chart table w/ storage.

Color-coordinated Formica counter tops.

Two-burner, gimballed kerosene stove.

Insulated ice box.

Stainless steel galley sink.

Enclosed Wilcox Crittenden marine head.

w/Microphor sewage treatment system.

Large storage area forward w/ separate anchor chain locker.

Hanging locker in head.

Manual bilge pump.

Specifications:

LOA
29′2½″

LWL
23′

BALLAST
4200 lbs.

DISPLACEMENT
9300 lbs.

SAIL AREA/MAIN
429 sq. ft.

SAIL AREA/GHOSTER
220 sq. ft.

POWER
13 hp. 2 cy. Diesel

MAST HEIGHT, ABOVE DECK
33'6"

Bristol Yachts
Bristol, Rhode Island 02809

BRISTOL 32

Designed by Ted Hood

Features:

HULL AND DECK
Molded high-impact fiberglass reinforced polyester resin . . . largely woven roving . . . hand layup, the best construction available. No fillers are used. Hull and deck thicknesses vary to suit structural demands. Deckhouse, deck and cockpit are integrally molded. Thru-bolted deck clamp and cove stripe molded with hull. Teak toe rails (unvarnished). Non-skid pattern molded into deck, seat and cabin top. Dorade boxes molded onto trunk cabin. Opening forward hatch (translucent) with molded gasket, receptacle, hatch lock and main cabin opening ventilator hatch. Hinged lazaret hatch. Molded seahood for main companionway hatch . . . with spray rail. Mounting base for companionway dodger.

COCKPIT
Molded as part of deck. Seat level enough below deck level to provide high coaming for comfortable back rest. Self-bailing cockpit. Cockpit drains fitted with seacocks. Molded cockpit seat hatch, completely scuppered to prevent leakage, is fitted with security hasp. Coamings and other trim . . . first quality teak.

DECK HARDWARE
All fittings are highest grade stainless steel, chrome-plated bronze with brushed satin finish, or special corrosion-resistant aluminum alloys. Many items are custom-made to our own designs. Custom stemhead fitting with integral chocks. One docking cleat fore and two aft. Bristol-type winch bases . . . with handle storage in bases. Main sheet traveler. Edson wheel steering.

INTERIOR
Satin-finished mahogany is used extensively on the interior because of the natural beauty of wood. There is generous drawer and locker space throughout. Doors are paneled and fitted mahogany. Bulkheads available in satin-finished mahogany or muted shades of easily-maintained Formica. Cabin floor is laid teak and holly inlay. Underside of deck in main cabin finished with smooth fiberglass "headliner."

Main cabin is equipped as follows: Pull-out berth port. Berth (starboard) has pipe berth over (with mattress). All berths have 4" polyfoam mattresses with breathable covers. Many convenient lockers and cabinets behind and above berths in forward and main cabins.

GALLEY
Located starboard aft . . . contains two-burner recessed alcohol stove . . . with hinged cover. Molded icebox (with polyurethane insulation) is on port side. Space for dishes, pots, pans, and canned goods is outboard of icebox. Additional lockers are located behind stove and sink. Stainless steel sink (14" x 10" x 6" deep) is equipped with high-capacity, self-priming pump . . . has swing-away spout. Sink outlet is fitted with 1½" seacock. All galley countertops are Formica.

HEAD
Located port-athwartships . . . contains large linen locker and counter with stainless steel wash basin. Outlet leads to seacock. Towel bar, mirror and hooks are conveniently located. A hanging locker provides additional storage area nearby.

FORWARD CABIN
Contains two (2) full-length berths with 4" foam mattresses. Each has drawer and storage bin built in under it. Full length shelves are run over each berth. Sides of hull are sheathed in nylon pile . . . with lockers above.

FOREPEAK
Located forward of forward cabin berths . . . contains ample storage space for anchor lines, sea bags, etc.

ENGINE INSTALLATION
Yanmar 15 HP. Diesel Bronze propeller shaft runs in Bristol-type rubber-mounted shaft log. Muffler exhaust. Throttle and reverse controls installed on cockpit side and connected to engine with rattle-proof ball joints. Instruments are located on aft side of cabin house. Two-bladed sailboat propeller. Over-sized, non-breakable fuel filter . . . as well as natural forced draft ventilation. Coast Guard approved.

ELECTRICAL SYSTEM
Heavy-duty system consisting of alternator on engine; two (2) 12-volt marine batteries; fused circuits; master disconnect battery switch; centrally-located electrical panel.

Seven (7) interior lights. Bow, stern and side running lights. Dockside 110-volt power and 4-way battery switch.

TANKS
Water tank (fiberglass) has 75-gallon capacity. Fuel tank has 18-gallon capacity.

SPARS AND RIGGING
Anodized aluminum mast and boom. Mast extrusion (Bristol design) with extruded sail track. Mast fitted with welded aluminum masthead fitting. Sheaves machined from solid stock. Standing rigging . . . stainless steel with swaged terminals and stainless steel turnbuckles. Main and jib halyards are stainless steel with Dacron tails. Running rigging is Dacron. Flag halyard. Main sheet arrangement includes a traveler. Sheet and halyard winches are standard.

COLORS
Owner has color options . . . may specify colors (from standard color selections) to be molded into hull and deck. Owner may also select from a variety of available colors . . . for boot-top, anti-fouling bottom paint, cove stripe and mattresses.

Additional Standard Equipment:
Yanmar 15 HP Diesel, Edson Steerer, Dockside Power, Manual Bilge Pump, Electrical Bilge Pump, Bow Pulpit, Stern Rail, Lifelines and Stanchions, 1 Lifeline Gate, Vinyl Mattresses, 2 Burner Recessed Stove, 1 Opening Port, Head, Interior Handrails, Exterior Teak Trim Fore Deck Light, Masthead Light, Anodized Mast and Boom, Genoa Track w/Block on Slide, Teak Sole, Extra Battery w/ 4 Way Switch, Electrical Package, Anchor Roller Stemhead, 1 #8 Lewmar Winch, 1 #16 Lewmar Winch, 2 #30 Lewmar Winches, 1 Standard and 1 Lock-In Winch

Handle, 5" Ritchie Compass, Jiffy Reefing.

Specifications:

MODELS
Sloop or Ketch

LOA
32'1"

LWL
22'0"

BEAM
9'5"

DRAFT
Keel–4'8"
Cbd up–3'6"
Cbd down–7'6"

BALLAST (LEAD)
4000#

DISPLACEMENT
11,300#

SLEEPING CAPACITY
5–6

SAIL AREA (SLOOP)
464 sq. ft.

SAIL AREA (KETCH)
505 sq. ft.

BRISTOL 35.5

Designed by Ted Hood
The Bristol 35.5, a medium displacement keel-centerboard designed to provide a responsive yet comfortable racer-cruiser. The hull, cockpit and deck draw on Ted Hood's experience in designing a long line of successful racer-cruisers. While current measurement rules are taken into consideration, the hull is in no way distorted around measurement points. The end result is a graceful hull with a classically modern appearance for those who appreciate a good looking boat with 6'4" headroom and a comfortable layout giving an uncramped, uncluttered feeling when above or below decks.

The dimensions of the full bodied hull give ample volume for a large comfortable arrangement. The interior provides accommodations for six people in a well thought-out layout. The efficient galley features a sink, large ice box, and two burner recessed stove. The navigation area combines a seakindly quarter berth with a full-sized chart table.

The main cabin features a large dining table with generous seating for a comfortable living area below decks. An extension dinette berth and an optional extension starboard settee berth provides sleeping accommodations for three or four in the main cabin. Forward of the main cabin there is a comfortable head with sink and a good sized forward stateroom, with a large V-berth for two and ample storage for their gear.

The deck layout is clean and simple. The large cockpit provides wide comfortable seats long enough for sleeping out under an awning. The trunk cabin protects the cockpit from breaking seas yet is below eye level when sitting in the cockpit. The wide side decks permit easy passage forward to the foredeck for efficient sail handing.

Each of the three arrangements available (for up to six people) show Ted Hood's experience and attention to detail. The main cabin comes with a choice of one, two or no pilot berths . . . plus a settee and drop-leaf cabin table. The galley, located aft for good ventilation and to keep the cook in close contact with the cockpit, provides ample storage space. The oversized quarter berth at the navigation station provides comfortable seating, while there is room for chart storage under the large lift-top table. Outboard shelves handle books and electronics.

A good sized head (optional shower) is located between main cabin and forward stateroom (with its hanging locker and privacy for two). Good ventilation provided throughout. Cockpit provides large storage lockers; an optional LPG Locker; and long, wide seats for comfortable cockpit sleeping. Standard power is diesel. Fuel capacity is 31 gallons. Water tank holds 56 gallons. With optional bow tank to 110 gallons.

Features:

Hulls made by hand layup process using full-strength resin; best available spars and rigging . . . up to off-shore cruising specs; anodized spars . . . ports are Almag 35 high tensile aluminum alloy (not plastic) with outside finishing ring; teak hand-laid cabin soles in most interiors; generous use of Philippine/Honduras mahogany and best available teak; exposed interiors of hull are gel-coated for easy cleaning; top grade marine hardware (Schaefer Marine, Nicro/Fico, Rostand ports, Edson steering systems, Merriman turnbuckles, etc.); Bomar hatches; stainless steel anchor roller stemhead; seacocks on all thru-hull fittings; Woolsey marine finishes . . . Woolsey Vinelast® bottom paint; heavy ⅜" lifelines; heavy pelican hook; stainless steel fastenings on all deck and hull hardware; welded bow and stern rails; Lewmar winches; plus a long list of other standard and optional equipment for customizing your Bristol 35.5.

Standard Equipment:
Yanmar 22 hp. Diesel
Edson Steerer
Bow Pulpit
Stern Rail
Lifelines with One Gate
Manual Bilge Pump
2 Burner Recessed Stove
1 Opening Port in Head

Interior Handrails
Exterior Teak Trim
Masthead Light
Combination Bow/Foredeck Light
Anodized Mast and Boom
Inboard Genoa Track w/Block on Slide
Electrical Package
1 #8 Lewmar Winch
1 #16 Lewmar Winch
2 #40 Lewmar Winches
1 Standard and 1 Lock-in Winch Handle
Jiffy Reefing
Anchor Roller Stemhead
31 Gallon Fuel Tank
Vinyl 4" Mattresses

Specifications:

LOA
35'6"

BEAM
10'10"

LWL
27'6"

DRAFT
Keel–5'9"
Cbd up–3'9"

DISPLACEMENT
15,000 lbs.

BALLAST (LEAD)
6500 Keel
7000 C/B

SAIL AREA
589 S.F.

IOR RATING
25.9 Est.

BRISTOL 40

Designed by Ted Hood

Features:

HULL AND DECK
Molded hand lay up fiberglass rein-

forced polyester resin . . . largely woven roving, strongest material available. Hull and deck thicknesses vary to suit structural demands. Deckhouse, deck and cockpit are integrally molded. Deck clamp and cove stripe molded with hull. Nonskid pattern molded into deck, seats and cabin top. Deck layout reflects careful planning. Consider these points when you comparison-shop. Opening hatch forward (hinged to open either forward or aft) is large enough to handle sail bags. Molded sea hood is standard. Molded rail from sea hood aft is perfect mount for dodger. All rails, coamings and trim are teak . . . natural finish. Dorado boxes for cabin ventilation (forward) are molded and cowl scoops for engine room vents are provided.

COCKPIT
Cockpit seat hatches are scuppered. Molded winch bases with cockpit cutouts provide handy storage for winch handles. Main sheet traveler is molded on bridge, in cockpit or optionally mounted forward of main hatch.

DECK HARDWARE
All hardware is chrome-plated bronze, stainless steel or high-strength alloys.

INTERIOR
Many options allow you to get the exact decor you desire. The all-wood interiors can be tailored to your taste. Just tell us what you want. The main cabin is finished with varnished, hand-rubbed mahogany. Choose from a variety of arrangements. To port, choose from a convertible dinette, pilot and pull-out transom berths, or a pull-out double berth. To starboard, a transom lower and pipe berth is standard. On request, a quarter berth with navigator table and station is also available. The cabin sole is hand-laid teak and holly inlay. Exceptionally roomy

storage spaces and a large chart drawer are also standard. A variety of colors are available for the 4″ foam mattresses.

GALLEY

Galley (aft) layout provides generous working space away from main companionway. Galley features include: pressure hot and cold water; cold water hand pump; 3-burner alcohol stove with oven; and storage drawers. Large hanging area aft of ice chest area is perfect for wet gear and boots. Forward cabin has second hanging locker, a stand (5 drawers) with shelf and large cabinet behind.

HEAD

Ample head compartment has two (2) doors providing private access from either forward or main cabin. Head is fitted with 10 (ten) drawers for storage and two (2) shelf compartments for linens. Entire head floor of molded fiberglass . . . makes excellent shower facility and simplifies cleaning. Hot and cold pressure water system is standard for both wash basin and shower.

FORWARD CABIN

Offers two (2) V-berths; dressing area; hanging locker; and separate access to spacious head.

ENGINE INSTALLATION

Westerbeke 40 diesel (4-108) is standard. Other diesel engines are available as options. All wiring, exhausts and grounding are underwriter-approved. Manual and electric bilge pumps are standard.

ELECTRICAL SYSTEM

Heavy-duty system consisting of alternator on engine and two (2) 12-volt marine batteries with four-way switch; bow, stern and side running lights; eight (8) interior lights; and 110-volt shore plug . . . six (6) 110-volt outlets.

TANKS

Pressure water system (6-gallon high recovery heater) has two (2) fiberglass water tanks (130 gallons) with deck fill. Fuel tank (aluminum) . . . 31-gallon capacity.

SPARS AND RIGGING

Anodized aluminum mast. Stainless steel standing rigging. Stainless steel wire halyards. Jiffy rigging.

COLORS

Owner has color options . . . may specify colors (from standard color selections) to be molded into hull and deck. Owner may also select from a variety of available colors for boot-top, anti-fouling bottom paint, cover stripe.

ADDITIONAL STANDARD EQUIPMENT

Westebeke Diesel 4-108, Edson Steerer, Dockside Power, Manual Bilge Pump, Electric Bilge Pump, Bow Pulpit, Stern Rail, Life lines and Stanchions, 1 Gate for Life lines, Vinyl Mattresses, 3-Burner Stove w/Oven, 1 Opening Port, Head, Interior Handrails, Exterior Teak Trim, Deck Light, Masthead Light, Anodized Mast and Boom, Genoa Track w/Block on Slide, Teak Sole, Extra Battery w/4-Way Switch, Electrical Package, Anchor Roller Stemhead, Hot and Cold Pressure System w/Shower, 2 #8 Lewmar Winches, 2 #40 Lewmar Winches, 1 Jib Halyard #16, 1 Standard and 1 Lock-In Winch Handle, 5″ Ritchie Compass, Jiffy Reefing.

Specifications:

MODELS
Sloop or Yawl

LOA
40′2″

LWL
27′6½″

BEAM
10′9″

DRAFT
Keel–5′4½″
Cbd up–4′0″
Cbd down–7′10″

BALLAST (LEAD)
6500#

DISPLACEMENT
17,580#

SLEEPING CAPACITY
6

SAIL AREA
Sloop–694 sq. ft.
Yawl–707 sq. ft.

BRISTOL 45.5

Designed by Ted Hood

Features:

HULL AND DECK

Molded high-impact fiberglass reinforced polyester resin . . . largely woven roving, strongest material available. Hull and deck thicknesses vary to suit structural demands. Deckhouse, deck and cockpit are integrally molded. Deck clamp and cove stripe molded with hull. Non-skid pattern molded into deck, seats and cabin top. Deck layout reflects careful planning. Opening hatch forward is large enough to permit handling sail bags. Molded sea hood is standard and molded rail from sea hood aft is perfect mount for dodger. All rails, coaming covers and trim are teak . . . furnished natural, sealed or varnished (optional).

GALLEY

The efficiency galley, located adjacent to the companionway includes deep sinks, stainless steel ice box, and 3 burner propane gas range with oven (all standard equipment) . . . with racks, storage drawers, and generous working space designed to keep the cook

happy. Hot and cold pressure water and 12V Crosby Refrigeration are also provided.

MAIN SALON

The "open space" look is especially notable in the large main salon where the L-shaped dinette, and ample room for chairs or transom berth makes an ideal setting for below-decks socializing. Teak and/or varnished, hand rubbed mahogany and fine appointments give it the appearance of an exclusive club . . . which in essence it is . . . just you and your closest friends or family. At night this area converts to sleep three people . . . besides those in the two private double-staterooms. Ample storage space helps keep everything shipshape during long cruises.

AFT CABIN

The skipper will get special delight in showing off this handsomely designed and crafted area. There's plenty of room, with sitting area, double bunks, hanging locker and storage drawers. Add the private head with tile stall shower (hot and cold pressure water) and you'll know justifiable pride.

FORWARD CABIN

The forward cabin, with its V-berth arrangement, features just a little more elegance than you'd normally expect. Fine woods are crafted into the closets, drawers, berths and V-berth filler. Head is well appointed. Hot and cold water is under pressure. No one can complain about these private accommodations.

Other Standard Equipment:

HULL

Hand lay-up, with alternate layers of mat and woven roving.

DECK

Hand lay-up, with mat and cloth, balsa core with wood paneling, gel-coated liner and vinyl.

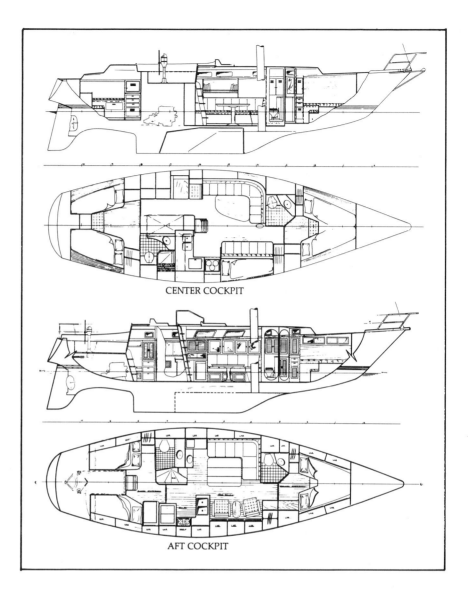

CENTER COCKPIT

AFT COCKPIT

BALLAST

Lead, internally cast.

CENTERBOARD

Fiberglass, molded with bronze pin through pipe and stainless wire rope through fiberglass pipe to Merriman C/B winch on cabin house.

RUDDER

Fiberglass, molded around bronze stock with welded pates bearing on skeg, at hull and top of stock.

MACHINERY: ENGINE

Westerbeke 60 with 2:1 short profile sailing transmission, 1¼" bronze shaft, cutlass bearing.

Mounted on fabricated glass, mahogany and stainless steel beds. Water lift muffler. Oil and water alarms.

PROPELLER

3 Blade.

ENGINE COMPARTMENT

Insulated, lead-lined, ventilated with 2-4" vents.

FUEL TANKS

100 gallon, stainless steel.

ALTERNATOR

2-12 Volt, 55 amp each.

EDSON STEERER

With controls, pedestal guard, and

brake mounted on pedestal and compass (6" Ritchie, black non-glare finish).

DOMESTIC WATER TANKS (3)
1 Bow—80 gallons. 2 under sole port and stbd—55 gallons each.

PRESSURE PUMP
12 Volt Par pump with:

HOT WATER HEATER
12 gallon with heat exchanger polyurethane on cold water system.

SINKS
Double stainless steel 10" x 14" x 9¾" deep in galley with mixing faucet.
Oval sink in bar with foot pump.
Porcelain sink in heads.

SHOWERS
1 in each head with Lovett sump pump for discharge.

INTERIOR JOINER WORK
Teak cabin sole, hand layed, screwed, glued and bunged.
Bulkheads—choice of teak or brunzeel mahogany glassed in place with either teak or Honduras mahogany trim.
Formica color for counters and head available for owner's selection.
Head soles—ceramic tile.
Finished bulkheads and trim sealed and hand rubbed varnish.
Cabin sole—sealed.
Dinette Table—fixed with drop leaves.

EXTERIOR
Teak trim, grab rails and toe rails.

DECK HARDWARE
Stainless steel, satin chrome or anodized.
Stemhead—fabricated stainless steel with tack and chocks.

CLEATS
2-12" Bow
2-9" Midship
2-9" Aft

Nicro Fico Ball Bearing Traveler.
Double bow and stern rails, lifelines and stanchions with 2 gates.
Cast ports with opening in heads.
Genoa Track—Merriman "T" track 1¼" bolted inboard.
Blocks—Schaefer Series #9 and #11.
Hatches—Bomar in forward cabin and midships.
Sliding fiberglass hatches for companionways with sea hoods and rails.

WINCHES (Lewmar)
2 #55 Jib Sheet
1 #40 Main Sheet
1 #44 Jib Halyard
1 #40 Main Halyard

ELECTRICAL
12 Volt grounded throughout.
Bass panel—with 26 DC circuit breakers, 7 AC breakers, 4 indicators and 1-30 amp shore power outlet. 7-110 V outlets.
3 Batteries—165 amp hours, total 495 amp hours in 2 banks, one for engine, 2 for ships service with switch for emergency start.
Bilge pump—electric
Constavolt—LaMarche 40 amp.
12V Crosby refrigerator with cold plates in stainless steel box.
Lighting—fluorescent fixtures with cone and dome lights in appropriate areas.

SPARS
Fabricated aluminum extrusions, anodized with stainless steel fittings, internal halyards, tapered spreaders.

STANDING RIGGING
Stainless steel with Navtec turnbuckles.

STOVE
Propane, 3 burner with oven.

OPTIONAL EQUIPMENT
Icerette and Wet Bar

Chrome Ventilators

Dorade Boxes

Teak Cockpit Grate

Varnished Teak Exterior (5 Coats)

Varnished Cabin Sole (5 Coats)

2 Swivel Chairs

Opening Ports

Higher 4" Flared, Tapered Toe Rails

Curtains

Hood Stowaway Mast

Hood Sea Furl

Ketch Rig

Roller Furling Jib

Fold-down Table

Radio Telephone

RDF Win and Speed inst.

Specifications:

MODELS
Sloop or Ketch

LOA
45' - 3"

LWL
37' - 3"

BEAM (max)
13' - 2½"

DRAFT (CB up)
4' - 11"
(CB down): 11' - 0"

DISPLACEMENT
34,660#

BALLAST
15,000#

MAIN
445 Sq. Ft.

130% Genoa
680 Sq. Ft.

150% Genoa
791 Sq. Ft.

SPEED UNDER POWER
8.0 knots.

P
50

I	J	E
56	18.5	18

Cape Cod Shipbuilding Company

P.O. Box 152
Wareham, Massachusetts 02571

MERCER 44

Designed by William H. Tripp
The Mercer 44 sleeps seven, the same as many smaller yachts, but the difference is that in 44 ft. the Mercer has accommodations for seven people. She has hanging lockers, linen lockers, food storage, water and fuel capacity for a lengthy cruise. The flush deck gives ample space for all to participate in the sunshine and fresh air, while the spacious main cabin with full headroom makes mealtime and evening games comfortable, without claustrophobia.

When not made up, the upper berths in main cabin are out of the way. If not needed, they can even be used as bookshelves, or for other storage. Since they are not fully extended unless in use, the cabin does not resemble a pullman train.

The galley is roomy and easy to work in, no feet in your face as someone comes down the main hatch.

Cape Cod is now in its 23rd year building fiberglass boats. The Mercer hull is built double thickness to the waterline, and the deck is double with a foam core for rigidity and insulation.

To our knowledge, no Cape Cod built Mercer 44 has had any structural failures. Flush deck construction has always been considered much stronger than trunk cabin which is used mostly to get full headroom in small yachts. The Mercer is large enough to utilize this able construction yet retaining full headroom. The stem is double from deck to keelson, giving assurance that you'd have to wear off about 6″ before you could cause a leak there. The lead keel is on the outside where good builders have been putting it since Nathaniel Herreshoff, 100 years ago, decided it was not only the best ballast, but also good protection.

Selected African mahogany in the interior and Burma teak trim on the exterior are in the tradition of finest yacht construction, combining beauty with ease of maintenance.

Cabin Interior—Standard 7 berth lay-out, with 4″ foam mattresses and covers. In doghouse: Quarter berth to starboard 6′6″ with large galley to port. Ample storage for food. Large shelves for dishes and racks for cups. Top and front doors to icebox. Engine room is under 2 large hatch covers beneath teak and holly inlaid sole.

Main cabin very spacious for a 44-footer. Four (4) berths, with 12 personal lockers. Drop leaf table with silverware drawer and bottle storage.

At starboard main cabin area: Desk-chart table with cabinets over and drawers and locker under. At port is dresser and large drawers

with lockers. Waterproof carpet over fiberglass floor. Water tank under cabin sole.

Head to port W/C Imperial toilet, stainless steel wash basin, formica counter top with individual drawers and linen storage. Double hanging lockers opposite the head.

Forward cabin has two berths, seat, two drawers and 6 lockers.

Standard Equipment:

Zephyr anodized aluminum mast

Aluminum spinnaker pole

Stainless steel standing rigging

Roller reefing on sitka spruce boom

Port, starboard, bow, and stern running lights

Polished stainless steel bow and stern pulpits

Double lifeline with gate

Complete engine instruments

12 volt electrical system—3 heavy duty batteries

Mahogany drop leaf table in main cabin with fiddle rails

Seven 4″ thick foam rubber mattresses covered

Sea cover over sliding hatch

Flag halyard to masthead

16′ Genoa track with 4 cars and turning blocks

All running rigging, Dacron®. Necessary blocks and cleats for mainsail and jib.

Winches:
2 for genoa sheets
1 #2 for mainsheet
1 #2 for main halyard (wire)
1 #3 for jib halyard
1 #2 for spinnaker halyard

Bilge Pump

Stainless steel galley and toilet sinks

Hot and cold water pressure system in head and galley

Topping lift

5 Teak hatches—4 with screens

Three 5″ vents with Dorade type water traps

2 Teak deck storage boxes

Wood trim on deck is teak

7 Life jackets

Anchor with Rode 150′ ½″ Nylon

4 Dock lines

2 Dry chemical extinguishers

Specifications:

Dimensions:

L.O.A.
44′0″ DRAFT 4′3″

L.W.L.
30′0″ DRAFT

BEAM
11′9″ (board down) 9′0″

SAIL AREA
Yawl: 902 sq. ft.—Sloop: 885 sq. ft.

DISPLACEMENT
27,000 lbs.; keel 8,600 lbs. lead secured to hull with 11 stainless steel bolts 1″ dia.

EDSON PEDESTAL STEERER with 28″ destroyer wheel and emergency tiller, 5″ compass and hood.

RUDDER
Fiberglass on 2″ stainless steel post.

CENTERBOARD
285 lbs., high-aspect ratio, cast manganese bronze with specially designed worm gear winch mounted just above waterline and Monel IWRC 6 x 37 cable.

HULL AND DECK
Fiberglass with color molded in. All hand lay up with foam sandwich reinforcement.

POWER
Gasoline engine with controls and full instruments. Westerbeke diesel optional extra.

GALLEY

Seagoing with excellent light and visibility in doghouse. Large icebox with triple access hatches. Shipmate (or equal) 3 burner with oven and double stainless steel sink.

HOT AND COLD RUNNING WATER

In galley and head.

REFRIGERATION

Available as extra (electrical or mechanical).

MONEL FUEL TANKS

68 gal. with gauges. 110 gal. water tank located in keel section.

12 VOLT SYSTEM

60 amp alternator, ten interior lights, spreader lights with fused panel and 2 master switches.

STAINLESS STEEL STANDING RIGGING

Swaged terminals and bronze turnbuckles. All rigging grounded to keel.

Cape Dory Yachts
160 Middleboro Ave.
East Taunton, Massachusetts
02718

CAPE DORY 25

Designed by Carl Alberg
The Cape Dory 25's handsome sloop design is both swift and seaworthy. She is another proud member of the "full keel" Cape Dory fleet . . . the result of Cape Dory's craftsmanship, engineering and attention to detail.

Sailors appreciate her easy motion and certain tracking, the result of a hull with fine lines and a "full keel" with attached rudder. Her graceful hull responds to the gentlest breeze or sudden gust. Cape Dory designed her to give ex-

cellent performance over a wide range of conditions. Her self-bailing cockpit is big enough for crew, 2 sail lockers and lazarette. A bridge deck helps make a safer cockpit and drier cabin. The locking lazarette hatch on her afterdeck covers a motor well that is spacious enough for optional outboard and fuel tanks. Molded-in non skid helps make sure footed crew movement over wet decks.

The Cape dory 25 is sloop rigged with a beautifully balanced, moderate sailpin. Her main is roller reefed for easy sail handling and efficient sail trim. Her anodized spars and "overbuilt" rigging are careful-

ly engineered and constructed to meet requirements often specified for much larger boats. She's fitted with the finest hardware and winches.

The thoughtful planning and painstaking efforts of Cape Dory designers and craftsmen are immediately evident below decks.

In the main cabin, there are comfortable bunks to port and starboard. A teak dining room table stows away; the galley is located directly below the main companionway hatch for extra room, light and ventilation. The top-loading icebox is located beneath the companionway stairs for easy access.

The galley is also equipped with a deep stainless steel sink, teak shelves, and ample storage areas. There is room for an optional two burner stove.

Between the main and forward cabins is a hanging locker and enclosed head. The forward cabin sleeps two and is complete with bronze opening ports and hatch.

Every hull and deck is built using Cape Dory's "quality engineered" methods. Every piece of fiberglass woven roving is hand laid in a precise location; the molding resin is carefully worked in by hand.

Deep into each hull, we securely fiberglass the molded ballast. A fiberglass liner or inner structure is permanently joined to the hull for added strength. It also becomes a moisture barrier that results in dry storage lockers that are easy to clean, as well as a drier boat.

Hull and decks are joined with Cape Dory's special bonding materials which incorporate the teak toe rail, assuring a solid, permanent joint.

The quality of every boat is carefully controlled through close inspection at every phase of construction. From start to finish, over 360 "quality control" inspections are made.

Standard Equipment:

Hull Molded in One Piece
Full Keel with Attached Rudder
Solid Stainless Steel Rudder Post
Bronze Rudder Shoe
Internal Molded Ballast (1700 lbs.)
Painted Boot Top
Anti-Fouling Bottom Paint (2 coats)
Shipping and Storage Cradle
Balsa Cored Deck

Molded-in Non Skid (Contrasting color)
Teak Rub Strakes
Teak Toe Rails
Teak Taff Rail
Teak Coamings
Teak Drop Board
Teak Companionway Trim
Self-bailing Cockpit
Bridge Deck
Sail Lockers
Outboard Motor Well
Scuppered Seat Hatches
Companionway Hatch Seahood
Forward Opening Hatch
8" Bow Cleat, Bronze
Bow Chocks, Locking
6½" Stern Cleats (2) Bronze
Genoa Track
Genoa Winches
Winch Bases, Bronze
Bronze Sheet Cleats
Main Sheet Traveler
Bronze Opening Ports (6)
Welded SS Pulpit
Anodized Spars
Mainsail and Working Jib
Double Lower Shrouds
Single Spreader Rig
Jib Halyard Winch

Pre-stretched Rope Halyards
Roller Reefing, Mainsail
Adjustable Outhaul
Adjustable Topping Lift
Sheets and Blocks
Main and Jib Sheets
Circuit Breakers-D.C.
Electrical Panel with Battery Volt Meter
Interior Lights
Navigation Lights

Fore Deck Light and Steaming Light on Spar
1 Water Tank (24 gal. total)
SS Galley Sink with Pump
Cockpit Seat Scuppers
Bronze Valves on All Underwater Thru Hulls
Teak Joinerwork
Berths for four
Privacy Door Between Main Cabin and V Berth
Teak and Holly Sole
Opening Hatch over V Berth
Space for Marine Head
Insulated Ice Box
Area for Stove
Galley Storage
Six Opening Bronze Ports
Interior Cushions
Bow Pulpit with navigation light
Molded-in Non Skid on Deck
Roller Reefing
Bridge Deck
Large Cockpit Scuppers
Teak Toe Rails
Teak Grab Rails
Navigation Lights
Deck Light
Main Hatch Seahood

Specifications:

LOA
24'10"

LWL
18'0"

BEAM
7'3"

DRAFT
3'0"

DISPLACEMENT
4,000 lbs.

BALLAST
1,700 lbs.

SAIL AREA
264 sq. ft.

MAST HEIGHT ABOVE WL
31½"

CAPE DORY 28

Designed by Carl Alberg

The Cape Dory 28's combination of exciting performance, luxury, and rugged quality construction have made her the "class of the fleet." She's another product of Carl Alberg's successful sea-tested design and Cape Dory's constant refinements in construction and detail. The Cape Dory 28 answers the cruising sailors call for uncomplicated sail handling, spacious "big boat" liveability and lasting value.

With a full keel and attached rudder, the Cape Dory 28 is stiff and stable, with superb tracking and precise downwind control. Her graceful hull responds to the gentlest breeze and builds to exceptionally good speed when the wind picks up.

In an age when "look alike"

boats fill the harbors, her bronze ports and hardware, teak coamings, toe rails and trim set her apart as a classic beauty.

Topsides, the crew goes forward sure and secure. Wide uncluttered non-skid decks are equipped with teak grab rails, and lifelines. She is equipped with a bowsprit with anchor roller. Bow and stern pulpits are also standard. The large cockpit is self-bailing and features a bridge deck and two large lockers for easy access to sails and gear.

The Cape Dory 28's sloop rig is the perfect complement to her full keel cruising underbody. With shorter mast, longer boom, and self-tending jib, she is powerful without being overpowering. She's a joy, not a job to sail. Once trimmed the Cape Dory 28 can be tacked without having to tend any sheets! Mainsheet is lead to an aft traveler. Jiffy reefing, anodized spars and heavy duty rigging are standard. All standing rigging is lightning grounded.

Down below, the thoughtful planning and painstaking efforts of Cape Dory designers and craftsmen are immediately evident. The interiors of few yachts compare to the luxury and quality joinerwork found in the Cape Dory 28. The warm inviting teak interior is light and airy, and tastefully accented with a teak and holly sole and colorful decorator cushions. Ventilation is provided by eight bronze opening ports and two Lexan hatches. Every inch of her spacious interior has been human engineered for maximum comfort, convenience and space utilization.

Accommodations include a slide out double berth to port, a wide single berth to starboard and a large private V-berth forward. The aft galley offers plenty of work and storage space, deep stainless steel sink, well insulated ice box, and two burner alcohol stove. Meals are served on her bulkhead mount-ed table. A spacious "walk through" lavette with head, wash basin and hanging locker separates the main and forward cabins.

Standard Equipment:

Teak rub strakes

Teak toe rails

Painted boot top

Anti-fouling bottom paint (2 coats)

Internal molded ballast (3,500 lbs.)

1⅛" Solid stainless steel rudder post

Bronze rudder shoe

U.L. listed bronze seacocks

Seacock handles

Full keel with attached rudder

Hull molded in one piece

Shipping and storage cradle

Balsa cored deck

Molded-in non skid

Teak taff rails

Teak coamings

Teak grab rails

Offshore cockpit

Sail lockers

Scuppered seat hatches

Companionway hatch seahood

Teak drop boards

Teak companionway framing

Ash hardwood bow sprit

8" Bow cleats (2) bronze

Large locking bow chocks (2) bronze

8" Stern cleats (2) bronze

Stern chocks (2) bronze

4' Genoa track

Genoa sheet cleats (2) bronze

Main sheet traveler

Jib sheet winch

Jib club pedestal, bronze

Aluminum Lexan deck hatch

Maincabin skylite

Bronze opening ports (8)

Teak Dorade ventilator

Bowsprit anchor roller

Anchor warp deck pipe (bronze)

Welded SS pulpit

Welded SS stern rail

Life lines

SS life line stanchions

Life line boarding gate (stbd)

Anodized spars

Single spreader rig

Mainsail and working jib

Double lower shrouds

Main halyard winch

Jib halyard winch

Pre-stretched rope halyards

Adjustable outhauls

Adjustable topping lifts

Jiffy reefing main

Main and jib sheets

Club footed jib gear

Volvo MD7A 13 HP diesel

1.91:1 Reduction gear

13 gal. fuel tank with gauge

Dual fuel filters

Waterlock muffler

Wire rein multiple exhaust hose

Adjustable engine mounts

Drip pan

1″ Bronze propeller shaft

Alternator

Full ventilation

Circuit breakers-D.C. electrical panel

Spare circuits

Battery

Battery voltmeter

Vaporproof battery switch

Ample interior lighting

Full navigation lighting

Fore deck light and steaming light on spar

Lightning ground system

Bonded underwater fittings

2 Water tanks (60 gal. total)

SS Sinks in head and galley

Foot pumps

Shower sump

U.L. Marine listed thrubolted seacocks with handles

Cockpit seat scuppers

Bronze cockpit sole scuppers

Flush mounted bilge pump

24 Gal. holding tank with head

All interior wood imported teak

Cape Dory's finest standard of joinerwork

Berths for 5

Teak and holly sole

Bi-folding door into forecastle

Opening skylight over V berth

Spacious head with sink

Teak shower grate

Cabinets

Hanging locker

3 Berth main cabin

Bulkhead mounted table

Ample storage

Deep SS sink

Large ice box

2 Burner alcohol stove

Ample galley storage

HiPressure laminant counter tops

4″ Foam cushions with decorator fabrics

8 Opening bronze ports

Main cabin skylight

Lifelines with offshore pelican hooks

Molded-in non skid on deck

Lightning ground system

Diesel power

U.L. listed bronze seacocks

Jiffy reefing

High capacity manual bilge pump

Bridge deck

Large cockpit scuppers

Teak toe rails

Teak grab rails

Non-slip teak cabin sole

Navigation lights

Deck light

Main hatch seahood

Vented grounded fuel tank

Engine room ventilation

Engine drip pan

Fused D.C. electrical panel

Bonded underwater fittings

Specifications:

L.O.A.
28′ 1¾″

L.W.L.
22′ 2½″

BEAM
8′ 10½″

DRAFT
4′ 0″

DISPLACEMENT
9,000 lbs.

BALLAST
3,500 lbs.

SAIL AREA
404 sq. ft.
Mast Height above W.L. 40′6″

CAPE DORY 33

Cape Dory 33 . . . the ultimate refinement and latest edition to Cape Dory's line of full-keel custom quality yachts. The Cape Dory 33 achieves a level of luxury, safety and sail handling ease few production yachts have attained.

Cape Dory 33 has a full keel and an attached rudder. A wider beam, extended well aft adds to her spaciousness on decks and below. Her tall sloop rig is a superb all-weather performer . . . quick in light-to-moderate air, yet stiff and stable when it blows. And when you're becalmed or it's time to maneuver into a crowded harbor, you can rely on her safe, powerful diesel. Shaft and prop are well positioned to provide maximum protection from lobster pots and underwater obstructions!

Her Cape Dory designed bronze cleats, opening ports and deck hardware accentuate her traditional elegance and set her apart as a premier yacht.

Her large cockpit provides comfort for the crew. Wheel steering

with guard and pedestal mounted engine controls are standard. Teak grab rails, double lifelines and stainless steel bow and stern pulpits add to the safety of moving around on deck.

Light and ventilation down below are provided by two smoked Lexan opening hatches, a companionway hatch with seahood, two dorades, and ten opening bronze ports.

The CD 33 carries 546 square feet of sail on a masthead sloop rig. She's designed to handle a large, full-hoisted standard or roller furling genoa for added speed and upwind performance. The rugged awl-grip coated mast is stepped on the keel.

Cape Dory woodworkers have painstakingly crafted teak and select hardwoods to create a warm, spacious interior, tastefully accented with teak and holly sole. The below deck's design has been meticulously considered and "human engineered" for maximum comfort, convenience, and space utilization. A comfortable "living area" in the main cabin includes a drop-leaf table flanked by two settee berths, one extending to a double. To starboard of the companionway is a convenient hanging wet locker, navigation station and roomy quarter berth. To port, is a U-shaped galley with generous work and storage space, deep double sink, large ice box, and gimballed 3-burner alcohol stove with oven.

By abandoning the traditional V-berth concept, Cape Dory designers have been able to create a spacious forward stateroom with large portside berth which converts to a double, a reading settee, bureau, hanging locker, and overhead shelves.

A fully enclosed head features ample cabinets for toiletries and towels, a hamper, shower with hot and cold pressure water and a washbin. A marine head and 35 gallon holding tank are standard.

Standard Equipment:
Teak Rub Strakes
Teak Toe Rails
Painted Boot Top
Anti-fouling Bottom Paint
Internal Molded Lead Ballast (5200 lbs.)
Solid 1½" Stainless Steel Rudder Post
Bronze Rudder Shoe
U.L. Listed Bronze Seacocks
Seacock Handles
Full Keel with Attached Rudder
Hull Molded in One Piece
Shipping and Storage Cradle
Balsa Cored Deck
Molded-in Non Skid
Teak Taff Rails
Teak Coamings
Teak Grab Rails
Offshore Cockpit
Sail Lockers
Lazarette
Scuppered Seat Hatches
Companionway Hatch Seahood
Teak Drop Boards
Teak Companionway Framing
Bronze Stemhead with Anchor Roller
Uni-directional Laminant in Highly Stressed Areas
Pedestal Wheel Steering
Pedestal Mounted Engine Controls
10" Bow Cleats (2) Bronze
Large Bow Chocks (2) Bronze
8" Stern Cleats (2) Bronze
Stern Chocks (2) Bronze
6' Genoa Track
2 Speed Genoa Winches
Molded in Winch Islands
Genoa Sheet Cleats (Bronze)
10" Lock in Winch Handle
Main Sheet Traveler
Aluminum Lexan Deck Hatches (2)
Bronze Opening Ports (10)
Teak Dorade Ventilators
Bowsprit Anchor Roller
Anchor Well on Forward Deck
Welded SS Pulpit
Welded SS Stern Rail
SS Life Line Stanchions
Life Line Boarding Gate (STBD)
Awl Gripped Spars
Keel Stepped Mast
Double Lower Shrouds
Single Spreader Rig
Main Halyard Winch
Genoa Halyard Winch
Jiffy Reefing Winch
Pre-stretched Rope Halyards
Adjustable Outhaul
Adjustable Topping Lift
Jiffy Reefing on Boom
Sheets and Blocks
Volvo MD 11C 23HP Diesel
1.91 Reduction Gear
21 gal. Fuel Tank
Dual Fuel Filter
Waterlock Muffler
Tachometer & Water Temperature
Wire Rein, Multiply Exhaust Hose
Adjustable Engine Mounts
Drip Pan
1" Bronze Propeller Shaft
Pedestal Mounted Engine Controls
Alternator

Full Ventilation

Sound-deadened Engine Compartment

3 Water Tanks (84 gal. total)

SS Sinks in Head

Deep Double SS Galley Sink

Teak Grate Shower Sump

U.L. Marine Listed Thrubolted Seacocks with Handles

Cockpit Seat Scuppers

Bronze Cockpit Sole Scuppers

Flush Mounted Bilge Pump

Remote Alcohol Tank (1½ gal.)

35 gal. Holding Tank

Pressurized Hot & Cold Water System

Manual Backup Water System

Circuit Breakers-D.C. Electrical Panel

Spare Circuits

Dual Batteries

Battery Voltmeter

Vaporproof Battery Switch

Ample Interior Lighting

Full Navigation Lighting

Fore Deck Light and Steaming Light on Spar

Lightning Ground System

Bonded Underwater Hardware

Interior Wood Teak or Select Hardwoods

Cape Dory's Finest Standard of Joinerwork

Berths for Six

Teak and Holly Sole

Bureau in Forecastle

Drawers under V Berth

Opening Skylight over V Berth

Shelves over V Berth

Spacious Head with Sink and Shower

Shower Grate

Cabinets

Storage Locker

Hamper

Hanging Locker

3 Berth Main Cabin (1 Double)

Drop-leaf Dining Table

Ample Storage

Navigation Station

Navigator's Quarter Berth

"U" Shaped Galley

Deep Double SS Sink

Large Ice Box

Gimballed Stove with Oven & 3 Burners

Ample Galley Storage

HiPressure Laminant Counter Tops

4" Foam Cushions with Decorator Fabrics

10 Opening Bronze Ports

Main Cabin Opening Skylight

Emergency Tiller

Lifelines with Offshore Pelican Hooks

Molded-in Non Skid on Decks (contrasting)

Lightning Ground System

Diesel Power

U.L. Listed Bronze Seacocks

Jiffy Reefing

High Capacity Manual Bilge Pump

Bridge Deck

Large Cockpit Scuppers

Teak Toe Rails

Teak Grab Rails

Non-Slip Teak Cabin Sole

Navigation Lights

Main Hatch Seahood

Vented Grounded Fuel Tank

Engine Room Ventilation

Engine Drip Pan

Fused D.C. Electrical Panel

Bonded Underwater Hardware

CAPE DORY 36

The pride of the Cape Dory fleet. This 36 foot blue water cruising yacht is the product of the long partnership between designer Carl Albert and Cape Dory. The result is a perfect combination of solid workmanship and classic good looks with the practicality of modern low maintenance materials.

The long keel gives good tracking ability . . . an important consideration for long-distance, self-steering cruises . . . while also protecting the rudder from fouling or damage. The hull layup is superbly strong, with firm bilge sections and a long smooth run aft for effortless offshore cruising.

But the Cape Dory 36 is not just intended for blue water cruising. She performs equally well as an evening or weekend family sailer. The cutter rig and carefully planned deck layout make sail handling a joy.

Cape Dory 36 has two 10 inch through-bolted bow cleats and two large bow rollers for secure anchor handling. Lewmar 2 speed winches enable all members of the family to trim the sails. The steering system is Edson, with a Destroyer wheel and emergency tiller. To keep the crew safe in all kinds of weather, there are double lifelines securely fastened to solidly through-bolted bow and stern pulpits. Her decks are solid and wide for sure-footed crew movement.

The diesel engine is a 4 cylinder Perkins, fresh water cooled, with a 2 to 1 reduction gear. All necessary controls, gauges and switches are provided. The lighted engine compartment is sound-proofed and has large removable panels for easy access.

The Cape Dory 36 has 135 gallons of fresh water, two of the tanks are located in the bilge for extra stability. 43 gallons of fuel, plus a 24 gallon holding tank with deck pump out, comply with current Coast Guard requirements.

The forepeak chainlocker is divided to stow two anchor rodes with accessibility through the V-berth bulkhead.

The aluminum mast is 6061 T6 alloy, the finest available for marine use. The mast is awl-grip coated and stepped on the keel. The tangs are stainless steel, the turnbuckles forged bronze. All halyards are pre-stretched, ½ inch yacht braid.

Bulkheads and trim are finished in the finest quality teak with a teak and holly cabin sole. A choice of attractive fabrics is available for the interior decor. Special attention has been paid to storage areas, so the Cape Dory 36 has "a place for everything." Her large navigation station is complete with a hinged-top chart table, chart stowage areas and space to build in electronic navigational instruments.

The galley has a deep, double stainless steel sink, a gimballed three-burner alcohol stove with oven, a large top-loading, heavily insulated ice chest and ample stowage for food and utensils. Counter tops are covered with Formica.

The private head is complete with sink, mirror, lighting, laundry hamper, lockers, opening port, dorade, teak grating, and a shower.

Standard Equipment:

HULL
Teak Rub Strakes and Teak Toe Rails

Painted Boot Top

Anti-Fouling Bottom Paint

Internal Molded Lead Ballast (6050 lbs.)

Staysail Halyard Winch

Jiffy Reefing Winch

Pre-stretched Rope Halyards

Adjustable Outhauls

Adjustable Topping Lifts

Jiffy Reefing on Boom (2 sets)

Sheets and Blocks

Club Footed Staysail Gear

DIESEL AUXILIARY
Perkins, 4 cylinder, 4-108 Diesel

Fresh Water Cooled

2.1:1 Reduction Gear

42 Gal. Fuel Tank with Gauge

Dual Fuel Filter

Water Separator

Waterlock Muffler

Full Engine Instrumentation

Wire Rein. Multiply Exhaust Hose

Adjustable Engine Mounts

Drip Pan

1″ Bronze Propeller Shaft

Pedestal Mounted Engine Controls

Alternator

Full Ventilation

Soundproofed Engine Compartment

Engine Room Light

ELECTRICAL
Circuit Breakers-D.C. Electrical Panel

Spare Circuits

Dual Batteries

Battery Voltmeter

Vaporproof Battery Switch

Engine Room Light

Ample Interior Lighting

Full Navigation Lighting

ForeDeck Light and Steaming Light on Spar

Lightning Ground System

Bonded Underwater Hardware

TANKS & HARDWARE
4 Water Tanks (130 gal. total)

SS Sink in Head

Deep Double SS Galley Sink

Teak Shower Grate with Sump

U.L. Marine Listed Thrubolted Seacocks with Handles

Shower Sump Pump

Cockpit Seat Scuppers

Bronze Cockpit Sole Scuppers

Flush Mounted Bilge Pump

Remote Alcohol Tank (1½ gal.

.24 Gal. Holding Tank

Pressurized Hot & Cold Water System

Manual Backup Water System

Shower

INTERIOR
Interior Wood Teak or Select Hardwoods

Cape Dory's Finest Standard of Joinerwork

Berths for Six

Teak and Holly Sole

V Berth Filler with Cushion

Bifold Door in Forecastle

Solid 1½″ Stainless Steel Rudder Post

Bronze Rudder Shoe

U.L. Listed Bronze Seacocks

Seacock Handles

Full Keel with Attached Rudder

Hull Molded in One Piece

Shipping and Storage Cradle

DECK
Balsa Cored Deck

Molded-in Non Skid

Teak Taff Rails

Teak Coamings

Teak Grab Rails

Offshore Cockpit

Sail Lockers

Lazarette

Scuppered Seat Hatches

Companionway Hatch Seahood

Teak Drop Boards

Teak Companionway Framing

Teak Hardwood Bowsprit

Uni-directional laminant in highly stressed areas

DECK HARDWARE & FITTINGS

Pedestal Wheel Steering

Pedestal Mounted Engine Controls

Pedestal Guard

10″ Bow Cleats (2) Bronze

Large Bow Chocks (2) Bronze

8″ Stern Cleats (2) Bronze

Stern Chocks (2) Bronze

10′ Genoa/Yankee Tract

2 Speed Genoa Winches

Teak Winch Stands

Genoa Sheet Cleats (Bronze)

10″ Lock-in Winch Handle

Main Sheet Traveler on House

Main Sheet Winch

Club Footed Staysail Traveler

Staysail Sheet Winch

Aluminum Lexan Deck Hatches

Bronze Opening Ports (10)

Teak Dorade Ventilators (2)

Bowsprit Anchor Rollers (2)

Anchor Warp Deck Pipe (Bronze)

Welded SS Pulpit

Welded SS Stern Rail

Double SS Life Line Stanchions

Life Line Boarding Gates (P&S)

SPARS & RIGGING
Awl Gripped Spars

Keel Stepped Mast

Double Lower Shrouds

Intermediate Shrouds

Single Spreader Rig

Main Halyard Winch

Yankee/Genoa Halyard Winch

Bureau in Forecastle

Drawers under V Berth

Opening Hatch over V Berth

Spacious Head with Shower

Teak Shower Grate

Cabinets

Storage Locker

Hamper

Hanging Locker

3 Berth Main Cabin (1 Double)

Drop-leaf Dining Table

Ample Storage

Navigation Station

Navigator's Quarter Berth

"U" Shaped Galley

Deep Double SS Sink

Large Ice Box

Gimballed Stove with Oven & 3 Burners

Ample Galley Storage

HiPressure Laminant Counter Tops

4″ Foam Cushions with Decorator Fabrics

10 Opening Bronze Ports

Main Cabin Opening Skylight

SAFETY GEAR
Emergency Tiller

Lifelines with Offshore Pelican Hooks

Molded-in Non Skid on Deck

Lightning Ground System

Diesel Power

U.L. Listed Bronze Seacocks

Jiffy Reefing

High Capacity Manual Bilge Pump

Bridge Deck

Large Cockpit Scuppers

Teak Toe Rails

Teak Grab Rails

Non-Slip Teak Cabin Sole

Navigation Lights

Main Hatch Seahood

Vented Grounded Fuel Tank

Engine Room Ventilation

Engine Drip Pan

Fused D.C. Electrical Panel

Bonded Underwater Hardware

Specifications:

L.O.A
36′1½″

L.W.L.
27′0″

Beam
10′8″

Draft
5′0″

Displacement
16,100 lbs.

Ballast
6,050 lbs.

Sail Area
622 sq. ft.

Mast Height above W.L.
46½′

Charter/Sail
Highway 7 North
Richland, Missouri 65556

BANDIT 19

Bandit 19's cabin is large and spacious. Four 6'4" people can live and sleep aboard. Ample cold and dry storage are located under the peak and quarter berths. The "pull-out" galley table seats four and is conveniently located to the optional galley unit. An optional portable head is located under the peak berth.

The interior of the Bandit 19 is like a second hull—a fully molded maintenance-free fiber glass part, making the interior smooth, attractive and easy to keep tidy. Colorful, foam-filled berth pads are color coordinated with the "non-wetting" floor rug. A translucent foredeck hatch and 42" windows in the cabin sides provide plenty of light. Soft upholstery on the interior cabin top warms the interior and covers the wiring to the night light in the cabin.

The only seam in the Bandit 19 is at the deck level where all three parts (hull, interior and deck) are bonded. The keel is molded as part of the hull with the ballast placed inside after molding making the

keel as maintenance-free as the fiber glass hull—no centerboard trunk to obstruct the interior. A sump within the keel molding collects water that may get to the interior in heavy weather or by rain through the hatches.

The Bandit 19 has the power to drive through heavy seas and carry through tacking without being stopped by waves. A proper ballast to weight ratio coupled with reasonable form stability permits the Bandit 19 to heel a moderate degree easily. At about 15° of heel angle the ballast begins to prevent further heeling, and even substantial increases in wind velocity only require minor attention to prevent further heeling. In heavy weather the cockpit floor, lee seats and under seat storage lockers are self-draining.

The Bandit 19 will sail on two feet of water. Beaching is further enhanced by a "kick-up" rudder. The shallow draft low-aspect ratio keel make loading or trailing a snap with the keel setting flat on the trailer.

Standard Equipment:

4 oz. Dacron main and jib

Stainless steel standing rigging

Running lights

Anchor light

Hinged mast step

Teak toe rail

Kick up rudder

Interior cabin light

Tempered glass foredeck hatch with screen

Dark bronze cabin windows

Genoa winches

Gel Coat waterline, coving stripe cabin trim

Bunk cushions

Cold storage and dry storage compartments

Specifications:

LENGTH OVERALL
19'2"

LENGTH WATERLINE
17'3"

MAXIMUM BEAM
7'0"

DISPLACEMENT
1600 lbs.

BALLAST
400 lbs.

SAIL AREA-MAIN (sq./ft.)
85

SAIL AREA-JIB (sq./ft.)
70

SAIL AREA-GENOA (sq./ft.)
115

DRAFT
26"

Cherubini Boat Company
222 Wood Street
Burlington, New Jersey 08016

CHERUBINI 44

This yacht is designed to comply with the timeless laws of Neptune. The sweep of her sheer, low freeboard and rake of her spars echo the great clippers and schooners of yesteryear.

Yet she is a yacht for today. Built of fiberglass using the latest state of the art techniques, the 44 is a fast, comfortable passagemaker capable of 10 knots under sail, yet set up for easy handling by a couple. The Scheel® keel gives her deep draft performance yet allows her to slip into the most inaccessible anchorages.

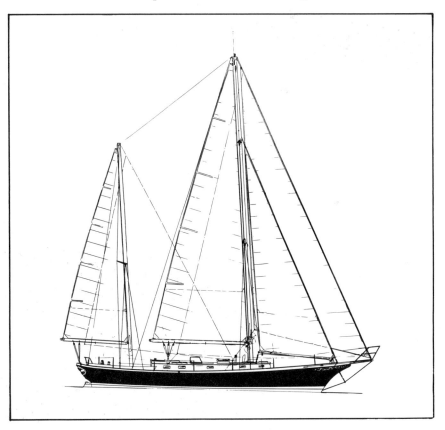

Each Cherubini is custom-tailored to meet the exacting requirements of her new owner. Every detail on board is carefully designed and built by craftsmen who know and respect the sea. As you step aboard on launch day, you'll know that here is a yacht that is truly yours, a reflection of your own personal tastes and desires.

Now in its third generation of boat design and building, the Cherubini family builds each boat as if it were their own.

Specifications:

LENGTH ON DECK
44'

LENGTH ON WATERLINE
40'

BEAM
12'

DRAFT
4'10"

BALLAST
12,000 lbs.

DISPLACEMENT
28,000 lbs.

WATER
200 gals.

FUEL
83 gals.

CHERUBINI 48

Here is a classic schooner that incorporates the latest design technology to ensure swift, comfortable passage-making.

Built of fiberglass, the 48 has an efficient staysail schooner rig that can be handled easily by two people. The only sail that isn't self-tending is the small main staysail.

The proven Scheel® keel will provide deep draft performance, yet allow her to slip into the most inaccessible anchorages.

There are single and double trunk deck plans available. Although there is a standard interior plan, the 48 is basically a custom yacht with design and construction flexibility to accommodate the varying requirements of each owner.

Specifications:

LOA
48'9"

LWL
44'

BEAM
13'

DRAFT
5'

BALLAST
16,900 lbs.

DISPLACEMENT
37,000 lbs.

SAIL AREA
1,204 sq. ft.

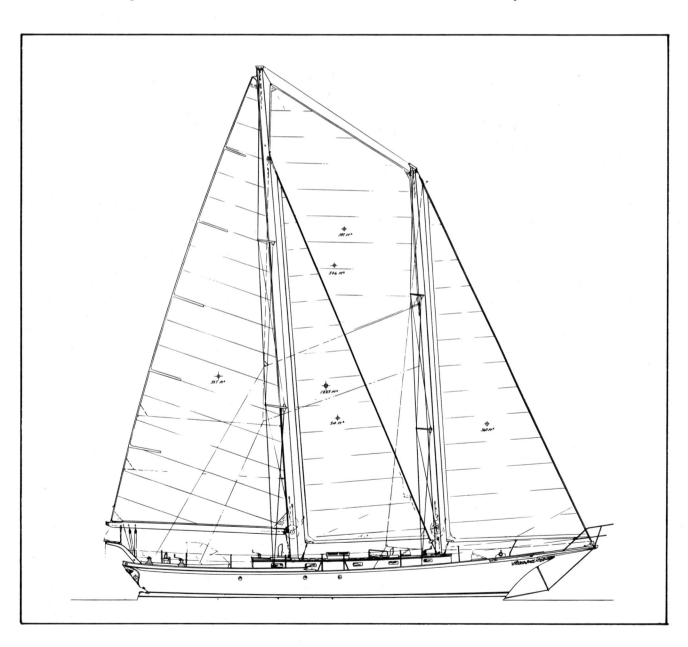

Gordon Douglas Boat Company, Inc.
Route 4
Oakland, Maryland 21550

FLYING SCOT

Designed by Gordon K. Douglas

The Flying Scot was designed by Gordon K. (Sandy) Douglas, the internationally known sailor, whom *Sail* magazine has called ". . . one of the best small-boat helmsmen this country has developed . . ." Sandy's distinguished career as designer and racer spans more than half a century. His Thistle and Highlander designs were outstanding successes.

The best features of all the boats that Sandy designed and raced were incorporated in the Flying Scot, which was designed for fiberglass construction; she is not a wood-to-fiberglass adaptation.

With her hard bilges and slightly tunneled hull, the Flying Scot has great stability and in a good breeze will readily lift up and plane easily. The high, crowned deck sheds spray instead of rolling it back into the cockpit. There are no splashboards; there is no need for them. The centerboard trunk is low, the boom is high, the decks are uncluttered. The rigging is ingeniously simple, and tremendously strong.

The Flying Scot can be easily sailed by one person, yet she'll carry eight people on a comfortable day's sail. Her hull and rigging can handle open water and heavy weather, yet she'll get you home when the water is a mirror. She can be trailered behind a compact car, and rigged by one person in minutes. And with increasing costs of slips and moorings, as well as decreasing availability, it's nice to

know you can let her sit on a trailer in your own backyard garage.

Many owners enjoy the thrill and excitement of keen competition. Racing a Flying Scot offers a challenge to the sailor and places the burden of success squarely on the boat handlers rather than the equipment. The Flying Scot is strictly a one-design boat, which means all hulls are the same, and changes in the Scot's hardware are restricted to occasional convenience items rather than go-fast gadgetry.

Racing takes careful planning and clever strategy. Estimating wind shifts, calculating tacks, and timing are mentally challenging. Racing excels as a family sport which encourages teamwork, and the Flying Scot excels as a family racer.

The Flying Scot Sailing Association sponsors more than 130 racing fleets across the country. The Scot has been selected regularly for the Adams and Mallory Cup races because she not only withstands rough weather and tough crews, but she also provides a true test of helmsmanship.

There are mid-winter regattas in Florida every year, but national championships are held every August in different locations around the country. The Junior North American championship for 13–17-year-old skippers is one of the most popular events. The Flying Scot is readily trailered to the various regattas which keeps the competition open and challenging.

The Flying Scot was intended to be sailed and raced by anyone, not just the highly skilled, the agile, and the young. This stable, forgiving sailboat was designed for family sailing and racing.

Specifications:

LENGTH, OVERALL
19 ft.

LENGTH, WATERLINE
18 ft. 6 in.

BEAM
6 ft. 9 in.

DRAFT, BOARD UP
8 in.

DRAFT, BOARD DOWN
4 ft.

WEIGHT, BARE HULL
675 lbs.

MAST HEIGHT ABOVE WATER
28 ft. 2 in.

SAIL AREA, MAIN AND JIB
190 sq. ft.

SAIL AREA, SPINNAKER (app.)
200 sq. ft.

Edey and Duff
10 Harbor Road
Mattapoisett, Massachusetts
02739

STONE HORSE

Designed by S.S. Crocker

The *Stone Horse*, which first appeared during the 1930s, is a Crocker masterpiece—a small keel sloop designed for the rough, shoal waters and fresh breezes south of Cape Cod. The boats became popular before World War II, being tough, seaworthy, comfortable, and marvellously fast. The war, of course, brought a temporary end to all yacht building, and the postwar period provided no lasting recovery for the traditional methods of construction. Rising costs prevented new building in almost all the pre-war classes, except those with large and enthusiastic racing organizations. Consequently, wooden *Stone Horses* are rare today. Those that exist are old boats beloved for their virtues, by experienced owners, who properly regard them as irreplaceable.

The fiberglass *Stone Horses* have a salty and traditional appearance, and do not look as though they belong in a bathroom or supermarket. On the other hand, they are not "character boats" in the sense of boats which perform poorly, and exist mainly as sentimental evocations of a vanished era.

Sam Crocker designed a perfect hull more than forty years ago. It is the kind of achievement which does not become obsolete. The sea hasn't changed much since then.

There are no extreme characteristics in the *Stone Horse* hull; everything is moderate and wholesome. Dimensions are given on page three. The lines were dictated by the realities of sea and weather, not by measurement rules or fashions. They show a hull which is easily driven, and therefore fast. Firm bilges, good beam, and substantial ballast provide stability. Draft, at three and a half feet, is shallow enough to permit her to go almost anywhere, and yet her long keel provides plenty of lateral plane to hold her on the wind. It also holds her on course, insures good balance under various distributions of sail area, and facilitates self-steering. The bow is graceful, buoyant, and dry. It keeps the water where it belongs. You will enjoy sailing in shirtsleeves, watching the crews of other boats wrapped in oilskins and drenched with spray. The transom stern is narrow and well-formed to minimize drag when heeled down. The rudder is hung outboard where you can keep an eye on it and get at it any time you want without hauling.

The *Stone Horse* cockpit is the full width of the boat, with high, sturdy bulwarks. The dimensions of seats and foot well were beautifully calculated by the designer to fit human bodies of many sizes. You are comfortable and well braced at any angle of heel.

A lazarette in the transom seat provides stowage for deck gear, life preservers, fenders, and so on. On either side of it is a watertight locker designed to hold a portable fuel tank. These lockers are scuppered to the cockpit sole, so any spilled fuel can't find its way below.

A raised deck may contribute more to the comfort of a small boat's interior than any other single feature.

On most boats the deck is at the sheerline, and there is a trunk cabin. This is a fine arrangement on larger boats. You get standing headroom under the trunk, and sitting headroom under the side decks, where the berths or seats

are. The side decks are usually low enough so that you can reach the water, or climb aboard relatively easily. The trunk cabin, with a grab rail, provides something to hang on to as you move forward in a seaway. A low profile, for most of us, is more beautiful. There may be less windage than with a raised deck, if the trunk is not too high.

Alas, fashion and custom decree that small boats be designed to look like bigger boats, but the dimensions of the human body stubbornly refuse to shrink in proportion. Thus, there are twenty-three footers with trunk cabins and side decks, suited only for children or midgets. They provide neither standing headroom under the trunk nor sitting headroom over the berths. When you sit down, you must sit perched on the edge of a berth, bolt upright, or even lean-

ing forward. This may not disturb you for a few minutes at the boat show, but after a while you want to lean back and relax. Being prevented from doing so can be irritating beyond endurance.

The disadvantages of a raised deck do not exist in a small boat. You can reach the water from the deck anyway. Going forward is a matter of a few steps, and you can grab the mast as soon as you are out of the cockpit. The comparative increase of windage is small. And there are advantages beyond accommodation. Construction is simpler and stronger. Higher topsides contribute enormously to stability and buoyancy when heeled.

Only one potential problem remains—appearance. Many raised-deck boats look clumsily high-sided. But Sam Crocker was famous for the grace of his raised-deck de-

signs. He had a knack for lovely proportions which makes the *Stone Horse* look low and sleek, despite all that space and comfort below.

The working sail area of a cruising boat ought to be generous, as opposed to that of a racer-cruiser, which ought to be as small as possible in order to keep rating low. The racer-cruiser can perform well only by setting a variety of additional sails, mainly spinnakers and large headsails. Extra sails are usually unnecessary for a good small cruising boat. They are merely an expensive nuisance. Her ordinary working sails should be enough to move her smartly even in very light weather.

Clearly, this generous area must be easy to reduce when the breeze pipes up. Reefing must be simple and quick. The total sail area, moreover, should be distributed

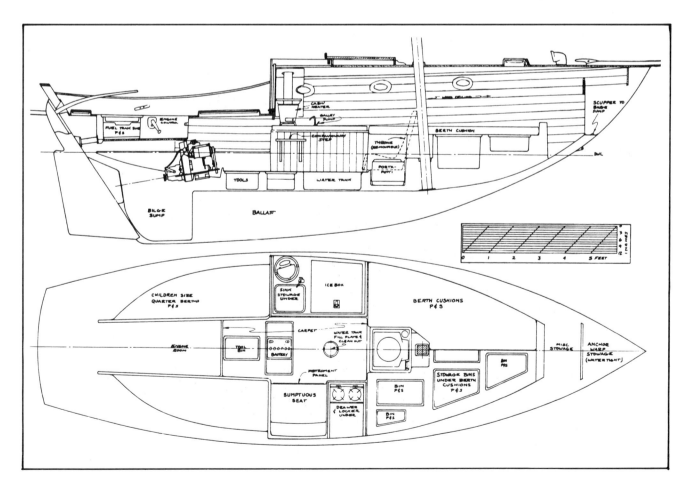

among the sails in such a way that any reduction in area has the smallest possible effect on balance, self-steering, and ease of handling.

The *Stone Horse* is a sloop with two headsails: jib and forestaysail. (Some people might prefer to call her a cutter. Her rig actually falls somewhere between the classic cutter and the ordinary sloop. Usage varies; it appears that either term may be used in this case.) Under main and staysail she will carry ample sail for moderate conditions, and the jib provides a generous additional area for light weather.

The purpose of this rig is to combine efficient performance with effortless handling. The jib has roller-furling gear, so that it can be rolled up on its luff-wire and left permanently hoisted. You need not go on deck at all to do this. (If you sail a racer-cruiser, you have to go forward, take one headsail in, bag and stow it, get out another, and set it in place of the first.) The staysail is set on a club and need not be trimmed every time you come about—a great convenience to the single-hander, or to the wife busy with her book or knitting. The staysail also has a downhaul running from the cockpit forward along the deck, through a fairlead, and then up to the head of the sail. You use it to bring the sail down without having to leave the cockpit, by merely casting off the halliard and hauling on the downhaul. Once lowered, the staysail is held snugly on its club and can't go overboard or get into trouble, even in a breeze. The club, in turn, is held firmly between its topping-lift and sheet. It can't bang on the deck. You can use it to hang on to, or brace yourself against, when you go forward at your leisure to furl the sail.

The main is of good area, so you can sail and maneuver in a tight spot without needing headsails at all.

This rig requires a short bowsprit and boomkin to provide an adequate base. The bowsprit is also the finest kind of help for handling ground tackle. Some wise old salts have bowsprits on their boats for this reason alone, even if the rig doesn't require one.

A sound principle of rigging is that there should be as little of it as you can get away with. Wire and rope create a quite astonishing amount of windage. On the other hand, a clever piece of running rigging can save a quite astonishing amount of work.

The *Stone Horse* mast is stepped on the keel. It has sufficient bury in the hull to stand without any rigging at all, though we emphatically suggest you never try sailing this way. Standing rigging, therefore, can be limited to forestay, backstay, and an upper and lower shroud on either side. All, of course, are of stainless steel 1 x 19 wire and have stainless steel tangs.

The *Stone Horse* interior, since it is not designed to provide berths for more people than can be comfortably accommodated, is rather different from the layout usually found in small fiberglass boats. It is the result of many years and thousands of miles cruising in various small craft.

Way forward is a small bulkhead forming a stowage bin for the anchor warp. A low bulkhead slightly further aft forms the foot of the berths. Between the two is a space for duffle, sailbags, spare rope, bedding, or anything you might stow in an all-purpose forepeak. The berths are of more than ample size—six and a half feet long. Their cushions are of polyurethane foam with inner linings of muslin and outer covers of pre-shrunk and mildew-proofed marine duck. Beneath the cushions are no fewer than nine separate bins for clothing, laundry, stores, or any miscel-

laneous items. If you prepare for a cruise by packing in an open-top canvas bag or two, you can come aboard, slip the bags into the bins, and be off without any delay caused by sorting or stowing.

One of two comfortable seats is immediately abaft the mast, between the berths. The other seat is on the starboard side, just forward of the main bulkhead. The head is exposed by lifting the midship seat (or "throne" as it has been dubbed). It is a Porta-Potti self-contained holding tank type that sits in its own seamless and easily cleaned watertight well.

There are generous formica counters on both sides of the cabin. The cooking stove is on the starboard counter. The icebox is on the port side. It opens from the top, and its lid forms part of the counter.

The sink is also on the port side. It is a plastic dishpan resting in an opening cut in the counter, and is easily portable. You can use it wherever you want, including out in the cockpit on a pleasant evening. Since it requires no drain, the potential danger of an extra hole through the hull is avoided. A drain is unnecessary in a small boat. You can empty the sink over the side even from below.

There is also plenty of room on the port-side counter for installation of a little heating stove. You stoke it up with charcoal, and it produces plenty of warm comfort during spring and fall cruising.

The cabin sole is carpeted. Old salts sometimes raise an eyebrow at the notion of carpet on a boat. We would have felt the same, years ago when synthetic fabrics were uninvented, and leaks and bilge water over the floorboards a common nuisance. But now we enjoy a carpet under our bare feet in cold weather, and the ease of quick cleaning by simply shaking the carpet over the side.

Drawers and lockers under the counters will contain most of your stores and galley equipment. Coffee mugs are best hung on hooks under the cabin top. Additional hooks by the counter can keep can openers, pot holders, ladles, and such small galley items out of the way and yet within easy reach.

A big stowage hammock can hang alongside each berth for clothes that ought to be quickly available, like sweaters, oilskins (when dry), and warm socks.

The water tank is amidships under the cabin sole, where its weight is as low as possible. It fills through a deck plate in the sole, and a pipe carries water up to a pump at the galley sink.

Specifications:

HULL LENGTH
23'4"

TOTAL LENGTH
28'3"

WATERLINE LENGTH
18'4"

BEAM
7'1"

DRAFT
3'7"

FREEBOARD
2'0"

HEIGHT
32'4"

SAIL AREA
339 sq. ft.

DISPLACEMENT
4490 lbs.

BALLAST (lead)
2000 lbs.

Florida Bay Boat Company
270 N.W. 73rd Street
Miami, Florida 33150

MARSH HEN

With a heritage dating to the working watercraft of Chesapeake and New England, Florida Bay Boat Company's new double ender, Marsh Hen, combines the simplicity and utility of those earlier times with state of the art engineering and construction. Marsh Hen is stiff, strong, and lightweight (600 pounds for easy trailering). Her cat-rig with free-standing tapered aluminum mast makes her simple to rig and sail. With her center-board raised, Marsh Hen sails in less than one foot of water and is easily beached . . . with her board down, a three foot draft lets her beat ably to windward. The 150 square foot sail has vertical slab reefing to quickly (one minute or less) reduce sail area to 85 square feet.

Comfort and utility are primary considerations in the design of Marsh Hen's full liner. A high

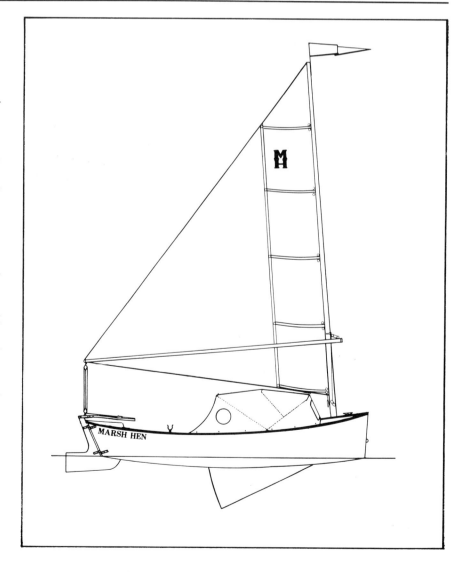

the seats and deck where you can stow your scuba gear, fishing tackle, outboard, a couple of sea bags and a portable MSD.

Extremely shallow draft lets you explore all those waters closed to deeper draft vessels. Add the optional canvas dodger with back flap and screen, and Marsh Hen converts to a roomy weekender allowing you to spend the night in comfort in that special anchorage away from the crowd.

Standard Equipment:

Dacron sail, Dacron running rigging, bilge pump, 2 mooring cleats, bow eye, 3 lifting rings, 3 cu. ft. ice chest, PVC rub rail, 6 opening hatches.

Optional Equipment:

Custom cockpit cushions, outboard motor bracket, 7' canvas dodger with zippered roll-up flap aft and screens for over-nighting, trailer, portable MSD, stainless steel lifting bridle, Silva Universal compass.

Specifications:

LOA	17'
LWL	16' 3"
BEAM	6'
DRAFT	6" Bd. up 3' Bd. down
WEIGHT	600#
SAIL AREA	150 sq. ft. 85 sq. ft. (reefed)

Spars: Aluminum
Sail: 4.5 oz. — Dacron
Tiller: Seasoned ash
Trim: Teak
Hardware: Stainless steel
Running rigging: Dacron

coaming surrounds the 12 foot cockpit keeping her dry while providing security and giving the skipper and crew comfortable back rests. There's room to lounge or sunbathe, nap, fish or whatever, without rubbing elbows with your companions.

A three cubic foot built-in ice box keeps a weekend's worth of beer and groceries cold. Six hatches give access to space under

Force Engineering
5329 Ashton Court
Sarasota, Florida 33583

STILETTO

Advanced technology from the aerospace industry makes Stiletto the fastest trailerable cruiser in America. It's 1,100 pounds (sail-away) light. And strong. Because Stiletto is made from the same pre-impregnated epoxy/fiberglass skin and honeycomb core that gives lightness and strength to Boeing's 747, the F-111 and the Space Shuttle.

Beyond the high strength-to-weight ratio, Stiletto's unique construction makes her totally unsinkable and rot proof. Maintenance is nil.

Standard Equipment:

(Some items optional or not available on all models)

SAILS
Main: 7 oz. cloth (230 ft.²) with reef points. Fully battened.
Jib: 6½ oz. cloth (106 ft.²).

MAIN SHEET
Harken 7-part with hexratchet.

TRAVELER
3-part roller bearing with full length anodized track.

JIB SHEET
Harken 2-part with hexratchet.

ADJUSTABLE TILLER EXTENSION
Anodized aluminum.

KICK-UP RUDDERS
Unique design has automatic return to locked-down position.

INTERNAL WIRE HALYARD WITH ROPE TAILS
Main and jib.

LINEAR POLYURETHANE COATING
Rotating mast, cross beams, boom and all molded fiberglass parts coated in durable polyurethane for long lasting beauty and protection.

JUMPER STAY
Allows fine tuning while preventing overbending of mast.

LUFF FEEDER
Stainless steel sail guide eases mainsail raising.

FORWARD TRAMPOLINE
Polypropolene mesh. The ultimate sun lounger. Doubles usable deck area.

DELUXE FINISHED INTERIOR
Luxuriously lined with Ozite's Aqua Tuft II marine carpeting for the ultimate in cozy comfort.

FULL LENGTH BERTHS
Complete with storage access panels.

DELUXE BERTH CUSHIONS
3" P-65 firm density foam. Covered in long lasting Herculon.

DELUXE ELECTRICAL PACKAGE
Navigational lights, anchor light, spreader light, interior lights, all controlled from built-in switch console with voltmeter. Battery and battery box.

DELUXE GALLEY
Simple and functional. Formica surfaces, stainless steel sink, 2 gallon water tank, hand pump, drawers and additional storage space.

DELUXE HEAD
Self contained portable toilet in handy-but-hidden compartment.

FLOOR BOARDS
Exotic teak and holly. Classy and traditional. Removable.

CHAIN LOCKER
Hide-away design for anchor, chain and rope storage.

STORAGE SHELVES
Located in each nacelle, these shelves provide convenient storage for wallets, sunglasses, keys and other keepables.

DECK HATCHES
Tough, light-weight Lexan. Provide added interior light, ventilation and cabin access.

BRIDGEDECK SEAT CUSHIONS
Comfortable 3" P-35 firm density foam covered with foam backed vinyl.

OUTBOARD BRACKET
Custom designed. Sturdy aluminum construction. Attaches at centerline of aft torsion tube. Up to 15 h.p.

BRIDGEDECK TENT
Custom tailored 4 oz. polyester oxford cloth, polyurethane coated. Encloses entire bridgedeck, including nacelles. Zippered windows with mosquito netting for added comfort and visibility.

SLEEPING TENT
Mounts on forward trampoline to provide on-deck sleeping area with protection against weather. Sitting headroom.

SUNSHADE
Covers entire bridgedeck (10 x 14). Includes adjustable whisker pole to support rear edge. Same roof as bridgedeck tent.

HEAD
Self-contained portable toilet and mounting platform. Mounts at aft end of nacelle.

GALLEY
Includes sink, water tank, hand pump, storage area. Removable for day racing.

REMOVABLE BERTHS
7' coated aluminum frame with vinyl webbing. Removable for use on bridgedeck or for bridgedeck or for beach lounging. Light, washable and mildew resistant.

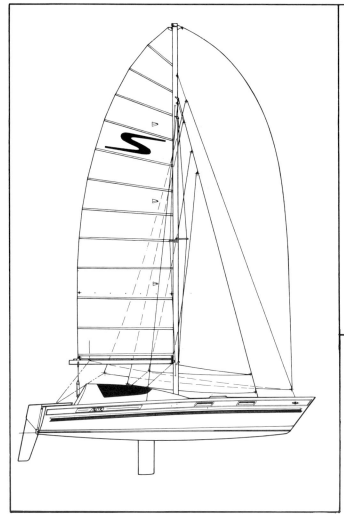

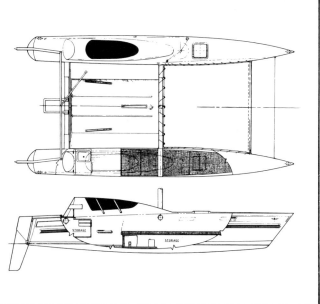

BERTH CUSHIONS
2″ foam pads covered in vinyl.

VENTILATORS
Low profile snap-in vents for added ventilation. Cover plates included.

VENTILATOR PACKAGE
Provides constant flow-thru ventilation. Scoop vents on foredecks and cowl vents on after end of nacelles.

COWL VENTS
Mounted on after end of nacelles.

PORTLIGHTS
Stylish and functional. Made of molded Lexan, they add a touch of class outside and tinted light inside.

COMPASS WITH MOUNT
Mounted on centerline of bridgedeck. *Unlighted.*

DUAL COMPASSES
Two deck-mounted Danforth "Corinthians." *Lighted.*

DUAL RACING COMPASSES
Two deck-mounted Suunto K-16 tactical compasses. *Unlighted.*

BOARDING LADDER
Light-weight folding ladder made of injection molded structural foam. Specially modified for Stiletto. Includes hardware.

TRANSOM STEPS
Injection molded "Zytel" steps permanently mounted to transom.

BOTTOM PAINT
U.S. MARINE Coating Polycop. Red, blue, brown.

JIFFY REEFING
Includes all necessary hardware and line.

SAFETY EQUIPMENT PACKAGE
All USCG approved. 6 life vests. 1 buoyant cushion. Two-fire extinguishers. 1 Viking aluminum anchor w/6′ vinyl coated 5/16″ chain and 100′ nylon line with end splices. 1 air horn with refill. 1 fog bell. 1 waterproof spotlight. 2 fenders 5″ x 20″. 1 marine signaling kit.

HALYARD WINCH
Allows easy mainsail raising.

WINCH HANDLE
Fits both halyard and deck winches.

TELEFLEX SINGLE LEVER OUTBOARD CONTROL
Single lever outboard motor shift and throttle control with removable handle.

RUBRAILS
Full hull-length protection against docks, pilings, etc.

VHF RADIO
Horizon 25 VHF radio with antenna, 25 watts of power.

DELUXE VHF RADIO
IMI 5500 VHF radio, 85 channel, fully synthesized with both international and U.S. channels. Antenna included.

VHF ANTENNA ONLY
Installed at mast head. Cable runs to electrical panel.

STEREO SYSTEM
IMI "Combi Standard" component stereo system. Includes 2 polyplaner waterproof speakers AM/FM stereo tuner with auto search. Stereo cassette deck with auto reverse and Dolby 40 watt amplifier. AM/FM amplified antenna.

DELUXE STEREO SYSTEM
IMI "Combi Plus" component stereo system. Same as above *plus* graphic equalizer.

SOLAR PANEL
Solar International 1270M panel. Peak power output 9 watts. Keeps battery at full charge 15" x 16½" x 1". Mounts on deck hatch.

GENOA
5 oz. cloth (159 ft²). Increases windward performance in light to medium air Complete with hardware. Uses standard halyard and sheets (w/window add $20.00).

REACHER DRIFTER PACKAGE
1½ oz. spinnaker cloth (265 ft²). Dramatically increases light air performance in off-wind conditions. Complete with rigging and hardware.
Hardware only.
Sail only.

QUICK DOWNHAUL
For jib and genoa 6:1 downhaul with lead to crew position on bridgedeck.

WINCHES
#6 deck mounted sheet winches

for reacher drifter and/or spinnaker.

WHISKER POLE
Adjustable 6' to 12' with self-latching hook on each end. Aluminum.

COLOR CODED SHEETS
Colors allow fast identification.

ROLLER FURLER
Schaefer's furling system specially adapted for Stiletto's reacher/drifter. Hardware included.

SPINNAKER PACKAGE
¾ oz. cloth (750 ft²) Assymetrical, poleless, masthead spinnaker with adjustable running backstays. Two #6 winches and handle, halyard, and all related hardware.

SAIL COVER
Full length protection. Stainless steel twist-lock snaps.

DUAL KNOTMETERS
Self-powered, 0–20 knots w/expand function. Paddle-wheel sensor. *Lighted.*

DIGITAL KNOTMETER
Datamarine "Corinthian" digital knotmeter 0–30 knots with tripmeter. Requires 12 v-power Model S-100KL. (With 10,000 mile non-resettable log, add $100 Model CL-100).

CUSTOM TRAILER
Designed with telescoping feature. Makes assembling and launching a breeze. Hot-dip galvanizing Twin Axles. Winch. Mast raising (and lowering) lever. Waterproof lights. Tie-down straps.

STORAGE COVER
Custom tailored 4 oz. polyester oxford cloth (beige) with polyurethane coating. Protects your Stiletto from the elements while she's in a trailering position.

Specifications:

LOA
26' 10"

LWL
24'

BEAM
13' 10"

TELESCOPED WIDTH
7' 11½"

SET UP TIME
1 hr.

DRAFT
9" board up
4' board down

SAIL AREA

Main
230 sq. ft. (fully battened)

Jib
106 sq. ft.

Genoa
159 sq. ft.

Reacher/Drifter
265 sq. ft.

Spinnaker
750 sq. ft.

HULL
Aircraft epoxy/fiberglass and honeycomb composite

WEIGHT
1,100 lbs. Std. Stiletto; 1,200 lbs. Championship Edition; 1,265 lbs. Special Edition

DESIGN SPEED
22 MPH +

MAST
Polyurethane coated aluminum extrusion (rotating airfoil design)

BRIDGEDECK
Fiberglass with molded seats

DAGGERBOARD
Centerline mounted

RUDDERS
Automatic kick-up and return

STANDING RIGGING
Stainless steel

RUNNING RIGGING
Harken blocks throughout, Internal halyards, Full length traveler

MISC. HARDWARE
Custom stainless steel

AUXILIARY
Custom bracket for up to 15 h.p. outboard

Golden Era Boats, Inc.
Marsh Road
Noauk, Connecticut 06340

PETREL

Petrel's history really began with a smaller predecessor. In 1914 Nathaneal Herreshoff designed a 12 foot 6 inch waterline boat for use by children on Buzzards Bay. Sailing qualities of this full keel gaff rigged sloop, initially designated the H-12½, quickly made it popular with sailors of all ages. Ultimately hundreds of these delightful boats were built; many of them surviving and being enjoyed to this day. Timelessness of the design encouraged two companies, Doughdish, Inc. and Cape Cod Shipbuilding Company, Inc., to build fiberglass versions which they currently call the H-12½, Doughdish and Bullseye.

Success of the H-12½ prompted Mr. Herreshoff in 1916 to design a larger version for those who wanted the same great sailing qualities but preferred a more roomy cockpit, greater speed, and a reasonable amount of covered storage. Waterline length of these boats was 16 feet and so, following its forerunner, it was called the Herreshoff 16 footer by the builder. Similarity of the boats is clear in the profile shape, transom form, and shearline. Although the boat was offered with a gaff rig akin to the

12½, most were furnished with a marconi mainsail. During the period between 1916 and 1925 forty of these 16 footers were produced. All were referred to as members of the Fish Class except for the last batch of seven which was called the Warick Neck Class. Several years later, in 1939, a few boats named Marlins were built with expanded accommodations. As with the H-12½, many of these boats have been held in such high esteem by their owners that they have been preferred and kept in service for more than fifty years. In the Mystic, Connecticut area alone there presently are six such gems, several of which are regularly entered in local around the buoy races.

Petrel is a reproduction of the Fish Class retaining the hull form, rig and appearance of its wood forbearer. The high maintenance wood hull and deck have been replaced, however, with seamless low maintenance fiberglass.

Main characteristics of the hull are its full keel, high ballast to displacement ratio, and full sections with substantial deadrise. This combination provides a high degree of lateral and directional stability and produces a soft, easy motion when under way. One gets the impression of being in a considerably larger boat. The hull is easily driven and nicely balanced with the rig. The helm is generally quite light and the boat obediently rounds up when the helm is released. The outboard rudder is simple in concept, readily dismounted, and easily maintained.

An exceptional feature of the boat is the cockpit. It is deep and roomy with wide seats, coamings suporting the back at the shoulder blades, and more than ample legroom. Seats, not including the lazarette top, are 6 feet 8 inches long and about 20 inches wide, thus corresponding in size to generous bunks. The arrangement gives the feeling of sitting in the boat rather than on it, promotes crew security and dryness, and permits many hours of sailing without undue fatigue. When the warm presence of

a good deal of wood is added the resulting cockpit is difficult to match in other boats regardless of size.

Two arrangements within the enclosed cuddy are available. In the standard version a watertight bulkhead is provided just ahead of the mast making the forward portion of the boat into a flotation chamber. This chamber, together with the hull foam core discussed below and sealed enclosure under the lazarette, provide positive buoyancy. The resultant cuddy is big enough for two adults to sit comfortably and for the dry stowage of a substantial amount of gear. A v-berth arrangement is also offered in which the watertight bulkhead is moved forward, flotation chambers built in under the berth to retain the positive buoyancy, and a cowl vent added on deck to increase ventilation.

Petrel's Standard Marconi main and jib provide plenty of sail area for ghosting along on ultra-light zephyrs. In winds up to 20 knots or so she'll go happily on all points with no adjustment of sail plan. Comfort and prudence would dictate tucking in a reef in more blustery conditions. Two rows of reef points are provided in the main for this purpose. Reefing may sound like a bother to some, particularly those who have never done it, but it is simple, can be done quickly by one person, and should be within every knowledgeable sailor's store of information.

It would be difficult to make the rig any more straight-forward. There are no winches or other complicated gear. All lines lead to the cockpit. The jib is self-tending so coming about amounts to nothing more than gently putting over the helm. Originally the boats had running backstays. However, on later models these stays were replaced with a second set of fixed upper shouds. This change was de-

finitely an improvement and a simplification and has been used on Petrel. Some of the original boats carried a gaff mainsail. Petrel can be provided with this sail plan if so desired. Sail area is the same as for the standard rig.

The hull is made using the foam cored fiberglass sandwich technique. As in typical fiberglass construction, the hull is built in a mold. After waxing and gel coating, layers of resin impregnated mat and woven roving are hand laid onto the coated mold surface. In ordinary construction the process would be complete at this point. However, in building Petrel a ⅜ inch thick sheet of Airex polyvinyl chloride foam is glassed to the layup with several layers of mat and roving subsequently applied on top of it. The result is a glass-foam-glass laminate which has been shown to be superior to normal fiberglass construction in several ways. Inclusion of the foam produces a stiffening effect similar to that achieved by the web in an I-beam. In a hull this stiffening markedly increases overall rigidity and impact resistance; factors which will prolong boat life and make the hull significantly more damage-proof. In addition, the foam, being very lightweight and being sealed within the hull, provides the several hundred pounds inherent flotation. Finally, the foam is an insulator thus reducing hull interior sweating and wave noise. The deck is of wood-epoxy construction. Marine grade plywood is laid over oak beams and coated on both sides with epoxy resin. The top is finished with a layer of fiberglass cloth set in epoxy to simulate canvas covering.

Ballast is lead, externally mounted and bolted through the hull. Fittings are mostly bronze with stainless steel being used where appropriate. A diaphragm type bilge pump is installed below

the cockpit sole. Spars are solid sitka spruce, sails are dacron, with the rigging being stainless steel wire or twisted dacron line. Cuddy sole, coamings, cockpit seats, sole and doors, transom inner liner, and let-in shear strake are oiled teak. The tiller and boom crutch are oak or ash. The rudder is mahogany treated with an epoxy coating.

Specifications:

LOA
20' 9"

LWL
16' 0"

BEAM
7' 1½"

DRAFT
3' 1½"

DISPLACEMENT
2850 lb.

BALLAST
1400 lb.

SAIL AREA
265 sq. ft.

East West Yachts
P.O. Box 9953
Marina del Rey, California 90291

HARDIN 45

The HARDIN 45 Auxiliary Ketch is ahead of her time . . . a breakthrough in design, style and performance, suited to gracious living aboard, entertaining and long range cruising. The expansive foredeck has room for sun-lounging, easy sail handling and anchoring. The Center-Cockpit concept permits a spacious, light-airy pilot-house area for the galley and dinette with see-out windows port, starboard and *forward*. The Owner's Cabin aft has a huge double berth and finely worked storage cabinetry.

In the HARDIN FLEET tradition the "45" has a heavily hand laminated hull, a one-piece house/deck and over-strength rigging and hardware. She is ketch rigged to be easily handled by man and wife.

Modern hydraulic steering gives fingertip control. Her unusual esthetic beauty tops off a high-stability hull with a moderate draft keel design for fast, stiff-upright sailing. (In selecting your personal yacht consider performance as well as interior arrangement—it becomes most significant later).

Integrity through-out is mirrored in the warmth and richness of carefully selected hardwoods. No unfinished fiberglass is visible from any of the living areas in a HARDIN 45. There is more interior room in this fine yacht than any yacht of her length today. She has two heads, two showers, holding

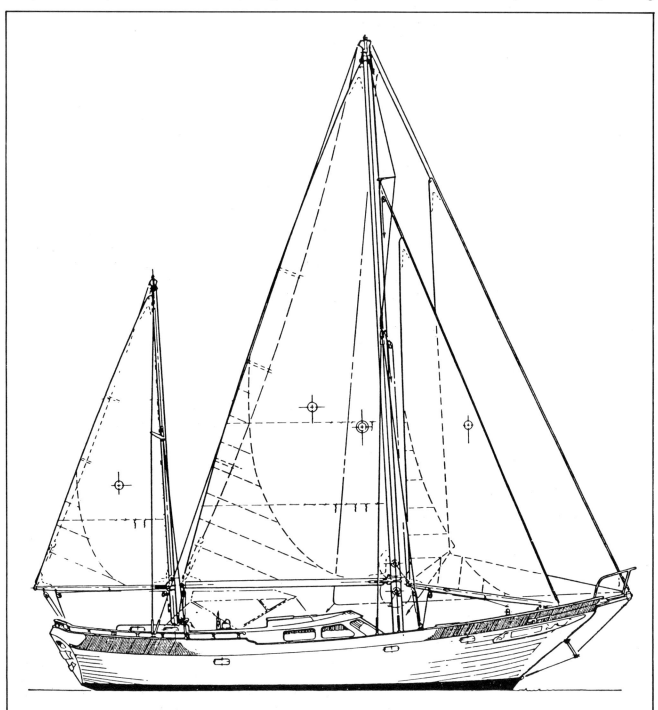

tanks, two walk-thrus, headroom and storage everywhere. (Overheard at a Boat Show, "Where have other designers been?").

The modern powerful diesel is openly accessible from both sides and with 180 gallons of fuel she can power at cruising speed for over 6 days and nights without a shutdown. All thru-hull fittings have sea cock valves. Tapping the 200 gallons of fresh water storage, hot water is supplied to the galley and both head basins. General construction follows recommendations of Gibbs and Cox and the American Bureau of Shipping standards.

Standard Equipment:

HULL
One piece molded fiberglass. Molded house with non-skid deck. Bronze through-hulls with sea cocks. Four hatches and all opening ports.

SAILS
Jib, Staysail, Main & Mizzen of 8 oz. dacron. High quality craftsmanship.

SPARS
Ketch rigged with club-footed staysail. Wood spars, painted are standard.

RIGGING
Over-strength S.S. standing rigging with S.S. turnbuckles of superior quality. Six winches (two are two-speed). Travelers and tracks/cars. Dacron running rigging.

DECK
S.S. bow pulpit, thru-bolted lifelines, cleats & chocks. Self-bailing center cockpit with wide teak seats and teak floor. Teak taff rail. Bow rollers. Non-skid standard, teak optional.

STEERING
"One finger" hydraulic. 30" teak wheel. Emergency tiller available.

ENGINE
Marine Diesel Auxiliary reduction & reverse gear. Alternator, filter, controls and instrument panel. Fresh water cooled.

TANKS
180 gallons fuel and 200 water in 2 fiberglass tanks each. Four deck fills and vents.

ELECTRICAL
12v lighting, running & spreader lights, with breakers. Ten 110v outlets.

GALLEY
Deep double S.S. sink, hot and cold pressure water, ice box and pull-out teak bar. Space for oven/range. Galley mate looks out windows.

PILOT HOUSE
Dinette w/4" cushions, see-out safety glass windows all around. Parquet floors.

SALOON
Settee berths port and starboard with uppers. Fourteen drawers over and under, 4 double and 3 single lockers. Opening ports and skylight hatch. Door louvered for ventilation and appearance.

FOREPEAK
Head and shower, spacious sail locker and access to chain locker. Opening ports. Hatch.

CHART ROOM
With ice box, chart area, engine access, drawers and hanging locker, opening port. Opening hatch over.

MASTER STATEROOM
56" x 78" double berth, 4" mattress, vanity with mirror, transom windows, access to rudder post fitting and Aqua-lift tank.

GUEST STATEROOM
Single or upper & lower w/drawers under. Engine access and opening port, privacy door to aft head.

Specifications:

LENGTH OVER DECK
45' 2"

LENGTH WATER LINE
34' 6"

BEAM AT DECK
13' 4"

BEAM AT WATERLINE
12' 6"

DRAFT
5' 6"

DISPLACEMENT
32,000 lbs.

BALLAST (IRON)
8,500 lbs.

SAIL AREA
809 sq. ft.

Harmonie Aluminum Yachts, Inc.
11368 Alfred, Montréal-Nord Quebec, Canada H1G 5B9

HARMONIE 11m

Designed by Robert Dufour
Designer's Comments:
The Harmonie 11m is probably the first aluminum sailing yacht in North America conceived specifically for production line construction techniques. Although the material has gained wide acceptance in Europe and is used extensively in one-off construction, (witness the 12 meters and many of the hot racing boats), it has not been used previously for production yachts principally because the construction techniques used required too many man-hours to produce a yacht that could be competitive price-wise even with the high quality fiberglass yachts let alone with the run-of-the-mill variety.

Typically, frames are required about every twelve inches. Lofting, cutting and fitting these diversely shaped pieces puts the labor cost sky-high and out of reach of all but the most determined or fortunate prospective boat owners. Yet, aluminum has much to recommend it as a highly desirable boat building material.

To make aluminum competitive price-wise with the higher priced fiberglass boats, a relatively new construction technique was chosen to design and build Harmonie 11m.

First, to ensure absolute precision and fairness of the hull surfaces, extensive use was made of mathematical tools to generate the hull shape allowing the determination of the exact hull offsets before the lines were in fact drawn. An added bonus is that the programs which allow for the determination of the hull shape in this fashion can also be used to design prefabricated modules and tremendously speed up the set-up of the production jigs as well as the construction of the prototype.

Secondly the boat is built around only seven web frames located at the bulkhead and two deep girders run from the transom aft to just forward the mast location. Additionally there are several closely spaced stringers to lend added rigidity to the hull panels between the main frames. To ensure accurate positioning and conformity of the hull to design dimension, several removable building jigs are installed during construction.

Speed and ease of construction is only one advantage of this building technique, the others are no less important; one is the uncanny fairness it gives the bare aluminum hull since it greatly reduces the effects of weld-induced plate distortion.

Thus the aluminum hull and deck unit can be produced at prices that remain competitive with fiberglass of the better variety and, as a bonus, give the boat owner access to the more desirable engineering properties of aluminum.

Harmonie 11m has the distinctive underwater profile of the modern racer, yet the IOR and assorted rating rules were never considered during the design stage. The aim was to produce a fast and powerful yacht of great strength and durability, allowing its owner comfort in port as well as at sea.

A displacement of 7819 kilos (17222 lbs) does not exactly put it in the lightweight category and would normally induce one to think its weight was in fact excessive until one realizes that it includes provisions for 100 gallons of water and fifty gallons of diesel fuel, a freezer, air conditioner, forced air heater, teak decks, heavy duty electrical batteries, an electric windlass hidden in the foredeck anchor locker, chain and warps and anchor rode enough for the most prudent skipper and a host of other niceties so necessary to well deserved enjoyment afloat. Coupled with a ballast displacement ratio of 40%, powerful aft section for good form stability and ability off the wind, a fine entry and highly efficient NACA airfoil type fin and balanced spade rudder, she won't need a team of heavyweights perched out over the weather rail to foot to weather in a blow. Yet excessive weight should not be tolerated aboard a yacht since it penalizes performance, and performance in itself is a major contributor to the crew's and the yacht's safety. Thus, the bulkheads and most of the accommodations are built with balsa cored panels, ultra light and expensive. In short, it's a question of priorities.

Priorities again enter the picture when considering the interior layout. It is well known that forward V-berths are totally useless at sea as a sleeping place and that the most comfortable part of the ship is midship and aft. It is probably the designer's Gallic heritage that leads him to ensure that the cook always has a preferred location on board in which to produce his much appreciated miracles. His location is near midships and he reigns over a compact but complete U-shaped domain, out of everyone's way and securely wedged in place only a step away from a huge freezer-frig compartment and an arm's reach away from the twin dinettes. A center folding panel can be installed to form one huge almost round dining table which would allow the spreading out of the most orgiastic feast for the palate. The tables can be removed and the owner has a large living room.

The dinette seats can be converted to berths: this should only be mentioned fleetingly. Harmonie was not conceived as a floating barrack but is intended to afford privacy to the owner and his guests. Thus, each couple has its own private aft cabin with a full width double berth, each with its own hanging locker. The owner's cabin has a decent chart table and ship's library whereas the guest cabin has a small settee in place of the table. The owner has access to the head directly from his stateroom, crew and guests use the same via the passageway entrance. Heads and Murphy's law being what they are, it was felt best to limit the occurrence of both aboard Harmonie, since too much of either does not necessarily make for true comfort.

What stowage space is lost aft is amply made up for by leaving all of the forepeak area free for sail bag stowage. Access to the deck is enhanced by using an extra large hatch and the use of two ladders, one to port of the hatch and one to starboard; thus, the crew can easily scamper up to the foredeck on either tack.

If below says comfort then topsides spells business. Harmonie sports a narrow cockpit with coamings that reach to armpit level when the crew are seated near its forward end. It doesn't make for a great ballroom floor but offshore the feeling of sheer security such a lay-out provides is uncanny. Noteworthy is the fact that the cockpit sports four 2½″ diameter drains. In spite of the two berths below there is still stowage under the cockpit seats for lines and fenders and a large locker is located under the helmsman's seat. Small objects can be stowed under the coamings.

All halyards lead aft to the cockpit as do the spinnaker pole topping lift and the foreguy. Jibing under spinnaker will be carried out using the dip-pole technique, thus,

the midstay has a quick release lever at its lower end. The mast is a two-spreader type which is not obvious from studying the sail plan. All rigging except for the midstay and the aft intermediate shrouds is Navtec rod. The backstay is split at its lower end to allow easy boarding access via a transom gate and a boarding ladder incorporated in the aft pulpit.

Harmonie sports wide side decks, totally unobstructed for easy and safe passage forward. Even when all the "spaghetti" for spinnaker handling is hauled out, there is only one line running forward along the starboard side deck: the foreguy lies completely flush and out of the way. While on the deck plan, it should be noted that each compartment of the accommodation has its own ventilation hatch as well as its own independent ven-

tilator. Additionally, each aft cabin has an opening portlight thru the aft bulkhead into the cockpit, which can be left open in all but the foulest weather and through which the navigator can communicate with the helmsman.

In these days of super bendy and super thin masts for fractional rigs, the return to the masthead rig must bear some explaining. First then is the fact that the boat has enough "heft" to take it and like it. Secondly is the designer's belief that an owner, worrying about all those funny curves his expensive spar is making up there when it begins to blow, is not worried enough about where he is, where he is going and how to get there best (priorities), but worried too much about whether he will get there at all. Thirdly is the belief that a main boom should, if possible, be kept

out of the cockpit area. When down in the sunny islands, it allows for the setting of a cockpit shade when underway, and, when gybing unexpectedly, it allows one to keep his head solidly on one's shoulders. Shareholders in Bayer may disagree, let them.

While on the subject of spars, it might be appropriate to mention that Harmonie's mast is a one piece extrusion and is totally anodized after all welding has been completed. There are no splices in the mast as is current with other anodized masts. A final note on the rig is that provisions are made for a hydraulic boom vang and backstay adjuster.

As is probably obvious, Harmonie 11m will not be an inexpensive throw-away boat. Were there any doubt left, then witness the special rudder quadrant construction. A rudder shaft of 5" diameter solid aluminum rod, a quadrant, that supports the suspended balanced spade rudder on custom roller bearings, ensure that first, there will be no Fastnet rudders aboard Harmonie 11m, and secondly, even under the most strenuous conditions, control will be fingertip smooth.

"Put the priorities in the right place," it wasn't exactly how the design commission was spelled out at the start, but, as contact between builder and designer progressed, that's just about how it turned out. Frankly, as a designer, it's a view I sort of like when it translates into a boat like Harmonie 11m.

Robert Dufour, SNAME

Standard Equipment:

Marine aluminum alloy hull and deck, all welded construction using inert gas techniques, structure is plating over web frames and longitudinal stringers.

Watertight collision bulkhead with door.

Cast lead ballast encapsulated in aluminum NACA type airfoil fin.

Suspended balanced spade rudder with 5" dia. solid aluminum shaft with custom roller bearing steering quadrant.

3" extruded aluminum toe-rail.

Large forward sail stowage compartment with large opening hatch and ladders, port and starboard, for easy access to deck.

3 cockpit lockers.

Coaming storage compartments.

Helmsman's seat with stowage under.

4 2.5" dia. cockpit drains.

Self draining cockpit seats.

Non-skid coachroof top.

Two hand-holds in forwards end of cockpit.

Foredeck anchor well.

4 mooring cleats.

6 mooring chocks.

Teak side decks.

Teak cockpit sole grating.

Teak cockpit steps.

Anti-fouling bottom paint.

Hull paint, two parts polyurethane.

Bilge painted.

Standard hull color graphics and matching boat topping.

Harmonie logo on hull.

Name and home port painted on hull (at builder's yard during construction).

Two bow rollers.

Bow and stern pulpits, double rail, welded aluminum, anodized or painted with stern gate and swim ladder and bow and stern navigation lights.

Stanchions, anodized or painted and double lifelines aluminum with stainless steel plastic covered wire rope, 30" above deck.

Six UFO type cabin ventilators.

Two Scoop type ventilators set on Dorade boxes.

Cabin side windows.

DECK HATCHES

MAIN SALON
Two 10 x 10 opening deck hatches

HEAD
One 10 x 10 opening deck hatch

GALLEY
One 10 x 10 opening deck hatch.

AFT CABINS
One 10 x 10 opening deck hatch, plus one opening port facing cockpit, port and starboard.

Translucent Lexan sliding main hatch.

Translucent Lexan drop boards and lock.

Pedestal steerer with 30" destroyer type wheel, engine controls and brake with Ritchie Globemaster 6" compass.

Emergency tiller with square lug on rudder shaft head.

Genoa tracks with genoa track cars and end stops.

Mainsheet traveller with car, blocks, and stops.

Primary cockpit winches: 2 Lewmar 48, 2 speeds self-tailing aluminum.

Secondary cockpit winches: 2 Lewmar 40, 2 speeds self-tailing aluminum.

Two winch handles lock-in type.

Deck organizers for all halyards.

Halyards lead back to cockpit.

Double turning blocks for genoa sheets with integral sheet stoppers.

Reefing winch on mainmast for reefing and outhaul.

Safety harness pad-eyes for helmsman in cockpit recesses.

Engine room surrounding lead backed fiberglass wool with aluminum liner.

Bukh 20HP diesel.

Hand crank.

Mechanic transmission and reverse gear ZF, 2.5: 1 reduction.

Stainless steel shaft with aluminum propeller.

Engine tool kit.

Engine spare parts kit.

Pedestal mounted engine controls.

50 gallons fuel tank.

Recessed engine instruments panel in cockpit: voltmeter, tachometer, oil pressure gage, water temperature gage, oil and water alarms and warning lights.

Aluminum anodized (hard or clear) mast and boom.

Navtec rod rigging for forestay, backstay, upper intermediate and single lower shroud.

Stainless steel wire rope intermediate headstay and runners. 1 x 19 type 316.

Mast wiring in conduit tubing.

Internal main (1), jib (2) and spinnaker dacron halyards (2).

Internal spinnaker pole topping lift.

Internal main boom outhaul.

Internal reefing lines.

Dacron main and genoa sheets.

Main and genoa halyards.

Spinnaker pole bell lift winch.

Boom vang.

Boom topping lift.

12V dc and 110V ac system.

Main dc disconnect switch with alternator protection.

61 amp alternator engine mounted.

One 12V 220 A.H. battery.

One 12V 110 A.H. battery.

12 and 110V electrical control panel including volt-ammeters.

QEMPAR automatic battery protection system to ensure that the engine can always be started electrically, includes automatic solid state battery charging priority select.

International rule navigation lights.

Deck floodlight.

Anchor and strobe lights.

12V cabin room lighting throughout including:

Waterproof chain well light

Night light (red and white) in forelocker

Neon lights in all accommodation compartments

Reading lights throughout

Variable indirect saloon lighting

Automatic lights inside all below-counter galley lockers

Manual lights inside hanging lockers

Lights in icebox (or freezer and fridge if fitted)

Chart table lights (1 neon, white and red and 1 flexible arm, white and red)

Engine compartment light

Lazarette light to illuminate rudder quadrant

Portable trouble drop light with 25ft extension

Spotlight plug in cockpit

Spotlight plug in anchor well

Cigarette lighter with light in galley

Compass light

Companionway night light (red and white)

110V system

20 amp battery charger with individual charging system

Shore power receptacle cord and adapter

Galvanic isolater

110V control panel with voltmeter-ammeter

Outlets throughout accommodation

Isolator transformer equipped razor outlet in head

S.R. Mariner NAV. 5 including:

Anemometer

Apparent wind direction indicator

Speedometer

Log

Close-hauled indicator

Depth sounder with alarms, for deep and shallow water and anchor alarm

Instruments pedestal mounted in cockpit

Repeater at navigation table

Thru-deck fitting for VHF coax cable and leader for coax in mast conduit

All matched wood interior finish with ash and walnut hand-rubbed to satin finish

Color coordinated cabin cushions with choices for main and aft cabin to owner's preference

Window curtains

Liquor cabinet

Large and airy main salon for lounging and dining

Four thick color coordinated cabin cushions (choice of color)

Upholstered backrest

One table each side of centerline passage with drop leafs

One additional seat in passageway to fo'c'sle

Plastic lined storage compartments under saloon settees

Headroom 6'3" average

Two aft cabins with double berths in each with hanging lockers, drawer and shelves

Navigation station in the starboard cabin with electric control panel and chart lights (2)

Chart stowage compartment in starboard cabin

Three burners gimbailed CNG stove with oven mounted in insulated stainless steel sheated space

Gas shut-off cock near stove and main shut-off on gas bottle

Stainless steel guard rail in front of stove

Two aluminum gas bottles

Double deep custom stainless steel sink, 12" depth

Pressure fresh water faucet with autoshutting

Sea water faucet

Top loading icebox

Dish and food stowage on shelves

Cutting board counter top

Waste container

Manual bilge pump, capacity 15 gal./min. operated from cockpit

Electrical bilge pump, automatic switch

Hundred gallons of fresh water in 5 tanks

Sea cock on the two thru-hull fittings below the waterline

Dockside fresh water connection

Manually operated head with holding tank (25 gal. appr.)

Custom stainless steel sink in vanity, 9" depth

Pressure fresh water system with autoshutting faucets

Mirror and locker

Towel bar

Paper holder

Grab rail and hand hold

Oilskin hooks

Private entrance from owner's cabin

Owner's manual in watertight pouch with drawings detailing electrical dc and ac circuits, plumbing, hydraulics and engine as well as all other equipment as supplied by equipment manufacturer. Contains sail plan dimensions for sailmaker

Ensign pole

One 20 lb. Danforth hi-tensile anchor

200 ft of nylon anchor rode

Two mooring warps of 50ft each

Four bumpers

One telescoping boathook

Safety belt for cook with attachment hooks

Harmonie logo for mainsail

Bosun's chair

Specifications:

LENGTH OVERALL
(36'1")

LENGTH WATERLINE
(29'6")

BEAM
(12'2")

DRAFT
(5'11")

DRAFT (SHOAL DRAFT KEEL)
(5'3")

DISPLACEMENT
(17000 lbs)

BALLAST, LEAD
(6957 lbs)

SAIL AREA (100% f. triangle)
(611 ft²)

MAINSAIL AREA
(260 ft²)

NO. 1 GENOA
(558 ft²)

NO. 2 GENOA
(470 ft²)

WORKING JIB
(360 ft²)

STORM JIB
(125 ft²)

SPINNAKER
(1299 ft²)

POWER

FUEL
(50 gal.)

FRESH WATER (5 separate tanks)
(100 gal.)

BALLAST DISPLACEMENT RATIO

DISPLACEMENT LENGTH RATIO

SAIL AREA DISPLACEMENT RATIO

FREEBOARD AT STEM
(4 ft)

FREEBOARD AT STERN
(3 ft)

Hinterhoeller Yachts Limited

8 Keefer Road
St. Catharines, Ontario, Canada
L2M 7N9

NONSUCH 30

Designed by Mark Ellis Design Limited

The Nonsuch 30 retains the traditional features of the catboat hull such as the almost plumb stem, a long, low sheerline and a cabin trunk that blends into the cockpit coaming. But from there on, it is different. The underbody is that of a dinghy—shallow and flat with a low-aspect ratio fin keel followed by a spade rudder that actually extends beyond the transom. Since you don't normally see the underbody, the appearance is that of a traditional catboat, but looks are deceiving.

Construction of the Nonsuch 30 is fiberglass sandwich with end-grain balsa core in the hull as well as the decks and top of the cabin. Unidirectional glass roving is incorporated in areas of high stress in the hull. The lead keel is external and bolted to the hull.

The interior of the boat has all of the roominess associated with the wide-beam catboats of earlier years combined with contemporary amenities. Single and double quarterberths aft plus convertible salon settees provide berthing for five persons. Midships is the galley to port and the head compartment to starboard with plenty of walking space between. The salon, with a large drop-leaf dining room table, is forward and can be closed off from the rest of the boat for privacy.

The forecastle/forepeak of a catboat takes on a grossly different appearance than other boats because it contains the mast step structure. Loads which normally are taken from the mast to the hull through widely spaced shrouds and stays, now have to be taken off the base of the cantilevered mast in a very constrained area. Hence, if you look into the forward end of the Nonsuch hull, you will see a very sturdy box-like structure that distributes mast loads into the hull.

This is not wasted space, however, for all the compartments between structural panels become storage bins of one sort or another. Entry to this area is gained through

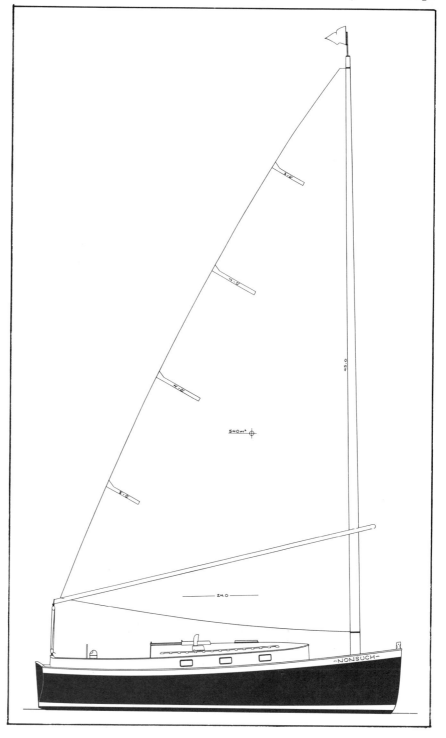

two hanging lockers, one on either side of the forward salon bulkhead.

Although the interior has an abundance of teak in it, the overall appearance is not dark because of the light-colored molded fiberglass headliner. The headliner covers the arched top of the cabin and extends down the trunk to the deck ledge where it terminates behind a fingergrip handrail running the length of the cabin on both sides.

The sailing rig is kept simple in line with the idea of a cat rig. What really differs from the earlier catrigged boats is the use of the wishbone boom instead of a foot boom. With the wishbone the sail is free-footed and the angle at which the boom hangs keeps the sail evenly tensioned.

Flattening of the sail is not accomplished with the conventional outhaul that pulls the clew of the sail towards the end of the boom, rather, the wishbone with clew firmly attached is pulled aft flattening the sail. The device that does this is called a choker and it is operated from the cockpit as a normal sail handling line. This is an improvement in itself over boom-footed mainsails that have the outhaul at boom level causing lazy crews not to properly shape the sail when changing points of sail.

The cat sail can be slab reefed similar to any mainsail except with the full-time lazyjacks installed; the reefed sail never gets away from you. These same lazyjacks are a real plus when lowering the sail. Just release the halyard and let the sail drop into the lazyjack pocket—nothing could be simpler.

Standard Equipment:

Molded Cove and Boot; Dark Blue.

Westerbeke 27 diesel Engine with vee drive; fresh water cooling, full instrumentation.

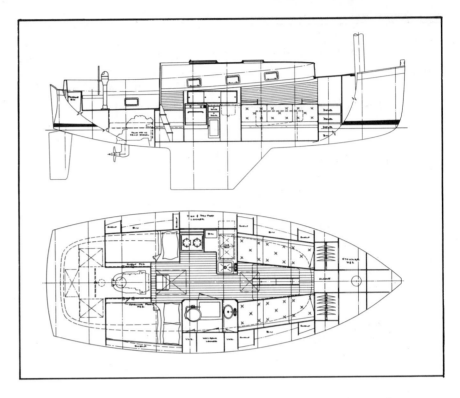

55 Amp Alternator.

Two 105 amp Batteries, with enclosure boxes.

Explosion proof master battery selection switch.

12 Volt accessory breaker panel with battery condition meter.

Fluorescent Lighting at head and Galley areas, and overhead in main cabin.

Regulation Offshore Running Lights.

Pedestal steering with integral shift and throttle controls, 28 inch stainless steel destroyer wheel.

5″ Binnacle compass with light and cover.

Self-tailing mainsheet winch on coaming.

Cold pressure water system with faucets at Galley and Vanity.

Fresh Water Foot Pump at galley.

Propane, stainless steel, gimballed 2 burner stove with oven.

Propane solenoid shut off system.

Safety bar across front of stove.

Teak grating and molded shower sump in head.

Stainless steel stanchions.

Upper life lines, stainless steel wire vinyl coated.

Double rail stern pulpit with integral boarding ladder.

Nine framed translucent opening ports with screens.

Aluminum framed translucent skylight hatch.

Curtain wires on all main cabin ports.

Double, flush drop leaf table with two deep storage wells.

Varnished teak cabin sole throughout.

Full length molded bulwarks with anodized aluminum toe rail cap.

Mooring bit at stem.

Large recessed side deck drains.

Four Barient winches and two handles.

Spin-tapered anodized aluminum, free standing spar.

Nicro-fico cup sheet main halyard led aft to cockpit.

Anodized aluminum wishbone boom.

Burgee halyard to masthead.

All reef lines and outhaul, led aft to cockpit.

Anchor light and steaming light on spar.

Lighting grounded spar.

2½″ closed flotation foam helmsman's cushion.

Teak handrails on cabin top.

Two lucite topped dorade boxes on cabin top.

Nosing trim around cabin house and cockpit coamings.

Three hanging lockers.

Eight drawers, all with varnished interior.

Full length teak grab rails in cabin.

Zippered, upholstered berth top cushions and backrests.

Companionway hatch panel with teak louvres, screen and cover board.

Teak finger pull rings on drawers and locker doors.

Side access to locker under forward settees.

Teak grab rails at companionway.

Swivel Reading Lights at settees and quarter berths.

Light in engine compartment.

Two fire extinguishers.

Varnished pine strapping accent over settee shelves.

Sacrificial Zinc on propeller shaft.

Midship mooring cleats and closed chocks.

Balsa cored hull and deck.

Detailed Owner's Manual.

Specifications:

LOA
30′4″

DWL
28′9″

MAXIMUM BEAM
11′10″

SAIL AREA
540 sq. ft.

DRAFT
4′11½″ (1.51 m)—shallow draft keel 3′11½

DISPLACEMENT
(approximately) 11,500 lbs.

BALLAST
(approximately) 4,500 lbs. lead

NIAGARA 31

Designed by Mark Ellis Design Ltd. The Niagara 31 is a dry sailing sloop rig which can be easily singlehanded or sailed comfortably by a couple. The cabin features a restaurant-like booth settee on the port side, facing a bench settee that converts to a berth. It has a fully enclosed head and large hanging lockers. The L-shaped galley has a two-burner propane stove, a deep stainless steel sink and ice box. Opposite the galley is a convenient chart table with swinging navigator's seat, combination red and white fluorescent lights overhead.

Standard Equipment:

Molded Cove and Double Boot; Dark Blue.

Westerbeke 21 diesel Engine with Vee drive; fresh water cooling; full instrumentation.

55 Amp Alternator.

Two 105 amp Batteries with enclosure boxes.

Explosion Proof Master Battery Selection Switch.

Regulation Offshore Running Lights.

12 Volt Accessory Breaker Panel with battery condition meter.

Fluorescent Light with red night light over chart table.

Fresh Water Foot Pumps at galley, and vanity sinks.

Deep Stainless Steel Sink at galley, oval sink at vanity.

Six Swivel, Reading Lights.

Fluorescent Lights in Head, Galley and Main Cabin areas.

Propane Gimballed stainless steel two burner stove.

Propanoid solenoid shut-off system.

Pedestal Wheel Steering with integral shift and throttle control; 30 inch stainless steel wheel.

5″ Binnacle Mounted Compass with light and cover.

Double Rail Welded Bow Pulpit.

Double Rail Welded Stern Pulpit with Integral Boarding ladder.

Stainless Steel Vinyl Coated Life Lines with Pelican Hook Gates at aft end.

Two Screened Translucent Opening Ports.

Large, Aluminum Framed Translucent Skylight.

Hatch and Foredeck Hatch.

Four large, framed Translucent Fixed Ports.

Six Barient Winches, Three Handles.

Large recessed side Deck Drains.

Molded, full-length Bulkwards with anodized aluminum Toe Rail cap and Integral Track.

Inboard sheeting tracks.

Teak Handrails on cabin top.

Four large anodized aluminum closed mooring chocks and cleats.

Fully enclosed mast wiring duct.

YACHTS

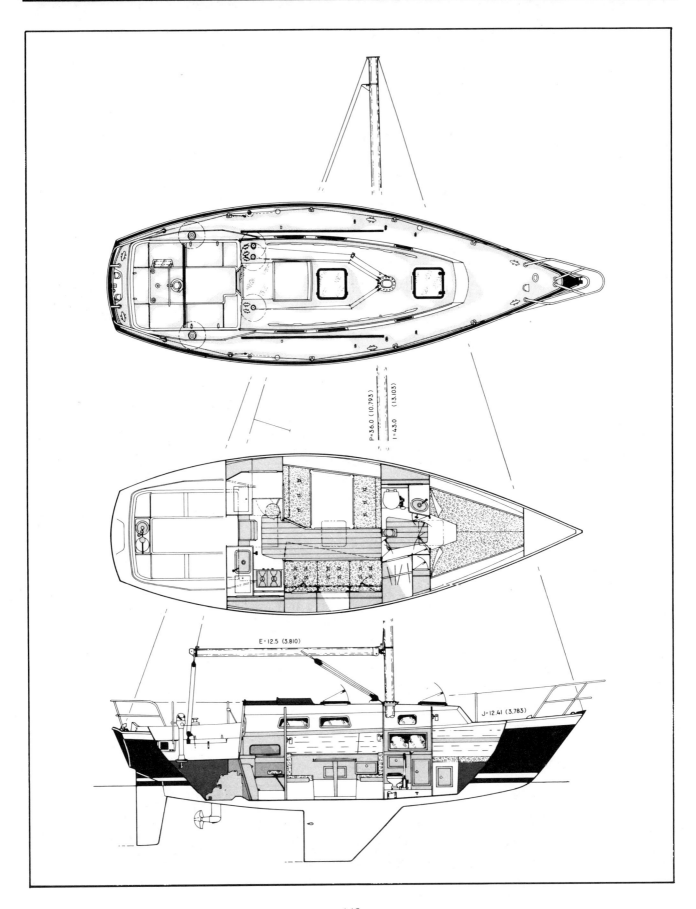

P=36.0 (10.793) I=43.0 (13.105)

E=12.5 (3.810)

J=12.41 (3.783)

148

Navtec stainless steel rod rigging.

Internal reef lines and clew outhaul, all led to aft cabin.

Clam Cleats for Primary Sheet Winches.

Boom Vang.

Spliced wire to rope main and genoa halyards.

Anchor light at masthead.

Steaming light and foredeck flood light on mast.

Anodized aluminum mast and boom.

Tapered, Air foil shaped aluminum spreaders.

Lightning grounded spar.

Varnished teak cabin sole, teak grating forward.

Zippered, upholstered cushions and backrests.

Five drawers, varnished inside.

Teak finger pulls on drawers and locker doors.

Side access to locker under forward dinette and settee.

Varnished pine strapping in bookcase over dinette shelf and over vee berth.

Bi-fold doors to head and to vee berth.

Large, fully insulated ice chest with teak grating, dividers and insulated lid.

Closed cell foam helmsman's bench cushion.

Two Fire Extinguishers.

Balsa Cored deck.

Sacrificial Zinc on propeller shaft.

Detailed owner's manual.

Specifications:

LOA
31'3" (9.53 m)

DWL
24'3" (7.39 m)

MAXIMUM BEAM
10'3½" (3.14 m)

DRAFT
5'0" (1.52 m)

SAIL AREA
(100% foretriangle) 491.82 sq. ft./ 45.67 sq. mtrs.

DISPLACEMENT
(approximately) 8,500 lbs. (3855 kg)

BALLAST
(approximately): 3550 lbs. lead (1610 kg)

NIAGARA 35

Designed by Mark Ellis Design Ltd. The Niagara 35 hull design is an external lead fin keel with a semi-balanced spade rudder. The decks are clean and cleared with plenty of seating and leg room in the large cockpit.

Three framed skylights, a translucent foredeck hatch and ten ports let loads of light into the salon and cabins. The ample galley boasts a three burner stove and a seven cubic foot capacity top loading ice chest with a double hinged, insulated lid. The cabin appointments are beautifully detailed making the Niagara a fine live-aboard boat. The luxury of a private captain's cabin adds to its appeal.

Standard Equipment:

Molded boot top; dark blue.

Westerbeke 27 diesel engine with Vee drive, fresh water cooling, full instrumentation.

55 Amp alternator.

Two 105 amp batteries with enclosure boxes.

Explosion proof master battery selection switch.

12 volt accessory breaker panel and battery condition meter.

Regulation offshore running lights.

110 volt, 30 amp shore power system.

Six swivel reading lights.

Fluorescent lighting at galley, head area, and over main cabin table.

Fluorescent light with red night light over chart table.

Cold pressure water system with faucets at galley and vanity.

Fresh water foot pump at galley sink.

Deep stainless steel sink at galley, oval stainless steel sink at vanity.

Propane, gimballed three burner stove with oven.

Propane solenoid shut off.

Pedestal steering with 32" stainless steel destroyer wheel.

Binnacle mounted compass with light and cover.

Double rail welded stainless steel bow pulpit.

Double rail welded stainless steel stern pulpit with integral fold-down boarding ladder.

Stainless steel wire vinyl coated life lines with pelican.

Hook gates at aft end, stainless steel stanchions, braces on aft stanchions.

Six screened framed translucent opening ports.

Three aluminum framed skylight hatches.

Large aluminum framed translucent foredeck hatch.

Four framed translucent fixed ports.

Six barient winches and three handles.

Two aluminum anchor rollers on bowsprit, anchor hawse pipe in foredeck to chain locker.

Large recessed side deck drains.

Molded full length bulwarks with anodized aluminum cap and integral sail track.

Inboard sheeting tracks for jib.

Teak handrails on cabintop.

Dorade box on deck with vents to head and galley areas.

Louvered companionway panel with screen and cover.

Four large aluminum fairlead chocks and mooring cleats.

Two aluminum midship mooring cleats with closed chocks.

Navtec stainless steel rod rigging.

Two internal outboard reeflines and clew outhaul, led aft.

Cunningham led aft.

Boom vang.

Spliced wire to rope main and genoa halyard.

Anchor light at masthead.

Steaming light and foredeck flood light on spar.

Anodized aluminum mast and boom.

Tapered air-foil shaped anodized aluminum spreaders.

Lightning grounded spar.

Fully enclosed wiring duct in spar.

Teak grating and molded shower sump in head.

Curtain wires on cabin windows.

Double drop leaf table with deep stowage wells.

Varnished teak cabin sole.

Zippered upholstered berth cushions and backrests.

Eight drawers, varnished inside.

Teak finger pull rings on locker doors and drawers.

Side access to lockers under forward settees.

Three full height cabin doors, one louvered.

Fully enclosed head area with separate access from both cabins.

Full length teak grab ledge in cabin at side deck.

Teak grab rails at companionway.

Varnished pine strapping over quarter berths and in book shelves.

Large fully insulated top loading ice chest with hinged insulated lid and teak gratings.

2½" thick closed cell flotation foam helmsman's cushion vinyl covered.

Two fire extinguishers.

Balsa cored hull and deck.

Sacrificial zinc on propeller shaft.

Detailed owner's manual.

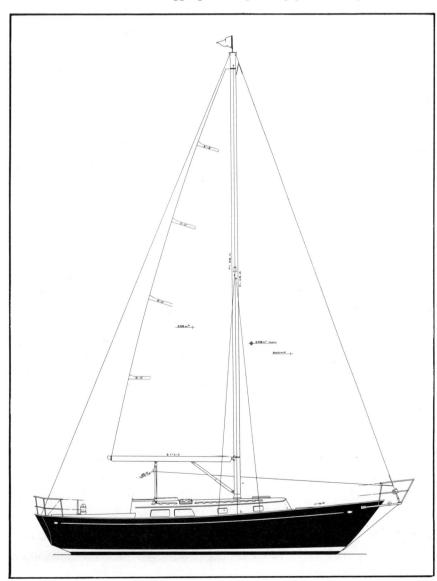

Homar Boats, Inc.
983 New Durham Road
Edison, New Jersey 08817

PHANTOM

The Phantom begins with a generous 4'5" beam. Parents and beginners welcome this as it provides outstanding stability and sailing ease. Should the Phantom capsize (you have to try hard to do it), it can be righted in a jiffy to make capsizing fun.

The simple lateen rig is easy to handle. Its fully drafted sail and sleeved luff is more efficient to give more driving power. Unlike the old-fashioned clip-on sail attachment, the sleeved method is easier, faster and much less trouble.

Other factors that contribute to the speed and performance of the Phantom are its special kick-up spade rudder and daggerboard. Both are molded from high impact plastic and hydrodynamically shaped for speed and maneuverability.

There's more beauty to the Phantom than its sleek graceful lines. A high sharp bow minimizes submarining downwind and optimizes upwind performance. Broad flat sections aft make the Phantom plane quicker and faster and offer stability not found on other boats of this type. This, combined with the capabilities of the Phantom to windward, is a racing skipper's delight.

The Phantom is quality construction throughout. Its rugged hand laid-up fiberglass hull and deck are beautifully finished with no rough surfaces or sharp edges. Weight is rigidly controlled for closer one-design racing. All hardware is bedded and backed with aluminum plates. Flotation is molded in. Every hull is factory tested with air pressure for watertight integrity.

Specifications:

LOA
14'1½"

LWL
10'6"

BEAM
4'5"

DRAFT
34"

SAIL AREA
84.5 sq. ft.

Hunter Marine
P.O. Box 1030, Route 441
Alachua, Florida 32615

HUNTER 19

The 19's roomy cockpit makes her an ideal and pleasant daysailer, but she is also capable of making two people comfortable overnight. A small-boat version of the famous Hunter CruisePac™ applies, with the cabin providing both a portable head and a removable ice box. A special convertible design allows port and starboard setees to be converted to a wide V-berth. A combination of broad beam and efficient sailplan makes the 19's performance both brisk and stable. And the convenient swing keel allows the 19 to be easily trailered, or sailed right up to the beach. Ventilation and forward access is provided by a tinted opening hatch.

On deck, a very complete selection of hardware provides good sail control, and there's even an on-deck anchor well, a feature rarely if ever found on boats of this size.

Specifications:

E (MAINSAIL FOOT)
8'4"/2.54 m.

J (FORETRIANGLE BASE)
6'6"/1.98 m.

P (MAINSAIL LUFF)
23'6"/7.16 m.

I (FORETRIANGEL HT.)
21'0"/6.40 m.

LOA
18'8"/5.69 m.

LWL
14'7"/4.45 m.

BEAM
7'4"

SAIL AREA
166 sq. ft.

DISPLACEMENT
1200 lbs.

DRAFT
board up 7"
board down 4'6"

HUNTER 22

The new 22 is a spacious, extremely well-equipped day sailer/overnight cruiser with big-boat features and a small-boat price. And she is easily trailerable. She is loaded with conveniences that make her a genuine pleasure to sail. There's a fold-out cockpit dinette table, for example, and an on-deck anchor well.

Nearly eight feet of beam allows generous space for a number of other exceptional features, including a complete galley with stove, sink and removable ice box; a drop-leaf cabin dinette table; and both a V-berth and two quarter berths for overnight accommodations. In addition, a great deal of storage has been designed in, including a unique "sea bag" system in the V-berth area. This feature allows various items to be stowed in separate pouches which are securely attached to the cabin sides, or they can be removed for easy packing or transporting. A top-quality portable head completes the cabin amenities.

The cockpit is unusually spacious and deep, providing secure, comfortable seating. A large cockpit locker portside is complemented by a fuel locker under the starboard seat, plus there's a built-in insulated cockpit cooler that is extremely convenient when under way.

Specifications:

E (MAINSAIL FOOT)
8'4"/2.54 m.

J (FORETRIANGLE BASE)
9'0"/2.74 m.

P (MAINSAIL LUFF)
23'6"/7.16 m.

I (FORETRIANGLE HT.)
27"/8.23 m.

LOA
22'3"/6.78 m.

LWL
18'4"/5.59 m.

BEAM
7'11"/2.53 m.

SAIL AREA
220 sq. ft./67.06 sq. m.

DISPLACEMENT
3,200 lbs./451.9 kg.

BALLAST (CAST INTERNAL)
1,300 lbs./589.8 kg.

DRAFT
Board up—23"/.58 m.
Board down—5'0"/1.52 m.

MAST HEIGHT
26'0"/7.92 m.

MAST HEIGHT FROM WATERLINE
30'3"/9.22 m.

HUNTER 25

The Hunter 25 appears to have been designed especially for cruising families with limited budgets. Big boat features such as two-burner alcohol stove, stainless steel sink with fresh water pump, folding dinette table, insulated icebox and even a fully enclosed private head are standard on this spacious 25. In addition, wide settee berths port and starboard, a quarter berth, and a large V-berth provide generous accommodations.

There are also many highly desirable standard features on deck: full length, black-anodized toe rail; winches; bow pulpit and stern rail; full lifelines; even three cockpit stowage lazarettes. And a particularly convenient feature rarely found on a boat this size is the on-deck anchor well.

Hunter even goes so far as to provide Coast Guard required equipment including lifejackets, enabling the new owner to use his boat immediately following purchase.

Specifications:

E (MAINSAIL FOOT)
8'0"

J (FORETRIANGLE BASE)
10'6"

P (MAINSAIL LUFF)
24'9½"

I (FORETRIANGLE HT.)
30'0"

L.O.A.
25'0"

L.W.L.
20'2"

BEAM
8'0"

SAIL AREA
256 sq. ft.

DISPLACEMENT
4,400 lbs.

BALLAST
   Shoal–2,000 lbs.
   Deep–1,800 lbs.

DRAFT
   Shoal–2'11"
   Deep–3'11"

MAST HEIGHT
28'8"

FROM WATERLINE
34'1"

HUNTER 27

Hunter Marine designed the popular Hunter 27 with cabin and deck layouts that provide big boat features on a mid-size cruiser. The 27 offers a T-shaped cockpit with wraparound coaming and pedestal steering, a stern rail swim ladder, double lifelines, and extrawide side decks for easy access forward. These features, normally standard only on much larger boats, join other very desirable features such as diesel auxiliary, 110-volt dockside power, and a tall rig for better sail performance.

Below, the Hunter 27 presents one of the largest cabins available. And as on deck, the appointments give a feeling of being on a much larger boat: standing headroom, teak and holly cabin sole; complete galley, large hanging locker, and even a navigator's station. Excellent lighting and ventilation are provided by four large screened, open ports.

Specifications:

E (MAINSAIL FOOT)
9'4"

J (FORETRIANGLE BASE)
11'3"

P (MAINSAIL LUFF)
32'4"

I (FORETRIANGLE HT.)
37'8"

L.O.A.
27'2"

L.W.L.
22'0"

BEAM
9'3"

DISPLACEMENT
7000 lbs.

BALLAST DEEP
3000 lbs.

SHOAL
3200 lbs.

SAIL AREA
360.2 sq. ft.

DRAFT SHOAL
3'3"

DEEP
4'3"

MAST HEIGHT
36'3"

FROM WATERLINE
40'11"

HEADROOM
6'1"

HUNTER 30

The Hunter 30 has proven itself to be an ideal combination of stable, efficient performance and spacious, live-aboard comfort. The deck features a wide and comfortable T-shaped cockpit with wraparound coaming and an interior/brightening, Lexan® sliding companionway hatch. Pedestal steering is standard, complete with engine control and lighted compass. Double lifelines are also standard, as is the stern rail swim ladder and on-deck anchor well.

Below-deck amenities are very compatible with living aboard, and include full standing headroom, teak and holly cabin sole, hot-and-cold pressure water, and plenty of stowage in all the right places. A complete galley, enclosed head with vanity and stand-up shower, folding dinette table, and sit down chart table are also standard.

Generous accommodations are provided by the forward cabin V-berth, port and starboard settee berths and the aft quarter berth, while excellent light and ventilation come from the nine screened, opening ports and two large hatches. Also standard is 110-volt dockside power, as is the dual 12-volt battery system.

In addition, a tall rig enhances sailing performance; and internal halyards, jiffy reefing, and a full complement of winches make sail handling easy. Auxiliary power is supplied by an economical two cylinder diesel engine.

Specifications:

E (MAINSAIL FOOT)
10'9"

J (FORETRIANGLE BASE)
12'10"

P (MAINSAIL LUFF)
37'0"

I (FORETRIANGLE HT.)
42'0"

L.O.A.
29'1½"

L.W.L.
25'9"

BEAM
10'1½"

DISPLACEMENT
9700 lbs.

BALLAST
Shoal–4000 lbs.
Deep–4000 lbs.

SAIL AREA
473.1 sq. ft.

DRAFT
Shoal–4'0"
Deep–5'3"

MAST HEIGHT
40'6"

HEADROOM
6'4"

HUNTER 33

The Hunter 33 combines the sleek lines of an offshore racer with functional live-aboard features that make her the ideal family cruiser. The "T" shaped cockpit provides plenty of space for friends, and pedestal steering, with lighted compass and engine control, is standard equipment.

Sail handling is also a pleasure. Standard features include internal halyards, recessed mainsheet traveler, inboard chainplates, two halyard winches and two 2-speed jib sheet winches. All standard.

Below decks, a unique floor plan creates three distinct living areas. The forward cabin, with private accommodations for two; the main salon, where twin settee berths and a large drop-leaf table create comfortable dining for six; and aft, the fully equipped, L-shaped galley. A gimballed, two-burner alcohol stove is complete with oven. There is generous counter space, and of course, hot-and-cold pressurized water. Eleven screened opening ports and two large hatches supply good lighting and ventilation.

Also located conveniently aft is a fully enclosed head with sink, vanity and shower with standing headroom; as well as a permanent navigation table with seat.

Specifications

E (MAINSAIL FOOT)
10'9"

J (FORETRIANGLE BASE)
14'0"

P (MAINSAIL LUFF)
37'1"

I (FORETRIANGLE HT.)
42'6"

L.O.A.
32'8"

L.W.L.
27'1"

BEAM
10'1½"

DISPLACEMENT
10,600 lbs.

BALLAST DEEP
4,100 lbs.

SHOAL
4,300 lbs.

SAIL AREA
496.7 sq. ft.

DRAFT SHOAL
4'0"

DEEP
5'3"

MAST HEIGHT
41'

HEADROOM
6'4"

HUNTER 36

The Hunter 36, now in its fourth year of production, was expressly designed to cruise four people in absolute style. Rather than using the majority of the cabin space for extra berths that might never be used, Naval Architect John Cherubini concentrated on making four people extremely comfortable.

Below decks, the luxurious accommodations include a private V-berth forward and wide settee berths port and starboard in the main salon. The starboard settee is part of a U-shaped dinette, which is designed so that lowering the table to bunk height creates a broad double berth.

Stowage is extremely generous, and both a large hanging locker and chest-of-drawers is situated on the port side forward. Many other drawers and shelves are conveniently located throughout.

The roomy head, with stand-up shower, includes a clothes hamper as well as refuse receptacle built into the vanity. And the U-shaped galley features both standard and deep sinks for easy washing and rinsing. The gimballed stove provides an oven and two top burners, and the very large icebox can also be filled from the cockpit.

To starboard is the navigation station, which is L-shaped to provide plenty of working area. An adjustable "bucket seat" insures secure seating, even in a seaway.

On deck, the 36 is designed and rigged for comfortable, easy handling. Main and jib halyards are led to the cockpit as is the mid-boom mainsheet. Roller furling and a spray dodger are standard, as are the anchor roller and recessed anchor well. Two large hatches and ten opening ports provide plenty of ventilation.

Wraparound coamings make the T-shaped cockpit dry and comfortable; and pedestal wheel steering is standard, complete with grab bar, table and compass. Primary winches are positioned on winch islands molded into the coamings. Other desirable features include 110-volt dockside power, European running lights, and hot-and-cold pressure water.

Specifications:

E (MAINSAIL FOOT)
12'9"

J (FORETRIANGLE BASE)
15'3"

P (MAINSAIL LUFF)
41'0"

I (FORETRIANGLE HT.)
46'6"

L.O.A
35'11"

L.W.L
29'6"

BEAM
11'1"

DISPLACEMENT
13,500 lbs.

BALLAST
6,000 lbs.

SAIL AREA
621 sq. ft.

DRAFT
4'11"

MAST HEIGHT
45'6"

HEADROOM
6'5"

Irwin Yacht and Marine Corp.
13055 49th Street North
Clearwater, Florida 33520

CITATION 31

Offered with a full keel for performance capability, shoal draft or centerboard configurations for coastal cruising, the 31's hull construction is Irwin gel coat over woven mat roving. The list of standard equipment includes a set of sails, 15 hp Yanmar diesel, auxiliary shore power, 12 v. electrical system, two burner gimballed propane stove, 110 A.C. for shore power and two 75 amp/hour batteries. On the deck the 31 features midship-mounted mainsheet traveler, tiller steering (wheel optional) and self-draining cockpit. The sleek exterior hides a roomy accommodation plan below, with sleeping space for five, nav station, U-shaped galley with propane stove, teak and holly sole, and plenty of storage.

Specifications:

LOA
31'2"

LWL
28'3"

BEAM
11'

CRAFT
full keel: 6'
shoal w/centerboard: 4'
board down: 8'1"

DISPLACEMENT
(approximately)
9,300 lb.

BALLAST FULL KEEL
(approximately)
3,750 lb.

SHOAL DRAFT KEEL
(approximately)
3,800 lb.

FUEL (approximately)
30 gal.

WATER (approximately)
40 gal.

POWER
Yanmar 15 hp diesel

SAIL AREA
495 sq. ft.

MAINSAIL AREA
222 sq. ft.

100/FORE
272 sq. ft.

CUT BACK MAIN
6 in.

REEFING
1 quick-reef point

P
37'0"

I
42'0"

E
12'0"

J
13'0"

MAIN MAST
¾' flat internal

BOOM
grooved

Islander Yachts
1922 Barranca Road
Irvine, California 92714

BAHAMA 28
Designed by Robert Perry

Construction:

Hull and deck are hand laminated reinforced fiberglass. Colors are permanently molded into the hull and deck during the laminating process. Non-skid surface is permanently molded into the deck. The interior is modular construction using marine grade plywood. The modular components, floor timbers, engine beds, bulkheads and other structural members are bonded with fiberglass to the hull and to the deck where it is appropriate. The keel ballast is lead, externally bolted to the hull. The rudder is high density foam blade with a stainless steel rudder post.

PROPULSION
Yanmar 2GM raw water cooled 15 HP diesel engine.

Engine instrument panel features tachometer, charging indicator light, oil pressure light, fuel gauge and water temperature light.

Bronze strut.

Two blade bronze propeller.

Fuel tank—20 gallon welded aluminum with deck fill.

ELECTRICAL
Wiring—Color coded.

One heavy duty battery with vapor proof switch.

D.C. electrical control panel featuring circuit breaker electrical system.

A.C. system—110V with double pole main breaker and outlets conveniently located throughout.

Lighting system 12V.

Navigation lights 12V.

Anchor light on mast.

PLUMBING
Water tank—20 gallon polyethylene located under starboard settee.

Foot pump and faucet in galley and head for fresh water system.

Polybutulene fresh water distribution system.

Bilge pump 15 gal.—min. diaphragm type operated from cockpit.

All thru-hulls and ball valves are Dupon Zytel to minimize electrolysis. All valves are clearly tagged.

Manual operated head with 15 gallon marine holding tank with manual pump for either deck or overboard discharge.

GENERAL INTERIOR
Oiled teak bulkheads and joiner trim.

Cabin sole carpeted.

Formica countertops.

Padded vinyl headliner with zippers for access to deck hardware and wiring.

Fabric cushions.

Curtains on large windows in main salon.

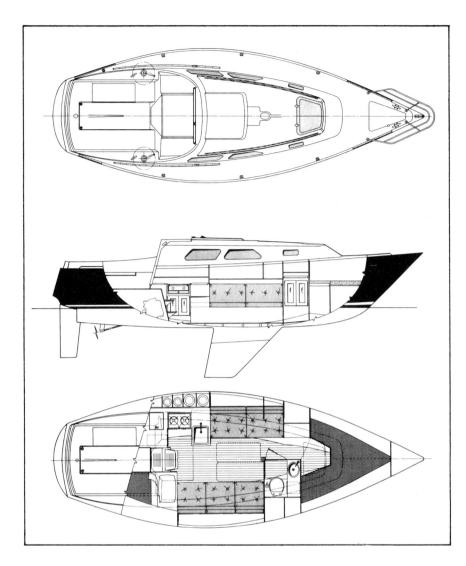

Double rail bow and stern pulpits with double lifelines, stanchions and boarding gates, port and starboard.

Swim ladder.

Full length anodized aluminum toerails bolted through overlapping hull to deck joint.

Two bow and stern mooring cleats.

Inboard genoa tracks with lead blocks.

Mid-boom ball bearing adjustable main sheet traveler.

Two opening ports with screens.

Fiberglass sliding main hatch with sea hood.

Translucent forward hatch.

Oiled teak exterior trim and handrails.

Laminated wood tiller.

WINCH PACKAGE

	Lewmar
2 Jib Sheet	30-A
1 Jib Halyard	8-A
1 Winch Handle	10″

SPARS AND RIGGING

Aluminum mast and boom with tunnel track.

Conduit tube for mast wiring.

Stainless steel tangs.

Stainless steel standing rigging with swaged fittings.

Internal main and jib halyards, pre-stretched dacron.

Boom-topping lift, short pennant swaging to backstay.

Mast winch refer-to winch package.

Anchor light.

Dacron main and jib sheets.

Sails—Dacron sails, main with reef points and 110% jib.

Slab reefing.

FORWARD CABIN

Hanging lockers with panel doors port side.

HEAD COMPARTMENT

Pullman with stainless steel sink.

Foot pump and faucet.

Two drawers and locker with panel door below countertop.

Mirror.

Towel bar.

Paper holder.

MAIN SALON

Fold up table that serves both settees.

Shelves over port and starboard settee.

Large quarter berth on starboard side.

GALLEY

Deep stainless steel sink.

Drawers and locker with panel door below.

Counter top and generous storage for all galley needs above countertop.

Foot pump and faucet.

Two-burner gimballed alcohol cooktop stove.

Large cubic foot insulated ice box with ventilated clear plastic shelf.

DECK

Anchor well.

Islander Yachts
1922 Barranca Road
Irvine, California 92714

FREEPORT 36

Designed by Robert Perry

The Freeport 36 Center Cockpit sloop by Islander Yachts is a new design of the highly successful Freeport 36 raised house model that numbers more than 150 in just a few years. Bob Perry has given the hull pleasing lines with fine entry and a profound flare forward for dryness. The rounded sections provide an easily driven hull and fair into a keel that is neither too long, too deep or too massive and exhibits none of the fin keel nervousness which requires constant attention of the helmsman. The rudder is protected by a full skeg that will make the Freeport 36 center cockpit track as confidently as her sistership. There is plenty of sail area to make her fast, exhilarating, responsive and is easily handled by two people. She is powered by a Pathfinder 50 diesel and will cruise more than 300 miles on her 50 gallons of fuel.

The comfortable bunk-sized cockpit with clear visibility is recessed well into the deck to avoid that "fly bridge" feeling prevalent on many center cockpit boats. An optional dodger or fixed spray shield will help keep the cockpit dry. Other features on deck are lockers for two propane bottles that vent overboard, anchor well, three miscellaneous lockers, four translucent deck hatches, eleven screened opening ports, ventilators, adjustable traveler, genoa tracks, and teak hand rails.

As you go below you'll realize that it is only a few easy steps into the light and spacious all teak interior. The headroom is 6′6″ throughout and there are six long berths in two staterooms, each with its own private head and shower and at night the main salon converts into a spacious cabin for two.

The seagoing intentions are clearly expressed in the Freeport 36 Center Cockpit. The galley has a vast amount of counter space and features a double sink, three burner gimballed propane stove/oven, large ice box, built-in dish locker and ample storage space for extended cruises. There are 150 gallons of hot or cold pressurized fresh water in three separate stainless steel tanks. There is ample locker and storage space as well as stand-up room in both the walk-thru and machinery room; a unique feature for a boat of this size. The machinery is accessible from either the walk-thru or cockpit.

The Freeport 36 Center Cockpit sloop is priced fully equipped—some of the standard equipment includes: Sails, jib furling gear, self-tailing winches, bow and stern rails, lifelines and swim ladder.

Features:

CONSTRUCTION
Hull and deck are hand laminated reinforced fiberglass.

Colors are permanently molded into the hull and deck during the laminating process.

Non-skid surface is permanently molded into the deck.

The interior is modular construction using marine grade plywood. The modular components, floor timbers, engine beds, bulkheads, and other structural members are bonded with fiberglass to the hull and deck where it is appropriate.

The keel ballast is internal, fiberglass bonded in place.

The rudder is a high density foam blade with a stainless steel rudder post.

PROPULSION
Pathfinder 50 (VW Rabbit) fresh water cooled 42 HP diesel.

Enclosed engine instrument panel features tachometer, hour meter, volt meter, fuel, oil pressure and water temperature gauges with audible warning system.

1″ stainless steel propeller shaft.

Two-blade bronze propeller.

Fuel tank—50 gallon welded aluminum with deck fill.

Muffler is an aqua-lift type.

Sound proofing in engine room.

ELECTRICAL
Wiring—color coded.

Two heavy duty batteries with vapor proof switch.

D.C. electrical control panel featuring circuit breaker, protected electrical system, battery monitoring volt meter.

Engine room light.

A.C. system 110V with double pole main breaker and outlets conveniently located throughout.

Lighting system—12V.

Courtesy lights at cabin sole.

Ice box light.

Navigation lights—12V.

Anchor light on mast.

Combination steaming and deck light on mast.

Companionway light and switch independent of main D.C. electrical panel.

PLUMBING
Stainless steel water tanks totaling 120 gallons.

Hot and cold pressure water system with six gallon water heater.

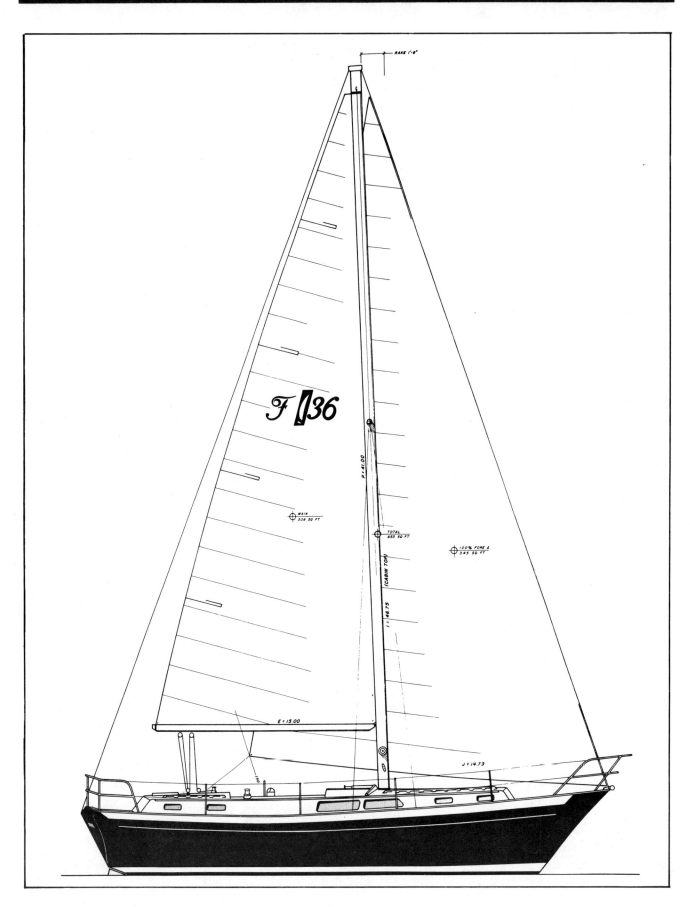

Foot pump and faucet in galley for fresh water system.

Two telephone type showers with hot and cold pressure water.

Bilge pump, 15 gal min., diaphragm type operated from cockpit.

Electrical bilge pump with automatic float switch.

All thru-hulls and ball valves are Dupont Zytel to minimize electrolysis. All valves are clearly tagged.

Two manually operated heads with a 17.5 gallon holding tank with manual pump for either deck or overboard discharge.

GENERAL INTERIOR
Oiled teak bulkheads and joiner trim.

Teak and holly main cabin sole.

Cedar lined hanging lockers.

Formica countertops.

Padded vinyl headliner with zippers for access to deck, hardware and wiring.

Grab rails on cabin trunk sides.

Deluxe fabric cushions.

Curtains on large windows in main salon.

FORWARD CABIN
Privacy door to forward head.

V-berth filler cushion.

Four drawers below V-berth.

MAIN SALON
U-shaped dinette that converts to a large double berth.

Teak framed mirrors.

GALLEY
Double stainless steel sink with hot and cold faucet. Four drawers and two lockers with louvered door below countertop. Generous storage area for all galley needs above and outboard of the countertop with sliding cane doors.

LIQUOR LOCKER
Foot pump and faucet.

Three-burner propane stove and oven with solenoid shut-off and safety valve.

Large 7.8 cubic foot insulated ice box with ventilated clear plastic shelves and light.

WALK-THRU TO AFT CABIN
Privacy door to aft cabin.

The electrical power center and access door to the engine room is located on the port side of the walk-thru.

Main salon hanging locker on starboard side.

HEAD COMPARTMENTS FORE AND AFT
Mirrors.

Towel bars.

Paper holders.

Hanging locker for forward cabin.

Linen storage area and three drawers.

Telephone type shower with hot and cold pressure water, faucets and curtains.

AFT CABIN
Large hanging locker on starboard side with louvered doors.

Settee between double and single berth with storage under the settee and berths.

Chart table with shelf for radio/ electronics.

DECK
Anchor well.

Anchor roller.

Double rail bow and stern pulpits with double lifelines, stanchions and boarding gates—port and starboard.

Stern pulpit with teak corner benches.

Full length teak cap rails bolted

through overlapping hull to deck joint.

Two bow and two stern mooring cleats with chocks.

Recessed inboard genoa tracks with lead blocks.

Two Dorade ventilators.

Fiberglasss sliding main hatch with molded-in sea hood.

Forward cabin hatch.

Two hatches over main salon.

Oiled teak exterior trim and handrails.

Ball bearing adjustable mainsheet traveller.

Eleven screened opening ports.

Aft cabin hatch.

Pedestal steering with 28" stainless steel wheel, engine controls, brake, 5" compass and emergency tiller.

Teak coaming caps.

WINCH PACKAGE
Choice of either Barient or Lewmar Package

SPARS AND RIGGING
Aluminum mast and boom with tunnel track.

Mast and boom have a baked-on painted finish for durability and appearance.

Conduit tube for mast wiring.

Stainless steel tangs to receive T bar type terminals.

Stainless steel standing rigging with swaged fittings.

Internal main and jib halyards with wire to rope splices.

Boom topping lift.

Mast winches—refer to Winch Package under Deck Category.

Anchor light.

Combination steaming and deck light.

Dacron main and jib sheets.

Jib roller furling gear.

Sails, dacron main with double reef row, 130% roller furling genoa with sewn on sail cover.

Main salt cover with Freeport 36 logo.

FREEPORT 36 OPTIONS
Anchor windlass.

Bimini top.

Boom gallows.

Cockpit cushions.

Cockpit dodger.

Contrasting non-skid color.

Hatches over each head.

Pedestal guard.

Pedestal guard with table.

Salt water anchor and deck wash down.

Teak cockpit grate.

Windshield.

Air conditioning.

Battery charger.

Generator.

Ice box refrigeration system.

Teak and holly sole throughout.

Bunker load.

Shipping cradle.

Specifications:
LOA
35'9"

LWL
27'6"

BEAM
12'0"

DRAFT
5'3"

DISPLACEMENT
17,000 lbs.

BALLAST
6,300 lbs.

VERT. CLEARANCE
53'0"

BALLAST/ D
37%

D/L
365

SA/D
15.8

SAIL AREA
653 sq. ft.

Main 308 sq. ft.
100% Fore Δ 345 sq. ft.

POWER
Diesel

FUEL
50 gallons

WATER
120 gallons

FREEPORT 36 RAISED HOUSE

Designed by Robert Perry

Features
Interior "A"

FORWARD CABIN
Privacy door to main salon.

V-berth filler cushion.

Three drawers and drop door below V-berth.

Hanging locker with louvered door.

HEAD COMPARTMENT
Privacy curtain to separate head compartments.

Separate shower stall with drain and teak grating.

Telephone type shower with hot and cold faucet and curtain with teak bench.

Teak framed mirror.

Pullman with stainless steel sink with hot and cold faucet.

Three drawers and locker with louvered door below countertop.

Outboard lockers with cane doors above countertop.

Towel bar.

Paper holder.

MAIN SALON
Hanging locker forward on starboard side with louvered door.

Table with hinged leaves and liquor locker that accommodates both settees.

Magazine rack on port bulkhead forward.

Port settee converts to double berth

Book shelves and locker with cane doors over both settees.

Chart table on starboard side with electrical control panel outboard. Four drawers below chart table.

Quarter berth on starboard side.

GALLEY
Double stainless steel sink with hot and cold pressure faucet. Four drawers and two lockers with louvered doors below countertop. Generous storage for all galley needs above and outboard of countertop with cane doors.

Foot pump and faucet.

Three-burner propane stove and oven with solenoid shut-off and safety valve.

Interior "B"

FORWARD CABIN
Deep "his" and "her" hanging lockers separated by a vanity with five drawers.

Queen berth port side enclosed by louvered doors. Two drawers and storage lockers with hinge down door below berth.

HEAD COMPARTMENT
Telephone type shower with hot and cold faucet, curtain, teak grating and bench.

Pullman with stainless steel sink and hot and cold faucet.

Four drawers and locker with louvered door below countertop.

Two lockers with cane doors separated by mirror above and outboard of countertop.

Large locker with louvered door.

Towel bar.

Paper holder.

MAIN SALON

L-shaped dinette on port side.

Fold-away table with hinged leaves that will accommodate seating for starboard settee.

Starboard settee converts to double berth.

Chart table on starboard side with electrical control panel, and a large shelf outboard for electronics. Shelves with louvered door below chart table.

Teak framed mirror in main salon.

SPARS AND RIGGING

Aluminum mast and boom with tunnel track.

Mast and boom have a baked-on painted finish for durability and appearance.

Mast head, winch pads, and fixed gooseneck are welded to mast.

Conduit tube for mast wiring.

Stainless steel tangs to receive T-bar type terminals.

Stainless steel standing rigging with swaged fittings.

Internal main and jib halyards with wire to rope splices.

Boom topping lift.

Mast winches—refer to Winch Package under Deck Category.

Anchor light.

Combination steaming and deck light.

Dacron main and jib sheets.

Slab reefing.

OPTIONS

Cockpit cushions.

Pedestal guard with/without table

Cockpit dodger with removable clear side curtains and roll up forward clear curtain.

Teak cockpit grating.

Teak and holly sole in forward cabin in lieu of standard carpet.

Battery charger/converter to shore power.

Ice box refrigeration system.

Anchor windlass.

Contrasting nonskid color.

Cradle (non returnable).

Bunker load.

Specifications

LOA
35'9"

LWL
27'6"

BEAM
12'0"

DRAFT
5'3"

DISPLACEMENT
17,000 lbs.

BALLAST
6,300 lbs.

VERT. CLEARANCE
53'0"

BALLAST/D
37%

D/L
365

SA/D
15.97

SAIL AREA
660 sq. ft.

> **Main** 268 sq. ft.
> **100% Fore △** 392 sq. ft.

POWER
Diesel

FUEL
55 gallons

WATER
100 gallons

ISLANDER 36

Designed by Alan Gurney

Features

CONSTRUCTION

Hull and deck are hand laminated reinforced fiberglass.

Colors are permanently molded into the hull and deck during the laminating process.

Non-skid surface is permanently molded into the deck.

The interior is a molded fiberglass liner incorporating marine grade plywood. The modular components, floor timbers, engine beds, bulkheads and other structural members are bonded with fiberglass to the hull and to the deck where it is appropriate. The keel ballast is lead, externally bolted on with steel bolts in either a standard or shoal draft configuration.

The rudder is a high density foam blade with a stainless steel rudder post.

PROPULSION

Pathfinder 50 (VW Rabbit) fresh water cooled 42 HP diesel.

Enclosed engine instrument panel features tachometer with hour meter, volt meter, fuel, oil pressure and water temperature gauges with audible warning system.

1" stainless steel propeller shaft.

Bronze strut.

Two-bladed bronze propeller.

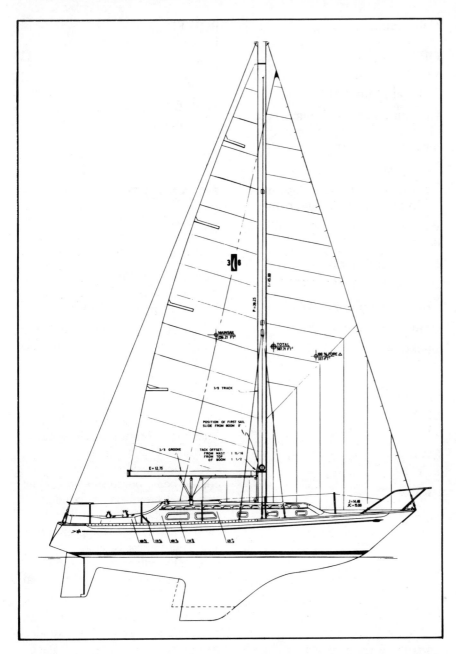

light on mast.

Companionway light and switch independent of main D.C. electrical panel.

PLUMBING

Two 27 gallon stainless steel water tanks located under settees with deck fills.

Hot and cold pressure water system with six gallon water heater.

Foot pump and faucet in galley for fresh water system.

Telephone type shower with hot and cold faucet and curtain.

Polybutylene fresh water distribution system.

Bilge pump 15 gal/min. diaphragm type operated from cockpit.

Electric bilge pump with automatic float switch.

All thru-hulls and ball valves are Dupont Zytel to minimize electrolysis. All valves are clearly tagged.

Manual operated head with 17.5 gallon marine holding tank with manual pump for either deck or overboard discharge.

GENERAL INTERIOR

Oiled teak bulkheads and joiner trim.

Teak and holly cabin sole.

Formica countertops.

Padded vinyl headliner with zippers for access to deck hardware and wiring.

Grab rails on cabin trunk sides.

Deluxe fabric cushions.

Curtains on large windows in main salon.

FORWARD CABIN

Privacy door to main salon.

V-berth filler cushion.

Three drawers and drop door on starboard side below V-berth.

Fuel tank—32 gallon welded aluminum with deck fill.

Muffler is aqua-lift type.

Sound proofing in engine room.

ELECTRICAL

Wiring—color coded.

Two heavy duty batteries with vapor proof switch.

D.C. electrical control panel featuring circuit breaker protected electrical system, battery monitoring volt meter located aft of galley.

A.C. system 110V with double pole main breaker and outlets conveniently located throughout.

Lighting system 12V

Courtesy lights at cabin sole.

Ice box light.

Navigation lights 12V.

Anchor light on mast.

Combination steaming and deck

Hanging locker with louvered door.

HEAD COMPARTMENT

Fiberglass shower pan with drain.

Telephone type shower with hot and cold faucet and curtain.

Teak framed mirror.

Pullman with stainless steel sink with hot and cold faucet.

Three drawers and louvered door below countertop.

Towel bar.

Paper holder.

MAIN SALON

Hanging locker forward on starboard side with louver door.

Fold-up, hide-a-way table serving both settees.

Teak framed mirror.

Shelves over port settee enclosed by sliding cane doors, and three convenience drawers.

Chart table on port side with large shelf outboard for electronics. Liquor cabinet and shelves below chart table with louvered doors.

Large quarter berth on port side with shelf.

GALLEY

Deep stainless steel sink with hot and cold faucet with four drawers and locker.

Generous storage for all galley needs above and outboard of countertop with cane doors.

Foot pump and faucet.

Three-burner gimballed alcohol stove and oven.

Large 6.5 cubic foot insulated ice box with ventilated clear plastic shelves and light.

DECK

Anchor well.

Anchor roller.

Double rail bow and stern pulpits with double lifelines, stanchions, and boarding gates port and starboard.

Swim ladder.

Full length anodized aluminum toerails bolted every 4" through overlapping hull to deck joint.

Two bow and two stern mooring cleats.

Recessed inboard genoa tracks with lead blocks.

Mid-boom ball bearing adjustable mainsheet traveler.

Six screened opening ports.

Fiberglass sliding main hatch with molded-in sea hood.

Translucent forward and mid cabin hatches.

Three seat locker hatches with locking hasps.

Oiled teak exterior trim and handrails.

Pedestal steering with 28" stainless steel destroyer wheel, engine controls, brake, 5" compass and emergency tiller.

Winch Package—

Choice of either Barient or Lewmar Package

SPARS AND RIGGING

Aluminum mast and boom with tunnel track.

Mast and boom have a baked-on painted finish for durability and appearance.

Mast head, winch pads, and fixed gooseneck are welded to mast.

Conduit tube for mast wiring.

Stainless steel tangs to receive T-bar type terminals.

Stainless steel standing rigging with swadged fittings.

Internal main and jib halyards with wire to rope splices.

Boom topping lift.

Mast winches, refer to winch package under Deck Category.

Anchor light.

Combination steaming and deck light.

Dacron main and jib sheets.

36 OPTIONS

Cockpit cushions to match deck color.

Pillow style cushions.

Varnished interior/exterior.

Pedestal guard with table.

Shoal Draft.

Folding propeller.

RACING PACKAGE

Spinnaker pole with bridles

Spinnaker pole chocks on deck

Spinnaker halyard block

Spinnaker halyard

Topping lift block

Topping lift

Foreguy

Foreguy/staysail track and block on foredeck

Two spreacher blocks

Spinnaker halyard winch on mast, Barient 22C or Lewmar 40C

Two secondary winches, Barient 25A's/Lewmar 42A's

Cradle (non-returnable).

Specifications

LOA
36'1"

LWL
28'3"

BEAM
11'2"

DRAFT
Standard–6'0"
Shoal–4'9"

DISPLACEMENT
    Standard–13,450 lbs.
    Shoal–13,600 lbs.

BALLAST
    Standard–5,450 lbs.
    Shoal–5,600 lbs.

Kady-Krogen Yachts, Inc.
3315 Rice Street, Suite 7
Miami, Florida 33133

KROGEN 38 CUTTER

The Krogen 38' Cutter is a yacht designed as a powerful sailing ma-chine with excellent up-wind per-formance and solid directional sta-bility. Rigged as a cutter, it is easily handled by a short crew and very versatile in its sail combinations. The center board, in the shoal draft version, has a sophisticated "hi-lift" hydro-dynamic section to achieve good "lifting" qualities when working to weather. On the other hand, it is designed in such a manner, that as the boat is trimmed off the wind, the board's drag coefficient is reduced. In addi-tion, there is a "trim" board aft. This allows the skipper to move the center of lateral plane aft when sailing off the wind, thus produc-ing a balanced helm on all points of sail.

The standard rig is: hanked on genoa, staysail and slab reefing mainsail. At owner's option, a roller reefing/furling rod head stay, roller furling stay-sail and roller reefing/furling (inside the mast)

mainsail (or any combinations thereof) can be fitted.

While sailing characteristics have been a prime consideration in the design of this yacht, her appointments below have had equal attention. The jointer work, materials and workmanship are of the highest quality. The decor is traditional in concept, reminiscent of the fine craftsmanship of some of America's finest shipyards. It features teak and holly cabin soles, teak panelled bulkheads, teak trim, lockers and beam caps, plus carefully selected fabrics and a delightful layout. This boat was designed for sailors by sailors, but offers all the conveniences and privacy desired by our lady "first mates."

The hull is hand layed up of FRP "PVC Foam" sandwich construction. This method is the highest quality available in the present state of the art. Ballast is 7,000 lbs. of lead. (Iron, in keel version.)

The interior of this boat is tastefully designed in the traditional manner of the truly fine sailing yachts of our time. The hand-rubbed teak decor is enhanced by the exquisite jointer work. Indirect lighting is used throughout the boat. The artfully decorated saloon boasts teak panelling and lockers, a "U" shaped settee and table plus a fireplace!

The fully enclosed master stateroom aft includes an over-size double berth, hanging locker, storage lockers, drawers and private lavatory.

The guest stateroom forward has two large single "vee" berths, hanging locker, storage lockers, drawers and private lavatory.

Both rooms reflect the creative use of hand-rubbed teak, complemented by teak and holly cabin soles.

The separate shower compartment and spacious "head" on the port side forward has hot and cold

pressure water which is piped throughout the boat.

The galley, starboard side aft, is equipped with a stove and oven, two insulated top-loading food storage spaces which can be used with ice or fitted as a refrigerator and freezer at the owner's option. Completing this area is a double stainless steel sink with hot and cold pressure water, in addition to ample locker and drawer space.

Engine: diesel, Pathfinder, 30 H.P., 2:1 reduction gear; muffler, hydro lift. The engine compartment is insulated and readily accessible all around for servicing and routine maintenance.

Steering gear: Edson with 28" teak wheel, with "Destroyer" outer ring. All thru the hull fittings below water line are fitted with bronze sea cocks.

Standard Equipment:

Aluminum Spars

Stainless Steel Rigging

Dacron Running Rigging

Halyard Winches

Centerboard Winch

Life Lines, Stanchions, Gates

Bow and Stern Pulpit

Wheel Steering

Nine Opening Ports

Gas Bottle Stowage Locker

Four Sudbury "Sky Vents"

Two Rope Deck Pipe Fittings

Bow Chocks

Stern Chocks

RIG
(Optional) Roller Furling/Reefing Gear for Jib, Staysail, & Mainsail is available at additional cost.

Hot and Cold Fresh Water Pressure System with (2) 75 Gallon Tanks

Propane Stove with Oven

Double Stainless Sink in Galley

Two Stainless Steel Wash Basins

Lancer Yacht Corporation
1939 Deere Avenue
Irvine, California 92714

LANCER 25 MKV

Designed by Shad Turner

The Lancer 25 MK V is a rare combination of beauty, roominess and sailing performance in a trailerable yacht. Ingenious use of interior space gives this 25 footer standing head room without the use of ungainly and unseaworthy "pop tops".

The Lancer 25 has a shallow-draft fixed keel underbody with a permanently mounted inboard rudder. There are no center boards, swing keels, flip up rudders, etc. to complicate your life. The Lancer

25 tracks well, steers easily and sails to windward as well as many deep keel yachts. She was designed by W. Shad Turner, a bright young yacht designer noted for his custom and production racing designs. Shad has endowed the Lancer 25 with a fine entry, carefully faired aft quarters and a thoroughly researched shallow-draft keel design. The net result is a hull that points well, is fast, yet stable, and is trailer launchable from any good ramp. The Lancer 25 sails where others must retract their keels.

The quality of the interior finish and detail is outstanding when compared to other craft of about this size. The bulkheads are "real" teak, not a "photo wood" imitation. The cabinet doors are teak with cane panels for beauty and

ventilation. The teak and holly sole is standard and there is a custom tailored soft headliner with foam insulation to eliminate the condensation problem associated with most fiberglass headliners.

The Lancer 25 MK V's modern new fractional rig with its standard internal reefing system for two reefs and internal outhaul is highly versatile. The boat will balance and sail nicely under main alone for "nonchalant" cruising and has smallish easy to handle head sails that add the extra power for outstanding sailing performance.

Standard Equipment:

HULL
Fiberglass, with Hand Laminated Woven Roving

Standard Colors—White Hull—Red, White and Blue Boot Top—Blue Sheer Stripe

KEEL
1300 lbs. of Internal Ballast Bonded Securely in Place

RUDDER
SS Rudder Shaft with Integral Steel Backbone—Surrounded with High Density Foam—Fiberglass Covered.

DECK
One Piece Fiberglass—Plywood and Balsa Core Reinforced

Molded Non Skid Surfaces

Large Self-Draining Cockpit

Lazarette Hatch

Sliding Main Hatch with Seahood

Lockable Flush Fitting Forward Hatch

Foredeck Self-Draining Anchor Locker

STANDING & RUNNING RIGGING
Aluminum Mast, Boom & Spreaders—Fractional Rig

SS Mast Tangs—Chain Plates & Stern Fitting

SS 1x19 Wire with Swedged Fittings (Standing)

Main & Jib Halyards—Prestretched Dacron with Spiced-on Fittings.

Ball Bearing Main Sheet Traveler with Control Lines

Main & Jib Sheets—Yacht Braid

Split Back Stay

A "Super Boom" with an Internal Outhaul and an Internal Jiffy Reefing System for Two sets of Reef Points.

Baked White Polyester Coating on Mast & Boom

SS Boom Vang Bails on Boom & Base of Mast

ELECTRICAL
12 Volt Die Hard Marine Battery with Fused Panel

4 Interior Lights

International Navigation Lights

TANKAGE
15 gallon water Tank with Deck Fill

INTERIOR
Teak & Holly Sole in Main Cabin

Beautifully Crafted Cane Panel Cabinet Doors for Superior Ventilation

Enclosed Head Compartment with Divider Curtain, Two Vanity Cabinets & Hanging Locker

Main Cabin—Single Berths, Port & Starboard

Galley—Foam Insulated Ice Box, Stainless Steel Sink, Teak Dish Lockers—Port & Starboard, Recessed Stove compartment

Two Quarter Berths, Port & Starboard

All Teak Interior

Plush 3" Cushions on all Berths—Upholstered Back Rests in Main Cabin.

EXTERIOR
Bow Pulpit

Stern Pulpit

Lifelines & Stanchions

Exterior Wood Trim of Oiled Teak

2 Bow & 2 Stern Mooring Cleats

Full Length Anodized Aluminum Toerail

Inboard Jib Tracks with Cars

Laminated Tiller

Tinted Ports

Dacron Mainsail with Two Sets of Reef Points, Fiberglass Battens, Leach Line & Draft Stripe.

Dacron #4 Jib with Windowed Tell-Tails, Leach Line, Sail Bag and Draft Stripe.

Stainless Steel Tabernacle Mast Step

Teak Cabin Top Handrails

Electrical Bilge Pump

Hasp on Main Hatch for Padlock

Stainless Steel Bow Eye

2 Opening Ports with Screens (Galley Area)

Specifications:

LENGTH OVERALL
24'8"

LENGTH WATER LINE
20'1"

BEAM
8'0"

DRAFT
3'0"

DISPLACEMENT
3,600 lbs.

BALLAST
1,300 lbs.

HEAD ROOM
Standing

BRIDGE CLEARANCE
36'0"

LANCER 28-TMK V

Designed by Shad Turner

The Lancer 28-T MK V is one of the most outstanding yachts of her type. The designer, W. Shad Turner, noted for his performance designs, has given the Lancer 28 a long waterline for speed under sail and power and the beauty of a low sleek cabin profile while still maintaining better than 6'2" standing head room. A ballast to displacement ratio of about 50% makes her sail without an excessive angle of heel. Modest draft and 8' beam make those out of the way places accessible and also make her trailerable, putting even those distant cruising waters within practical vacation range.

The interior has an enclosed head and sleeps up to seven in a teak crafted interior. Cane panel teak doors add beauty as well as providing superior locker ventilation to combat mildew. A custom tailored soft headliner with foam insulation makes for a warm, comfortable, luxurious feeling below.

The Lancer 28 MK V's new fractional rig is versatile and practical. It has easy to handle, smallish headsails and a mainsail large enough to drive the boat by itself in complete control for "nonchalant" cruising. Internal jiffy reefing and an internal outhaul are standard as is the beautiful baked on mast finish.

Standard Equipment:

HULL
Fiberglass, With Hand Laminated Woven Roving

Standard Colors—White Hull—Red, White & Blue Boot Top—Blue Sheer Stripe

KEEL
2600 lbs. of Internal Ballast Bonded Securely in Place

RUDDER
SS Rudder Shaft With Integral Steel Backbone—Surrounded With High Density Foam—Fiberglass Covered

DECK
One Piece Fiberglass—Plywood & Balsa Core Reinforced

Molded Non Skid Surfaces

Large Self-Draining Cockpit

Lazarette Hatch

Sliding Main Hatch with Seahood

Foredeck Self-Draining Anchor Locker

Lockable Flush Fitting Forward Hatch

STANDING & RUNNING RIGGING
Non Masthead Fractional Rig

Aluminum Mast, Boom & Spreaders

SS Mast Tangs—Chain & Plates & Stem Fitting

SS 1x19 Wire with Swedged Fittings (Standing)

Main & Jib Halyards—Prestretched Dacron With Spliced-on Fittings

Ball Bearing Main Sheet Traveler with Control Lines

Main & Jib Sheets—Yacht Braid

Split Back Stay

A "Super Boom" With an Internal Outhaul and an Internal Jiffy Reefing System for Two Sets of Reef Points

Baked White Polyester Coating on Mast & Boom

SS Boom Vang Bails on Boom & Base of Mast

INTERIOR
Teak & Holley Sole in Main Cabin

Beautifully Crafted Cane Panel Cabinet Doors for Superior Ventilation

Enclosed Head Compartment with Divider Curtain, Stainless Steel Sink, Hanging Locker & Cabinet

Main Cabin—Single Berths, Port & Starboard

Galley—Foam Insulated Ice Box, Stainless Steel Sink, Teak Dish Lockers, Port & Starboard, Recessed Stove Compartment

Two Quarter Berths, Port & Starboard

All Teak Interior

Upholstered Headliner

Plush 3" Cushions on all Berths—Upholstered Backrest in Main Cabin

ELECTRICAL
12 Volt Die Hard Marine Battery With Fused Panel

5 Interior Lights

International Navigational Lights

TANKAGE
15 Gallon Water Tank With Deck Fill

EXTERIOR
Bow Pulpit

Stern Pulpit

Lifelines & Stanchions

Exterior Wood Trim of Oiled Teak

2 Bow & 2 Stern Mooring Cleats

Full Length Anodized Aluminum Toerail

Laminated Tiller

Tinted Ports

Dacron Mainsail With two sets of Reef Points, Fiberglass Battens, Leach Line & Draft Stripe

Dacron Jib With Widowed Tell-Tails, Leach Line, Sail Bag & Draft Stripe

Stainless Steel Tabernacle Mast Step

Teak Cabin Top Handrails

Electrical Bilge Pump

Hasp on Main Hatch for Padlock

Inboard Jib Track with Cars

Stainless Steel Bow Eye

2 Opening Ports with Screens (Galley Area)

Specifications:

LENGTH OVERALL
27'8"

LENGTH WATER LINE
23'11"

BEAM
8'0"

DRAFT
3'0"

DISPLACEMENT
5,200 lbs.

BALLAST
2,600 lbs.

HEAD ROOM
6'2"

BRIDGE CLEARANCE
38'0"

LANCER 36

Designed by Bruce Lee and Bruce Farr

The Lancer 36 is a high performance, high sail area yacht with a light displacement hull form, generous beam with powerful sections, and a fine bow. The powerful hull coupled with a deep, modern NACA shaped keel with the center of gravity of the ballast only 17″ from the bottom of the keel, will be very stiff and ensure excellent performance to windward, especially in rough water. The generous beam, light displacement and high sail area to displacement ratio will guarantee a fast, exhilarating ride downwind and reaching with easy control.

The rig is a development of the non-masthead swept spreader arrangement used successfully on previous Bruce Farr racing and cruising yachts—no complicated runners, easy to handle, smallish headsails and a mainsail large enough to drive the boat by itself in complete control for "nonchalant" cruising. A slightly higher fore-triangle height compared to mainsail luff will give more direct control of forestay sag and will make backstay adjustment less critical.

By combining and blending the talents of two outstanding yacht designers and utilizing a proven hull form along with a sail plan that will produce an extraordinary high power ratio (sail area to displacement), the Lancer 36 should prove to be an impressive performer.

The standard interior has a straight forward arrangement well proven on many ocean racing yachts of around this size. Features of note are the two large double quarter berths, a full size chart table that measures 3′9″ by 2′6″, a very large head compartment, and sail storage area forward. The main cabin area has two pilot berths and two settee berths with a large drop-leaf table on the centerline. Countless lockers throughout the yacht, along with an 18 cubic foot ice box, should afford adequate provision storage for a large crew for an extended cruise or a long distance ocean race.

The optional cruising interior layout is quite unique in that it has a separate and private owner's stateroom aft, with a 6′9″ long double berth and direct access to a large head area with a separate stall shower compartment. The navigation area has a full size (2′ x 3′) sit-down chart table and a double quarter berth. The galley has approximately 18 square feet of counter space, a 12 cubic foot ice box (refrigeration option), lots of lockers and drawers, a gimballed stove with oven and a double stainless steel sink. The main cabin area is unique, to say the least; it has 17 linear feet of plush upholstered lounge area for entertaining. The lounge can be used for either 2 large single berths, 7′6″ long, or can be converted to 2-7′6″ long double berths. Cane panel locker doors, a solid teak drop-leaf table, two 5′ long book case alcoves and fine teak joiner work make for a roomy, inviting social area.

Perhaps the most important advantage of the Lancer 36 is its lightweight. This just makes everything easier—for the same power and greater speed, the sails are smaller and thus easier to handle, the winches are smaller and easier to crank, the sheets are lighter, and everything is just simpler and less expensive. The boat is particularly responsive and easy to steer, and the family can comfortably take it out for an afternoon race or an extended cruise, without needing a highly talented racing crew.

Standard Equipment:

HULL

Fiberglass, with hand laminated woven roving, full balsa core sandwich construction

Standard colors—white hull—red, white and blue boot top—blue sheer stripe

KEEL

4000 lbs. of internal ballast bonded securely in place

RUDDER

Schedule 80 SS rudder shaft with steel backbone—surrounded with high density foam—fiberglass covered

DECK

One piece fiberglass, plywood and balsa core reinforced

Molded non skid surfaces

Large self-draining cockpit

Sliding "skylight type" main hatch with seahood

Locking forward "skylight type" aluminum frame hatch

Foredeck self-draining anchor locker

STANDING & RUNNING RIGGING (MASTHEAD RIG)

Aluminum mast, boom, & air foil spreaders

SS chain plates & stem fittings

SS 1 x 19 wire with swedged fittings (standing)

Internal upper and lower shroud tangs (gib hooks)

Internal main and jib halyards pre-stretched dacron with spliced-on fittings

Special stainless steel mast step fitting with provision for up to 14 turning blocks and/or halyard attachments

Ball bearing main sheet traveler with control lines

Main & jib sheets—yacht braid

Split back stay

A "Super Boom" with an internal outhaul and an internal reefing system for two sets of reef points

Baked white polyester coating on mast and boom

SS boom vang bails on boom & base of mast

ELECTRICAL
12 volt die hard marine battery with fused panel

14 interior lights

International navigation lights

Engine room lights

TANKAGE
40 gallon fresh water tank

INTERIOR
Forward cabin area—five cane door lockers, two book cases, two berths (that convert to doubles), hanging locker, bureau with drawers, and sail storage locker,

plush 5″ color coordinated cabin cushion, upholstered back rests with storage lockers behind

Separate owner's cabin with drawers, hanging locker, and double berth

Navigation station-full size chart table with chart storage under, and double quarter berth

All teak interior

Beautifully crafted cane panel cabinet doors for superior ventilation

Teak companionway interior handrails

Upholstered headliner

Fully enclosed head compartment with teak door, vanity sink, and sliding locker

Complete galley with deep double SS sink, foam insulated ice box, teak dish lockers, drawers, fresh water pump & gimballed stove with oven

Electric ice box drain pump

Teak ceilings (hull covering) forward cabin, owner's cabin & navigator's quarter berth

Solid teak drop leaf table

Mirror in head compartment

Aromatic cedar lined drawers in galley, forward owner's cabins

EXTERIOR

Exterior wood trim and handrails of oiled teak

2 bow & 2 stern mooring cleats

Full length anodized aluminum toerail

Inboard genoa track with surfline wide sheave blocks

Pedestal wheel steering system with SS wheel, Danforth Corsair compass, & engine controls

Tinted translucent forward and main hatch

Hasp on main hatch for padlock

Bow pulpit

Stern pulpit

Lifelines and stanchions

Mainsails with two sets of reef points, fiberglass battens, leach line, cunningham and draft stripe

4 genoa with windowed tell-tails, leach line, sail bag and draft stripe

Four opening ports with screens, owner's cabin, navigation, head and galley areas

2-cockpit storage lockers with sliding covers (approximately 5 cubic ft. of storage area each)

Flush sliding transparent cover over cockpit engine instrument panel

LANCER 42

Designed by Herb David
The Lancer 42's long water line length, high sail area to displacement ratio, modern N.A.C.A. shaped keel, and a high stability factor (2225 lbs. of righting moment at 1° angle of heel) contribute greatly to her all around sailing performance. Speeds under power with either single or twin diesel engines will be in the 8 to 12 M.P.H. range, up to about 40% faster than other cruising yachts.

Sail handling has been simplified to the point where you can handle all halyards, reef lines for both reefs, boom vang, boom topping lift, and main sheet from the cockpit, using custom Schaefer designed line stoppers and a standard Lewmar #30 self-tailing winch. You'll never again have to leave the safety of the cockpit to reef the mainsail.

The cockpit is quite roomy and includes a pedestal steerer with engine controls, a 5″ compass with binnacle and pedestal guard, a teak fold-up cockpit table and an engine access hatch which measures about 3′ x 5′, affording you walk around space in the engine room.

The interior accommodation plan is also quite unique for a sailing yacht of this size—a very large owner's cabin is located forward. The cabin takes up the full width of the yacht and includes a queen size berth, hanging locker, drawers and is adjacent to a head compartment with a separate shower stall. A separate and private guest cabin with a hanging locker and a double berth with drawers under is incorporated into the design.

Another interesting and unique design feature is the separate navigator's area which includes a full size sit down chart table with chart stowage under, a 6′8″ long quarter berth, electrical panel and an electronic shelf. As an option, this area may be partitioned off with teak bulkheads and a raised paneled teak door to become a private Captain's cabin.

The "U" shaped galley is a delight. Over 25 square feet of counter space provide the room to prepare meals for a large crew for an extended voyage. An electric refrigerator with freezer compartment is standard as is a propane stainless steel gimballed stove with oven, hot and cold pressure water, a deep double stainless steel sink and a six plus cubic foot load top ice box that can be converted into a deep freeze. The main salon includes two transom berths that convert to two doubles, a fold-a-way teak table, 2 book case alcoves with hull ports—so that you can see out when seated in the salon and a teak and holley sole.

All in all, the Lancer 42 should be an outstanding cruising yacht both under power and sail. Her race winning hull and the ability to power in the 8 to 12 knot M.P.H. area encompasses performance parameters that few, if any cruising yachts, can match.

Standard Equipment:

HULL
Fiberglass, with hand laminated Woven Roving–Full Balsa Core Sandwich Construction

Standard Colors–White Hull– Red, White & Blue Boot Top– Blue Sheer Stripe

KEEL
7000 lbs. of Internal Ballast Bonded Securely in Place

RUDDER
Schedule 90 S/S Rudder Shaft with Integral Steel Backbone– Surrounded with High Density Foam–Fiberglass Covered

DECK
One Piece Fiberglass–Plywood and Balsa Core Reinforced

Molded Non-Skid Surfaces

Large Self Draining Cockpit

Teak Main Companionway Door & Hatch

Sliding "Skylight Type" Main Hatch with Seahood

Locking Forward Cabin & Amidships "Skylight Type" Aluminum Frame Hatches

Bow Roller for Anchor & Mooring Bit

Foredeck Self Draining Anchor & Storage Locker

STANDING AND RUNNING RIGGING
Aluminum Mast & Boom with Air Foil Spreaders

Internal "Gib Hook Type" Tangs for Standing Rigging

Stainless Steel Chain Plates and Stem Fitting

S/S 1 x 19 Wire with Swedged Fittings Standing Rigging

Prestretched Dacron Running Rigging with Spliced on Fittings

Internal Main & Jib Halyard

Ball Bearing Main Sheet Traveler with Control Lines

Split Back Stay

Baked White Polyester Coating on Mast & Boom

A "Super Boom" with an Internal Outhaul and an Internal Reefing System for Two Sets of Reef Points

S/S Boom Vang Bails on Boom & Base of Mast & Boom Vang Tackle

All Halyards, Main Sheet, Boom Vang, Reefing Lines for Both Reefs, and Main Boom Topping Lift are Led Aft to a Custom Schaefer 10 Gang Line Stopper and a Self-Tailing #30 Lewmar Winch with Handle

ELECTRICAL
4-12 Volt Marine Batteries with Perko Selector Switch to Isolate Batteries into Two Banks

Interior Lighting (12 Volt)

Electric Marine Head & Holding Tank with an Electric Off Shore Pump Out System

110 Volt Electrical System– includes O Duplex Outlets, 20 AMP Battery Charger, Marine Deck Connector and Circuit Breaker

One Electric Bilge Pump with Automatic Feature

International Navigation Lights

Engine Room Lights

Hot and Cold Pressure Water System

TANKAGE (approximate)
One 104 Gallon Fuel Tank

One 225 Gallon Water Tank (Below Water Line)

INTERIOR
Owners Cabin—Queen Size Double Berth, with 5″ Cushion, Hanging Locker with Cane Door, Bureau with Cedar Lined Drawers, Teak Ceilings (Hull Covering) Teak and Holley and Carpeted Sole; 2 Bookcase Alcoves, Four Opening Ports with Screens—"Sky Light" Ventilating Hatch, Full Length Mirror

Guest Cabin—Double Berth With 5″ Cushion, Hanging Locker with Cane Door, Full Length Mirror and Drawers, Two Opening Ports With Screens, Teak and Holley Sole

Head Compartment—Opening Port With Screen, Vanity with Mirror, S/S Sink and Drawers, Separate Stall Shower Compartment with Hot & Cold Water–Shower Drain Pump and Seat

Galley—Norcold 110 & 12 Volt Refrigerator with Freezer Compartment, S/S Gimballed Stove With Oven–Propane System with Two Aluminum Tanks and Solonoid Safety Shut Off System, Deep Double S/S Sink–Pressure Hot and Cold Water–Opening Port with Screen–Sliding Storage Lockers, Drawers, Teak & Holley Sole– Top Load 6 Cubic Foot Ice Box with Electric Drain Pump

Main Salon—Two Berths that Convert into Doubles–Two Bookcase Alcoves with Hull Ports–Hanging Locker–Plush 5″ Color Coordinated Cabin Cushions, Upholstered Back Rests with Storage Lockers Behind–Teak & Holley Sole– Hide-A-Way Fold Out Solid Teak Table Measuring About 3′ x 5′

Navigation Area—Full Size Sit Down Chart Table with Chart Storage under–Electrical Panel and Electronics Shelf

General—All Teak Interior– Beautifully Crafted Cane Panel Cabinet Doors for Superior Ventilation–Upholstered Headliner–Aromatic Cedar Lined

Drawers in Galley, Head Compartment, Guest Cabin and Owners Cabin—Teak & Holley Sole Throughout—16 Opening Ports with Screens

EXTERIOR
Exterior Wood Trim and Handrails of Oiled Teak

Two Bow, 2 Stern and 2 Amidships Mooring Cleats

Full Length Anodized Aluminum Toerail

Double Bow and Stern Pulpits and Double Life Lines with Gates Port and Starboard

Flip Down Boarding Ladder in Stern Pulpit

Inboard Genoa Tracks with Wide Sheave Blocks

Pedestal Wheel Steering System with S/S Wheel, Danforth 5" Compass with Binnacle, Engine Controls, Pedestal Guard, and a

Solid Teak Fold-Up Cockpit Table

Tinted Translucent Forward-Amidships and Main Companion Way Hatches

Hasp on Main Hatch for Pad Lock

Main Sail with Two Sets of Reef Points–Fiberglass Battens–Leach Line, Cunningham–Draft Stripes and Windowed Tell Tails

120% Genoa with Windowed Tell Tails, Leach Line, Draft

Stripes and Sail Bag

2 Cockpit Storage Lockers with Sliding Covers

1 Cockpit Seat Hatch

Flush Sliding Transparent Cover Over Cockpit Engine Instrument Panel

Specifications:

LENGTH OVERALL
42' 7"

LENGTH WATER LINE
35' 3"

BEAM
13' 9"

DRAFT-STANDARD KEEL
6' 0"

DRAFT-SHOAL DRAFT KEEL
4' 11"

DISPLACEMENT
21,000 lbs.

BALLAST
7,000 lbs.

BRIDGE CLEARANCE
60' 0"

Legnos Boat Building Company, Inc.
973 North Road, Route 117
Groton, Connecticut 06340

MYSTIC 20

The Mystic 20 is a nineteenth-century classic built with twentieth-century methods and materials. She is available rigged either as a cat or sloop. With the mast stepped well up in the bow, she is a cruising cat whose fine lines set her apart from her boxy, square-sterned working sisters. The rig is irreducibly simple. She balances well and, with all lines leading to the cockpit, she handles easily.

Rigged as a sloop and fitted with a bowsprit, the Mystic 20 resembles the graceful Noank sloop, designed in the 1800's for fishing off the Connecticut coast. She is versatile, she points well and she is steady in a seaway. Her sailing motion is that of a much larger vessel.

Whichever rig you choose, you get the same hand lay-up in the wood spars and bronze hardware, reflecting careful planning and expert craftsmanship. The cabin and cockpit best represent our philosophy of maximum utility and usable

space in minimum overall size. The area is spacious, with full sitting headroom and ample ventilation through a forward port, a large sliding hatch and removable companionway doors. A cabinet on the starboard side accommodates a portable head. To port, a counter includes a galley sink with storage under. A large teak cap in the centerboard trunk provides and ideal seat or work area. There is additional stowage under each 6' 6" berth, as well as a locker forward with two storage compartments and shelf. The cockpit is deep and roomy, offering security and comfort rarely found on a vessel this size. With companionway doors stowed and hatch open, there is

room for additional seating in the cabin, making it possible to take a large group daysailing.

The boat is quick, maneuverable and balances well, due to the shallowness of her forefoot and slackness in her forward sections. The optional inboard diesel engine offers security when the wind disappears and the added pleasure of leisurely cruises around the harbor. The raked, wineglass transom, inboard rudder, sweeping sheer and rounded cockpit make the Mystic 20 pleasing to the eye.

Specifications:

LOA
20'

BEAM
8'

DRAFT
(board up) 2' 1"
(board down) 4' 3"

DISPLACEMENT
3000 lbs.

SAIL AREA
Cat 282 sq. ft.
Sloop 273 sq. ft.

COCKPIT
7' 7" long

BUNKS
6' 6" long

McConnell Marine Limited
Rural Route #1
Nobel, Ontario, Canada
P0G 1G0

GEORGIAN 34

Bruce Kirby has drawn on his experience with the Laser's freestanding mast, added the convenience of the wishbone boom, the simplicity of the catboat and the safety of the ketch rig to produce the Georgian 34. Of classic catboat design, the beamy centreboarder will be as much at home in the coves of her native Georgian Bay as reaching down the Tongue of the Ocean with 1000 square feet of sails set.

The spacious deep cockpit will seat a crowd or provide shelter for an offshore crew. Below she has the space of a 42 footer. Eighteen feet of 6' 4" headroom with an open concept that will never give that closed-in feeling. Twelve opening ports and hatches, and two dorades will keep the cabin

fresh and light. Each of the sleeping areas has its own dresser with drawers and lockers. The starboard quarter berth can be closed-off to make a private cabin with its own entry into the head.

The sturdy Yanmar 23 hp diesel with 30 gals. of fuel will push the Georgian through the lumpiest seas for hour after hour. The generous sail plan and the ability to fly a staysail from the mizzen will keep her moving in the lightest air or surfing down an ocean roller.

Standard Equipment:

HULL AND DECK
Hull and deck fully cored with Klegecell P.V.C. foam for rigidity, insulation and elimination of water absorption by the core.

Extensive use made of uni-directional and woven materials rolled and squeegeed to assure high glass content for light weight and maximum strength.

Extra uni-directional materials installed and oriented for

maximum strength in highly stressed areas.

Unpigmented gelcoat used below the waterline to minimize blistering potential.

Molded non-skid in traffic areas textured for ease of cleaning and maximum safety.

High strength FRP floors installed in the hull to provide optimum strength combined with light weight.

Hull and Deck mechanically fastened and bonded with fiberglass tape to assure the strongest and most leakproof joint possible.

DECK HARDWARE AND TRIM
Molded bulwark with teak railcap.

Teak capped stainless steel bowsprit with bow roller.

Aluminum cleats and chocks for bow, spring and stern lines.

Full length teak handrails on coachroof for security on deck.

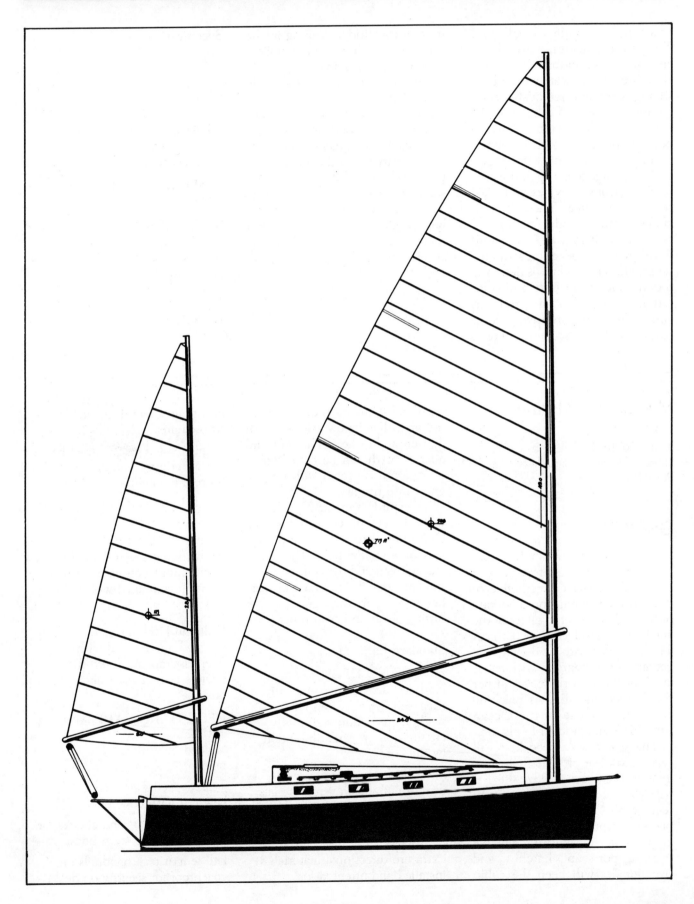

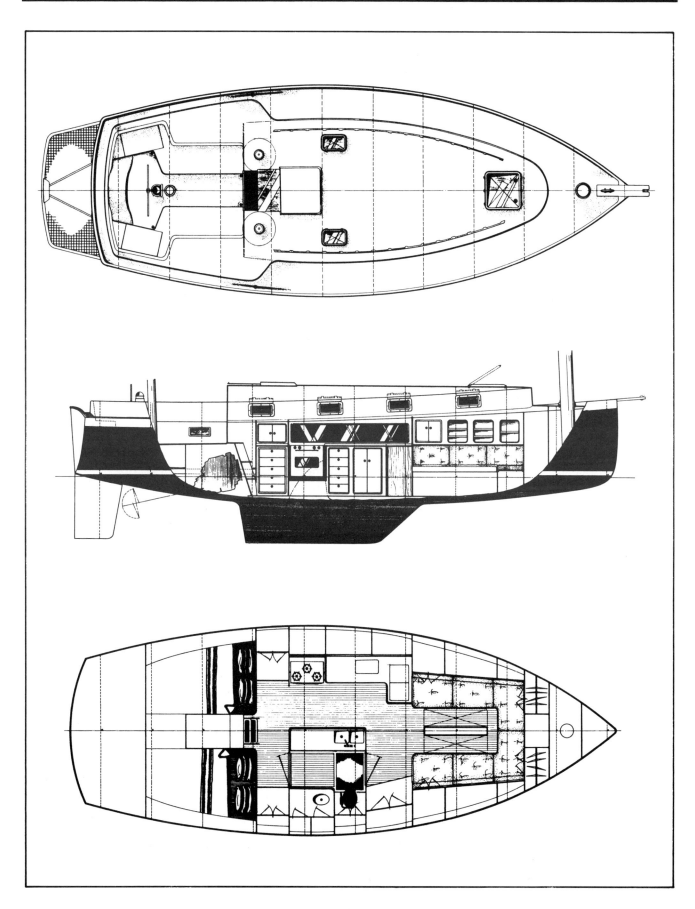

Stainless steel bow and stern pulpits, stanchions and stanchion bases. Bases fabricated to sit in deck-bulwark corner for extra rigidity. Vinyl covered stainless steel lifelines.

Large aluminum framed hatch over the main cabin-salon area, two aluminum framed hatches over the galley and head. Twelve aluminum framed opening ports including two in cockpit area to light and ventilate the quarter berth area, all with removable screens.

Two FRP cockpit hatches providing access to stowage, and self-draining propane tank locker.

Two generous stowage compartments in the cockpit coamings for winch handles etc.

Teak helmsman's seat. Stainless stern platform with dacron trampoline.

Lewmar winches with stoppers for halyards and control lines mounted on the coachroof.

Stainless steel boarding ladder.

INTERIOR
Bulkheads of teak and high pressure laminate with teak trim.

Teak and hardwood stripped plywood sole.

Panel type full height cabin doors with louvres.

Teak frame locker doors with rattan panels for proper ventilation of stowage areas.

Tinted acrylic sliding locker doors in the galley and head.

Bare teak tread ladder with handholds.

Teak handrails around the entire cabin for security below.

Two dry hanging lockers and one generous wet gear locker.

4″ polyurethane foam cushions with removable covers.

Wide range of fabric options.

Pine slat ceilings with Owner's choice of finish.

Top loading dry food locker.

Three burner gimbled propane range with large oven, one 25 lb. propane tank stored aft in self draining locker. Provision for installation of propane demand hot water heater standard.

Stainless steel grab rail around stove alcove.

8 cu. ft. reefer with highly efficient poured foam insulation, food grade FRP liner, with Adler-Barber "Cold Machine" refrigeration.

Teak drop leaf table with condiment and liquor stowage.

PROPULSION
Yanmar 3GM 3 cylinder, 23 HP diesel engine with 35 Amp alternator, full instrumentation, flex mounted.

Pedestal mounted engine controls, Water-lift exhaust system.

Extra heavy engine mounts to minimize vibration and noise.

Lead-on-foam sound insulated engine enclosure.

30 gallon fuel tank, extra primary water separater fuel filter, installation includes provision for direct sounding of tank. Fuel gauge standard, gauge at helm position.

Martec propeller standard equipment.

ELECTRICAL
Two 105 Amp hour batteries mounted in acid proof covered boxes, securely contained in position, provision for third battery.

Three position explosion proof selector switch. Battery space vented to deck.

16 position breaker panel with master breaker, voltmeter and battery test switch.

IMCO running lights.

Mizzen mounted deck flood light.

Interior footlights.

Indirect and direct lighting provided by incandescent and fluorescent lights.

PLUMBING
64 gallon fresh water capacity in three molded polyethylene tanks, individually filled and vented.

2″ diaphragm bilge pump mounted for on deck use, with screened intake mounted in deep sump moulded into hull. Wilcox Crittenden "Imperial" head, discharging into 30 gallon holding tank.

Seacocks on all through-hulls

Double stainless steel galley sink, single stainless sink in head.

Sump for shower and head sink with automatic pump.

"Telephone" style shower head.

Pressure water system standard.

Manual fresh water pump in galley.

KEEL AND CENTERBOARD
6000 lb. lead keel with stainless keel bolts bedded with two part polysulphide compound.

FRP centerboard trunk moulded integrally with the hull.

Solid FRP centerboard with stainless steel pin, stainless pennant led to winch on deck.

RIGGING
Tapered spun aluminum spars with welded mastheads.

Internal halyards, Aluminum luff groove track.

Lewmar blocks.

Prestretched dacron halyards, Yacht braid sheets and control lines.

Sheet winches and centerboard winch self-tailing type.

EQUIPMENT
Four approved dry chemical fire extinguishers.

5″ back lighted Ritchie Compass, pedestal mounted.

A.H. Moody and Son, Ltd., Southampton
Imported by Impex Marine Enterprises, Ltd.
P.O. Box 445
Reading, Pennsylvania 19603

MOODY 29

Designed by Angus S. Primrose

The Moody 29 is designed for simple handling but in such a way as not to detract from performance. Angus Primrose has designed a fast hull with a good ballast ratio so that she is both stiff and seaworthy. A substantial 20 h.p. diesel gives impressive performance under power.

The accommodation comprises 6/7 berths in two cabins. In the saloon the table folds away to provide additional living space and to enable the starboard settee berth to convert to a double. There is plenty of stowage everywhere and two hanging lockers. The separate toilet has decent headroom and its own washbasin. The galley has full cooking facilities with icebox, stove (with grill and oven), sink and plenty of stowage and there is a separate fixed chart table with chart stowage.

For a 29 footer to have this sort of space below usually means some compromise on deck, but this is not the case with the Moody 29. The foredeck well, so successful on the larger Moodys, and which makes sail handling so much simpler and safer, has been included. Side decks are generously wide and by utilising a transom hung rudder the cockpit is the sort of size you would expect to find on much larger craft.

The interior is finished in teak and to the same general standards as on the larger Moody craft, the equipment specification also has not been skimped, winches are up to the size needed, an alloy toerail is fitted, items such as compass and bilge pump are standard supply, and each boat comes with a Lloyds Register Certificate.

Standard Equipment:

SPARS AND RIGGING
Spars in silver anodised aluminum, mast incorporates winches and cleats for main and foresail halliards, internal halliards, aerofoil spreaders, integral spinnaker track and slider, deck foodlight and steaming light, boom complete with slab reefing hooks, three integral stoppers, internal reefing lines and clew outhaul. Standing rigging in stainless steel wire with stainless steel rigging screws, terylene halliards, kicking strap, burgee halliard and topping lift.

DECK EQUIPMENT
Aluminum alloy toerails incorporating alloy lifeline stanchions, stainless steel pulpit and pushpit and integral fairleads. Stemhead fitting with chain roller and anchor stowage arrangement. Chainpipe. Mooring cleats for'd and aft (4). Deck fuel and water fillers. Teak handrails to coachroof. Double stainless steel lifelines. Mainsheet track and slider. Genoa sheet tracks, sliders and turning blocks. Two Lewmar 24 two speed genoa winches and cleats. Ventilite vents to forecabin, toilet and main saloon. For'd hatch. Main hatch and garage. Teak washboards.

SAILS
Mainsail and No. 1 jib supplied as standard, complete with bags, tack and hanks.

COCKPIT
Large self draining cockpit, tiller steering, sail locker, self venting gas locker with space for 2 bottles, bilge pump.

HULL AND SUPERSTRUCTURE
Hull finished in white high gloss self coloured gelcoat, gold cavita line, waterline and flash painted, hull antifouled. Superstructure in pale blue with moulded integral non-slip surface.

ENGINE/ELECTRICAL
Bukh DV20ME 20 h.p. diesel flexibly mounted and acoustically silenced, two bladed propellor. Alternator charges twin heavy duty "Freedom" (no maintenance) batteries via 4 way master switch. Common earthing system to sacrificial anode. 12 V lighting in for'd cabin, toilet and main saloon. Chart table light. Full set navigation lights, compass light, deck light, steaming light.

ACCOMMODATION
For'd cabin comprising two berths, shelves above berths, stowage below. Toilet compartment with marine w.c., washhand basin, stowage space. Two hanging lockers. Main saloon with two settee/berths (one converts to double), foldaway table, stowage lockers behind berth, drinks locker. Galley with cooker (2 burners, grill and oven), stainless steel sink, f.w. pump, icebox, stowage for cutlery, crockery etc., quarter berth (cosy double) with stowage below, chart table with chart and navigation book stowage.

FURTHER STANDARD EQUIPMENT
Bilge pump (through cockpit mounted), porthole compass, dry

powder fire extinguishers (2), 25 lb. anchor complete with 15 fathom chain.

Specifications:

L.O.A. (excl. rudder)
28' 6"

L.W.L.
23' 7"

MAX. BEAM
10' 6"

MAX. DRAUGHT
4' 6"

DISPLACEMENT
7,300 lbs.

BALLAST
2,750 lbs.

SAIL AREAS

Main Sail
164 sq. ft.

Fore Sail
203 sq. ft.

No. 1 Genoa
322 sq. ft.

FUEL (approx.)
20 gallons

WATER (approx.)
40 gallons

MOODY 36

Designed by Angus S. Primrose

Interior Features:

CONSTRUCTION AND FINISH

Varnished teak bulkheads and trim throughout interior.

Main salon, galley, forecabin and aft cabin have white vinyl headliners.

Structural bulkheads bonded to hull.

Removable varnished marine plywood floors with carpet (teak sole optional)

Stainless steel brass hardware and locks on all doors and cabinets.

Stainless steel grabrails throughout interior.

Fiberglass molded settees, forward V-berths, and aft double berth with partitions bonded to hull for added strength.

All closets are woodlined and ventilated, thereby preventing condensation.

Blue vinyl storage bags are mounted under all seats and berths.

All bilges are finished with two coats of marine paint.

FORECABIN

Access to forepeak for stowage of anchor chain.

Two 6'4" single berths with 4' foam cushions and removable designers covers with seat in between.

V-berth insert provided to make double berth.

Ample shelf space with dividers over—and storage lockers under berths.

Two swivel reading lights mounted on bulkhead.

Large translucent opening, aluminum-framed hatch with vent over cabin.

Headroom—6'2".

Two hanging lockers aft of V-berth to port.

Solid core teak-faced door to head compartment, hung in laminated curved teak door entrance and bulkhead.

HEAD

The walk-thru head compartment is finished in attractive, easy to maintain formica, and teak varnished trim.

Marine Lavac toilet on starboard with extra hanging locker behind.

Washbasin with pressure cold/hot water, shower, teak grating, curtain, separate sump and pumpout on port.

Various storage cabinets, mirror, towel ring, glass-toothbrush and toilet tissue holder.

Overhead 12V. light and Dorade vent.

Teak faced door to main cabin, hung in laminated curved teak door entrance and bulkhead.

MAIN CABIN

L-shaped settee on starboard.

Large double leaf teak table with storage compartment in center.

6'5" settee on port.

All seat backs open to large outboard lockers, and above are bookshelves and closed cabinets.

Under the settees there is abundant storage capacity.

Fixed ports with drip rails, dorades and vents.

Large translucent hatch in center of cabin.

Overhead dome lights.

GALLEY

L-shaped galley near the companionway with gimballed stove, broiler and oven operated on LPG. St/steel sink with hot/cold instant hotwater heater.

Icebox and electric refrigerator.

Food lockers and drawer.

Dish storage above counter.

Separate liquor and glass cabinet.

TUNNEL

This protected area gives access to the engine room and has a comfortable pilot bunk, and large navigation table, with chart storage, storage shelves and instrument mounting space.

MASTER AFT STATEROOM

Large double berth, with full storage around and under area.

Vanity table, hanging locker, reading lights, overhead dome light and translucent opening ventilation hatch, with extra vent.

The head compartment is equipped with a marine Lavac toilet, separate holding tank, washbasin, lockers and optional shower.

Hot/cold pressure water system, mirror, towelrack, toilet tissue holder.

The head is finished in maintenance free formica.

Standard Equipment:

HULL AND DECK
Moody blue deck with white hull and blue sheer line and boot stripe.

Molded-in gold cove stripe, non-skid and non-glare decks.

Handlaid solid fiberglass (mat and woven roving) hull and deck according to Lloyd's approved construction.

Inward flanged hull to deck joint sealed and thrubolted to aluminum toerails and track.

Separate 2 bottle propane tank storage on deck.

Teak handrails mounted on cabin tops.

Blue anti-fouling bottom paint.

Bolted-on fin keel.

Extra reinforced cockpit seats.

Enormous cockpit lazarette locker under port seat.

Five interior bulkheads.

Unique forward deck well with drains, for ease of sail-or anchor handling.

Slanted cockpit coamings for comfortable seating.

DECK HARDWARE
Stainless steel pulpit and pushpit with gate.

COR type anchor with 20 fathoms of chain, hawse pipe with cover and anchor bow roller.

Hand windlass.

Four oversized bow and stern, midship mooring cleats with fairleads.

Stainless steel wire double life lines.

Aluminum stanchions bolted to toerails.

Companionway hatch with molded cover.

Dodger, stainless steel handrails.

Teak drop boards for main cabin entrance.

Aluminum encased windows with interior drip rails.

Aluminum framed, tinted Lexan forward and aft cabin hatches.

Fully removable cockpit sole for vertical access to engine room

Stainless steel Tannoy vents (3) and Dorade boxes (3) with PVC vents.

RIGGING—SLOOP
Proctor, heavy wall extruded aluminum mast and boom.

Mast stepped on deck over reinforced bulkhead.

Aluminum spreaders.

Oversized SS/rigging; tangs and turnbuckles.

Oversized SS/chainplates.

Wire conduit with messenger inside mast.

Internal roller reefing gear in boom.

Pre-stretched, internal main, jib and topping lift halyards.

Lewmar blocks, mainsheet traveller and winch.

Lewmar 2-speed sheet winches and halyard winches, handles and pockets.

Boom vang: 4:1.

Deck mounted genoa tracks.

Mast mounted spinnaker/track and eye.

Main and Jib sails.

Sailcover and color coded sail bags.

Fiberglass battens.

Lewmar blocks, main and jib sheets.

Mooring lines and fenders (3).

ENGINE, STEERING AND OTHER EQUIPMENT
40 HP fresh water cooled British Leyland, 4 cylinder Diesel.

Fully insulated engine room with access from tunnel.

Built-on engine oil removal pump.

Water injected wet exhaust system, with stainless steel waterlift muffler.

Recessed, lighted instrument panel in cockpit area.

Two-bladed left hand, folding propeller.

Stainless steel propeller shaft 1¼".

Rudder shaft stainless steel 1¾".

Orion rudder system with easy accessibility to entire system in aft cabin.

Steering pedestal with stainless steel destroyer type wheel and compass.

Emergency tiller.

Single-lever engine controls.

Single fuel-tank with clean-out plates, dip stick, 60 US gallons.

Central grease cylinder with twist lock to stuffing box.

Complete engine manual and instructions.

Sumlog with mileage day counter.

Depthfinder on stainless steel swing bracket.

Fire extinguishing system Halon in engine room.

Tool kit.

Log book and first aid kit.

ELECTRICAL SYSTEM

12 Volt D.C. electrical control panel with fuse box and explosion proof battery selector switch.

Four heavy duty 12 Volt batteries (90 AMP each) with easy access from engine room.

International navigation lights.

Deck light.

Steaming light.

All circuits wire coded.

Engine room light.

12 Volt interior cabin and reading lights.

PLUMBING

Pressure water system hot/cold to heads, showers and galley.

Instant, unlimited hot water supply LPG system.

Steel water tanks with clean-out plates 75 US gallons.

Waterfill plate on deck.

Manual 15 GPM bilge pump.

Lavac marine toilets with holding tanks.

Deck and overboard discharge.

Thru hull fittings are bronze.

Bronze seacocks, with grounding device.

Four self-draining cockpit scuppers.

Specifications:

LOA
36'0"

LWL
30'0"

BEAM
12'4"

DRAFT
5'0"

DISPLACEMENT
14,700 lbs.

FUEL CAPACITY
Approx. 60 gal.

WATER CAPACITY
Approx. 75 gal.

SAIL AREAS
Main–243 sq. ft.
Working Jib–263 sq. ft.
No. 1 Genoa–467 sq. ft.
Storm Jib–94 sq. ft.

MOODY 36S

Designed by Angus S. Primrose
Built for A.H. Moody and Son, Limited, Southampton
Imported by Impex Marine Enterprises, Ltd.

Standard Features and Equipment:

GENERAL

Hull and superstructure in GRP to Lloyds specification. 8 berth 4 cabins, aft cockpit, sloop rig, diesel inboard engine, separate toilet compartment with shower.

FO'C'SLE

2 berths convertible to a double as an option, stowage lockers, finished in teak veneer and teak trim. Emergency escape hatch.

TOILET

Marine WC with inlet and outlet seacocks, basin and pressurised hot and cold water system, towel rail, mug and paper fitments, cupboards, hanging locker with zip curtains in waterproof material. Finished in wipe clean laminates.

SALOON

'L' shaped settee/berth with second settee/berth opposite, table shelves and lockers. Fixed chart table. Finished in teak veneer and teak trim.

GALLEY

Gas cooker comprising two burners, grill, oven with flame failure device, gimballed with clamp type fiddle rail, stainless steel double sink with pressurised hot and cold water system. Good crockery and cutlery stowage space.

AFT CABINS

One port and one starboard running under cockpit. Double berth, locker space, wardrobe space. Completely separate from main saloon. Finished in teak veneer and teak trim.

AFT PEAK

Emergency steering position and stowage space.

FORE PEAK

Chain stowage.

COCKPIT

Seating both sides, access to locker/sail bin. Steering pedestal, engine instrument panel, and controls. Double gas locker.

ENGINE

Thornycroft T90 35 h.p. diesel engine with 1.8:1 reduction, or comparable replacement, with standard instrumentation and single lever control. Dipstick to fuel tank, shaft in stainless steel, two-bladed propeller in bronze.

ELECTRICAL

Charging by way of 12v alternator on engine. 2 heavy duty 12v batteries with 4 way switch. Electric lighting in cabins. Port/starboard, stem steaming and deck flood lights.

DECK EQUIPMENT

Stemhead fitting with chain roller, pulpit, 8 stanchions and sockets, lifelines, stern pulpit, chain plates, 4 mooring cleats and 4 fairleads, 2 genoa sheet winches with cleats, one main sheet traveller and cleat, 2 genoa tracks, sliders and blocks, handrails and ventilators, forehatch, fuel and water fillers. Anodised aluminum toerail.

SPARS

In silver anodised aluminum and comprising mast with winches and

cleats for main and foresail halyards, topping lift and burgee halyard. Main boom with reefing system.

RIGGING

Standard rigging in stainless steel wire, running rigging comprising halyards for main and foresail, topping lift and burgee in terylene.

SAILS

In terylene from a well known sailmaker complete with bags, tacks and hanks. Mainsail and working jib supplied as standard.

GENERAL EQUIPMENT

1 diaphragm type bilge pump, 1 set settee cushions and mattresses, fitted carpets, 3 dry powder fire extinguishers, 3 mooring warps, 3 fenders, anchor with 15 fathoms of

non calibrated chain, wheel steering, compass, Sumlog, echo sounder on swinging bracket, tool kit, first aid kit, log book, emergency tiller, mainsail coat, spray hood, cool box.

The above specification is intended to fairly represent the Moody 36S. However the right to amend this specification without notice is reserved.

Specifications:

Dimensions

L.O.A.
36'

L.W.L.
30'

BEAM
12' 04"

DRAFT
5'

DISPLACEMENT
14,700 lbs.

FUEL CAPACITY
c. 40 gal

WATER CAPACITY
c. 60 gal

Sail Areas

MAIN
243 sq. ft.

WORKING JIB
263 sq. ft.

WORKING JIB
467 sq. ft.

STORM JIB
94 sq. ft.

MAINSAIL
Standard

WORKING JIB
Standard

MOODY 41

Designed by Angus S. Primrose
With her three separate sleeping cabins the Moody 41 can sleep six in gracious style, or by using the saloon this number could be increased to nine without loss of comfort. Sailing performance is ensured by a good sail area/displacement ratio, a long waterline and high prismatic coefficient of the hull, while her longer fin keel combined with the balanced rudder, which is positioned well aft, maintains her directional stability.

The hulls of the Moody 41s are built in the Lloyds approved factories of Marine Projects (Plymouth) Ltd. and every Moody 41 carries a Lloyds Hull Construction Certificate. Marine Projects are firmly established as one of Britain's finest productions. Boatbuilders and the care and attention to detail upon which their reputation is based is clearly reflected in the internal fitting out which is all in teak. All fittings supplied are chosen to be more than suitable for their purpose and are obtained from world renowned manufacturers. A robust 48hp diesel engine from Thornycrofts gives the Moody 41 an appreciable turn of speed under power.

Standard Features and Equipment:

FORE PEAK
Chain Locker.

FORECABIN
A comfortable, spacious sleeping cabin with two single berths in a "V" formation with an upholstered seat in between. An infill piece to convert these berths to a double is available. A good sized hanging locker is to starboard with a dressing table unit in front. Stowage is also provided for along the ship's sides and underneath the berths. The cabin is fitted out in teak with fitted carpets on the floor areas and an opening hatch is fitted in the deckhead.

FORWARD TOILET
The forward toilet which is situated to starboard is fully fitted out with a Marine WC with inlet and outlet seacocks, washbasin and shower with hot and cold pressurized water system. The shower is fitted complete with tray, teak grating, curtain and electric pump. Also supplied are towel rail, tooth mug and brush holder and loo paper holder. There is plenty of stowage space and lockers all in easily wiped clean materials. An opening hatch is fitted in the deck head.

FORWARD GUEST CABIN
Is to port opposite the toilet. Two generous single berths are fitted against the ship's sides with a hanging locker on the forward bulkhead, and dressing table all finished in teak and with fitted carpet to the floor area. Ventilation is provided by an opening deck hatch.

SALOON
The Saloon on the Moody 41 is a particularly spacious area and great attention has been given to provide comfort and practicality. Two "L" shaped, deep buttoned and contoured settee berths are fitted to port and starboard which can be used as sleeping berths if required. Alternatively, the Port settee could be converted to a double as an optional extra. The table is split into two fixed units with leaves, which when raised form a really large dining table. Lockers are fitted all around the ship's sides. The saloon is again fitted out in teak with fitted carpets to the floor, although teak flooring can be fitted at additional cost if desired.

GALLEY
The galley is to the aft of the saloon on the port side and is separated from the saloon by a semi bulkhead. The "U" shaped arrangement of this area allows for an efficient and comfortable working space and at the same time provides for the protection of the cook from being thrown around the boat. A fully gimballed, lockable, gas cooker is supplied with two burners, oven and grill and with a safety bar fitted to the front. Twin S.S. sinks are fitted with one cover so that when one of the sinks is not in use there is extra working space. A top opening ice box and hot and cold pressurized water system is standard. Stowage for food, crockery, cutlery, etc. is plentiful.

NAVIGATOR'S AREA
Opposite the galley on the starboard side immediately adjacent to the companionway, and is completely self-contained with a large chart table and fixed navigator's seat. Care has been taken to make sure that adequate space is available for instruments and books. The panel for the boat's electrical system is positioned in this area.

OWNER'S STATEROOM
Reached from the Saloon through a passageway to starboard which is fitted with lockers and hanging space and from which access is to be gained to the engine compartment. The Owner's Stateroom is a truly comfortable and well appointed cabin with a large double berth surrounded on three sides by panelling above which is a stowage shelf and reading lights. An upholstered corner seat is next to the berth with the dressing table fitted to the forward bulkhead. As with

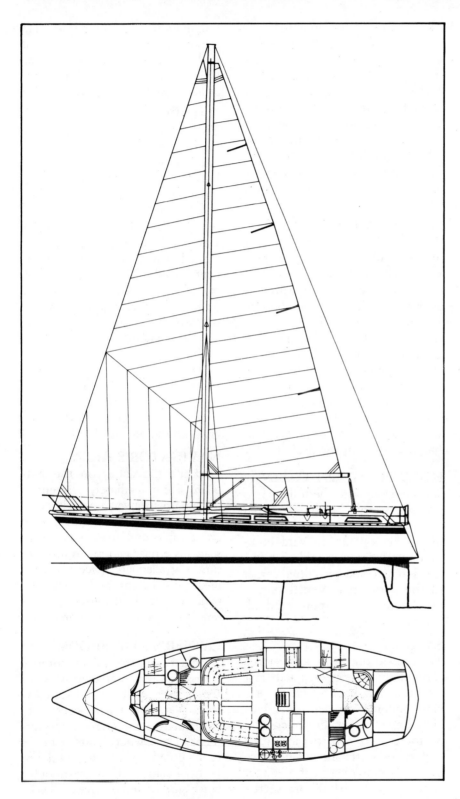

COCKPIT

The large cockpit has seating on both sides and aft with high combings to give added protection. The equipment fitted to the cockpit includes the steering pedestal, engine instrument panel, engine controls, navigation instrument console. Stowage available is really generous with a "step-in" and "stand up" locker large enough to take sails, all gear, fenders and even a deflated rubber dinghy. The double gas bottle locker is fully self-contained and has direct drainage.

ENGINE

Thornycraft T108 48 b.h.p. diesel engine with 1.8:1 reduction gearing. Hurth gear box (or comparable replacements). Standard instrumentation and single lever control. Sight glass or electrical gauge for fuel tank. Shaft in stainless steel and two bladed propeller in bronze.

ELECTRICAL

Charging is by way of a 12v alternator on engine, 3 heavy duty 12v batteries with four way change over switch. Electric lighting to cabins and navigation lights. Port/starboard stern/steaming and deck flood lights.

DECK EQUIPMENT

Stemhead fitting with chain roller, pulpit, alloy toe rail, stanchions and sockets, guard rails, pushpit, chain plates, 6 mooring cleats, 6 fairleads, 2 three speed headsail sheet winches with cleats, 1 mainsheet traveller with cleat, winch, 2 genoa tracks, sliders and rollers, handrails and ventilators, five opening hatches over forward toilet, forecabin, guest cabin, saloon and aft cabin. Fuel and water fillers, S.S. safety guard around mast.

SPARS

In silver anodized aluminum and comprising mast with winches and

all other cabins the Owner's Stateroom is furnished in teak with fitted carpets. An opening hatch is fitted in the deck head for light and ventilation but which also allows for emergency exit. The owner's private toilet compartment is fitted out to the same high specifications as the forward toilet with all fittings duplicated.

cleats for main and foresail halyards, topping lift and burgee halyard. Main boom with clew outhaul. Slab reefing.

RIGGING

Standing rigging in stainless steel wire, running rigging comprising sheets and halyard for main and foresail, topping lift and burgee halyard and terylene.

SAILS

1 Mainsail with 3 rows of reef points and cover, 1 Working jib. All sails in terylene complete with bags, tack, hanks and set of battens for the mainsail, from a well known sail maker.

GENERAL EQUIPMENT

Main compass, Echo Sounder with repeater in cockpit. Sumlog. Hand windlass. Anchor with 15 fathoms chain, Diaphragm type bilge pump, 3 dry powder fire extinguishers, 1 automatic fire extinguisher in engine room, 3 mooring warps, 3 fenders, 1 set of cushions/mattresses. Fitted carpets, wheel steering. Binnacle guard to steering pedestal, first aid kit, log book, emergency tiller.

Mooney Marine, Inc.
Route 33, P.O. Box 280
Deltaville, Virginia 23043

DEPARTURE 35

Designed by Charles Wittholz
Designed to produce good sailing characteristics on all points of sail, with 5′ draft, she is deep enough for upwind bluewater work yet shoal enough for lots of gunk-holing. At a moderate displacement of 16,480 pounds, she will be easily driven by her 600 square feet of sail. The cutter rig is quick to respond in light airs and easy to handle as the wind picks up. With the cut-away fore-foot and full keel she has a well balanced helm and tracks downwind true to her course. Her fine sailing balance and outboard rudder will make self-steering simple. If preferred, she may be ketch rigged but with either rig this design has the capabilities to go anywhere.

The bluewater interior calls for two quarter berths aft and two berths in the main cabin, providing comfortable accommodations for four. Two upper berths may be swung over the main cabin berths for that extra weekend crew. A wet locker where you need one, shelves, lockers and two large hanging lockers give ample stowage. The enclosed head forward does not close off the forward cabin

when in use and provides sail storage where a little dampness won't matter. A large chart table to starboard, and galley to port completes her practical arrangement.

Interiors are normally built on a semicustom basis, to order, and therefore tailored to every owner. For those owners who wish to extend their budget, we offer "kits" or packages, from the sail-away/motor-away to our popular Package "A", the completed hull, deck and cabin steelwork, including major deck hardware plus our beautiful Awlgrip custom paint work.

Understanding the problems owner/builders encounter, we have refined the DEPARTURE to simplify owner completion. After completion of the steelwork, the hull is ready for interior woodwork and equipment. Here again, STEEL offers advantages that no other material can match. Our STEEL hulls are structurally complete with a predrilled framing system for bolting in interior components. The first step is simply bolting firring strips to the frames. Then, with solid STEEL cabin sole beams already installed, a level, sturdy cabin sole is quickly laid. Bulkheads and partitions are put into place, followed by the installation of bunks and cabinetry. Finally, a wood strip or plywood ceiling finishes what is now a beautiful wood interior.

Specifications:

LOA
35' 0"

DWL
29' 0"

BEAM
11' 0"

DRAFT
5' 0"

DISPL
16,480 lbs

SAIL AREA
600 sq. ft.

Steel Scantlings:

FRAMING: TRANSVERSE
¼" x 3" flat bar on 42" centers

FRAMING: LONGTITUDINAL
¼" x 1½" flat bar on 12" centers

KEEL SHOE AND STEM
½" plate

KEEL SIDES
3/16" plate

HULL AND CABIN SIDES
10 ga. (.134")

CABIN TOP AND DECK
12 ga. (.105")
Hulls are sandblasted and cold galvanized inside and out. Built with all flat bar framing to eliminate hidden and hard to get at areas assuring total hull protection.

Morgan Yacht, Inc.
7200 Bryan Dairy Road
Largo, Florida 33543

MORGAN 32

Designed by Morgan Yacht, Inc.

The Morgan 32 is a sleek, strong and superbly stable yacht that sails the seas with supreme authority. An adventuress whose hull was designed for speed and comfort. Her interior for offshore luxury. And all her features and systems for durability and dependability both at sea and dockside. Under sail she's a dramatic beauty. And when the sails are furled she's quietly driven by a 20 hp diesel engine.

The Deck features a T-shaped cockpit with large self-draining scuppers, two seat lockers, teak coaming caps, and single-handled sail controls. There are four screened Lexan opening ports, two large fixed port lights, teak-capped bulwarks, and a translucent ventilation hatch forward.

The Interior is a show of luxury. The salon has teak veneer paneling throughout, teak and holly cabin sole, even a teak drop-leaf table. Its starboard settee converts to a double berth. There's an oversized quarter berth aft, and a chart table with hinged extension top. Behind a teak privacy door is the forward cabin, with a V-berth which converts to a double berth. The U-shaped galley has a deep double stainless steel sink, a 7 cubic foot ice box, and lots of storage space. The head also has a stainless steel sink, plus mica countertops, a fiberglass shower pan, and teak door.

Plumbing and electrical: All the plumbing is polybutylene tubing. The wiring is BIA color coded. The 12-volt DC electrical panel has indicator lights for each function. Included is a 65 amp battery with a vapor-proof switch.

Construction: The hull features hand laid-up fiberglass construction throughout and fire-retardant resin. The internal lead ballast is fully grouted into place and completely fiberglassed over for a "double bottom" effect. All thru-hulls below the waterline are recessed to minimize underwater resistance. The large skeg-protected rudder provides full control on downwind legs. (A shoal or deep draft keel is available.)

Standard Equipment:

HULL
Designed by Ted Brewer, Jack Corey and the Morgan Design Team

Laminate, hand-laid up with substantial structural re-inforcing

Fire retardant resin

Wood structures below cabin sole treated and sealed w/resin

Performance oriented, airfoil keel and skeg sections

Large rudder w/stainless steel post and steel reinforcing web

Bronze rudder heel casting

Shoal draft keel and rudder—4' 0"

Boot stripe blue (w/matching cove available)

U.L. approved sea valves on all thru-hull fittings below the water line

Fiberglass double bottom system over internal lead ballast

PVC drain from chain locker

Fwd. sole access for transducer installation

DECK & EXTERIOR HARDWARE
Bulwarks w/teak cap and aluminum rubrail

Mooring cleats fore and aft

4 opening ports (non-corrosive w/ Lexan glazing and screens)

Large fixed ports in galley and navigation areas

St. Stl. stern rail w/centerline gate opening and international navigation light

St. Stl. bow rail w/international nav. light

Lifeline gates port and starboard

Fwd. ventilation hatch of translucent acrylic, (w/closed cell neoprene gasketing) hinged, with adjustor and dogs

St. stl. stem and tack fitting (including headstay chainplate)

Fiberglass companionway hatch cover w/teak inlay

Fiberglass companionway spray hatch shield

Teak handrails port and starboard on cabin trunk

Large weather deck surfaces

White isopthalic gel deck w/white nonskid

Deck re-inforcing in way of all hardware

(4) Deck scuppers thru bulwork

Teak eyebrow on cabin edge

COCKPIT
Comfort designed seats and coamings

T-shaped foot wall for level-footed steering and winching

Large self-draining cockpit scuppers

(2) large, hinged seat lockers (canvas locker liners available)

Teak coaming caps—port and starboard

Steering system inspection through aft helmsman's seat

Steering pedestal w/5" illuminated compass w/anti-glare shield

28" stainless steel destroyer wheel

Traveller w/slide car, bridge deck mounted

INTERIOR
Carpet cabin sole

Teak veneer paneling on main bulkheads

Mildew resistant and fire retardant vinyl hull liner

6' 3" maximum headroom

Custom fabricated foam cushions

Decorator co-ordinated fabrics

Teak companionway ladder

Teak handrails

Vinyl covered berth tops

Teak fiddles throughout

All teak surfaces hand rubbed and oiled

12 volt DC decorator lighting

Engine room access on (3) sides

GALLEY
U-shaped galley

Galley located near companionway hatch

7 cu. ft. all fiberglass lined ice box w/hand pump to overboard discharge (shelving available)

3" maximum ice box foam insulation

Insulated ice box lid w/gasketing

Deep stainless steel sink

Stove, 2 burner alcohol, gimballed

Pot/pan stowage under stove

Dry stowage food locker, countertop opening

(2) sliding door dish lockers

Mica countertops

Manual water w/foot pump (pressure water available)

Utensil drawer w/locker under

MAIN CABIN
Chart table w/hinged extension top

Wet locker under chart table

Electrical locker outboard of chart table

Oversized quarter berth aft. of nav. station (stowage under)

Settee berth to port, stowage outboard (fuel tankage & stowage under)

Settee berth to starboard w/ removable backrest (converts to double berth) stowage outboard (water tankage and stowage under)

Teak, bulkhead mounted dinette table

(2) opening ventilation ports

PASSAGEWAY
Large teak hanging locker

(1) opening ventilation port

VANITY & HEAD
Mica countertop vanity w/st. stl.

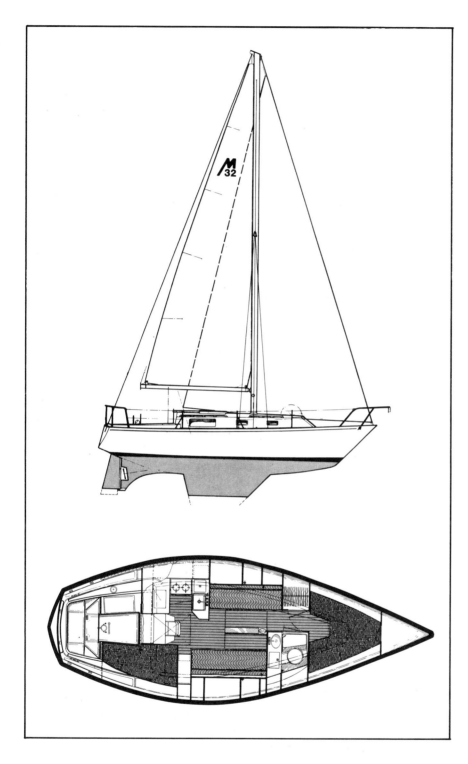

Teak privacy door

Mica bulkheads

FORWARD CABIN
V-berth with filler cushion to form double

(2) large stowage drawers

Bin stowage under berth

Teak hanging locker

Overhead, translucent ventilation hatch

Teak access door to chain locker

BILGE
Reinforced cast aluminum mast step

All lead ballast—no ferrous metal punchings

Wiring conduit for electronics from mast to panel

Sole access for cleaning and servicing

Mast step and chain locker only drain into bilge

SPARS AND RIGGING
Sloop rig

Mast stepped on keel

Mast/boom—glass peened (hardened) surface for increased strength & corrosion resistance

PVC wiring conduit w/messenger inside mast

Air foil section, aluminum spreaders

Complete standing & running rigging pkg. including genoa sheets

Extruded aluminum boom w/fixed gooseneck

Topping lift

Internal pre-stretched dacron rope halyards

Mainsheet w/6:1 purchase through Harken blocks

SAIL HANDLING EQUIPMENT
(2) 2-speed Lewmar 40 winches

sink, stowage locker under & bulkhead mirror

Top opening hamper outboard

Stowage locker outboard

Manual water w/foot pump (pressure water avail.)

Fiberglass shower pan

Marine, manual toilet w/lever pump

Holding tank w/deck pump-out

(1) opening, ventilation port light-port

(1) 10″ winch handle

(2) Lewmar 8 main and jib halyard winches

Genoa track w/slide car port and starboard

1¼″ x 8′ 0″ (inboard tracks available)

PROPULSION, STEERING & CONTROLS

Yanmar 3 GM 3 cylinder 22.5 hp diesel engine, complete w/tool kit, row water cooled

Fiberglass engine drip pan

1¼″ propellor shaft

Fiberglass stuffing box w/bronze boaring

3-blade propellor

Edson cable steering

Fiberglass cannister type, water cooled exhaust system w/transom mounted port

Bronze sea water strainer

Engine control panel, bridge deck mounted, complete w/ tachometer, and audio visual alarm for engine oil and water, compass light, blower and bilge pump switches on separate panel

Provision for optional emergency tiller

TANKAGE & PLUMBING SYSTEM

35 gal nominal polyethylene water tank w/inspection port

Semi-rigid polybutylene, corrosion proof fresh water lines

Fresh water filter

(1) manual water w/foot pump in galley

(1) manual water w/foot pump in head

Marine approved fuel line hoses & connections

27 gallon nominal baffled aluminum fuel tank w/weather deck fill, overboard venting and in-line fuel filter

Automatic bilge pump w/manual override switch

ELECTRICAL SYSTEM

All wiring ABYC color coded

(1) 70 amp, 12 volt marine battery

12 volt DC engine blower w/ supply and exhaust vents

International running lights on bow and stern rails

Mast head, foredeck and compass lights

Master battery switch

12 volt DC electrical panel w/ indicator lights for each function

Specifications:

L.O.A.
31′-11″

BEAM
11′-6″

DWL
25′-0″

SHOAL DRAFT
4′-0″

DEEP DRAFT
5′-6″

DISPLACEMENT (approx.)
10,000 lbs.

BALLAST
4,000 lbs.

MAST HEIGHT ABOVE WATER
45′-8″

FREEBOARD FORWARD
4′-4″

FREEBOARD AFT
3′-4″

SAIL AREA

Main
207 sq. ft.

Foretriangle
277 sq. ft.

Total
484 sq. ft.

AUXILIARY
Diesel

MORGAN 46

The Morgan 46 is a high performance yacht that can take any kind of weather with undoubted authority. You'll find that she is ideal for cruising the Caribbean or cruising to Tahiti. She's an exceptionally large 46 footer, stretching over 39 feet at the waterline and 13½ feet at the beam. Her proven hull design is fast, comfortable and directionally stable, with good interior volume. With the generous standard 60′4″ sloop rig and skeg rudder or the optional ketch rig, she sails and tacks beautifully. And under power, she moves ever so easily with her quiet, smooth 65 horsepower Perkins diesel.

The interior finish is warm and attractive with teak and holly cabin sole throughout, and teak bulkheads and trim. Her interior arrangement has been designed to insure live aboard comfort as well as entertaining guests at sea or ashore. The standard three stateroom accommodation plan features a plush owner's cabin with generous stowage and hanging lockers and a complete head with tub and shower. The forward stateroom will challenge yachting industry standards established for an owner's cabin. Complete privacy is again assured with a separate head complete with shower.

The standard passageway stateroom includes an over/under double berth plus a privacy door forward and aft head access door.

The Morgan 46 main salon will be the center of many activities. Her large L-shaped dinette invites elegant dining experiences serviced from her gourmet-styled galley. Opposite the dinette there is a pilot berth and combination set-

tee/double berth. Just aft of the settee is the pride of every serious sailor; a navigation station designed to fulfill your every need without compromise.

Features:

SYSTEMS

All the plumbing is polybutylene tubing and rigid PVC. All the wiring is color-coded to the recommended American Boat and Yacht Council standards and wired through a custom 115V AC, 12V DC modular electrical panel which contains hydraulic/magnetic breakers. The large fuel and water tanks make long extended passages a cinch. The easily adjusted main sheet traveler and three-speed Lewmar sheet winches make sail handling a joy. The optional Hyde rod roller furling system makes sail handling even easier, especially for short handed crews.

CONSTRUCTION

The deck and hull are both laminated solid fiberglass, with added sandwiched plywood coring in the deck. The keel houses internal cast lead ballast which is grouted around and fully glassed over for the extra protection afforded by this double bottom effect. All cabinetry and bulkheads are double bonded to the hull sides for their entire lengths with heavy 20-oz. woven roving. To create a unitized construction system for additional strength and stiffness, all cabinetry components are also bonded to each other. In addition, all exposed metals below the waterline are bronze to resist electrolysis.

Standard Equipment:

HULL

Hand laminated w/mat, woven roving and fabmat

Solid glass laminate throughout

Special mat sequence at hull centerline to add thickness and

improve resistance to leaks induced by impact

Shoal draft—5′ 3″

Internal cast lead ballast (8400 lbs.) grouted into deep cavity and fully glassed over

Substantial reinforcement in way of keel, chainplate attachments, centerline, mast step and sheer

White Isopthalic gel topsides w/ contrasting Imron blue boot and cove stripe

Structural non-corrosive heavy wall fiberglass shaft log

Cast bronze shaft strut and bronze shaft

U/L approved sea valves on all thru-hull fittings below the water line

DECK & EXTERIOR HARDWARE

White isopthalic gel deck w/white nonskid

Hand laminated w/mat, woven roving, fabmat and plywood coring.

St. stl. anchor roller chock assembly providing stowage for two anchors w/single hawse pipe and mooring cleat

Custom welded double rail st. stl. pulpit and pushpit w/gate in pushpit

European style international running lights pulpit and pushpit mounted

St. stl. lifeline stanchions w/ vinyl-coated st. stl. wire double lifelines and backup plates

Lifeline gates port and starboard

Forward hatch aluminum 21 x 21 frame hatch w/st. stl. Vent-o-mate, mounted on 2″ FRP boss molded into deck

Main salon hatches (2) 21 x 21 aluminum frame hatches

Midship cabin hatch (1) 10 x 10 aluminum hatch

Aft cabin hatches (2) 10 x 10 aluminum ventilation hatches w/ starboard hatch having a st. stl. Vent-o-mate

Forward and aft head—Acrylic light panels w/st. stl. Vent-o-mates

Galley (1) 10 x 10 opening aluminum hatch

Forward companionway hatch to be sliding w/FRP hatch cover and teak removable hinged doors

Aft companionway hatch to be FRP sliding hatch w/hatch cover, teak drop-in boards and st. stl. hand rails port and starboard

Flush mounted FRP lazarette hatch with drains from well

Sealed and vented deck stowage locker

FRP cockpit seat hatch w/FRP liner

Coaming locker

Opening parts on cabin sides (14) w/screens, sill drains

FRP steering pedestal w/5″ compass, engine controls, instruments and 36″ destroyer wheel

St. stl. pedestal guard

Cockpit deck plate for lifting engine from above deck

Four cockpit drains

Teak coaming caps

Teak deck handrails

Full length teak toerails w/ scuppers and six integral chocks

Teak taffrail

Four mooring cleats fwd. & aft, 2 midship cleats

Back-up plates on deck hardware

45 lb. CQR anchor w/ground tackle

MAIN SALON & STATEROOMS

3 stateroom arrangement

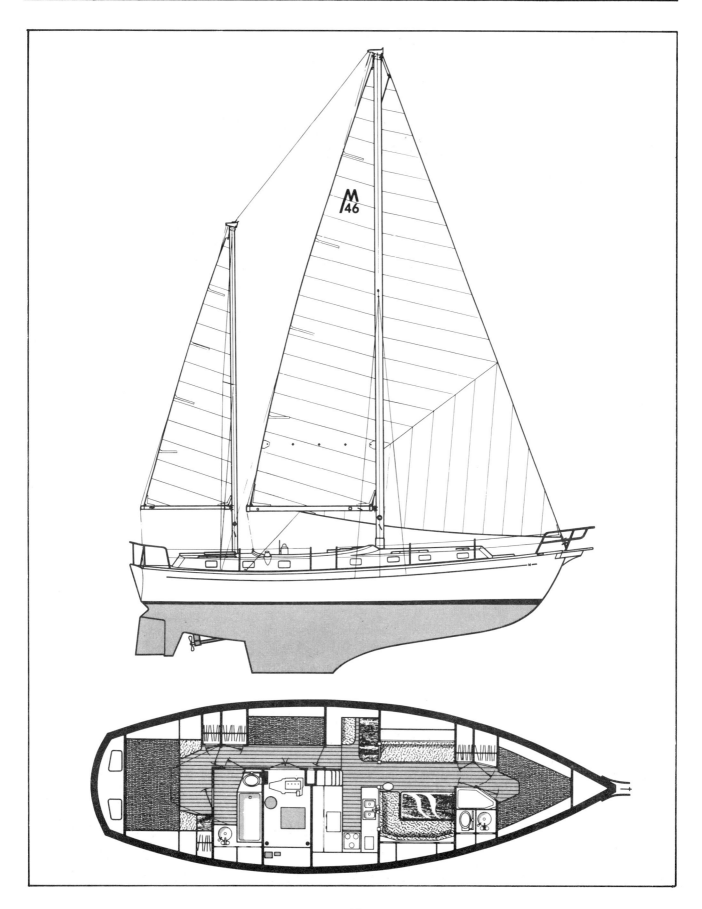

L-shaped dinette w/bulkhead mounted table

Settee/berth and pilot berth opposite dinette

Entire sole underside and bilges are painted with gelcoat for easy maintenance

Headroom 6'-2" minimum, except 5'-10" passageway/midship cabin

Maximum accessible stowage areas, drawers, bins and lockers

Vinyl covered berth tops

Teak and holly plydeck cabinsole throughout

Cabinsole on two levels w/ elevation change at nav. station

Custom fabricated 4" foam cushions w/deluxe color coordinated fabric in all cabins

Teak veneer paneling on main bulkheads and vertical partitions

Mildew resistant and fire retardant vinyl hull liner, partition coverings and hanging locker liner

Fiberglass and padded vinyl headliner

Teak forward companionway ladder, interior handrails, door frames & trim

Teak & st. stl. aft companionway folding ladder

Removable joiner work surrounding engine room to facilitate engine removal through forward companionway hatch

Forward stateroom with flat V-berth and insert, bureau, double hanging locker, drawers and shelves over berths

Midship walkthru area is a private stateroom w/over-under dbl. berth, hanging locker, drawers and oilskin locker

Aft stateroom w/large double berth, hanging lockers port & starboard, drawers under berth,

lockers above berth outboard w/ bin storage and cushioned valet seats port & starboard, w/sloped aft bulkhead

GALLEY
Large U-shaped galley

FRP stovewell - two burner st. stl. stove w/oven and gimballs

Double st. stl. sink with standard faucets

Emergency fresh water hand pump

17 cu. ft. divided top loading icebox with two access lids, larger compartment has rubber coated shelves & racks, 3" foam insulated, 2 pcf density urethane foam with a manual drain pump leading overboard and special insulated counter surface for max cold storage

Top loading pot locker

Mica covered counter surfaces

Food and dish storage lockers above counters

Drawers and lockers below counters

Custom fit cabinets for flatware and dishes

Custom area to fit 20 gal. garbage container

Water system control valves under galley sink cabinet

Dust bin in galley sole

Piping conduit from aft deck locker to stove well

HEADS
Joiner work mica covered with teak trim

Aft head has a tub/shower and a telephone style shower head

Forward head has a shower pan w/slot teak grate and telephone style shower head

Both tub & shower pan drains lead overboard via electric pumps

Holding tanks on both toilets w/ deck pump-out fittings

Emergency fresh water hand pumps in both heads and large home-size toilets w/lever pumps

Framed mirror in each head and vanity stowage cabinets with sliding doors

NAVIGATOR'S STATION
Full size athwartship chart table w/hinged top over chart stowage and locker below

Fixed navigator's seat

Outboard reference shelf

Electrical panel w/locker below and radio shelves outboard

Undersole conduit from mast step to nav. station

ENGINE ROOM & BILGES
Dual access to engine room thru passageway doors and aft head door

Removable joinerwork to facilitate engine removal

All tank fittings and clean-out holes accessible through sole drop-ins

PROPULSION & STEERING
Perkins 4-154 diesel engine w/ 2.73:1, Hurth reduction gear, fresh water cooling & 60 amp alternator

1-¼" bronze propellor shaft w/ intermediate bearing

Three bladed bronze propeller

Bronze sea water strainer

Pedestal mounted engine controls and instruments including tachometer, oil pressure and water temperature gauges, voltmeter and hour meter

Audio/visual temperature/pressure alarm

Engine bed thru bolted to hull stringers

Pedestal mounted hydraulic

steering unit w/st. stl. 36" destroyer wheel

Fiberglass rudder w/st. stl. shaft, cast bronze heel, and bearing, rudder cored w/polyester syntatic foam for light weight, high strength and maximum adhesion to rudder skins

Deck lights, navigation lights, bilge pumps and engine room blower controlled from steering pedestal

PLUMBING

Pressure water system distribution thru polybutylene tubing and filter at pump

7 gal. hot water heater w/engine bypass and 115 volt element

Marine heads w/manual pump to holding tanks or direct overboard discharge

Water tankage: 195 gal. nominal in FRP tanks, lined w/ sanitaryware gel and fully baffled-tanks are dipstickable w/central manifold, deck fills

Fuel tankage: 175 gal. nominal in fire retardant FRP tank, dipstickable & full baffled

All plumbing connections thru top of tank, deck fill 1750 gph submersible (2) bilge pumps

All standard tanks below the sole for improved weight distribution

ELECTRICAL SYSTEMS

All ABYC color coded wiring

All interior circuits wired thru one main junction panel

Custom 115 v AC/12 v DC modular electric panel w/ hydraulic/magnetic breakers & indicator lights 115 v 30 amp shorepower receptacle w/50 ft. cord

Ground fault circuit protection on wall receptacle

115 v duplex receptacles throughout

2—165 amp hr. marine batteries

4 position vapor-proof master battery switch

12 v lighting throughout

12 v engine room blower

12 v navigation lights including running lights, compass light, masthead light, foredeck light & bilge pumps controlled at pedestal

12 v receptacle at forward companionway to accommodate cockpit or deck light

Running lights are European style, international style, mounted on the pulpits

Night light system

110 v polarity protection

RIGGING
Sloop Rig

Mast & boom one piece aluminum extrusions w/maximum corrosion resistant satin-peened finish

PVC wiring conduit w/messenger inside mast

Aluminum airfoil section spreaders

Boom w/fixed gooseneck

Topping lift on boom

SAIL HANDLING EQUIPMENT
Two 3 speed Lewmar #48 sheet winches

Two 2 speed Lewmar #16 halyard winches

One Lewmar #16 mainsheet winch

Mainsheet traveler w/car and movable and stops

One 10" winch handle, one 10" lock-in winch handle

Genoa lead blocks on 1-1/4" x 12' T-track mounted on toerails

Deck mounted genoa sheet turning blocks

Specifications:

LOA
46' 6"

LWL
39' 3"

BEAM
13' 6"

DRAFT

SHOAL DRAFT
5' 3"

DEEP DRAFT
6'

DISPLACEMENT (APPROX.)
30,000 lbs.

BALLAST (LEAD)
8,400 lbs.

SAIL AREA: SLOOP
   100% of Fore Triangle–545 sq. ft.
   Mainsail–367 sq. ft.

SAIL AREA: KETCH
   100% of Fore Triangle–476 sq. ft.
   Mainsail–281 sq. ft.
   Mizzen–119 sq. ft.

PROPULSION
65 hp Perkins 4-154 Diesel

TANKAGE
   Water–95 gal.
   Fuel–175 gal.

MAST HEIGHT ABOVE DWL
   Sloop–60' 4"
   Ketch–56' 6"

OUT ISLAND 41

The new 416 version of Out Island 41 demonstrates a new expression of comfort and performance in a popular cruising yacht. So what's different? Her interior. Morgan changed things around to add to your cruising comforts and convenience.

Some things you'll see right off are additional seating in the salon

and a separate L-shaped galley. Some things you won't see are the extra storage space and up-graded electrical, plumbing and mechanical systems.

Of course, you'll still find a huge master stateroom with private head and shower. An enlarged forward guest stateroom with additional head and shower. Plus, an engine room, with room to get in and out. You'll also appreciate the large work bench across from the engine access doors.

And you'll still find deep shag carpeting in the staterooms. Teak sole in the main cabin. Teak bulkheads throughout.

There's liberal use of satin mica on counter tops and horizontal surfaces. And the entire interior is designed to offer maximum natural lighting and ventilation.

Top side, her big uncluttered deck is unchanged. There's still plenty of room to stretch out under the sun, plus a big center cockpit that gives you lots of room to maneuver.

You will also experience improved performance with the new 41's standard ketch rip. Her main and mizzen masts were relocated and she now carries 878 square feet of sail with a tailer double spreader mast.

Her hull is heavy, hand laid-up fiberglass with fire retardant resin and molded-in boot-top and sheer stripe. She has a full length keel with lead ballast, large fiberglass rudder with stainless steel post and her molded fiberglass deck and cabin top are sandwich cored with plywood construction for added strength and rigidity, as well as insulation. And for added safety and strength, deck hardware is through bolted.

Her big-wheeled, freshwater cooled Perkins diesel gives her performance and maneuverability most often associated with ocean going cruisers. She can go up to approximately 500 miles between refuelings. And she's highly maneuverable with her redesigned rudder—even in close quarters. Docking is a breeze.

Standard Equipment:

HULL
Solid fiberglass hand lay-up laminate, substantially reinforced in way of keel and all chainplates

Internal cast lead ballast securely fiberglassed into molded keel

Hull color white, with contrasting boot and sheer

Full length solid molded rubrail with aluminum cap

U/L approved sea valves on all thru-hull fittings below water line

Structural non-corrosive heavy wall fiberglass of shaft log

Interior wood construction treated with wood preservative below cabin sole

Fire retardant resin

DECK & EXTERIOR HARDWARE
White isopthalic gel deck with contrasting nonskid

Deck, cockpit and cabin are a plywood-cored sandwich construction, fully hand-laid with mat and roving into a single fiberglass molding

Aluminum anchor roller chock assembly with large roller

Pulpits are all stainless steel welded construction

Stainless steel lifeline stanchions with vinyl coated stainless steel double lifelines

Lifeline gates port and starboard

Deck hatch forward—21 x 21 cast aluminum frame hatch

Galley hatch—aluminum frame hatch

14 opening ports with Lexan glazing, non-corrosive frames, integral sill drains and screens

Two transom opening ports with screens

Two sliding fiberglass companionway hatches

Teak companionway drop-in boards fore and aft

Aft cabin hatch aluminum 21 x 21 frame hatch

Fiberglass helmsman's seat over beverage locker

5″ illuminated compass with anti-glare shield

Teak deck handrails

Full length aluminum toerails, slotted for finite adjustment of genoa block location

35 CQR Plow anchor with ground tackle

Fiberglass seat locker

Deck prism in cockpit sole to engine room

INTERIOR
Two double private staterooms

Forward stateroom with V-berth and locker

Aft stateroom with double berth, two hanging lockers, linen locker, bureau and dressing seat

Main salon with L-shaped dinette and settee opposite

Bulkhead-mounted folding dinette table

Settee convertible to sea berth with padded bunkboard

Dinette area converts into double berth

Two full-length shelves and storage locker in main salon

Teak interior trim and handrails

Mildew-resistant and fire-retardant vinyl hull liner and partition covering. Vinyl lined lockers

Large mirrors in both heads

Teak companionway ladders to main and aft cabins

Both heads with separate shower areas and fiberglass shower pans

Custom fabricated 4″ foam cushions with deluxe color coordinated fabrics

Teak and holly sole in galley and main salon

Carpet in private staterooms and passageways

Teak veneer paneling on main bulkheads and vertical surfaces

Vinyl covered berth tops

Teak chart table with 7 cu. ft. ice box, drawers and chart stowage below. Shelf above chart table with space available for electronics. Chart table adjacent to main companionway

Large engine room with maximum access to machinery

Double engine room access doors

Hand rubbed teak oil on all teak surfaces

Passageway work bench

GALLEY
Large L-shaped galley with bulkhead forming third side of "U"

Two burner stainless steel alcohol stove with oven and gimbals

Double stainless steel sink

Emergency fresh water hand pump on galley counter

Ten cu. ft. icebox, top-loading with flush-mounted lid

Compartmentalized shelf and storage lockers outboard of stove and over counter

Dry food storage locker under companionway ladder

Mica on counter surfaces

Hand pump for each ice box drain under galley sink

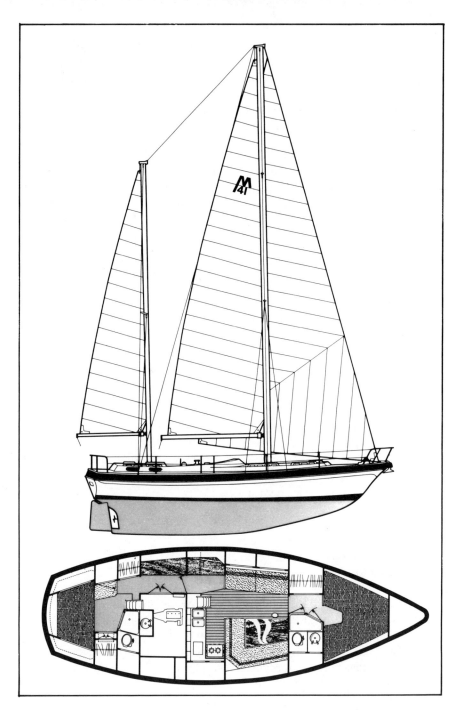

RIGGING
Ketch rig with complete standing and running rigging—all wire rope stainless steel

Masts and booms one piece aluminum extrusions with maximum corrosion resistant satin-peened finish

PVC wiring conduit with messenger inside masts

Aluminum airfoil section spreaders

Booms with fixed gooseneck

SAIL HANDLING EQUIPMENT
Two 2-speed Lewmar 42 sheet winches

Two 2-speed Lewmar 16 mast-mounted halyard winches—main

One Lewmar 8 mast-mounted halyard winch—mizzen

Two 10″ winch handles

Two soft-shell snatch blocks for genoa sheets

Deck-mounted genoa turning blocks

Main and mizzen boom topping lift

Main and mizzen sheet tackle

PROPULSION, STEERING & CONTROLS

Perkins 4-154 (62hp) diesel engine with 2.57:1 reduction gear with fresh water cooling & 60 amp alternator

1—¼″ diameter bronze propellor shaft w/intermediate bearing

3-bladed bronze propellor

Pedestal-mounted Hynautic hydraulic steering unit with stainless steel destroyer wheel

Fiberglass rudder with 1-¾″ diameter stainless steel shaft and ⅜″ gudgeon plate. Rudder is cored with syntatic polyester foam for light weight, high strength and maximum adhesion to rudder skins

Deck lights, navigation lights, compass light, bilge pumps and engine room blower controlled from steering pedestal

Bronze sea water strainer

Audio/visual alarm for engine oil and water

PLUMBING SYSTEMS

Pressure water distribution system with polybutylene plumbing and filter at pump

Water heater with engine by-pass and 115 v element

Marine heads with manual pump to holding tanks or direct overboard discharge. Holding tanks plumbed to deck plates

Water tankage—200 gal. nominal in 2 polyethylene lined FRP tanks

12 volt oil change pump

Fuel tankage—90 gal. nominal in 2 FRP baffled tanks

12 volt bilge pumps (2)

12 volt shower pumps, which pump directly overboard

Fuel and water gauges

ELECTRICAL SYSTEM

All ABYC color coded wiring

All interior circuits wired thru one main junction panel

Custom 115 v AC/12v DC modular electric panel with AC polarity protection

Hydraulic/magnetic breakers (MIL spec) with "on-off" indicator lights in main panel

115 v, 30 amp shorepower with 50 ft. cord and adaptor

Ground fault circuit protection on wall receptacle

115 v duplex receptacles throughout

Marine batteries—two 165 amp hr—12 volt

4-position vapor-proof master battery switch

12 volt lighting throughout

12 volt, engine room blower

12 volt navigation lights including European style running lights pulpit and pushpit mounted, masthead lights, foredeck light controlled at pedestal

Specifications:

LOA
41′3″

LWL
34′0″

BEAM
13′10″

DRAFT
4′2″

DISPLACEMENT
27,000 lbs.

BALLAST (INTERNAL)
9,000 lbs.

SAIL AREA: KETCH
100% of Fore Triangle–413 sq. ft.
Mainsail–312 sq. ft.
Mizzen–153 sq. ft.

PROPULSION
62 H.P. Perkins 4-1542.57:1 R.G.

TANKAGE:
Fuel–90 gal.
Water–200 gal.

OUT ISLAND 51

Morgan's Design Group was challenged to redesign the Out Island 51—already a proven world cruiser of exceptional performance—and make it the luxury standard of discriminating yachting.

Topside, the OI-512 features Morgan's outstanding contemporary Out Island styling—with a cockpit generous enough for entertaining dockside or sail handling maneuvers underway on any sea anywhere. A simplified rig makes extended passage or leisurely island hopping equally easy. Additional ondeck stowage and cockpit locker space keeps necessities at hand without having to go below.

But be prepared when you do go below! You'll find a new dimension in spaciousness, lighting and ventilation. The main salon features plush wrap-around seating, port and starboard, concealing generous outboard lockers. Overhead hatches and large windows in the main salon bring the outside inside. For entertaining, there's a large liquor locker and space for an icemaker—and for an optional fireplace! Teak joiner work and plush carpeting complete the salon's sense of true luxury.

The separate galley is a cook's delight with its two-door refrigerator/freezer, deep double sink, space for a microwave oven, extra lockers and storage areas, mica countertops and enough ports and hatches to far exceed normal ventilation standards.

To starboard of the galley is the family-size dinette area with comfortable seating for five. With more opening ports and an overhead hatch. Forward is the guest stateroom: large double berth, bureau, hanging locker for two and a complete guest head with dual entrance to allow guests access without entering the main living/entertaining areas. Inside the head is an enclosed shower stall with seat, vanity and space for the larger marine toilet.

To port of the forward head is a full workshop compartment with work bench and bifold doors closing it out from the main areas.

Aft from the companionway to starboard is a navigation center with chart table, shelves for complete electronics, opening port to cockpit and outboard, plus drawer bank, hanging locker, storage under the hinged table top and a bulkhead-mounted seat.

Inboard of the passageway is the engine room—large enough to accept the machinery necessary for a yacht this size and eliminating the servicing nightmares of many other sailing vessels.

Aft is the owner's suite—and more luxury. The queen-sized berth is surrounded on three sides by lockers. There's a settee with more storage under. There's even a giant cedar-lined hanging locker. A bureau and drawers in the berth face add to the abundance of storage space. Plush carpeting, overhead ventilation and opening ports surrounding the entire stateroom,

complete this luxurious area.

To starboard is an overly-spacious head with a separate bathtub/shower area, vanity with deep sink, mica countertops and storage locker under, outboard linen lockers, opening ports and an overhead hatch.

Features:

The new 51 features a hot-cold pressure water system, with all fresh water fed through polybutylene tubing. The two-panel AC/DC electrical system is in an ABYC-approved enclosure. The system also features hydraulic magnetic function breakers with indicator lights.

The hull is solid hand laid-up fiberglass. Airex®-cored for maximum strength and thermal-sound insulation. The internal cast-lead ballast is fiberglassed into the molded keel. All the below-waterline sea valves are bronze. All the interior wood construction below the sole is treated with preservative, including the 1½" plywood structural main bulkheads.

Standard Equipment:
HULL
Hand laminated construction thru-out

Airex sandwich core construction

Solid glass laminate in way of all thru-hulls

Solid glass laminate in way of all attached chainplates

Fiberglass double bottom system over internal lead ballast

All interior wood construction below sole is treated

Structural, non-corrosive FRP, heavy wall shaft lag w/bronze bearing & stuffing box

Choice of boat top and sheer stripe color

Rubrail—clear anodized

aluminum half round on solid molded-in FRP boss

Bronze sea valves on all thru-hulls below waterline

DECK & EXTERIOR EQUIPMENT
Plywood cored laminate

Aluminum fabricated anchor roller assembly w/chrome bronze chain deck pipe

Custom welded S.S. bow rail

Custom welded S.S. stem rail w/gate

Stanchions w/vinyl coated double lifelines

Lifeline gates—P&S

(8) aluminum frame deck hatches w/tinted Lexan (6) 21" x 21" double opening, (2) 10" x 10" ventilation

"Oversized" companionway hatch w/teak inlay

Teak hinged companionway doors

Teak deck handrails

Insulated FRP cockpit beverage box w/drain

(3) Cockpit stowage lockers w/FRP liners and drains

(1) side deck stowage locker w/fiberglass liner

(2) Cockpit coaming stowage bins w/teak retainers

Large cockpit drains

Cleats—bow & stern (12" anodized aluminum)

Cleats—midship springline—P & S (12" anodized aluminum)

5" illuminated compass w/sunshield

(24) opening portlights (w/tinted glazing & screens)

Lo-glare cockpit lighting on steering pedestal

(4) large, fixed windows

Perforated aluminum toe rail

(1) large opening port—above starboard cockpit footwell, for communication to nav. area

INTERIOR CONCEPT

Live aboard interior accommodation plan

Custom upholstered foam cushions

Teak veneer on all bulkheads in living and sleeping quarters

Mica bulkheads in fore and aft heads

Teak trim thru-out

Low maintenance mica countertops and shelf areas

Teak interior handrails

Archway, teak cabin doors with laminated trim thru-out

Deck beams thru bolted to all major structural bulkheads

Sole drop-ins for easy access to bilge, tank fittings and thru-hulls

Indirect fluorescent lighting around entire perimeter of yacht with teak valance

Teak parquet sole in areas of galley, companionway ladder and nav. station

Teak companionway ladder

Deluxe, plush carpet in living and sleeping areas

Protective chase tubes for all primary plumbing and wiring runs under sole

Hand rubbed oil on all exposed teak

Teak and/or mildew resistant vinyl lined lockers

Oilskin locker, adjacent to companionway

(4) hanging lockers (teak or cedar lined)

Teak ceiling panels around upper perimeter of hullside, in coordination with foam padded, leather grain vinyl on lower areas of ceilings

All berth taps vinyl covered

INTERIOR CONCEPT

Double treatment headliner with a combination of stretched leather grain vinyl and fiberglass with matching pattern. Removable vinyl panels in areas of deck hardware and for access to underside of weather deck.

FORWARD STATEROOM

Double berth with 6″ foam mattress

Drawer and bin stowage under

Port side locker with mirrored sliding doors and mica shelf

"Oversized" teak retainer on locker shelf

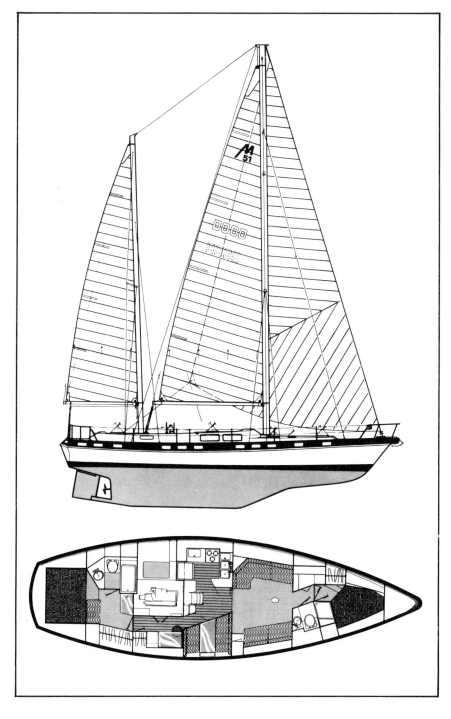

Teak lined hanging locker with interior light

Teak bureau with drawers and bin

Privacy door from forward passageway

Separate privacy door from stateroom to fwd. head

12v bulkhead lighting

(2) opening portlights with screens

(1) 21″ x 21″ overhead hatch

Plush carpeted sole

FORWARD HEAD

Separate FRP shower stall with teak slat seat

Mica covered outboard locker with large shelf

Mica bulkheads

Mica vanity top with S.S. sink

Hand held shower with bulkhead bracket

Re-inforced FRP sole pan and head mounting platform

Shower curtain track

Shower light

Lockers with shelves outboard

(2) Opening portlight with screen

(1) 10″ x 10″ ventilation hatch

Vanity mirror with fluorescent lighting

WALK-IN HANGING LOCKER

Cedar lined

MAIN SALON

Open, spacious entertainment, living area (approx. 8′ x 12′)

Oversized, deep settees for lounging or sleeping (approx. 30″) with 5″ cushions

"L" shaped settee (port side) with stowage bins under

Mica shelves with teak fiddles outboard

Starboard settee with stowage bins under (space for opt.

fireplace fwd. of this settee on bulkhead)

Mica shelves with teak fiddles outboard, full length of settee

Teak bulkheads with laminated trim

Liquor locker with "mixing" shelf at aft end of starboard settee, locker under for additional stowage (space for opt. icemaker)

Indirect fluorescent lighting

12v bulkhead lighting

(6) opening portlights with screens

(4) double opening 21″ x 21″ overhead hatches

(2) Large fixed windows for additional light

Plush carpeted sole

DINETTE

Dining area, on raised platform, across from galley

Condiment locker outboard

Drawer (1) and bins (3) stowage under each seat

Additional stowage outboard under seats

Teak table on hi-lo pedestal (converts to form an oversized double berth)

4″ foam cushions and backrests

(2) opening portlights with screens

Indirect fluorescent lighting

12v bulkhead lighting

(1) large fixed window

GALLEY

Large U-shape for fingertip convenience

Fiberglassed lined icebox (approx. 10 cu. ft.) with insulation on all sides including underside of top and lid. Compartmentalized w/ plastic coated shelving.

Gimballed, 3-burner alcohol range with oven

Two door, upright 12v/110v refrigerator, freezer. Full door storage, vegetable bins, door locks. Freezer with door stowage, ice cube trays and door lock.

Concealed, garbage bin with large removable container

Mica countertops

Double, extra deep S.S. sink

Auxillary manual water pump

Dry stowage locker

(3) drawer teak cabinet

Food and dish stowage lockers outboard w/mica shelves

12v fluorescent lighting

(2) Opening portlights with screens

(1)Large fixed window

NAVIGATOR'S STATION/ WALK-THRU

Teak top chart table, hinged w/ chart stowage under

Full length mica shelf outboard for electronics

2 stowage drawers, 1 bin stowage

Large, teak lined hanging locker at aft end of area; interior light, mica shelf top

(2) Opening portlights with screens

(1) Large opening portlight to cockpit

Teak parquet sole

Double door access to engine room inboard

Deluxe electrical panel on inboard bulkhead, adjacent to navigator

Aircraft style, chartlight on spiral extension cord

12v bulkhead lighting

OWNER'S STATEROOM AFT

Queen size berth w/6″ foam mattress. Access to steering & stowage under. Teak lined lockers on (3) sides surrounding berth w/

mirrored doors to stowage lockers. Mica shelves w/oversized teak retainers (3)

Double door cedar lined hanging locker w/interior lighting

Teak bureau w/drawers and bins

Large mica shelf spans hanging locker & bureau

Settee w/4" foam cushion w/ stowage under

Teak vanity/desk w/stowage locker & shelves and drop down surface for desk use

(5) opening portlights w/screens

(1) double opening 21" x 21" hatch

Plush carpeted sole

Bulkhead mounted teak steps for emergency exit thru overhead hatch

Large cedar lined linen stowage drawer

12v bulkhead reading lights

Indirect flourescent lighting

AFT HEAD
FRP sole & head platform unit

Mica bulkheads in bathtub/shower area

FRP bathtub w/hand held shower

Mica locker outboard of tub w/shelf top

Mica vanity top w/S.S. sink; stowage locker under

Linen lockers outboard w/sliding doors

Vanity mirror w/fluorescent lighting

12v bulkhead lighting

(2) opening portlight w/screen

(1) 10" x 10" ventilation hatch

Shower curtain track

SPARS/RIGGING
Ketch rig, single headsail

Roller furling rod headstay

Split backstays w/link plate

All extrusions 6061-T6 aluminum alloy

All spars glass peened (hardened) for strength and corrosion resistance

Tapered main mast

Double spreader rig, aluminum airfoil sections w/full length intermediate shrouds

PVC wiring conduit inside main mast

Fixed goosenecks on main and mizzen booms

S.S. 1 x 19 standing rigging

Navtec double toggle stainless steel turnbuckles

SAIL HANDLING EQUIPMENT
(2) Jib self-toiling winches—Lewmar 48

Mainsheet traveler w/car, adjustable and stops, (1) Lewmar 40 winch and sheet cleat

Mainsheet—⅝" dacron (1) w/5:1 purchase

Jib sheet—⅝" dacron (2)

Internal—wire/rope halyards (2) main mast

(2) Main mast halyard winches—Lewmar 16

Mizzen halyard (1) w/Lewmar 8 winch

⅞" sail track on all spars

Outhaul cars on main & Mizzen booms

Main & Mizzen topping lifts

Mizzen sheet winch #16 Lewmar with cleat

Genoa roller furling winch #16 Lewmar w/cleat

PROPULSION/STEERING/CONTROLS
Perkins 4-236 (85 hp) diesel engine w/Hurth, 2:1 transmission

1-½" S.S. propellor shaft

Bronze sea water strainer

Hydraulic steering system

Fiberglass steering pedestal w/single control lever, engine instrument panel, engine start and kill buttons, 5" compass

S.S. pedestal guard

S.S. rudder stock (2-½" diameter)

Structural fiberglass shaft lag

3-blade bronze propellor

Water lock exhaust system

PLUMBING/MECHANICAL SYSTEMS
Hot/cold pressure water system

FRP water tanks (2) with 265 gal. approx capacity individual deck fill plates & valve system

FRP fuel tank (1) with 235 gal. approx capac., deck fill plate, fittings plate to accommodate main engine and optional generator supply and return

Bilge pumps (2) 12v, heavy duty 1750 gpm, submersible

Manual head w/holding tank waste system w/deck plates (2)

Emergency water hand pump in galley

Fresh water distribution thru polybutylene tubing

Engine room sound and heat insulation

Water heater—12 gal. 110 v. w/engine by pass

Shower/tub drain pumps w/overboard discharge

ELECTRICAL SYSTEMS
(2) panel AC/DC electrical system in ABYC approved enclosure

Hydraulic/magnetic function breakers w/indicator lights for all systems, including option functions

12v DC panel equipped w/60 amp main, bilge alarm indicator and amp/volt meters

115v AC panel equipped with (2) sets of amp/volt meters for (2) standard 30 amp shore power lines, and includes all necessary switches and/or equipment for optional generator installation as standard, including freq. meter

Nine pole power selector for ship or shore power w/built in polarity protection

(2) 50' —30 amp shore power cords

60 amp battery charger

Specifications:

LOA
51'6"

LOW
43'0"

BEAM
15'0"

DRAFT
5'6"

DISPLACEMENT
46,000 lbs.

BALLAST (LEAD)
12,000 lbs.

SAIL AREA
  Main–384 sq. ft.
  Mizzen–209 sq. ft.
  100% of Foretriangle–494 sq. ft.

PROPULSION
85 HP Perkins Diesel

TANKAGE
  Water–300 gals.
  Fuel–265 gals.

MAST HEIGHT ABOVE DWL
64'6"

Nordic Yachts, Inc.
5481 Guide Meridian
P.O. Box 964
Bellingham, Washington 98225

NORDIC 40

Designed by Robert H. Perry

Designer's Comments:
With the plug for the "44" tooling still warm, the Nordic group commissioned the design of a 40 footer to be called, of course, the Nordic 40. Rather than simply parrot the characteristics of the 44 I chose to push the concept farther towards the area that seemed to be responsible for the success of the 44. That area is performance. Modern hull design technology has taught us that with the appropriate longitudinal distribution of hull volumes we can optimize speed potential without reducing the useable living space in the accommodations. This involves a midship section with a hard turn to the bilge for stability and fairs into a relatively flat bottom to reduce superfluous displacement. I have used a moderately high prismatic coefficient of .55 on the 40 and coupled this

with a medium/low displacement to length ratio of 234. While it is not uncommon today to find displacement to length ratio dipping down below 100, care must be given if the effect on interior comfort is to be avoided. Below 200 the room for incidental items such as tanks, lockers and bilge sump starts to disappear. My experience has shown me that tanks, lockers and bilge sumps are not exactly incidental to the accommodation of cruising yachts. I keep my displacement to length ratios between 260 and 200 when given the chance.

"The keel configuration of the 40 is near identical to the 44 and this has proven very effective. Outside ballast is used and again I reiterate that there is no substitution for outside ballast where safety is concerned.

"The rudder is slightly raked aft which can be justified by hydrodynamics but in truth was done to facilitate construction and insure a proven rudder/skeg shape. I anticipate that the 40 will be a fast boat with excellent speed off the wind due to the broad stern. The fine entry and stability of the boat should insure good on-the-wind speed.

"It is not unusual today to find three cabin layouts on forty foot boats. In the Nordic 40 we incorporated a stateroom aft with a double quarter berth to starboard. This area could be left open in the traditional manner or closed in with some variation. The galley is large and incorporates a wet locker into the forward counter thus providing extra space for a larger than usual ice-box. The V-drive installation of the engine allows the accommodations to be pushed aft and opens up more available space than straight drive installations. The head is large and includes a separate shower stall.

"There is nothing 'trick' or novel in this interior. As our experience grows we are slowly evolving a set of basic standards for interiors that result in adaptive and spacially effective layouts. The Nordic 40 utilizes our proven basic layout with the inclusion of subtle refinements and innovations. For instance, note that the mast is moved forward to an area where it does not conflict with the components of the main cabin area.

"This slightly forward position of the mast on the Nordic 40 is a development of something we have been working on very intensely. There is a critical balance between fore triangle area and mainsail area in terms of ease of handling. True, the large fore triangle will add a tenth of a knot or two on the wind, but the negative side of this is that large genoas are difficult to handle and the rig will require reefing earlier to maintain good helm balance. I have moved the mast slightly forward on the Nordic 44 and the result is a boat with a feather light helm and the feel of a much smaller boat in terms of helm pressure. While fore and aft lowers could be used if an owner demanded, current sailing practice has taught us that performance can be substantially increased if there is some control over the mast bend. To this end I have designed the 40 with centerline lowers and a baby stay. The running backstays that show on the sail plan will be needed very infrequently and only when the wind and sea conditions require the additional fore and aft stiffness to reduce the mast pumping.

"Close study will show that the entire cockpit area was lifted from the 44 mold, as is, and used again for the 40. While this was economically advantageous of course, the prime reason for the adaptation was the fact that we feel the Nordic 44 cockpit is very close to the 'ideal.' The seat backs are curved and the seat tops follow a changing camber to allow for a flat footing surface at the bridgedeck and gradually fair into very comfortable contoured seats aft. Seat lockers are huge and the T-shape allows

for an immense wheel."

Standard Equipment:

Universal Model 5432 diesel (32hp) w/Hurth 2:1 reduction V-drive. Engine is mounted on aluminum foundation and thru bolted to longitudinal stringers. Engine is fresh water cooled.

12 Volt 55 AMP Motorola alternator w/transistorized regulator.

Pedestal mounted throttle and shift controls with Morse jacketed cables.

Water cooled exhaust system with Vernatone fiberglass muffler. Seawater intake system is provided with valve and in-line seawater strainer.

1¼" stainless steel propeller shaft through cast bronze stuffing box and fabricated shaft log which is bedded and thru bolted to hull. Propeller is 2 bladed bronze. Strut is cast bronze with rubber cutless bearing.

55 gallon aluminum tank mounted to stringers. Piping is copper tubing with flex line attachment to engine. Fuel filter/water separator is Racor Model 200 FF. Fuel fill is mounted in cockpit sole to facilitate measuring fuel level with dip stick provided. Shut off valves are provided at tank and fuel filler.

1 each type 30-H-24 (90 A.H.) engine starting battery. 1 each type 8-D-24 (204 a.h.) ships power battery. Guest 2401 battery isolator allows alternator to charge batteries as required without switching. Perko Model 9601 switches provide disconnect and battery paralleling function. Power distribution is provided by master panel located at navigation station.

Includes 50 ft. cordset providing power to A.C. section of master panel located at navigation station. A.C. outlets are located in head, aft stateroom, galley and forward stateroom.

Controls and monitors all A.C. and D.C. power functions. Voltmeters and ammeters are provided for both A.C. and D.C. Breakers are provided for most equipment which would normally be installed on a vessel of this size. Additional space is provided for installation of breakers for extra equipment. The A.C. main breaker section includes polarity indicator. Indicator lights mark critical functions. 20 AMP automatic battery charger.

All underwater fittings are properly bonded to sacrificial aincs which are attched to strut.

All lighting is 12 volt. Fluorescent overhead lighting is provided in head and galley. Incandescent overhead lighting is provided in sa-

lon, staterooms and navigation station. Incandescent reading lights are provided at berths in both staterooms. Engine room light, shower light and chart table light are provided. All navigation lights are high intensity type. Port/starboard (red/green) mounted on bow pulpit. Stern light mounted on stern pulpit. Combination bow light/deck flood light mounted on mast. Anchor light mounted on mast head. Red compass light.

Aqua Meter 199 Galaxy compass, w/stainless steel case and cover.

Two stainless steel tanks with 130 gallon total capacity. Tanks are properly baffled and vented. Jabsco pressure pump with filter and accumulator tank. 6 gallon hot water tank (110 volt and engine heated).

Pressure hot and cold faucets at head sink and galley sink. Fresh water foot pump at galley. Oval stainless steel sink in head. Deep double stainless sink at galley.

Molded fiberglass shower stall with seat in head. Alsons personal shower with mixer valve.

Wilcox No. 1460C water closet, 16 gallon holding tank with dockside pumpout connection. Selector valve allows waste to be discharged directly overboard or into holding tank.

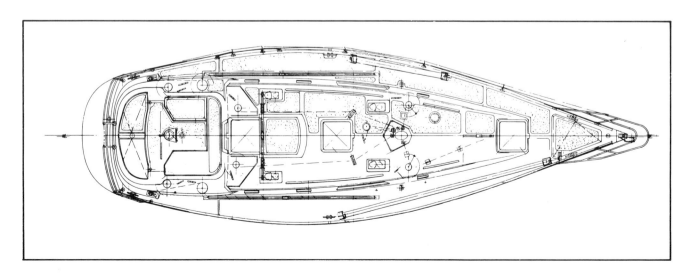

Deep bilge sump accommodates all drainage. 1 each Rule 1500 G.P.H. automatic bilge pump is provided. 1 each Guzzler 500V manual bilge pump and 1 each Edson 638 (1 gal/stroke) are provided with suction lines in sump. Suction lines are fitted w/strainers.

Underwater fittings are flush mounted bronze thru hulls with ball valves. Hoses attached with stainless steel hose clamps.

All cabinetry is teak veneers and solid teak. Formica covering is provided on working surfaces and berth flats. Cabinet doors are provided with positive finger latches. Finish is minimum 3 coats hand rubbed teak oil. Doors are provided with retaining hooks and swing stops.

Foam and suede vinyl covered detachable headliner panels for access to wiring, deck hardware fastenings, etc.

All cushions polyfoam. Aft stateroom berth cushion is laminated foam. Wide selection of covering fabrics and urethans offered for customer selection.

3 burner gimballed Hiller propane stove with oven. 5 gallon propane tank mounted in lazzarette propane well (room for two tanks). Solenoid actuated shut-off valve at tank is operated with switch mounted on master electrical panel. System is thoroughly tested after installation.

Molded fiberglass ice box with 8.5 cu. ft. capacity. Insulated with minimum 3" polyurethane foam. Wrapped with polyethylene vapor barrier. Drained to bilge sump. Shelves are provided for food storage.

All hatches are Golot with tinted plastic. Companionway 28" x 28". Foredeck 28" x 28". Main cabin 23" x 23", aft of mast.

4 dorade boxes molded integrally with deck. Fitted with 4" Nicro flexible cowls. Screw in cover plates provided on interior.

Ample teak hand rails on interior and exterior.

Two fixed windows with trim rings. 6 each Vaassen opening portlights.

4 each 10" anodized aluminum mooring cleat, thru bolted with backing plates.

Chocks or chafe plates where applicable.

Welded and polished combination stem fitting/anchor bow roller. Roller is machined polyethylene with stainless steel shaft.

Anodized Goiot toe rail thru bolted (hull and deck) every 4¼"/ Coordinated Goiot stanchion bases, chocks and end fittings are used.

1¼" Merriman T-track with Merriman wide block Genoa lead cars. Blocks are predominately Schaefer.

28" bow and stern pulpits are welded and polished stainless tubing. Intermediate rails are provided. 28" stainless steel stanchions support double life lines which are P.V.C. coated stainless wire. Lifeline fittings are stainless steel. Lifeline gates are provided port and starboard.

All winches are Lewmar chrome plated brass, 3 each winch handles are provided.

Primaries (2)—48C, Genoa halyard—40C. Main halyard (1)—40C, Main sheet (1)—42C, Reef (1)—30C, Outhaul/Flattener—8C.

Denouden composition non-skid matting is applied to recessed areas of deck with recommeded adhesive. Color is gray.

Main traveler track and babystay track are Nicro-Fico #1169. Main traveler car is 6 wheel Nicro-Fico #1391. Babystay car is 4 wheel Nicro-Fico #1162.

Mast and boom are extruded aluminum with linear polyurethane paint coating. All halyards, reeflines, outhaul and topping lifts are led internally. Provision is made for 1 each main halyard, 2 each Genoa halyard, 2 each Spinnaker halyards, 1 each pole topping lift, 1 each boom topping lift and 3 each reef lines with jam stoppers. Mast is tapered. V.H.F. Coax and Messenger for wind instrument cables are provided in mast.

Standard rigging is navtec stainless steel rod with appropriate end fittings, turn-buckles and toggles. Removable link is provided in backstay for future backstay adjuster installation.

Running rigging is braided dacron with stainless wire where applicable. Main halyard with shackle. Main topping lift. Main sheet. Traveller control lines. Outhaul. Reefing lines (2). Genoa halyard. Halyards may be left aft to cockpit if desired.

Norseman Yachts
14025 Panay Way
Marina Del Rey, California
90291

NORSEMAN 447

Designed by Robert H. Perry

The hull form of the Norseman has been designed to accentuate control, comfort and speed. The compromises required to achieve this balance of characteristics are slight. Control is assured by the proven mid-length keel/vertical rudder on skeg combination. The key is directional stability and maneuverability. Too often in the full keel yacht you have directional stability at the expense of maneuverability. Keel fin length is designed to provide accurate lateral plane for windward ability, suffic-

ient volume for internal ballast and a substantial platform for haul outs under less than optimum conditions. Comfort at sea is a function of stability, dryness, the ability to make safe and quick passages and a comfortable motion resulting from stability charcteristics.

The speed of the Norseman comes from its sharp entry and powerful quarters and clean run. The basic hull shape is not oriented toward any singular sailing condition or point of sail, but to general all around good performance. There is no sacrificing downwind safety and control for upwind speed.

Possibly one of the most interesting aspects of this design is the deck configuration. The simple, hackneyed phrase, "form follows function" somewhat inadequately describes the design origins of this

deck. The "form follows function" approach possibly describes the base origins of this deck but to this beginning careful design has been added to insure an aesthetically pleasing and no less functional result. For lack of a better term they have dubbed this deck configuration the "pickle fork shape." The "pickle forks" extend forward of the short cabin trunk to partially enclose and provide security, storage bins and integral dorade boxes in the working area around the mast. The forks don't detract from the partial flush deck appearance of the Norseman. The usual price for the beauty of a flush deck forward is headroom, but the Norseman's deck incorporates a subtle bubble between the forks to retain full standing headroom throughout the interior while adding to the aesthetic complexity of the deck.

Note there is no anchor well forward. Perry is convinced that anchor wells on yachts over 40 feet unreasonably limit ground tackle options. Note too the plethora of open hatches. The cockpit features contoured seats and seat backs plus large hatches for access to the lazarette and aft stowage areas. There is a slight raised bossing in the top of the cabin trunk to aid in the installation of a dodger. Another touch you might not notice is the faceted corners on the cabin trunk aft. This treatment enhances the appearance while reducing superfluous bulk in the deck structure.

The big question in planning accommodations is should the design orient itself towards comfort offshore under adverse conditions or comfort at the hook, in the most tranquil of bays? The two criteria need not result in polarized accommodation plans. Of course, stacked quarter berths are best for sleeping offshore and voluminous dinettes best accommodate the cocktail hour at anchor. But between these extremes the Norseman provides an interior that has a double quarter berth, in its own stateroom that can be divided to provide two very comfortable sea berths or, undivided, a very roomy owners' berth. Opposite the owner's stateroom is a head with separate enclosed shower stall and large wet gear locker. Special attention has been paid to storage in the galley and the comfortable dinette can be left set up without hindering movement forward. This interior maximizes privacy, open spaces and versatility while not resulting in a layer cake type exterior.

Standard Equipment:

(Sloop Rig)

Main, jib (Cutter rig optional).

Internal lead ballast.

Molded one piece hull and deck.

Balsa cored deck.

Vetus non-skid recessed on house, deck, and cockpit.

Six anodized aluminum Goiot hatches.

Nine Vassen anodized aluminum opening ports.

Five Simpson/Lawrence tempered glass deck prisms.

Five Lewmar winches, two #55 primaries, two #40 halyard winches, one #42 main sheet, all hard anodized aluminum.

Mariner blocks, track, and traveler.

Yacht Specialties cable quadrant steering w/32" wheel.

Stainless steel bow and stern pulpits.

Double life lines with tapered S.S. stanchions.

Recessed area provided for navigation instruments.

Vented compartment for two 5 gal. LP.PG. tanks.

U.S. tapered aluminum mast with internal halyards and reefing, L.P. paint, anchor and steaming lights, foredeck light.

Stainless steel tie rod.

American standing and running rigging.

Navtec turnbuckles.

Navigation lights to International specifications.

Five molded dorade vents with Nicro Fico flex vents.

Contoured cockpit seats.

61 h.p. F.W.C. lehman diesel engine with V-drive and 2:1 reduction.

Strainer on salt water intake.

Vernalift exhaust system.

Racor spin filter.

Electric fuel pump.

Two Henderson manual bilge pumps.

One Par electric bilge pump.

4 Whale foot pumps.

Two Par shower sump pumps.

Pressure water system with Par pump.

Ten gallon American water heater.

Two Par (ITT) marine toilets w/ 15 gallon holding tank.

Two 120 amp marine batteries.

110V shore power connector with eight outlets.

US manufactured master electric panel with circuit breakers and metering indicators.

Interior lighting: ten dome lights, eight reading lights.

Stainless steel bow roller system (double).

Six anodized Schaefer mooring cleats (four 10", two 8").

Accommodations for seven in 3 cabins.

Three hanging lockers.

Contoured interior seating with vinyl covers.

Navigation station with contoured seat.

Separate wet locker.

U-shaped galley with pantry, trash bin, double sinks.

Area provided for cabin heater in main salon.

Six fixed tinted acrylic windows.

Teak and satin finished formica interior.

Interior teak satin varnished.

Teak and holly cabin sole with satin Varathane.

Teak interior hand rails.

Exterior teak gloss varnish.

All exterior surfaces are gelcoat.

Four stainless steel water tanks, 120 gal.

Two black iron fuel tanks, 100 gal.

One FRP holding tank, 15 gal.

Note: All tanks are removable thru companion way hatch.

Three fire extinguishers.

Six life jackets.

One horn.

One ship's bell.

Five mooring lines.

One emergency tiller.

Two fenders.

Specifications:

LOA
44'7"

DWL
37'6"

BEAM
13'0"

DRAFT
6'4"

DISPLACEMENT
28,000 lbs.

BALLAST (LEAD)
INTERNAL
12,000 lbs.

SAIL AREA
937 sq. ft.

ENGINE
61 hp F.W.C. Lehman Diesel

Pacific Seacraft Corporation
3301 So. Susan St.
Santa Ana, CA 92704

CREALOCK 37

Designed by W.I.B. Crealock

The Crealock 37 is, in a sense an orphan, denied the usual parentage of builder and seller. Crealock designed her simply because he thought she might appeal to those who wanted a boat to go anywhere with true speed and safety and, above all, without the handling problems that speed so often brings. "I did not worry about long-waterlines or short-waterlines or I.O.R. bumps or distorted ends or revered classic features," Crealock says. "I seem to remember Shakespeare saying ' . . . there is a destiny which shapes our ends . . ." Well, her ends were shaped by her destiny, and if drawing them out gave her a little more elegance and seakindliness, then they were drawn out.

Thirty years of designing and many years of deep water cruising lie behind the 37.

"Let's face it," Crealock says, "every builder of cruising boats claims that their product approaches the speed of light under way, sails straight into the wind, is built to smash ice, has a penthouse within it, and is sold by a nonprofit organization."

So how can one make a choice? Don't go by the claims, go by results. For speed look at Dave White's 37, which placed second

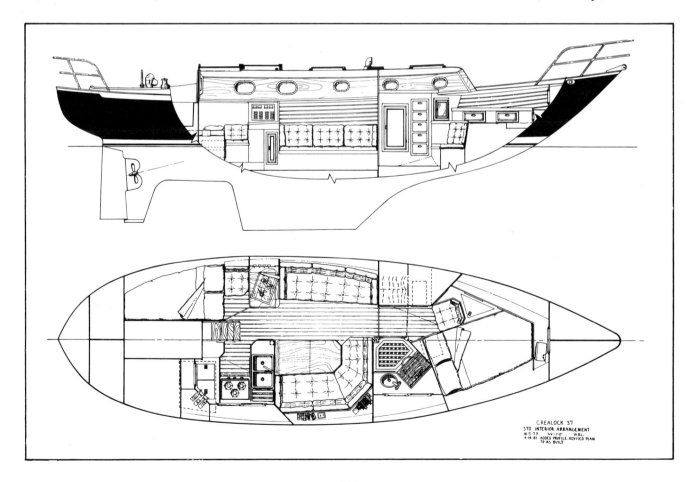

overall in the single-handed Trans Pac against many larger boats, and for close-windedness one can look at the tests to which she was put by two sailing magazines. For her strength and integrity, you have Pacific Seacraft's reputation.

Crealock feels that the "split underbody deserves some comment, since it may appear unconventional to some in a cruising boat designed to go anywhere. "We really put a great deal of thought into the exact configuration of the keel and bustle and skeg," says Crealock. "The danger there is that the keel and skeg of a racing boat will simply be transplanted onto the cruiser. But the requirements are quite different and the sections chosen should also be different if directional control is not to be sacrificed—as it sometimes is. I think we succeeded because two owners have complained that because the boat steers so well, it was a waste to choose a wheel instead of a tiller."

Crealock does not believe there is any magic shape of bow or stern for a cruising boat, but that a well designed example of any type will serve well. "However, I do feel," he says, "that there are levels of performance. You have transom sterns and counters, lifeboat types and Colin Archers, the cruiser sterns and the canoe, and when you analyze them all I feel that the canoe, if it has sufficient overhang, offers the most advantages. It gives appreciably better lines to the hull than the other double-enders, and it offers that vital factor of reserve buoyancy without presenting too much of a rump to the seas; it does take a lot of care in the designing. If you would judge a stern, realize first that it will have more effect on the motion of the boat than will the bow, secondly, when the going gets really tough, your stern will probably have to serve as your bow; remember this when you are dreaming about running under

bare poles from your neighborhood hurricane."

Rig, Crealock feels, is very much a personal choice, and Pacific Seacraft offers sloop, cutter, staysail cutter, yawl, and double-headed yawl. Given a good hull and rig that provide an acceptable level of performance, there are one or two factors Crealock feels are not usually given enough consideration in the choice of a cruising boat. "I feel that sometimes one gets so caught up in the concept of the fast passage that one loses sight of the fact that the passage itself should be one of the pleasures of the cruise, and I think there are three factors that contribute to that goal. The first is motion; a boat with an uncomfortable motion not only brings fatigue to its crew, but it makes it difficult to regard the passage as more than a necessary interlude during which one holds tight and longs for the landfall, instead of a time for relaxation and enjoyment. Displacement and hull shape are the principal factors (after size) that affect motion, and except for boats designed for special purposes or for those hardy individuals who are unaffected by motion, you are going to suffer if your displacement drops too low. Hull shape means primarily bow and stern and midship section shape and it is up to the designer to weigh these factors in the initial concept. The second factor is balance, that elusive quality which makes a boat responsive under almost any conditions and which means that the crew does not have to fight the boat every yard of the way. When you are shorthanded and you grow weary of those long night watches, a balanced boat can make a world of difference. Thirdly, there is the cockpit—a most vital factor on a long cruise. This is the heart of the boat—the clubroom, the patio, so why, in heavens name, be content

with a flat, straight-backed seat?"

"And what of the cockpit size? In my opinion, when people promote the advantages of the small footwell cockpit, they are simply saying 'sorry, we didn't have room for a decent cockpit.' Consider the safety aspects of a spacious cockpit with a barrier between it and the accommodation below. Let's assume it fills with water. If the boat has a properly buoyant stern this will mean a temporary aft trim lowering the stern several inches—hardly catastrophic. There will also be a loss of stability of perhaps 5 to 10%. As soon as the boat heels, or if she is already heeled, which is more than likely under such conditions, most of the water is spilled out of the upper part of the cockpit and the loss of stability is rapidly reduced. Any possible danger from such a flooding is surely far less than the danger of being swept out of a shallow cockpit. I know what it's like to spend long night watches trying to lean against a seven-inch coaming. Give me a comfortable, secure cockpit every time."

During the entire production process, Pacific Seacraft has worked directly with Crealock to deliver the closest rendering of the designer's specifications possible. Her hull is one-piece hand-laminated fiberglass of enormous strength, achieved by alternately hand applying layers of woven roving and mat, then squeezing out all excess resin to obtain the maximum glass-to-resin ratio. Deck strength and insulation are increased with balsa core and wood stiffening. Finish beauty, both inside and out, and fine joiner work are hallmarks of Pacific Seacraft.

The vital hull-to-deck connection is engineered with a double flange completely bedded in polyurethane compound and then thru-bolted with 18-8 stainless steel bolts. It is the strongest, most watertight connection available.

On going below, you'll find a warm interior designed for long, comfortable ocean cruising. From her 6'3" headroom to her teak-and-holly sole, no comfort has been spared. Teak and oak are used throughout for all cabinet and joiner work within. All upholstery is first quality decorator fabric selected for beauty, durability, and stain resistance.

Specifications:

LOA
36'11"

WL
27'9"

BEAM
10'10"

DRAFT
5'4"

DISPLACEMENT (APPROX.)
16,000 lbs.

BALLAST (LEAD)
6,000 lbs.

SAIL AREA
573 sq. ft.

YAWL
619

CUTTER
708

HEADROOM
6'4"

Pan-Oceanic Marine, Inc.

2575 South Bayshore Drive
Miami, Florida 33133

OCEANIC 46

Designed by Ted Brewer

The Oceanic 46 Pilothouse Cutter is one of a family of four offshore cruising yachts designed exclusively for Pan-Oceanic Marine by Ted Brewer. Pan-Oceanic states their prime objective is to build into every boat the qualities knowledgeable sailors care about: safety, comfort, performance—value.

Hull and rig are constructed to exceedingly strong specifications. The hand-laid fiberglass hulls and decks are constructed of alternating layers of woven roving and matt, with laminate well squeegeed to ensure a consistently high glass-to-resin ratio. The securely engineered hull-to-deck joint, thoroughly bedded, is through-bolted at five-inch centers. Down below, beneath this solid exterior, lie spacious and well-appointed accommodations that have delighted all those who have stepped aboard. The joinery and superb wood finishes are of the quality you would

expect from expert craftsmen working with select materials. Pan-Oceanic will work with you on any special modifications you feel will best suit your needs. Onboard systems are to highest U.S. Marine standards and are specifically engineered to provide safe and reliable service. The popular pilothouse cutters offer full-size aft-cockpits and the luxury of an extra, completely independent steering station out of the weather. Pan-Oceanic builds, commissions, and sells and services each of their yachts themselves. They fit the finest equipment and hardware they can find. The specifications of the 46 are indicative of the whole family: Oceanic 41, Oceanic 43, Oceanic 46, and Oceanic 55. Shoal draft options and a center-cockpit version of the Oceanic 43 are available.

Standard Equipment:

Main with double reef points.

Yankee jib.

Staysail.

Staysail boom and fittings.

Main boom gallows.

Mainsheet traveller.

Staysail traveller.

Sail covers and bags.

Two #28 jib sheet winches.

Two #24 sheet winches.

Three #20 halyard winches.

Genoa tracks and snatch blocks.

Jiffy reefing.

Dacron running rigging.

Stainless steel cleats.

2 station steering with full engine instrumentation.

S.S. Destroyer wheels.

Two 5" compasses.

Anchor, chain and rode.

Welded stainless steel bowsprit.

Teak grate bowsprit platform.

Two bronze anchor rollers.

Stainless steel bow pulpit.

Stainless steel stanchions and bases.

Double lifelines and gates.

USCG safety equipment.

Dorade boxes with cowl vents (7).

13 bronze opening ports.

4 bronze hawse pipes.

PVC tubing in mast for nav. wiring.

Spreader lights.

Masthead light.

International navigation lights.

12 Volt pressure water system.

Hot water, 110 Volt and engine heat exchanger.

Copper hot water plumbing.

Two showers and sumps.

Two US heads with anti-siphon on outlets.

12 Volt bilge pump.

Manual diaphram bilge pump.

Choice of stove type.

Teak cutting board.

Teak deck (Non-skid option).

Teak rub rail, toe rail, cockpit seats and grating.

Six cast aluminum cabin hatches.

Teak companionway hatch.

Teak and holly cabin sole.

Padded vinyl overhead.

Fully lined lockers.

Teak boarding ladder.

Fabric covered interior cushions.

S.S. mast rail.

Sea chest.

Divided chain locker.

Specifications:

LOA
45'8"

LWL
38'6"

BEAM
13′6″

DRAFT
5′10″

DISPLACEMENT
33,500 lbs.

BALLAST
11,500 lbs.

BAIL AREA
1,093 sq. ft.

Parker Dawson
Corporation
55 Park Road, South Shore Park
Hingham, Massachusetts 02043

PARKER DAWSON 26

Designed by Bob Finch

Designed on the West Coast by Bob Finch and tank tested at Lockheed Aircraft Company, the hull form gives excellent stability in heavy weather and the low wetted surface and unique swing keel design provide exceptional light wind performance. She is easy moving and pulls very little wake with almost no quarter wave.

She's close winded and tracks very well. She goes where she's pointed and her excellent wheel steering keeps her on course for long periods of time "hands off." When her course needs adjusting, because of her big rudder positioned all the way aft, only a slight touch is needed for correction and she'll answer her helm when other boats would have lost steerageway. She tacks readily under all conditions, even when sailing under working jib alone. In fact, we've discovered that often instead of reefing with the modern "jiffy" reefing that's provided with the boat, it's easier just to drop one sail (either the main or the jib) alto-

gether and just keep sailing with the other alone. With just the jib (or, for that matter, just the mainsail) alone, the Parker Dawson/26 beats to windward and tacks and comes about and still balances as well as many boats do by reefing. With either full or shortened sail, she is lively and responsive and sails without much heeling.

The Parker Dawson/26 has proven to be an especially easy transition boat from power to sail for people with less experience. The diesel auxiliary starts instantly and is quiet. The boat answers her rudder very fast, even at very slow speeds. She literally turns in her own wake, just as she does under sail. It never fails to astonish people to find that she will steer in reverse and that she will even do tight controlled figure "8"s backwards! Not a particularly useful maneuver, but a measure of how easily she handles alongside a dock or in a crowded harbor! She cruises at about six knots, with almost no wake or quarter wave. Fuel consumption is very small, between ¼ and ⅜ of a gallon an hour! We've estimated she gets about twenty miles to a gallon of diesel fuel, with a cruising range of over three hundred miles under power.

The Parker Dawson/26 has comfortable main and aft cabins, each available with its own head, a welcome arrangement usually associated only with vessels of a much larger size. Optional cockpit enclosures provide virtually a third "convertible" cabin for additional protection in port, underway, or even while trailering.

All four berths (two forward and two aft) are 6′5″ long. The table in the forward cabin can be folded or removed, providing more than fifteen feet of continuous settee, or a fifth berth. The well equipped galley has generous headroom. Plenty of stowage room is provided in the galley drawers and lockers, the

lockers under each bunk, and the semi-enclosed shelf space running the length of both sides of each cabin.

The separated aft cabin gives unmatched privacy for group cruising; or, as a "bedroom-kitchen" arrangement for two. Available with its own head (located under the entrance step), vanity with doors and shelves, stainless steel sink with running water, underbunk stowage, and generous shelf space, the cabin is a completely self-contained, separate living unit.

The Parker Dawson/26 has a mast-stepping and unstepping system that can be used underway. The mast heel is hinged to lower forward, using the boom as a gin pole with the four-part sheet, furnished extra long for the purpose, to provide an easy pull. A special wire bridle and turnbuckle is provided and rigged to keep the boom on the center-line during the process. It's easy for a husband and wife or can be done alone.

While the Parker Dawson/26 was never designed for the purpose, it is interesting to note that many owners who trail the boat use it as a quite comfortable camper on route. Many of the same amenities which make the vessel so pleasurable in the water actually apply equally well on land.

Probably the most innovative and important feature of the Parker-Dawson/26 is her swing keel. This is superbly designed and engineered, the heart of the PD/26's performance capability. The keel is of cast iron, streamlined shape, tapered and heaviest at the bottom, where it counts most. The upper and forward end of the cast keel has flat cheeks that bear against the inside of a heavy stainless steel hanger box, bushed and held tightly by spacer panels. The keel hangs from a 1″ stainless steel pin directly from the hanger box. This lets the keel move up and down freely, but eliminates the side play "klunking" and wear that so plague other swing keel or centerboard boats.

The top of the hanger box holding the keel is tightly bolted up inside and through the heavy fiberglass trunk that is molded integrally with the hull. Because the hanger pin does not go through the fiberglass, it can't leak. The position of the keel is controlled through a 50 to 1 worm gear oil bath winch to a ¼" stainless flexible wire pendant. This is attached through a heavy stainless machined thimble to a stainless pin far enough forward and high enough on the keel so it does not drag in the water to vibrate, hum or collect seaweed. The upper end of the wire leads to a special cast

winch drum/reel, lipped to prevent cable over-ride and with a different radius to provide mechanical advantage where it is needed to equalize the effort to raise the keel. All the mechanism is out of water. The high gear ratio means the keel will remain where it is positioned, without running away or having to use a dangerous ratchet or braking system. The draft is fully adjustable between 1'8" and 5'4", for shallow to deep water sailing.

Even fully raised, the keel extends below the bottom enough to provide lateral resistance for sailing, even to windward and tacking, and for protection for the propeller. The Parker Dawson/26 has been tested as self-righting, even with the keel all the way up! Fully down, with a 5'4" draft, the deep keel provides the super performance that is characteristic of the PD/26. Because there is no keel side play, the keel can be left down and the Parker Dawson/26 sailed and moored like a full keel boat all season long. We never raise our keel unless we're going into shallow water, beaching, or trailing. Finally, a heavy screw-in stainless insert pin is available to lock the keel down for offshore passages if you should want.

Specifications:

LOA
25'7"

LWL
22'2"

BEAM
8'0"

DRAFT
1'8" (keel up)
5'4" (keel down)

SAIL AREA
271 sq. ft.

MAST CLEARS
32'6" above W.L.

COCKPIT
6'0" long

HEADROOM UNDER BOOM
6'2"

DISPLACEMENT
5700 lbs.

KEEL (cast iron)
1200 lbs.

FUEL (diesel)
15 gallons

FRESH WATER
25 gallons

CABINS
2 (separated)

SLEEPS
5

CABIN HEADROOM
5'10"

AUXILIARY
Diesel inboard or gas outboard

Pearson Yachts
West Shore Road
Portsmouth, Rhode Island, 02871

PEARSON FLYER 30

Designed by William Shaw

Designer Bill Shaw says the new *Flyer 30* is designed to race as a one-design, yet over-night comfortably and do both at a low cost.

"Fast" hull graphics are standard on every *Flyer* in a variety of color combinations. Lifelines, bow pulpit and stern rail braces are also included as standard deck hardware.

The underbody shows a high lift fin keel and an outboard rudder. Below the sheer line are two fixed smoked ports concealed by hull graphics.

Her completely uncluttered deck sports two sheet winches and the jib halyard winch, which is led aft for easier sail handling. She has inboard and outboard genoa tracks, a teak toerail and a huge 8' cockpit. Harken mainsheet and traveler control system and Harken backstay tackle are other standard features.

The *Flyer 30's* fractional rig carries 456 sq. ft. of sail area, which

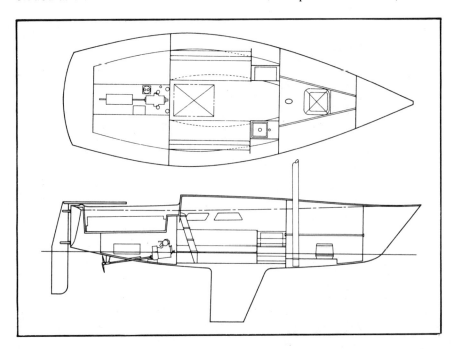

applied to its newest one-design. Class rules are now being developed and additional information is available through Pearson Yachts' dealers.

Specifications:

L.O.A.
29' 11"

D.W.L.
25' 0"

BEAM
11' ¾"

DISPLACEMENT
6,135 lbs.

BALLAST
2,700 lbs.

DRAFT
5' 9"

SAIL AREA
456 sq. ft.

POWER
BMW Diesel

PEARSON 37

Designed by William Shaw
One of the most difficult challenges of a naval architect has been met by Bill Shaw and the Pearson design group, with the introduction of the new Pearson 37 sloop.

They have combined high performance racing potential with comfort, good looks and rather elegant space belowdecks for cruising. All that really needs to be done to go from full race to full cruise is to change the crew.

Pearson Yachts has provided the P37 with a comfortable seven-berth layout. The versatile V-berth arrangement allows for comfortable sleeping when the berths are down and for sail stowage when folded up. There are four berths in the traditional main cabin, and a double quarterberth which forms a seat for the chart table.

should drive her as fast as her name implies. The *Flyer's* auxiliary is a 7 HP BMW diesel with single lever throttle/clutch control.

Belowdecks, the *Flyer* is simple, yet comfortable. Four full length berths provide the sleeping accommodations. The two salon berths are contoured for added comfort. A sink unit, optional stove and a portable cooler make up the galley. A zippered privacy curtain blocks off the head forward of the

galley. Outboard of the head unit is a large sail stowage area. Varnished mahogany bulkheads and a teak cabin sole make the belowdecks visually pleasing as well.

Her electrical equipment includes a 12V DC system with 55 AH battery, navigation and interior lights, master battery disconnect switch and a grounding system.

Pearson Yachts' reputation for building boats with structural integrity and durability has ably been

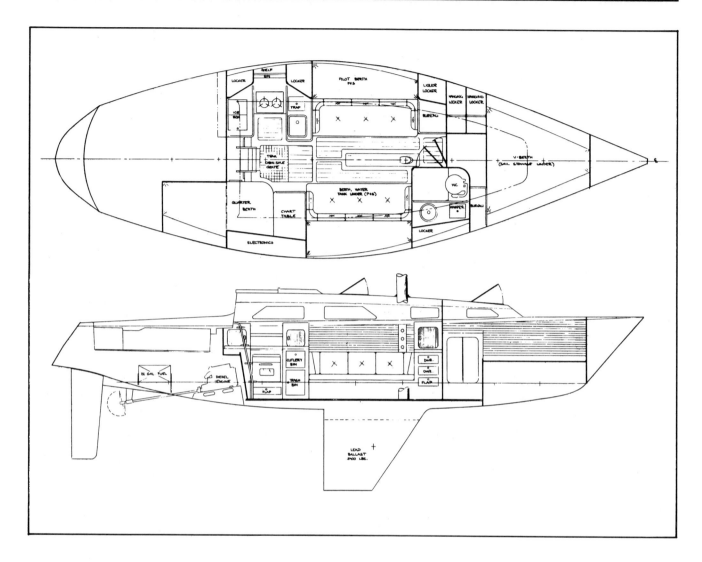

The interior has been executed in a very contemporary fashion with rounded corners to complement the blonde appearance of the varnished hickory. Joiner work has been acomplished with typical Pearson care, and there is a standard teak and holly cabin sole.

A further tribute to human engineering is the workable arrangement in the U-shaped galley to port. Lockers are angled for maximum space utilization with ample space for food preparation.

Specifications:

L.O.A.
36′11½″

D.W.L.
30′1½″

BEAM
11′10″

DISPLACEMENT
12,800 lbs.

BALLAST
5,400 lbs.

DRAFT
6′6″

SAIL AREA
639 Sq. ft.

MAST HEIGHT ABOVE D.W.L.
52′11″

WATER CAPACITY
70 gals.

FUEL CAPACITY
22 gals.

POWER
Diesel

Ross Marine, Inc.
44 Pasture Lane
Darien, Connecticut 06820

SONAR

Designed by Bruce Kirby

In a recent One-of-a-Kind Regatta in New Orleans, the Sonar tied for 3rd (resolved to 4th in a tie breaker) and was beaten only by hiking and trapeze-rigged Olympic boats. The Sonar has strong performance in all wind velocities—light, medium and heavy. An 11-foot self-bailing cockpit can seat 8 people. Seat backs are contoured for maximum comfort.

The Constitution, By-laws and Specifications have been reviewed by some of the top sailors in the U.S. with the result that the class rules are very stringent, effective and maximize one-design qualities. With its stability and simple sail handling, the Sonar can be easily handled by three people, but with its roominess, it is ideal for two couples. The Sonar has more flotation than required for positive buoyance (i.e., it is non-sinkable).

The Sonar gets her agility from a lighter hull and a 935 lbs. lead keel producing a very high ballast displacement ratio. The entire boat weighs 2,100 lbs. From the stability information, it can be seen that the Sonar is very stiff without need for hiking. Elaborate and duplicate sail controls are illegal under class rules, but there is no trim device missing on the Sonar that is necessary. There are only 3 sails: main, non-overlapping jib and spinnaker. The smaller jib makes tacking much easier and eliminates any need for sail changing, yet there is no sacrifice in speed.

For cleaning and limited haul-out regulations, the Sonar can easily be lifted on the average yacht club hoist. Two-wheel trailers are available. The Sonar is as easy to trail as any other mid-size one-design.

Specifications:

LDA
23'0"

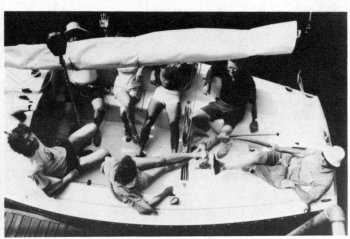

LWL	DRAFT	BALLAST
18'9"	3'11"	930 lbs.
BEAM	**DISPLACEMENT**	**SAIL AREA**
7'9½"	2,100 lbs.	250 sq. ft.

C.E. Ryder Corporation
47 Gooding Avenue
Bristol, Rhode Island 02809

SOUTHERN CROSS 28

Designed by Thomas Gillmer
Tom Gillmer's Southern Cross 28 is a canoe sterned, cutter rigged beauty with Scandinavian overtones. She has a modified full keel with an inboard rudder mounted on a substantial skeg. While her 8,500 pound displacement is moderate, she has the feel of a bigger vessel. Her helm is light and beautifully balanced, and she is quick in light air. Her flaring hull forward keeps her dry on deck and the sculptured stern leaves a wake almost undisturbed.

On deck, Southern Cross 28 is very similar in concept and appearance to our 31. Tom placed her wraparound cockpit well aft to maximize living space below and working space forward. The cockpit is snug, comfortable, and visibility is excellent. There is a seahood over the companionway hatch. And the high bulwarks help to keep the sea out and you in. The walkways are wide and make for a good working platform. Her deck is very functional and pleasing to the eye.

Her cutter rig is large enough to drive her well in light air and small enough to handle easily when it's time to batten down the hatches. And her self-tending staysail takes the work out of tacking out of a crowded harbor.

There is in this little ship a sense of timelessness and a feeling that this design will endure. She looks like a sailboat.

Below decks, Southern Cross 28 is finished in traditional oiled teak. The bulkheads are teak marine plywood and are solidly fiberglassed to hull using our own specially designed Airex fillet. Trim is solid teak. There are fully zippered fabric covers on all berth cushions. Everything is rugged, seaworthy, and functional. There is a handheld shower with fiberglass pan in the amidship head compartment, plenty of stowage space, a sizeable galley, and a navigation station back aft near the companionway. A sturdy drop-leaf table folds away conveniently against the main cabin bulkhead. All in all, she is a nice place to be when the wind is whistling outside.

Her hull is cored with Airex®, a resilient, semi-rigid foam that provides remarkable stiffness. Because of this construction, she is as quiet on the inside as a wooden boat and is well insulated from the heat in summer and the cold in winter. The insulating quality of Airex virtually eliminates condensation in the hull and makes those storage lockers under the bunks usable again. The ballast is cast lead. And the boottop and sheer stripe are Awlgripped.

Our Southern Cross hull-deck joint is the best there is. It is thru-bolted and set in fiberglass, and provides angle beam rigidity along the entire length of the gunwale.

The deck is cored for lightness and stiffness. There is enough teak on deck to add richness but not enough to add a lot of work when you should be sailing. The bowsprit is solid teak. All deck hardware is stainless steel, epoxy coated, or corrosion resistant synthetics. You may also choose polished bronze hardware, for that real go-to-sea look. A solid bronze Southern Cross insignia plaque is affixed to each boat. All portlights open and are fitted with screens.

Aluminum spars, Dacron® running rigging, and stainless steel shrouds complete the exterior. Turnbuckles are chrome plated forged bronze.

Standard Equipment (Cutter):

CONSTRUCTION
One piece hand laminated fiberglass hull with Airex core deck with molded-in non-skid surface, weather resistant ivory gelcoat on hull and deck, fiberglass rudder with bronze shoe.

One piece cast lead ballast bonded inside hull 3500 lbs.

Antifouling bottom paint: blue, green, red, or black

Awlgrip boottop: blue, green, or red

Awlgrip sheet stripe, blue green, or red

JOINERY AND ACCOMMODATIONS

Forward Cabin
Teak interior trim

Full length shelves

Vee berth mattress with storage under

Head Compartment

Formica on all surfaces

Fully enclosed head compartment with manual shower and sump tank

Stainless steel round head sink

Hanging locker and additional storage lockers to port

Mirror

Main Cabin

Pull out double settee berth to starboard

Settee berth to port

Full length shelves above both berths

Compartment storage behind backrests

Full head liner with teak hand rails

Bulkhead mounted fold down table

Foam filled, fully zippered fabric mattresses

Back rest cushions

Teak and holly sole

Dust bin—main cabin area

Galley

Stainless steel galley sink with lever action pump

Gimballed recessed alcohol two burner stove

Butcher block counter tops

Storage locker outboard

Storage locker under counters

Waste basket

Ice box with 3″ poured foam

Navigation Area

Unobstructed surface of ice box serves as chart table

Storage area outboard

MECHANICAL

11 HP universal diesel with flexible mounts

Twin blade propeller

Corrosion proof water lift muffler

15 gallon fuel tank

Fram fuel filter

Tobin bronze propeller shaft

PLUMBING

Manual fresh water system

Foot operated pump for the sink and shower in the head

Marine head with holding tank, USCG approved

Water capacity 47 gallons in keel tank

ELECTRICAL
12 volt electrical system

Fused electrical panel

Color coded electrical wiring system

85 Ampere marine battery

Navigational lighting group

Cabin lights

Three pole battery switch

Electrical bonding

DECK
Life lines (single) and stanchions

Bow and stern pulpit

Forward hatch

Teak cap rails

Black anodized or Epoxy coated deck hardware

Six portlights, all opening

Fuel fill deck plate

Drained rope locker in forepeak

Bronze tiller head with laminated tiller

Genoa sheet winches with handle

Mooring chocks, bow and stern

Mooring cleats, bow and stern

Midship hawse pipes

Large, self-bailing cockpit with scuppers

Sliding companionway hatch with teak trim, weather boards, and seahood

Cockpit sail lockers port and starboard with hasp

Engine controls

Deck mounted engine instrument panel

Teak bowsprit

Bilge pump

Teak dorade boxes

SPARS AND RIGGING
Anodized aluminum mast, boom, and staysail boom

Stainless steel chain plates and stemhead

Stainless steel 1 x 19 rigging

Dacron running rigging main, jib, and staysail sheets and halyards

Jiffy reefing

Halyard winches and cleats

Main boom topping lift

SOUTHERN CROSS 31

Designed by Thomas Gillmer
The Southern Cross 31 is a superb, fast, stable yacht brought to cruising perfection. Her deck and rigging configuration are traditional and proven, with safety and ease of handling prime considerations. The walkways are wide, and deck obstructions are held to a minimum. Stem-to-stem bulwarks help to keep the decks dry in a seaway. All sheets lead to the cockpit. A seahood encloses the companionway hatch. The mechanical and electrical systems are functional and rugged. Her construction is geared to men who are going to sea, for a weekend or a life-time.

Meticulous craftsmanship and fine materials combine with thoughtful, functional design to make the Southern Cross a luxurious home as well as a seaworthy vessel. Opening ports and hatches for ventilation below decks; a stainless steel sink, gimballed stove counter space and storage compartments make the galley easy to use. A comfortable navigation station is conveniently located near the companionway. The bordered dinette folds neatly on the starboard bulkhead and sleeping accommodations for five contribute to your comfort at sea or at anchor.

Standard Equipment (Cutter):

CONSTRUCTION
One piece hand-laminated fiberglass hull with Airex® core

Stiff balsa cored deck with molded-in nonskid

Weather resistant ivory gelcoat on hull and deck

Fiberglass outboard rudder with laminated tiller

Large self-bailing cockpit with scuppers

Sliding companionway hatch with teak trim, weatherboards, and sea hood

Bomar translucent forward and midship hatches

Black anodized or epoxy coated hardware

Teak toe rails, handrails, bowsprit, and cabin nosing

Eight opening ports with screens

Cockpit sail lockers with hinges and locking hasps

Aft cockpit seat locker

Antifouling bottom paint

Awlgrip boottop and sheer stripe

Thrubolted hull deck joint

INTERIOR
Choice of fixed chart table with storage under or foldaway with quarterberth

Oiled teak bulkheads

Solid teak interior trim

Lockers over berths in main and forward cabins

Full headliner

Four or five full-sized berths

Huge private forward cabin with hanging locker lined in cedar

Separate head compartment with stainless steel sink in vanity

Mirror in head

Manual shower and shower pan in head

Clothes hamper

Approved marine toilet with holding tank

Butcher block Formica counter tops

Teak and holly cabin sole

Storage lockers under counters

Storage under berths

Stainless steel double galley sink with footpump

Gimballed Shipmate 2-burner stove with oven, alcohol

Heavily insulated icebox

Foam filled, fully zippered fabric cushions

DECK HARDWARE, RIG, AND EQUIPMENT

Cutter rig with staysail and intermediate shrouds

Wear resistant anodized aluminum spars

Aircraft quality stainless steel standing rigging

Chrome bronze turnbuckles

Custom stainless steel stemhead with integral chocks and anchor rollers

Thrubolted stainless steel chainplates and bobstay

Prestretched Dacron® main, jib, and staysail halyards

Dacron® main, jib, and staysail sheets

Halyard and sheet cleats

Hawsepipes, stern and midships

Teak dorade boxes with cowl vents

Winch base storage compartments

Rope locker with deckplate

2 Slab jiffy reefing

Fixed topping lift

Navigation lighting group

Foredeck and anchor lights

Adjustable roller bearing mainsheet traveller

Barient mainsheet winch

Staysail traveller

Barient two-speed genoa sheet winches with handle

Genoa tracks with adjustable standup blocks

Barient main, jib, and staysail halyard winches on mast with handle

Stainless steel bow and stern rails

Lifelines (single) and stanchions

Cockpit mounted bilge pump

Custom bronze Southern Cross insignia

POWER, ELECTRICAL, AND WATER

22 HP Diesel, ready to run

Bronze propeller shaft

2-bladed sailboat propeller

Corrosion proof waterlift muffler and riser

34-gallon fuel tank

47-gallon fresh water keel tank

Dual 85-amp marine battery installation with battery boxes

Battery shutoff switch

Battery charge indicator

12-volt cabin lights

Marinetics electrical panel with circuit breakers

Color coded electrical wiring system

Electrical bonding

Bronze seacocks on all underwater fittings

Specifications:

LOA
34'6"

LOD
31'0"

LWL
25'0"

BEAM
9'6"

DRAFT
4'7"

DISPLACEMENT
13,600 lbs.

BALLAST
4,400 lbs.

SAIL AREA
447 sq. ft.

HEADROOM
6'2"

AUXILIARY
Diesel

SOUTHERN CROSS 39

Designed by Thomas Gillmer
The Southern Cross fleet is designed by Thomas Gillmer, one of the country's foremost Naval Architects. Educated at the U.S. Naval Academy and Johns Hopkins, Mr. Gillmer spent several years at sea as a Navy officer. He has served as Professor of Naval Architecture and Director of the Ships Hydrodynamic laboratory and of the Model Towing Basin, and has authored several definitive books on naval design.

Standard Equipment (Sloop):

CONSTRUCTION

One piece hand-laminated fiberglass hull with Airex® core

Stiff balsa cored deck with molded-in nonskid

Weather resistant ivory gelcoat on hull and deck

Fiberglass inboard rudder with bronze post

Large self-bailing cockpit with scuppers

Sliding companionway hatch w/ teak trim, weatherboards, and sea hood

Bomar watertight translucent hatch, forward and amidships

Black anodized or epoxy coated hardware

Teak toe rails, coamings, handrails, and bowsprit

All opening ports

Cockpit sail lockers with bronze hinges and locking hasps

Aft cockpit seat

Antifouling bottom paint

Awlgrip boottop and sheer stripe

Thrubolted, no leak, hull deck joint

DECK HARDWARE, RIG, AND EQUIPMENT

Wear resistant anodized aluminum spars

Aircraft quality stainless steel standing rigging

Chrome bronze turnbuckles

Custom stainless steel stemhead weldment with integral chocks

Thrubolted stainless steel chainplates and bobstay

Prestretched Dacron® main and jib halyards

Dacron main and jib sheets

Halyard and sheet cleats

Hawsepipes, bow, stern, and amidships

Teak dorade boxes with cowl vents

Winch base storage compartments

Rope locker with deckplate

2 Slab jiffy reefing

Fixed topping lift

Navigation lighting group

Foredeck and anchor lights

Adjustable roller bearing mainsheet traveller

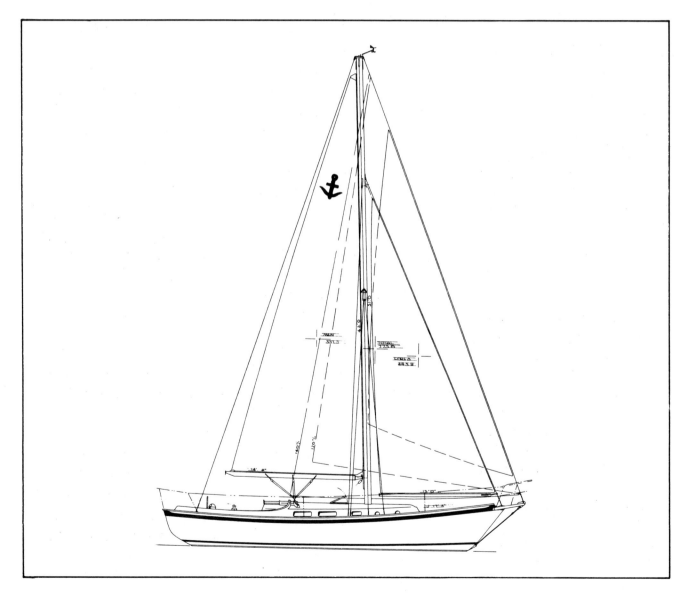

Barient mainsheet winch

Barient 2 speed genoa sheet winches with handle

Genoa tracks with adjustable wide sheave blocks

Barient main and jib halyard winches on mast with handle

Stainless steel bow and stern rails

Lifelines (double) and stanchions

Cockpit mounted bilge pump

Custom bronze Southern Cross insignia

Edson steerer with 5" Ritchie compass

Flag pole socket

Anodized aluminum mast partners

Stainless steel mast tie rod

INTERIOR

Choice of layouts

Waxed teak bulkheads

Solid teak interior trim

Lockers over berths in main and forward cabins

Full headliner

Full-sized berths for seven

Hanging locker lined in cedar

Separate head compartment with Dupon Corian® vanity top

Mirror in head

Shower and shower pan in head

Clothes hamper

Approved marine toilet with Mansfield holding tank

Formica counter tops

Teak and holly cabin sole

Storage lockers under counters

Storage under berths

Stainless steel double galley sink with footpump

Gimballed Shipmate 3 burner stove stainless steel with oven

Heavily insulated icebox

Foam filled, fully zippered fabric cushions

Waste basket and dust bins

Pine ceiling in main and forward cabins

POWER, ELECTRICAL & WATER

Westerbeke 50 HP Diesel, ready to run

Bronze propellor shaft

2 bladed sailboat propellor

Corrosion proof waterlift muffler and riser

50 gallon fuel tank

100 gallon fresh water keel tank

Dual 100 amp marine battery installation with battery boxes

Battery shutoff switch

Battery charge indicator

12 volt cabin lights

Marinetics electrical panel with circuit breakers

Color coded electrical wiring system

Electrical bonding

Sea cocks on all underwater fittings

Hot and cold pressure water

SAILS

Hood mainsail with 2 sets of reef points

Hood 110% lapper

Hood mainsail cover, acrylic

Specifications:

LOA
43'

LOD
38'7"

LWL
31"

BEAM
12'1"

DRAFT
5'4"

DISPLACEMENT
21,000 lbs.

BALLAST
7,676 lbs.

SAIL AREA
835 sq. ft.

HEADROOM
6'4"

AUXILIARY
59 hp Diesel

SEA SPRITE 23

Designed by Carl Alberg

This legendary New England boat sprang from the genius of Carl A. Alberg, one of America's foremost naval architects, over two decades ago. Boys have grown into men and taught their sons to sail on a Sea Sprite. Others have stared in envy. And, some have gone to sea.

On June 29, 1974, a lone twenty-one-year-old set sail from Wickford Harbor, Rhode Island, aboard his Sea Sprite sloop. Fifty-nine days later he tied up in Falmouth . . . England. Few will want to duplicate this trans-Atlantic passage in their Sea Sprite, but such a voyage is a tribute to the man and his boat.

The Sea Sprite is a perfectly balanced, full keel, lead ballasted sailing vessel reminiscent of larger offshore yachts. Her classic design, uncomparable beauty and superior performance have satisfied over 700 owners.

Her rig is simple: she can be easily sailed as a board boat, yet has the spirited performance to handle a crowd for an afternoon sail without compromise. Her wineglass hull form insures a fast-moving, highly maneuverable vessel that is, at the same time, stiff and stable in choppy seas. And the three foot draft makes her trailerable, opening up new waters for your sailing pleasure.

The walkways are wide and unobstructed. Her foredeck is huge for safe and easy handling of sails and anchors, or for just lying around the sun. Her deck is trimmed in easy-to-care-for teakwood, which gives her the feel and appearance of an expensive custom yacht.

Down below, the quarters are bright and spacious and are also trimmed with teak. Gleaming white fiberglass headliner and interior liner are easy to keep clean and require no maintenance. From her teak and holly cabin sole to her carefully thought out butcher block galley counters, Sea Sprite's appointments bespeak a simple elegance that you will be proud of.

Standard Equipment

CONSTRUCTION
One-piece hand-laminated fiberglass hull

Balsa cored deck with molded-in nonskid

Weather resistant ivory gelcoat on hull and deck

Fiberglass covered hi-density foam rudder with bronze post

Internally bonded 1400 lb. cast lead ballast

Sliding companionway hatch with teak trim and weatherboards

Translucent forward hatch

Black anodized, epoxy coated, or DuPont Zytel hardware

Teak toe rails, coamings, and cabin handrails

Two fixed ports

Sturdy bronze tiller head with teak tiller

Gas tank locker

Outboard motor well with hinged cover

Boottop and antifouling bottom paint

Molded-in gold cove stripe

Cockpit sail locker hatch

DECK HARDWARE, RIG, AND EQUIPMENT
Wear resistant anodized aluminum spars

Stainless steel bow pulpit

Aircraft quality stainless steel standing rigging

Stainless steel stemhead and chainplates

Prestretched Dacron main and jib halyards

Dacron main and jib sheets

Halyard and jib sheet cleats

Mooring chocks, bow and stern

Mooring cleats, bow and stern

Standup jib sheet blocks

Jib sheet winches and handle

Jiffy reefing gear

Fixed topping lift

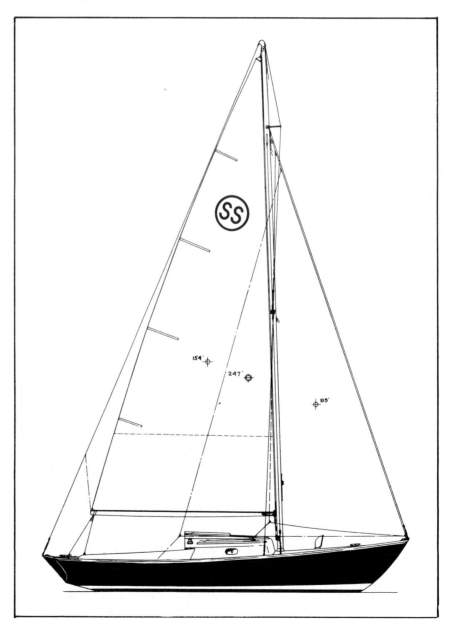

Navigation lighting group

INTERIOR

Teak interior trim

Full-length shelves

Gleaming white headliner

Easily cleaned, fully lined interior

Four full sized berths

Drained rope locker

Hinged head compartment

Butcher block Formica counter tops

Teak and holly cabin sole

Molded-in battery box

Hinged outboard motor storage compartment

Storage locker under counter

Storage under all berths

Stainless steel galley sink with galley pump

10-gallon fresh water tank

Insulated icebox

Interior lighting group

Foam filled, fully zippered, fabric cushions

Specifications:

LENGTH OVERALL
22'6"

LENGTH WATERLINE
16'3"

BEAM
7'0"

DRAFT
3'0"

DISPLACEMENT
3350

BALLAST
1400 lbs.

SAIL AREA
Total–247 sq. ft.
Main–154 sq. ft.
Jib–93 sq. ft.
Genoa–165 sq. ft.
Spinnaker–324 sq. ft.

AUXILIARY (OPTIONAL)
Diesel

SEA SPRITE 27

Designed by Bill Luders

The Sea Sprite 27 is a remarkable achievement in every sense. Her sweeping, graceful lines make her seem like she's in motion even when she sits dockside. But classic lines are merely show without performance—and the 27 is at her best under sail. The full keel and unique hull configuration make for uncompromising stability, without sacrificing maneuverability. She carries a four part main sheet on a traveler for easy sheeting, inboard stays for better performance, side decks are wide and unobstructed for fast, easy access to all parts of her sailing gear, auxiliary power comes from an economical diesel, she's rugged, she's as roomy and comfortable below decks as she is sleek and sassy above.

She's bright and spacious with all the comforts of home. You'll find the forward head with shower and vanity sink offers the luxury and privacy usually found only in much larger boats. The four opening ports and ventilated forward hatch provide cool cross-ventilation inside. The large forward berth and pull-out settee berth in the main salon are roomy, cool and comfortable on those long hot summer nights.

The galley with rich teak trim and butcher block counter tops is beautiful as well as functional. Two burner gimballed stove, deep stainless steel sink and double insulated ice chest make preparing meals or snacks just as easy at sea as dockside. Plus there are extra large storage areas for canned goods and cooking utensils. The six foot head room and wide comfortable salon make for an overall roominess that

will make lounging below as comfortable as your living room.

The Sea Sprite 27 is more than a fine sailing vessel—she's the experience of a lifetime. Her unique design and classic lines create an unparalled sailing experience. She points high on the wind for less tacking and straighter courses—with her full keel, her stability comes not only from her keel's ballast, but from the excellent hull design making her motion at sea easier even on those choppy days. But you'll never really know how it feels until you slip into that quiet island cove on a gentle summer afternoon, or spend a cool summer evening offshore with the moon in the sails and the wind at your back. Whether it's an afternoon on the bay, or a week or two exploring hidden coves and inlets—the Sea Sprite 27.

Standard Equipment (Sloop):

CONSTRUCTION
One-piece hand-laid full keel fiberglass hull

Stiff, cored deck with molded-in nonskid

Weather resistant ivory gelcoat on hull and deck

Full length rudder with bronze post and fittings

Laminated wood tiller

Large self-bailing cockpit with scuppers

Cast lead ballast bonded inside hull

Antifouling bottom paint: blue, green, red, or black

Awlgrip boottop: blue, green, or red

Molded-in cove stripe: red or gold

INTERIOR
Forward cabin
  Private forward cabin with full length shelves

Privacy curtain

V-berth filler cushion

Storage under V-berths

Oiled teak bulkheads and trim

Head compartment

Athwartships head compartment with full length door

Formica® covered interior bulkheads

Vanity with stainless steel sink and storage outboard

Fiberglass shower pan with teak grate over shower sump

Manual shower with footpump

Monogram® self-contained toilet

Hanging locker outboard of head

Mirror

Main cabin

Pull-out double berth to starboard

Settee berth to port

Full length shelves above main cabin berths

Storage behind backrests and under berths

Full headliner with teak drip-edge molding

Oiled teak bulkheads and trim

Foam filled, fully zippered fabric mattresses on all berths

Backrest cushions

Teak and holly cabin sole with dust bin under hatch

Sturdy bulkhead-mounted fold-down dining table

Galley

Butcher block Formica® counter tops

Solid teak trim

Stainless steel galley sink with pump

Gimballed 2 burner alcohol stove with chopping board

Food storage outboard

Pots and pans storage under stove

Heavy foam insulated icebox doubles as chart table

Solid teak companionway ladder

MECHANICAL

Universal 11 HP Diesel with 2:1 reduction

Adjustable flexible engine mounts

Bronze propeller (2-blade) and propeller shaft

Self aligning bronze stuffing box

Corrosion proof water lift muffler

Corrosion proof 12-gallon vented diesel fuel tank

Cockpit mounted engine controls and instrument panel

Fram® fuel filter

PLUMBING

Manual fresh water system

Water capacity 45 gallons in two tanks

Sea cocks on all underwater fittings

ELECTRICAL
12-volt electrical system

Fused electrical panel

Color coded electrical wiring

85-amp-hour marine battery in corrosion proof box

Navigational lighting group

Cabin lights

Heavy duty battery shutoff switch

Foredeck flood light

Electrical bonding

DECK HARDWARE
Bow rail and stern pulpit

Stainless steel stanchions and lifelines (single)

Translucent forward hatch with ventilator

Teak handrails on cabin top

Teak toerails and taffrail

Black deck hardware

Four opening ports with screens, two fixed

Fuel fill deck plate

Adjustable mainsheet traveller

Lewmar genoa sheet winches with lock-in handle

Genoa tracks with standup blocks

Cast bronze winch bases

Mooring cleats and chocks

Sliding companionway hatch with teak trim and weatherboards

Solid teak cockpit coamings and cabin nosings

Cockpit sail locker hatches with hinges and hasp

Lazaret locker with hasp

Cockpit mounted manual bilge pump

Seahood

SPARS AND RIGGING
Anodized aluminum mast and boom

Fractional rig

Stainless steel chainplates and stemhead

Stainless steel standing rigging

Dacron® running rigging

Jib halyard winch on mast with cleat

S2 Yachts, Inc.
725 East 40th Street
Holland, Michigan 49423

S2 7.3

Standard Equipment:

HULL & DECK
100% hand-laid fiberglass hull, 100% hand-laid fiberglass deck w/ balsa core sandwich construction, internal lead ballast, horizontal hull/deck joint, S2 custom non-skid deck and cockpit surfaces, large cockpit w/contoured seats and backrest with two drain scuppers, exposed fuel tank cockpit locker w/hasp, large lazarette locker w/hasp, spade type rudder, teak weather-grooved bentboards, black anodized toe rail track, and a chrome plated bronze tiller head w/ H & L varnished laminated tiller arm.

CABIN
Six large weather-tight bronze smoked acrylic main cabin windows, S2 clear acrylic foredeck hatch-double hinged & double dogged. S2 translucent acrylic sliding companionway hatch w/S.S. safety hand rail with brass lock, bi-fold hinged dinette table, "First mate approved" fabric covered foam berth cushions for four (choice of 2 colors), removable rudder-back cabin sole carpeting, six large under-berth storage lockers, forepeak locker w/teak door

Jiffy reefing

Main boom topping lift

Aluminum mast step

Forged chrome bronze turnbuckles.

and trigger lock, vinyl foam covered backrest cushions w/storage compartments in main salon, solid teak trim throughout cabin interior, moisture and mildew resistant hull and headliners.

GALLEY
Cabinetry w/two storage doors, stowaway stove, S.S. sink w/hand pump and 15 gallon water tank.

HEAD
Privacy area for future head w/ bunk extension cover.

SAILS
"North" mainsail with single reef, "North" 100% working jib.

SPARS, RIGGING & FITTINGS
Heavy duty S.S. chain plates w/ custom forward stem head plate, four 6" marinium cleats, two #7 Lewmar primary genoa sheet winches, genoa sheet blocks, genoa winch handle. Nicro Fico jib tack snap shackle, complete Samson "Yacht Braid" for running rigging and "XLS Halyard Braid" for halyards, 4:1 mainsheet system, mainsheet traveler system w/rubber cushioned adjustable stops. 2:1 Cunningham system lead aft to cockpit, complete S.S. standing rigging—5/32" 1 x 19 cable with #5 S.S. turnbuckles w/lock nuts. "Kenyon" black E.S.P. coated masthead spar, internal reef system, internal 3:1 outhaul system, internal halyards lead to aft cockpit, tubular shaped spreaders, S.S.

hinged mast base for stepping ease, S2 burgee.

SAFETY
Six custom S.S. lifeline stanchions thrubolted w/S.S. back-up plates, with single lifeline cable and Pelican hooks, custom S.S. bow pulpit w/welded bases and thru-bolted international navigation lights, master battery switch w/battery box, interior lighting package, S2 exclusive; 7' long recessed, "non-trip" teak hand rails w/S.S. supports.

HULL DECK COLORS
White hull & deck, standard. Optional: Laguna Sand hull & deck: Khaki/white: Navy/white

Specifications:
L.O.A.
23'10"

DWL
18'6"

BEAM
8'0"

SHOAL DRAFT
2'10"

DEEP DRAFT
4'0"

DISPLACEMENT
3250 lbs.

BALLAST LEAD
1300 lbs.

SAIL AREA
251 sq. ft.

MAST HEIGHT ABOVE D.W.L.
31'8"

HEADROOM
5'0"

COCKPIT LENGTH
6'10"

S2 11.0C/CENTER COCKPIT

Standard Equipment:
HULL & DECK
100% hand-laid fiberglass hull, 100% hand-laid fiberglass deck w/balsa core sandwich construction, internal lead ballast, horizontal hull/deck joint w/rigid crash rubrail, teak-capped molded-in bulwarks, S2 custom non-skid deck and cockpit surfaces, large cockpit w/contoured seats & backrest w/two scupper drains, skeg-rudder for excellent downwind tracking, hull color—Gull White w/Black gelcoat bootline stripe, double Black feature cove stripe, anti-fouling bottom paint. S2 bronze acrylic sliding companion hatch w/S.S. safety hand rail w/brass lock, fiberglass storm hatch-cover for main companionway hatch, solid teak weather-grooved bentboards, S2 bronze acrylic forward deck hatch & aft deck hatch w/non-skid teak strips—double-hinged & double-dogged, four large bronze acrylic weather-tight main cabin windows. Two rugged aft deck lockers w/S.S. piano hinge, forward anchor locker w/overboard drains, S2 custom built-in self-draining dorade vents, bronze seacocks on all thru-hull fittings.

CABIN
Solid teak trim & bulkheads, S2 custom draperies, teak & holly cabin sole, moisture & mildew resistant hull & headliners, ten opening self-draining port lights w/screens, eleven interior decorator cabin lights, seven large gelcoat-finished underberth storage lockers, four storage compartments behind main salon backrest cushions, port & starboard teak magazine racks, port & starboard teak lounge cabinets, five hanging lockers—three aft, two forward, solid teak dinette table with double drop-leaf

arrangement, complete navigator's desk w/teak bifold top, electronics area, chart lite w/ample chart storage, teak removable companion step, completely private v-berth, berths for six luxuriously covered in choice of three decorator-coordinated fabrics with v-berth filler cushion, completely private aft stateroom, full teak door, dressing area and teak framed mirror.

GALLEY
"First Mate-Approved" color-coordinated L-shaped galley, two insulated top-loading iceboxes, S.S. two-burner alcohol gimballed stove/oven, S.S. deep double sink w/80 gallon water pressure system, utensil tray, six utensil drawers, two large front-opening galley doors, one large storage compartment under stove for large cooking utensils, fiberglass pantry, large dish locker storage.

HEAD
Large fully-enclosed color-coordinated head, full teak door, head w/30 gallon fiberglass holding tank, vanity w/S.S. oval sink & telephone pressure shower, vanity storage compartments, fiberglass tub/shower w/sump pump, teak framed mirror.

SAILS
"North" mainsail w/double reef, "North" 100% working jib, custom mainsail cover.

SPARS, RIGGING & FITTINGS
"Hall" awl-grip masthead spar, double internal reef in boom, internal 5:1 outhaul system, internal halyards leading aft to cockpit, 4:1 Cunningham system leading aft to cockpit, fixed boom topping lift, airfoil single spreader rig, main & jib halyards 5/32" wire to 7/16" rope, "Samson Yacht Braid" for all running rigging, S2 custom S.S. mast collar w/halyard turning blocks. Complete set of certified rotary swaged S.S. standing rigging—all

lower shrouds ¼″ 1 x 19 S.S. cable swaged to #8 Johnson turnbuckles w/safety lockingrings; all uppers, forestay & backstay ⁵/₁₆″ 1 x 19 S.S. cable swaged to #10 Johnson turnbuckles w/safety lockingrings. S2 custom heavy-duty S.S. side chain plates & polished S.S. forward stem plate w/anchor roller, 6:1 "Harken" mainsheet system, mainsheet traveler system w/rubber cushioned adjustable stops, one #8 "Lewmar" main halyard winch, one #16 "Lewmar" two-speed jib halyard winch, two #42 "Lewmar" two-speed self-tailing primary genoa sheet winches, two self-locking winch handles, two "Nicro Fico" genoa snatch blocks, "Nicro Fico" jib tack snap shackle, two 1¼″ x 14′ black anodized genoa track & cars, complete "Schaefer" deck gear & hardware, four 12″ Marinium mooring cleats, "Samson"

docklines: 2—⅝″ x 20′; 2—⅝″ x 25′, S2 burgee.

SAFETY
Cockpit-operated manual bilge pump (gusher type), S2 custom welded S.S. double rail bow pulput & split stern rail w/fold-down swim ladder w/welded bases thru-bolted, eight custom S. S. double lifeline stanchions backed by alum. back-up plates thru-bolted w/double lifelines & S.S. pelican hooks, S2 exclusive; custom recessed "non-trip" teak deck handrails w/custom molded fiberglass supports, teak companionway entry handrails.

POWER, CONTROLS & ELECTRONICS
Pathfinder 42 h.p. 4-cylinder freshwater cooled diesel, pedestal engine controls, three batteries: 1 12-volt, 2 6-volt, master battery

switch, electric fuel gauges, 70-gallon alum. fuel tank, cockpit engine switch panel w/tachometer, S.S. 1″ marine shafting, bronze strut & shaft log. 2-blade bronze propeller w/S.S. nut & key, heat exchanger for hot-water system. "Edson" pedestal steering, 5″ Ritchie w/plastic cover, S.S. pedestal guard, pedestal brake, custom 30″ S.S. wheel, emergency tiller. International navigation lights, anchor light, engine compartment light. S2 custom master circuit breaker switch panel for 12-volt & 110-volt, battery condition meter, voltage meter, dockside 110v shore power w/ 50′ cord and adapter.

Specifications:
L.O.A.
11.0m 36′0″

241

D.W.L.
28'3"

BEAM
11'11"

DRAFT
4'8"

DEEP DRAFT
on request

DISPLACEMENT
15,000 lbs.

BALLAST LEAD
6,000 lbs.

SAIL AREA
625 sq. ft.

MAST HEIGHT ABOVE D.W.L.
49'0"

HEADROOM
6'3"

COCKPIT LENGTH
7'0"

Sabre Yachts

Hawthorne Road
South Casco, Maine 04077

SABRE 28

Designed by the Sabre Design Team

The Sabre 28 is a performance cruising yacht with legendary elegance. Years of innovative research and development plus over 450 Sabre 28's have led to an exceptional level of refinement. The luxurious teak interior and the pride of Maine craftsmanship distinguish a Sabre from others in the fleet.

The hull design is the result of an extensive tank testing program at the Stevens Institute. The Sabre 28 topped the performance charts in her size range. Low wetted surface and a fin keel provide exceptional light wind performance. The hull form gives optimum stability for heavy weather performance. Her skeg-rudder provides directional stability usually found only in traditional long-keel designs. A 3'10" shoal draft model is offered as an option.

The large, self-bailing cockpit is designed for maximum comfort on a long cruise, with careful attention to the correct seat height, seat width, distance between seats, backrest height, and visibility over the coach roof. Hatch covers pro-

vide access to two large storage lockers and a convenient storage bin under the port seat. The starboard cockpit locker has a large shelf for extra storage.

The Sabre 28 has cruising accommodations for six in two cabins, with full standing headroom. The comfortable forward cabin has two 6'4" vee berths, and a filler cushion to form a double berth. Excellent storage is provided by two deep drawers and two lockers plus full length storage bins by each berth.

The Sabre 28 washroom includes a marine head with a large hanging locker behind. A teak towel rack and a teak toilet paper holder are provided. To starboard are the vanity counter and sink with storage lockers outboard and a locker with shelf below. A mirror is mounted on the forward side of the cabin door. The main cabin has three 6'4" berths with upholstered berth backs and storage below.

All berths have fabric covered 4" foam mattresses. The port main berth extends to form a double. There are deep storage lockers and shelves behind the berth backs. The double leaf dining table folds up against a large magazine rack on the main bulkhead. A small storage locker is located on the starboard main bulkhead. Teak handrails in the main cabin are standard, along with accent trim below the windows.

The galley has a white formica countertop with teak trim, a two burner recessed alcohol stove with cutting board top and a deep stainless steel sink. The large, well insulated, ice box has a shelf to store smaller items, plus a discharge pump. Galley storage includes four drawers and four lockers. The built in wastebasket is a special Sabre feature.

The hull is a single unit, hand laminated fiberglass molding using alternate layers of mat and roving, with additional layers in high stress areas. The interior construction is of handcrafted wood using the finest and most meticulous boatbuilding methods. Oiled teak is used on most visible surfaces, with mahogany construction under the berth cushions and other concealed areas. All trim is solid teak. The entire cabin sole is striped teak.

The deck is hand laminated fiberglass with balsa core stiffening and non-skid deck surfaces molded in. The toerails, handrails, coaming caps and trim are all teak. The companionway hatch has a fiberglass spray hood for foul weather protection. A foredeck anchor well simplifies the handling of ground tackle. The stainless steel double rail bow pulpit, stern rail, stanchion posts plus upper and lower lifelines are all standard.

Standard Equipment:

The mast and boom are aluminum with a durable Awigrip finish. The

internal main and genoa halyards are led to Lewmar #8 winches mounted on the mast. The genoa sheets are fed to adjustable blocks on the 8'0" toerail tracks and then to Lewmar #30 two-speed winches mounted on teak coaming caps. The main sheet is led to a roller bearing traveler. The boom is equipped with two sets of jiffy reefing gear plus an internal clew outhaul and topping lift.

The 12-volt electrical system has two 74 ampere hour batteries with a full disconnect battery switch and a circuit breaker switch panel. There are two bulkhead mounted lights in the forward cabin, one ceiling mounted light in the washroom, and two bulkhead lights plus a galley ceiling light in the main cabin. Teak access panels are provided in the aft face of the headliner to facilitate the installation of navigational instruments in each cockpit face. Navigation lights and a masthead light are installed in accordance with Coast Guard Standards. All seacocks are grounded to the keel, and a heavy duty lightning ground system connects the mast and all chainplates to the keel.

The 20 gallon water tank is located under the forward berths. All through-hulls below the water line are protected by seacock valves with handles. A diaphragm bilge pump is located in the cockpit. Two fire extinguishers are standard, one mounted in the main cabin by the quarter berth, the second in the starboard cockpit locker. The marine head and a 22 gallon holding tank are standard. A Coast Guard approved waste treatment system which allows overboard discharge is offered as an option. The 13 H.P. Volvo MD7A diesel with 1.9:1 reduction drive is standard. Two fuel filters, a fuel gauge and a sea water filter are provided. The tachometer, ammeter, fuel, oil and temperature gauges

are recessed in the cockpit face below the companionway step. The galley top and front remove for easy engine access. Full ventilation is provided in accordance with Coast Guard Regulations. The heavy duty aluminum fuel tank, with side deck fill, has a capacity of 20 gallons.

Specifications:

LOA
28'5"

LWL
22'10"

BEAM
9'2"

DRAFT
Standard Model: 4'4"
Shoal Model: 3'10"

DISPLACEMENT
7900 lbs.

BALLAST
2900 lbs.

SAIL AREA
393 sq. ft.

COCKPIT LENGTH
7'2"

HEADROOM
6'0"

Sanford Boat Company, Inc.

Lower Pleasant Street
Nantucket, Massachusetts 02554

ALERION III

Designed by Nathanael Herreshoff In 1913, Nathanael Herreshoff's drawing on a lifetime of experience designed Alerion for his personal use. He owned her for seventeen years, sailing her alone into his eighties. He circumnavigated Bermuda, cruised the shoal waters of Florida and astounded contemporaries by ghosting through the unrippled waters of summer New England. Now she is on display at Mystic Seaport to be admired but not to be sailed.

Sanford Boat Company is producing a few near copies of this marvelous boat. Some differences: the Boat's one-piece cold molded epoxy/mahogany hull, her marconi rig, her availability. The similarities: the lines, the beauty and finish of the original turn of the century product, the exquisite performance.

Sanford Boat Company Inc.'s purpose is creating high performance seakindly sailboats engineered and built to become heirlooms. Such boats are not readily available today; they are only found as restored antiques or as custom boats where an experienced owner has found a competent builder and spent the year or two that it takes to build a great boat. Their boats are available on a semi-production basis to satisfy the needs of that small group of sailors who understand and want boats of superlative quality.

Rather than develop a new design for a 26' sloop, Sanford felt it more sensible to choose a boat that had already proven its ability and desirability. In the past, as today, most designs were strongly influenced by the current fashions or rating rules which distorted their shapes away from the fastest and most seakindly ones. From time to time, though, boats have been designed with only the sea as a rule and pleasure of movement as a goal. Such was N.G. Herreshoff's Alerion, a boat which gave him and her subsequent owners a satis-

faction that their present builders seek to reproduce.

Herreshoff had a fainting spell in her and gave up sailing alone. He sold her to Amory Skerry who called her "a sweet sailer and sweet to handle . . . For twelve years Alerion was a beloved member of the Skerry family. Then the war came . . ." After the war she went to Isaac Merriman. Francis Herreshoff reports that "in a letter to me, he said, 'I think she is one of the finest boats that was ever built', and he should know because he has owned some of the best of them." Merriman willed her to his son who after a period of years gave her to the Mystic Seaport.

The Seaport thought her important enough to have her com-

pletely refurbished, restored to her 1924 rig and put on permanent display. There she sits, admirable, but frustrating to those who would sail her.

Reproducing an old boat requires decisions as to how to render the old with the materials and processes available today. While an exact copy may be possible, it may also be inappropriate. Keeping in mind the aim to reproduce the satisfaction of the original's owners, Sanford made the following decisions: To retain the hull lines, cockpit and deck layout exactly. To use a single spar in place of the split spar of the 1924 sliding gunter rig, and to eliminate the running back-stays. To radically alter the construction from plant on frame

to stressed skin; and to adjust for the lighter hull by increasing the weight of the ballast keel. To choose deck fittings for availability as well as historical match.

The result is the speed, beauty, seakindliness and handling ease of the original in a boat that can be maintained practically today.

Reason for Alerion's performance is apparent from an analysis of her form. She has a large sail area, an easily driven hull, and a large deadrise angle coupled with concave floors and a sharp bow. The first two make her fast, the last makes her dry, stiff and easy.

Alerion's midship section is derived from the great "compromise sloops" of the 1880's, best exemplified by the Mayflower of Edward

Burgess. The "compromise" sloops took the best features from the shallow American sloops and the deep English cutters, and in Burgess' work derived from the best of the pilot cutters, Baltimore clippers and racing fishing schooners of the mid 1800's. They represent the ultimate development of the displacement sailboat for speed and sea-kindlyness. Like them, Alerion has moderately hard bilges and hollow floors for stability, high deadrise to prevent pounding and to be easily driven.

Alerion had three rigs during her lifetime. In 1912 she was designed with a traditional gaff rig. In 1924 Herreshoff, influenced by his sailing in Bermuda, changed her to a sliding gunter, a rig that is basically a marconi rig with a two-part mast. The gunter's advantage is that the mast is reefed when the sail is reefed and that each spar is small and light. The disadvantage is a greater total weight of spars and a greater interference with the luff of the sail. Isaac Merriman gave Alerion a marconi rig. Mystic Seaport, when they restored her, returned her to the gunter rig for historical reasons.

Alerion's rig has a large main and small jib—the most efficient distribution of sail on a sloop (e.g., catamarans and high performance one designs.) The jib is small enough to never need reefing so all sail reduction can be done without going forward. The jib is self tending, does not need a sheet winch. There are no lines to handle when coming about.

The cold molded hull of the Alerion Class Sloop is superior to the plank on frame one of the original because it is one piece and will not leak or rot. It requires only the maintenance required of a fiberglass hull. Furthermore, cold molded construction is superior to fiberglass or metal construction because the lightness of wood allows

a thicker hull than do the heavier materials. The basic thickness of the Alerion Class Sloop is ¾". Equal weights of fiberglass, aluminum, or steel would be ¼", 5/32", or 3/64". The thinner sections are considerably weaker than the wood notwithstanding the greater unit strength of the heavy materials. Additionally, the wooden hull is advantaged by low thermal conductivity and resistance to structure borne sound. The Alerion Class Sloop has her hull sheathed in Phillipine mahogany (the hardest of the light woods), she has beams of fir, uses ash where hardness is required, and has an aluminum or spruce mast.

Specifications:

LOA
26'0"

LWL
21'9'

BEAM
7'7"

DRAFT
2'5"/5'9"

DISPLACEMENT
6050 lbs.

SA
364 sq. ft.

DISPLACEMENT/(L/100)
260

SA/DISPLACEMENT 2/3
186

Scepter Yachts, Limited
4720 Cowley Crescent
Richmond, British Columbia,
Canada V7B 1C1

SCEPTRE 36

Designed by Heir Driehuyzen

Superbly detailed, roomy interior—wide, deeply upholstered settees with sloping seat backs—oiled teak and color keyed fabric and vinyl liners—pressure water shower—large gourmet galley. A yacht designed for enjoying the good things in life; for dinner with your friends by candle light and wine; for extended cruising in great comfort.

But don't be fooled by the Sceptre 36's luxurious accommodations! Hoist the sails and she transforms into an easily handled, spirited performer that wants to win races when the wind dies; her sleek hull and reliable diesel will get you to your destination at seven knots cruising speed.

Standard Equipment:

ENGINE
Yanmar 2QM20 20 HP Diesel; 2.14:1 reduction.

16 x 14 x 1" 2 Blade R.H. propeller

Lube oil & temperature alarm

Anti-vibration mounts

Engine compartment sound insulation

18 U.S. gal. fuel tank

Fuel-water separator/filter

Maximum speed 7.5 knots; cruising speed 6.5 knots

STEERING
EDSON wheel steering

30" S/S destroyer wheel

Engine controls on pedestal

Brake, guard & binnacle compass

BILGE PUMPS
Cockpit operated Henderson Mark V (manual)

Electric pump in engine bilge

Electric pump in keel stub bilge

PULPITS & LIFE LINES
Welded double bar bow & stern pulpits

Double life lines, 3/16" vinyl covered

Port, starboard & transom gates

HATCHES & PORTS
ATKINS & HOYLE 24" x 24" foredeck hatch with inside/outside locking

ATKINS & HOYLE 16" x 16" main cabin hatch

Plexiglass companionway slider with moulded F.G. storm cover

Plexiglass companionway hatch board

4 fixed plexiglass ports

4 opening ports 4" x 14"

1 opening port 4" x 10" in quarter berth

2 fixed plexiglass sky-lites

GRAB RAILS
4 teak cabin top grabrails

5 teak interior grabrails

teak post at galley

ELECTRICAL - 12 VOLT
Two 90AH 12 volt marine batteries

"MARINETICS" 12 volt distribution panel with 9 circuit breakers, battery condition meter & panel light

5 fluorescent cabin lights

2 incandescent cabin lights

Chart table goose neck light

Engine compartment light

Navigation & stern lights

Steaming and anchor lights

Wiring to chart table for VHF & tape deck

ELECTRICAL - 110 Volt
30 AMP power inlet & circuit breaker

3 duplex outlets

FRESH WATER SYSTEM
Two tanks, 74 U.S. gal. total capacity

Cross-over valve

"Par" B-36970-1000 water pressure system

Shower

Piping for optional hot water system

INTERIOR FACILITIES
a) *Forward Cabin:* V-berth with sail bag stowage under berth; step-in berth filler cushion;

separate seat; large hanging locker.

b) *Head:* Marine toilet (Canadian boats only); 12″ S/S sink; H&C faucet set, shower, mirror, toilet tissue holder, towel bar, various cabinets bins & lockers.

c) *Main Cabin:* L-shaped settee converts instantly to double berth 46″ x 6′-10″; fully fiddled teak table with removable drop leaf; table & leaf storage compartment; 6′4″ settee berth to port; shelves and cupboards P & S; large liquor cabinet.

d) *Galley:* U-shaped galley with 10″ deep S/S sink, H & C bar faucet, auxilliary F.W. foot pump; 6¾ cubic foot icebox with separate ice compartment—accessible from cockpit, sliding food tray; self stowing counter over stove alcove, s/s safety bar across stove opening; 3 drawers, 2 pots & pan lockers; large double tiered food locker; 5″–4″ long cupboards; push-through garbage hatch to 2 cu. ft. garbage bucket; paper towel holder.

e) *Navigation Station:* 28″ x 36″ chart table with chart locker; wet-gear locker under; separate locker suitable for propane instant hot water system; outboard shelf and lockers.

f) *Quarter Berth:* Large quarter berth with removable step-in cushions; opening port to cockpit "T" well.

g) *Cushions & Seat Backs:* 5″ tufted settee cushions, sloping seat back cushions, 4″ V-berth & Q-berth cushions. All cushions and seat backs fabric covered & zippered.

INTERIOR FINISHES
Oiled teak bulkheads & trim

Fabric hull liners

Vinyl deck head liners.

Teak & Holly cabin soles.

DECK STOWAGE FACILITIES
Fore-deck anchor well

Cockpit seat hatch

Lazarette seat hatch

Lazarette propane bottle well

MAST & RIGGING
"STEARN" tapered urethane coated mast with internal halyards, spinnaker cranes (2), spinnaker track; double airfoil spreaders (Mast is keel stepped)

"STEARN" boom, urethane coated; double tack hooks, adjustable internal topping lift; internal clew outhaul; internal slab reef pennants (2).

NAVTEC Rod Rigging; Intermediate shrouds to deck; Fore and aft lower shrouds; long aft turn buckle to accommodate optional backstay tightener.

Internal main halyard to cockpit; LEWMAR #30A 2 speed winch; halyard stopper.

Internal genoa halyard to cockpit; LEWMAR #30A 2 speed winch; halyard stopper.

Recessed bridge deck traveller, 4:1 mainsheet, roller bearing car with plunger stops.

Two jiffy reef pennants & cunningham to cockpit.

Inboard, recessed genoa tracks with cars; LEWMAR #42A 2 speed primary winches, two 10″ winch handles, two ½″ genoa sheets.

MISCELLANEOUS
Nylon anchor bow roller

Double tack hook bow fitting

Fire extinguisher

Emergency tiller

Thru-deck mast collar

S/S cockpit & side deck drains

Pettit UnipoxySuperslick bottom paint (#1690)

Four 8″ tie up cleats.

Specifications:

LENGTH OVERALL
35′6″

WATERLINE LENGTH
29′1″

BEAM
11′5″

DRAFT
6′0″

DRAFT (shoal)
4′11″

DISPLACEMENT
12,000 lbs.

BALLAST (lead)
5,500 lbs.

SAIL AREA
597 sq. ft.

W.D. Schock Corporation
3502 South Greenville Street
Santa Ana, California 92704

LIDO 14

There are now over 4700 Lidos sailing throughout the United States and Mexico. Lido owners have formed an outstanding class association with 70 very active fleets. The association plans exciting sailing activities for its members as it works to preserve the one-design characteristics of the Lido 14, thereby maintaining an unusually high resale value for the boat.

The Lido's cockpit is open and spacious. The contoured bench seats, which run the full length of the cockpit, are exceptionally comfortable and are completely unobstructed. Flotation is provided

by these seats and by the under-deck bow tank.

The Lido's hull and deck are fiberglass and the mast and boom are aluminum, so maintenance is a breeze. It is hand-laid up and molded in one piece for maximum strength and rigidity. Every piece of rigging and hardware has been carefully chosen and its effectiveness proven throughout the 20 years of production.

Being just 14 feet long, the Lido is easy to trailer. It is equipped with a specially designed hinge at the base of the mast and has an innovative tilt-up rudder.

Standard Equipment:

STANDARD COLOR/GRAPHICS SELECTION

Hull and deck may be any color selected from Color Chart dated 8/79.

Striping to be Graphics "B".

HULL

100% hand lay-up fiberglass.

High gloss gelcoat.

Seat tanks are fiberglass bonded to hull.

Bow flotation tank is fiberglass bonded to hull.

Full length rub rail.

DECK AND DECK HARDWARE

100% hand lay-up fiberglass.

High gloss gelcoat.

Wood, foam or additional fiberglass laminations in load bearing areas.

Deck is bonded and riveted to the hull.

Gold anodized bow fitting and mast hinge.

Jib cam cleats on stainless steel tracks with spring-loaded stops.

Easy adjust shroud chainplates that are below the deck.

Stainless steel mainsheet track with spring loaded stops.

Swiveling jib tack shackle.

Tank storage shelf under the deck.

CENTERBOARD

Fiberglass shell with high density foam core.

High gloss white gelcoat.

Centerboard is suspended by two stainless steel straps that insert into centerboard trunk.

Centerboard automatically jibes.

2:1 lift system with automatic shock chord centerboard drop.

RUDDER

Fiberglass shell with high density foam core.

High gloss white gelcoat.

Rudder is tilt-up design in a gold anodized aluminum casting.

Varnished oak tiller with tiller extension.

SPARS AND RIGGING

Mast and boom are gold anodized.

Adjustable gold anodized spreaders with rod rigging.

Shrouds are 1 x 19 vinyl covered stainless steel cable.

Forestay is 1 x 19 stainless steel cable.

Main and jib halyard are 7 x 7 stainless steel cable with spliced dacron tails.

Stainless steel halyard shackles are used with ball swages.

Jib halyard is 2:1.

Whisker pole padeye on the mast.

2:1 adjustable outhaul.

2:1 adjustable boom vang.

Roller bearing mainsheet blocks.

Lifting points for sling launching.

Mainsheet cam cleat with roller bearing block.

Specifications:

LENGTH OVER-ALL
14 ft.

BEAM
6 ft.

DRAFT—CENTERBOARD UP
5 in.

DRAFT—CENTERBOARD DOWN
4 ft. 3 in.

SAIL AREA (MAIN)
76 sq. ft.

SAIL AREA (JIB)
35 sq. ft.

SAIL AREA (TOTAL)
111 sq. ft.

TOTAL BOAT WEIGHT
310 lbs. (including all gear except sails.)

Additional Features:

Gold anodized aluminum spars.

Plastic covered stainless steel shrouds.

Dacron running rigging.

White Neoprene gunwale guards.

640 lbs. buoyancy.

SANTANA 23

Designed by Shad Turner
The Santana 23 is an uncompromising blend of the contemporary high-performance racer and the trailerable cruiser. This beautiful Shad Turner design is an internally ballasted daggerboard boat built to high standards of quality and equipped with the latest in racing hardware. The Santana 23 combines a high sail area to displacement ratio with an exceptionally

wide beam so she'll sail fast and dry. The boat is well balanced to assure a responsive helm and her relatively deep and narrow daggerboard ensures good lift to weather. Her retractable rudder and hinged mast make towing, launching and rigging a pleasure.

Below the Santana 23 is perfect for overnighters. The interior is beautifully finished and well equipped for four. There is a large V-berth forward and two seven-foot berths in the main cabin which run aft under the cockpit seats. Raised winch platforms above these berths provide a spaciousness seldom found in a boat this size. The galley is placed amidship and is equipped with sink, water tank, ice box, and stove compartment. Dropleaf shelves afford additional counter space. Two large lockers in the main cabin and compartments under each berth offer abundant space for storage. The area under the V-berth can accommodate a portable head.

The daggerboard is 170 lbs. of lead encased in high density foam and fiber-glass. The ballast is relatively light by design because of the self-righting characteristics of the boat. The daggerboard trunk is vertical and extends through the deck for maximum strength and rigidity. The trunk also acts as a compression post for the mast, distributing the loads from the mast down to the hull. It is reinforced in the lower section where the majority of the load is placed when the boat is sailing. The control line for the board is an easily serviced six-part block and tackle operated from the deck.

The trunk cabin design of the 23's deck offers clean straight leads for all the lines and provides wide side decks with hiking ramps. Nothing interferes with visibility from the cockpit. The windows and hatches are flush mounted and the main sliding hatch is made in two sections to create an especially large companionway.

The cockpit is a full eight feet long with wide, comfortable bench seats. Raised winch islands are immediately aft of the cabin. A roller bearing traveler bridges the seats and a T-shaped arrangement of the cockpit sole leaves an opening aft for easy installation and operation of an outboard engine. No outboard bracket is necessary.

The Santana 23 is of hand laid up fiberglass construction and is reinforced in areas of increased stress. The interior liner is bonded to the hull and the bulkheads are bonded to the hull and deck for increased rigidity. The rudder and daggerboard were designed and engineered for strength and performance.

Standard Equipment:

HULL
100% hand lay-up fiberglass.

High gloss gelcoat.

All fiberglass bonded cabin sole.

All flush through hull fittings.

BALLAST
850 lb. interior lead under the cabin sole.

250 fiberglass foam-filled, lead inserted daggerboard.

RUDDER
Fiberglass blade with a high density foam core.

Anodized aluminum rudder case blade.

Retractable rudder

Laminated oak and mahogany varnished tiller.

Tiller extension.

DECK AND DECK HARDWARE
100% hand lay-up fiberglass.

Balsa sandwich and marine plywood sandwich in load bearing areas.

Non-skid on deck, cabin top, cockpit sole and seat top.

Molded Hiking Ramps.

Tilted plexiglass main hatch.

Two tinted plexiglass windows.

Tinted plexiglass forward hatch.

Two Lewmar #16 AL genoa sheet winches.

One lewmar #8 AL genoa halyard winch.

One Lewmar #8 AL main halyard winch.

Two Lewmar 8 inch AL lock-in winch handles.

All deck blocks lead the halyards aft to the cockpit.

One double halyard stopper.

Two aluminum genoa tracks and lead blocks.

Roller bearing traveler and control lines.

Four mooring cleats.

Mast hinge.

All exterior trim in natural teak.

Two cockpit seat hatches for access to the lazerette.

Bow pulpit.

Lifelines and stanchions.

Stern rails.

Self-bailing cockpit.

Two cabin top plexiglas deck lights.

RIGGING
Black anodized aluminum mast and boom.

Four aluminum black anodized airfoil spreaders.

All internal halyards.

Main and genoa halyards are rope-to-wire spliced.

4:1 internal outhaul that is led aft to the cockpit.

Internal reef line that is led aft to the cockpit.

All standing rigging is stainless steel with sage fittings.

All the running rigging is dacron.

Spinnaker halyard is internal and led aft to the cockpit.

Internal spinnaker pole tropping lift and spinnaker pole car lift led aft to the cockpit.

6:1 adjustable backstay.

Two spinnaker sheets with snap shackles.

Two Harken hexaratchet spinnaker lead blocks.

12:1 boom vang.

Cunningham system led aft to the cockpit.

Headfoil II.

Windex.

4:1 Harken mainsheet cam cleat with ratchet block.

Two outboard genoa tracks with genoa sheet barber haulers.

Double bridle spinnaker pole.

ELECTRICAL
One 12 volt 90 amp hour battery.

Running lights.

Cabin lights.

Bow light.

Electrical panel with circuit breakers.

INTERIOR
Oiled teak bulkheads and cabinets.

Cane faced locker doors and varnished teak and holly cabin sole.

Stainless steel sink in the galley.

Fresh water pump in the galley.

3-inch cushions on all the bunks and fabric on cabin sides.

Interior cabinetry is fiberglass bonded to the hull and deck.

Two shelves in the forward cabin.

Synthetic fabric hull liner that is mildew-proof.

Specifications:

LOA
23'4"

LWL
20'7½"

BEAM
8'10"

DRAFT
5'3"

DAGGERBOARD RETRACTED
10"

DISPLACEMENT
2600 lbs.

BALLAST
1130 lbs.

SAIL AREA
100% FA., 283.5 sq. ft.